IRENE DUNNE

Irene Dunne, 1944. (Author's collection)

IRENE DUNNE
A Bio-Bibliography

Margie Schultz

Bio-Bibliographies in the Performing Arts, Number 19
James Robert Parish, Series Adviser

Greenwood Press
New York • Westport, Connecticut • London

Library of Congress Cataloging-in-Publication Data

Schultz, Margie.
    Irene Dunne : a bio-bibliography / Margie Schultz.
      p.   cm.—(Bio-bibliographies in the performing arts, ISSN 0892-5550 ; no. 19)
    Filmography
    Discography
    Includes bibliographical references (p.   ) and index.
    ISBN 0-313-27399-5 (alk. paper)
    1. Dunne, Irene, 1904-   . 2. Dunne, Irene, 1904- —
Bibliography. 3. Actors—United States—Biography.   I. Title.
II. Series.
PN2287.D85S38   1991
792'.02'8092—dc20
   [B]   91-21528

British Library Cataloguing in Publication Data is available.

Copyright © 1991 by Margie Schultz

All rights reserved. No portion of this book may be reproduced, by any process or technique, without the express written consent of the publisher.

Library of Congress Catalog Card Number: 91-21528
ISBN: 0-313-27399-5
ISSN: 0892-5550

First published in 1991

Greenwood Press, 88 Post Road West, Westport, CT 06881
An imprint of Greenwood Publishing Group, Inc.

Printed in the United States of America

The paper used in this book complies with the Permanent Paper Standard issued by the National Information Standards Organization (Z39.48—1984).

10 9 8 7 6 5 4 3 2 1

For
my father, William,
for introducing me to movie musicals
and
my mother, Margie,
for sharing her research skills

Contents

Illustrations	ix
Preface	xi
Acknowledgments	xv
Biography	1
Plays and Personal Appearances	29
Filmography	49
Radio	137
Television	151
Discography	171
Awards and Honors	179
Song Sheets	187
Annotated Bibliography	189
Appendix: Magazine Covers	289
Index	291

Illustrations

Irene Marie Dunn and her brother Charles.	2
Dr. and Mrs. Francis Griffin.	12
Alternate delegate to the United Nations.	22
Leading lady of Show Boat tour, 1929.	41
With Pat O'Brien in Consolation Marriage, 1931.	56
With Cary Grant and Ralph Bellamy in The Awful Truth, 1937	87
As Queen Victoria in The Mudlark, 1950.	128
The cast of You Can Change the World, 1949.	134
Irene Dunne and NBC microphone, circa 1935.	139
Scene from Frontier Circus, 1961.	166
With Rex Harrison at Grauman's Chinese Theatre, 1946.	181
With Melvyn Douglas in Theodora Goes Wild, 1936.	206
Recipients of the Kennedy Center Honors, 1985.	222
Irene Dunne and her mother.	257
Home at 461 North Faring Drive.	264

Preface

Irene Dunne often was called the First Lady of Hollywood, a title that not only referred to her long and dignified career, but to her private life as well. She could make audiences laugh or cry, with her understated dramatic characterizations, her deft comic timing, and her lilting soprano voice. Although her roles included a pioneer (<u>Cimarron</u>), a kept woman (<u>Back Street</u>), a princess-turned-dress designer (<u>Roberta</u>), a supressed racy novelist (<u>Theodora Goes Wild</u>), a sympathetic matriarch (<u>I Remember Mama</u>), and Queen Victoria (<u>The Mudlark</u>), Miss Dunne's portrayals were always sympathetic and ladylike. Off screen, she was married to the same man for thirty-seven years, almost a record in Hollywood. After she retired from the screen, she served as an alternate delegate to the United Nations, a position she considered the highlight of her career. Her affiliation with many civic and philanthropic causes, including the California Arts Commission, the American Red Cross, the American Cancer Society, and Saint John's Hospital, further enhanced her reputation. Although she received five Academy Award nominations, Miss Dunne considered Notre Dame's Laetare Medal a bigger honor, stating, "God does not read an actress's press clippings."

Irene Dunne began her career on the stage, achieving her first fame in Broadway musicals in the late 1920s. She was signed by a talent scout from RKO, who saw her in a touring production of <u>Show Boat</u> in 1930. After a less-than-auspicous screen debut in <u>Leathernecking</u>, Miss Dunne starred in the epic <u>Cimarron</u>, receiving her first Academy Award nomination. In 1935, she left RKO and became one of the first stars to free-lance, making one film a year for several different studios. Although her earliest films were melodramas or musicals, Miss Dunne proved that she was an adept comedienne in 1937's <u>Theodora Goes Wild</u>. Her dignified image played against the screwball antics, introducing her to a new legion of fans. In the late 1930s and 1940s, her comedic services were as sought after as those of Carole Lombard and Jean Arthur. During World War

II, Miss Dunne actively sold war bonds, entertained the troops, and visited hospitals. After retiring from films in 1952, she made sporadic radio and television appearances and worked for many civic and philanthropic causes.

Few actresses matched Irene Dunne's versatility. Although she had some formidable competition throughout her career, including Ann Harding, Norma Shearer, Jeanette MacDonald, Claudette Colbert, Katharine Hepburn, Greer Garson, and Myrna Loy, who could capably replace Miss Dunne in one genre or another, no other actress could perform equally well in epics, melodramas, romances, comedies, and musicals. When the Kennedy Center Honors recognized Miss Dunne in 1985, James Stewart pointed out that she was the only actress to receive three Academy Award nominations in three different genres. Through the years, many of her films have been remade, with Kathryn Grayson, Deborah Kerr, and Jane Wyman being the actresses most frequently cast to reprise her roles. Although Miss Grayson capably sang the parts Miss Dunne originated in <u>Roberta</u> and <u>Show Boat</u>, she could not have handled the comic maneuverings of <u>Theodora Goes Wild</u>. Despite the fact that Miss Kerr was properly cast in the remake of <u>Love Affair</u>, her singing had to be dubbed in the musical version of <u>Anna and the King of Siam</u>. And while Miss Wyman displayed her comic and dramatic talents in remakes of <u>The Awful Truth</u> and <u>Magnificent Obsession</u>, and proved herself as a vocalist in other films, it is difficult to imagine her attempting an aria.

This book is intended as an overview of Miss Dunne's life and career. It does not purport to be an in-depth biography. This volume is divided into nine sections, as follows:

(1) a brief <u>biography</u>;

(2) a listing of Miss Dunne's <u>plays and personal appearances</u>. This chapter includes plays performed on Broadway and on tour, as well as selected personal appearances made during World War II and at film tributes. Each listing is preceded by the letter "P." Cities played, dates of performances, production and cast credits, a short synopsis, and reviews are included when available;

(3) a <u>filmography</u> of the movies in which Miss Dunne appeared. Each feature film listing is preceded by the letter "F." Entries are arranged chronologically by year of American release. Studio, year of release, production and cast credits, a short synopsis, and reviews are included for each film. Short films are preceded by the prefix "FS" and appear in a chronological list following the features. Entries include the year of release, credits, and a brief description;

(4) a listing of Miss Dunne's national <u>radio</u> appearances. Each entry is precededed by the letter "R" and includes episode title, airdate, cast, a brief synopsis, and selected reviews;

(5) a listing of Miss Dunne's national <u>television</u> appearances. Entries are preceded by the letter "T" and include episode title, airdate, cast, brief synopsis, and

selected reviews. Additionally, this chapter includes an
episode guide for <u>Schlitz Playhouse of Stars</u>, which was
hosted by Miss Dunne for twenty-six weeks. Entries are
grouped together under <u>Schlitz Playhouse of Stars</u> (T-1)
and preceded by the prefix "SP." They include episode
title, airdate, a brief synopsis, and selected reviews which
mention Miss Dunne's participation;
     (6) a <u>discography</u> of recordings made by Miss Dunne.
This chapter is divided into three sections: 78s, LPs, and
CDs. Each listing is preceded by the letter "D" and
includes recording date, label, number, and songs performed
by Miss Dunne;
     (7) a listing of <u>awards and honors</u> bestowed upon
Miss Dunne. Each entry is preceded by the letter "A."
Listings include the name of award and approximate year of
receipt;
     (8) a list of film <u>song sheets</u> which feature Miss
Dunne on the cover. Listed chronologically and preceded by
the letter "S," each entry includes published songs from the
film and a brief description of the cover;
     (9) an annotated <u>bibliography</u> of writings by and
about Miss Dunne. This chapter includes reviews, articles,
and announcements from books, newspapers, magazines,
tabloids, and trade papers, showing the diverse publications
which have written about Miss Dunne's life and career. Each
entry is preceded by the letter "B."

     In addition, the book contains an appendix of selected
magazine covers which feature Miss Dunne. A complete index
of names and titles concludes the volume; index references
are to the entry numbers within the various section
listings. The career and biographical information contained
herein are correct as of March 31, 1991. Any additions or
corrections for future editions may be sent to the author in
care of Greenwood Press.

Acknowledgments

It takes the efforts of many people to gather the information for a book of this scope. I am very grateful to have had the support of so many, who shared their research facilities, collections, and memories to make this a fitting tribute to an often neglected actress.

Irene Dunne will always be remembered as a lady, both on and off screen. I appreciate her colleagues for sharing their thoughts and reminiscences: William Bakewell, Ralph Bellamy, Carol Bruce, Joseph Cotten, Elinor Donahue, Kitty Carlisle Hart, Allan Jones, Joan Leslie, Roddy McDowall, James Stewart, Vera Hamilton for Perry Como, and Martha Wilson for Garson Kanin.

A myriad of thanks to Barry Rivadue, whose imagination, wit, and research skills were invaluable. In addition to scouring New York libraries for references to Irene Dunne's stage appearances, he made a terrific sounding board for ways to improve this book. As a bio-bibliography veteran, he understood the pleasures and pitfalls of research - and he made it easy to laugh when things went awry.

Many people took time out from their own projects to contribute to the research for this book. I am particularly grateful to Carol Forsyth, Art Pierce, and Vincent Terrace for sharing their respective knowledge of photography, radio, and television. Further thanks go to Kim Altana; Earl Anderson; Connie Billips; Tom Bourgeois; James Taylor Breen; Beverly Bare Buehrer; Jack Buxbaum; Father John Catoir, the Christophers; Karin Fowler; Anthony Greco; Dorothy K. Halloran, Family Rosary; Chris Kershaw; Sharon Lindy; Joan Marcus; Brian Matteo; Amy F. Mihill and Connie Lewis, St. Louis Municipal Opera; Brenda Nelson-Strauss, Chicago Symphony Orchestra; Max Preeo, <u>Show Music</u>; Howard Prouty; and Sandy Weber. A special thanks to Allan Herzer, Ona Hill, and Doug McClelland for sharing their collections, and to Albert Koenig, Jr. for his endless enthusiasm.

I appreciate the many librarians who helped locate Irene Dunne material. They were: Art and Music Department, The Public Library of Cincinnati and Hamilton County; Joan L. Clark, Cleveland Public Library; William J. Dane, Art and

Music Department, Newark Public Library; Donald Draganski, Music Department, Roosevelt University Library; Simone Galik, New Jersey Division, Newark Public Library; Eleanor M. Gehres and Kay Wisnia, Western History Department, Denver Public Library; Alex Gildzen, Special Collections Department, Kent State University Library; Laura R. Keen, Washingtoniana Division, District of Columbia Public Library; Michael Lohmar, Fine Arts Department, St. Louis Public Library; Michael A. Lutes, Theodore M. Hesburgh Library, University of Notre Dame; Fauna Mihalko, Genealogy Library Department, Madison- Jefferson County Public Libary; Milwaukee Public Library; Helen A. Rowin, Music and Performing Arts Department, Detroit Public Library; Anne A. Salter, Atlanta Historical Society; Henry F. Scannell, Microtext Department, Boston Public Library; Wesley L. Wilson, Maryland Department, Enoch Pratt Free Library of Baltimore; and Maria Zini, Pennsylvania Department, Carnegie Library of Pittsburgh. A special thanks to Ned Comstock, USC Cinema-Television Library, University of Southern California; Kristine Kreuger, National Film Information Service, Academy of Motion Picture Arts and Sciences; and Reg Shrader, Film and Photo Archive, Wisconsin Center for Film and Theater Research.

My sincere appreciation to my adviser, James Robert Parish, and my editor, Marilyn Brownstein, for their help.

This book could not have been written without Irene Dunne, who died during its production. Although her health prohibited her from cooperating, her exemplary life and career proved inspirational. It is my hope that the book is a fitting memorial.

A final, very special thanks to my parents, William and Margie, for their encouragement, support, and love. Their belief in me has made me believe in myself, and, for that, I am very grateful.

IRENE DUNNE

Biography

Irene Marie Dunn was born on December 20, 1898 in her parents' home at 507 East Gray Street in Louisville, Kentucky. Her father was Joseph John Dunn, a Louisville native who was chief engineer on a number of riverboats, and later was appointed United States riverboat-boiler inspector. Her mother was Adelaide Antoinette Henry Dunn, an accomplished musician who hailed from Newport, Kentucky. Adelaide studied piano at the Cincinnati Conservatory of Music before her marriage.

Although Irene's birth variously has been reported as occurring as late as 1904, records at Louisville's St. John's Catholic Church showed that she was baptized in 1898. Genealogist Ward Harrison confirmed that census records also verify the 1898 birthdate.

According to the <u>Madison Courier</u> [Indiana], Irene was almost born on a riverboat. The Dunns were heading for Madison, where Adelaide's parents resided, when Irene's birth became eminent, forcing the Dunns to disembark at Louisville (see B-461). <u>Modern Screen</u> claimed that one of Irene's four aunts suggested her name. "Another aunt, leaning over the crib..., exclaimed, 'Oh, what a little lady-baby!'" Caroline Hoyt reported, a premonition of Irene's reputation throughout her life (B-197). Irene had a brother Charles, who was two years younger.

Irene spent her childhood in Louisville and St. Louis, where her father was transferred when he became supervising steamboat inspector. She was taught by the Sisters of Loretta at Saint Benedict's Academy in Louisville and the Loretto Convent in St. Louis. Classmates recalled that Irene had no show business aspirations while dwelling in St. Louis. She did not participate in school plays or pageants.

Joseph died of a kidney infection when Irene was eleven. Adelaide then moved the family to Madison, Indiana, where her father, Charles Henry, operated the boiler works which constructed and installed boilers in riverboats traveling the Ohio and Mississippi Rivers. The family resided at 940 Middle Drive. Irene graduated from the eighth grade from Madison Grammar School in the spring of

Irene Marie Dunn and her brother Charles. (Wisconsin Center for Film and Theater Research)

1913. She made her stage debut that same year as Mustardseed in a school production of Shakespeare's *A Midsummer Night's Dream*. She later appeared in a benefit performance of *St. Cecelia* for Madison's King's Daughters Hospital. The play was so successful that the cast traveled to Milton, Kentucky for a repeat performance, marking Irene's first "road show."

Adelaide encouraged Irene's musical and dramatic talents, giving her daughter voice and piano lessons. The fledgling Madison Current Events Club awarded Irene a scholarship for a musical course at the Oliver Willard Pierce Academy of Fine Arts in Indianapolis. She received her first real music lessons at the academy. Although Irene and her family attended St. Michael's Catholic Church in Madison, Irene sang in the First Baptist Church choir under the direction of Percival Owen. It was her first professional engagement, as she was paid ten dollars for each performance.

Irene graduated from Madison High School in 1916. The yearbook called her "Dunnie" and referred to her participation in girls chorus and as a senior commissioner. The yearbook quote described Irene as "divinely tall and most divinely fair." Although many sources date the spelling change in her name to the beginning of her professional career, Irene's last name was spelled "Dunne" in her high school yearbook. Programs and reviews continued to vary the spelling of her name, with the "e" being consistently in place only after *Show Boat* played Chicago.

According to the *Louisville Courier-Journal*, Irene earned a teaching certificate from St. Louis's Webster College (B-132). In September, 1918, she was en route to Gary, Indiana to accept a position as an art instructor when she stopped to visit some relatives in Chicago. She discovered a voice contest and decided to enter on impulse. Irene won a scholarship to the Chicago Musical College, where she studied voice, sight reading, harmony, Italian, and music history. Her voice lessons were paid for by H.M. Sydacker. The college, now part of Roosevelt University, was founded by Dr. Florenz Ziegfeld, father of theatrical entrepreneur Florenz Ziegfeld, who would later play a major part in advancing Irene's career.

Irene's goal in 1918 was to sing with the Metropolitan Opera. She studied coloratura roles like Gilda in *Rigoletto* and Juliet in *Romeo and Juliet*. She interviewed various managers during her first year in Chicago, hoping to begin her professional career. Although she was offered a role in the musical comedy *Chu Chin Chow*, the show's casting director advised her to continue her studies while on scholarship. Irene won a scholarship for a second year of study and followed the casting director's advice.

Irene was awarded a senior diploma on June 19, 1919. Her vocal degree included proficiency in harmony, sight reading, language, musical history, and pedagogy. She received a gold medal for her vocal excellence at the college's annual contest. The sixty-five-member Chicago

Symphony Orchestra accompanied the competition, which included Irene's rendition of "The Shadow Song" from <u>Dinorah</u>. Although Irene's name continued to vary in spelling until 1930, the graduation program listed her as Irene Dunne.

With a second scholarship in music history and continued support from H.M. Syndacker for her voice lessons, Irene returned to the Chicago Musical College for the 1919-20 school year. She doubled up on her voice lessons and added French to her curriculum.

At Adelaide's urging, Irene made her first trip to New York to audition for the Metropolitan Opera in 1920. She failed the audition, but began her professional career. <u>The Madison Herald</u> told the following story. During the summer of 1920, Irene sang for a railroad convention in Atlantic City, then joined her friend, Rosemary Pfaff, in New York. Rosemary was already beginning to establish a musical career. During Irene's visit, Rosemary auditioned for the lead in a touring company of the musical comedy <u>Irene</u>, but was turned down because of her height. Rosemary's mother, who accompanied her on the audition, suggested Irene for the role. After hearing Irene sing, the business manager gave her a script and asked her to read the lines of the first act with him the next day. Irene memorized the script and astounded the manager with an excellent interpretation. He promised her the title role in the musical if the choreographer approved of her. The choreographer said she lacked dancing talent and dismissed her. According to the <u>Madison Herald</u>, Irene was so upset that she left her bag at the theatre. When she returned for it, the manager and the choreographer promised her the role if she would study with the company's ballet mistress. She agreed and was awarded the title role in the touring company of <u>Irene</u> without any previous professional experience (B-244). <u>Modern Screen</u> told a similar story, with Irene replacing Broadway leading lady Patti Harrold for three evening performances and a matinee before embarking on the tour (B-197).

Despite these detailed accounts, <u>Variety</u> heralded Helen Shipman as the leading lady in the Chicago company of <u>Irene</u> when the musical opened in November, 1920. And although many sources claim Irene Dunne was with the tour for its entire five-month run, a program from March, 1921 does not list her in the cast. The University of Southern California Cinema-Television Library, to whom Irene donated her scrapbooks, scripts, and memorabilia, can find nothing about her role in the production. It is more than likely that Irene was in the chorus of the musical, but left when it moved from the Garrick Theatre to the Studebaker Theatre in March, 1921.

Adelaide convinced her daughter to go back to New York in 1921. Irene thought of returning to her first vocation, teaching music, but listened to her mother. In New York, Irene continued her musical studies while waiting for her next role.

Irene made her Broadway debut in the musical <u>The</u>

Clinging Vine on December 25, 1922. In the tiny role of Tessie, a secretary in a paint factory, Irene appeared for only four minutes during the first act. She was also the understudy for leading lady Peggy Wood. Although a theatrical newcomer, Irene understood the maneuverings of show business. She wrote a note to playwright Zelda Sears, thanking her for Tessie's brevity on stage, allowing Irene to have time to continue her musical studies. The note was well-circulated and brought Irene to the attention of many important figures in the world of musical comedy. During a 1924 tour of the production, Peggy Wood developed laryngitis. Irene was called to Cleveland to replace Wood until she recovered.

Irene became adept at stepping in for musical stars. After her experience in *The Clinging Vine*, Irene was hired to replace Gloria Dawn in the Broadway production of *Lollipop* in early 1924.

Irene's first association with Jerome Kern occurred in 1925 when she was cast in the Broadway production of *The City Chap*. As Grace Bartlett, Irene little suspected that someday she would be the foremost interpreter of Kern's music on film. *The City Chap* opened on October 26, 1925. Although earlier Playbills spelled her name "Dunne," *The City Chap* inexplicably listed her as Irene Dunn.

In March of 1926, Irene replaced Genevieve Tobin in the musical *Sweetheart Time* on Broadway. That summer Irene performed with the St. Louis Municipal Opera company for a season, gaining confidence and experience by playing a variety of roles. During 1926 she also appeared in Atlanta with a group of young singers from the Metropolitan Opera, whose repertoire included the works of Gilbert and Sullivan.

Irene went back to work on Broadway for the next few years. *Yours Truly* opened on January 25, 1927. Although she played the role of Diana when the musical opened, Irene succeeded leading lady Marion Harris as Mary Stillwell after the show had been running for two months. The following year Irene had a major role in *She's My Baby*, with Beatrice Lillie and Jack Whiting. The musical, with songs by Richard Rodgers and Lorenz Hart, opened on Broadway on January 3, 1928. Although Irene and Rodgers never worked together directly, their career paths continued to cross through the years, with Irene's first film being based on a Rodgers and Hart show, and Rodgers musicalizing two of Irene's films for Broadway. Additionally, Irene's career was connected to Rodgers's later partner, Oscar Hammerstein II, who wrote the lyrics and screenplays for several of her films.

Irene finally got the chance to originate the lead in a Broadway musical with *Luckee Girl*. Her work was praised when the show opened on September 16, 1928. But despite her enthusiastic notices, the show ran only eighty-one performances. She considered trading in her career for the new role of wife.

On July 16, 1928, Irene married Dr. Francis ("Frank") D. Griffin, a New York dentist. The ceremony took place in a little church on East 83rd Street in New York. They honeymooned in Europe.

Born in Northampton, Massachusetts in 1886, Frank Griffin was twelve years older than Irene. They met at a party at New York's Biltmore Hotel in 1924. According to Modern Movies, he was so taken with her charms that he bought an engagement ring the next day. Frank proved himself a hero when he rescued Irene a few months later. They were heading for a costume party in a hansom cab when a fire truck roared by and frightened the horse. Frank grabbed the bridle and prevented the animal from running away (B-84). Despite the fact that Irene later said that they fought for two years throughout their courtship, the Griffins' marriage was, by most accounts, one of the happiest in show business, lasting until his death in 1965.

Although Frank came from a conservative, non-theatrical background, he did not object to Irene continuing her work on stage. At first Irene planned to give up her career for marriage, but as her career gained momentum, Frank encouraged her to continue performing. "If she didn't have talent, I would have [asked her to drop her career]," Frank told the New York Herald Tribune. "I really didn't think marriage and the stage were compatible but we love each other and we were both determined to make the marriage work" (B-199).

Irene's next job turned out to be the catapult to a film career, but it came about quite unexpectedly. When Irene first went to New York in 1920, following her graduation from the Chicago Musical College, school founder Dr. Florenz Ziegfeld gave her a letter of recommendation to give to his famous son, theatrical producer Florenz Ziegfeld. Irene told Good Housekeeping that she tried to deliver the letter, but could not get past the showman's secretaries. One day while Irene was on her way to see a friend's rehearsal, she met the younger Ziegfeld in an office elevator. Irene recalled, "Mr. Ziegfeld got off the elevator before I did and looked mildly surprised that I wasn't going to his casting office." A few minutes later, Ziegfeld sent a secretary to find Irene. She gave him the letter and he offered her a job as a chorus girl in his Follies. "I was horrified and told him I wouldn't dream of taking such a position," she continued. "I was a serious singer. A chorus job was not my cup of tea" (B-45).

Despite Irene's refusal, Ziegfeld remembered her a few years later when he was casting the road company of his musical success Show Boat. He hired her to replace Norma Terris as Magnolia. Most of the other leading players on the tour had created the roles on Broadway. It was then quite common for shows to close in New York for the summer because the theatres were not air conditioned. Irene began the tour in Boston on June 1, 1929 and traveled for seventy-two weeks. While in Baltimore, Irene received a movie offer from RKO. The studio was achieving much success with its musical films and wanted to add another ingenue to its stable of stars, which included Ann Harding and Constance Bennett. Irene accepted the offer and moved to Hollywood.

Irene's first film was <u>Leathernecking</u>, a forgotten comedy based on <u>Present Arms</u>, a Broadway musical by Richard Rodgers, Lorenz Hart, and Herbert Fields. Despite its musical origins, by the time <u>Leathernecking</u> was released, most of its score had been pared, as musicals were quickly losing their popularity at the box office. The plot concerned an army private stationed in Hawaii, who pulled a series of tricks to impress a wealthy woman he wanted to court. Irene's role in <u>Leathernecking</u> was one that could have been played by other RKO contractees. James Robert Parish noted in <u>The RKO Gals</u> that <u>Leathernecking</u> served as a kind of screen test to examine Irene's future box office potential (B-343). The studio was not taking a chance with an unproven talent in a big-budget film.

In June, 1930, Irene was announced as one of the stars of RKO's production of Victor Herbert's <u>Babes in Toyland</u>. The film was scheduled to be directed by Luther Reed and choreographed by Pearl Eaton. In addition to Irene, the cast was to include Bert Wheeler and Robert Woolsey, Joseph Cawthorn, Dorothy Lee, Ned Sparks, Marguerite Padula, Edna May Oliver, and the Tiller Sunshine Girls. The production was postponed, due to the cost and the decreasing popularity of screen musicals. <u>Babes in Toyland</u> was made in 1934 by MGM with Stan Laurel and Oliver Hardy.

Fay Bainter was the top contender for Sabra Cravat, the leading female role opposite Richard Dix in <u>Cimarron</u>. Based on Edna Ferber's novel about the 1889 Oklahoma land rush, the film called for Sabra to age forty years. After Bainter had a disagreement with producer William LeBaron, the search was on for a new leading lady. Dix had seen Irene perform on stage in New York and suggested her for Sabra. According to James Robert Parish, Dix was exceptionally generous toward helping unknown and featured players boost their careers. Dix asked LeBaron to persuade director Wesley Ruggles and other RKO executives to give Irene the part. Meanwhile, Irene convinced makeup wizard Ern Westmore to transform her into Sabra, while cameraman Ernest Bracken photographed the aging. Bracken passed the shots along to Ruggles and she won the part.

<u>Cimarron</u> premiered at New York's Globe Theatre on January 26, 1931. Considered one of the best westerns ever made, the film won three Oscars. Until <u>Dances with Wolves</u> in 1991, it was the only western to win an Oscar for Best Picture. Irene received her first Academy Award nomination, but lost to Marie Dressler for <u>Min and Bill</u>. <u>Inside Oscar</u> reported that Irene was such a newcomer that her name was misspelled on the Academy Awards ballot (B-479).

Although RKO announced that Irene's third film would be <u>Heart of the Rockies</u>, she followed the epic <u>Cimarron</u> with a more conventional role in <u>Bachelor Apartment</u> (RKO, 1931). She played a prim stenographer who fell in love with her playboy boss in a comedy directed by the leading man, Lowell Sherman.

MGM borrowed Irene for her first musical role in <u>The Great Lover</u> in 1931. As an opera singer who must choose between her mentor, played by Adolphe Menjou, and a young singer, played by Neil Hamilton, Irene was able to display her dramatic and vocal talents.

Back at RKO, Irene starred in <u>Consolation Marriage</u>, proving her versatility on her home lot. While reigning RKO leading lady Ann Harding was only accepted on screen in sophisticated roles, Irene proved she was equally adept at playing shopgirls, aristocrats, or singers. The film concerned a marriage of convenience between two jilted lovers.

Despite Irene's film success, her husband chose to remain in New York where he practiced dentistry. During her first year in Hollywood, Irene kept her marriage a secret, fearing the disclosure might damage her career. When <u>Photoplay</u> discovered the truth in 1931, Irene said she was happy to finally be able to talk about Frank. Her only complaint about the arrangement was her high long distance bills. The movie magazines dispelled separation rumors by pointing out that Irene spent her vacations in New York with her husband and that her RKO contract had a clause that the studio had to provide her with ten days notice before beginning a movie. In 1964, a friend explained the situation, saying, "[Irene] always had a deep respect for Frank's profession, just as he always respected hers. It was a matter of practical necessity, during those years, that they be apart" (B-28). Others, like film historian James Robert Parish, have implied that the Griffins' was a marriage of convenience.

During the early days of the bi-coastal marriage, the Griffins kept the apartment they had lived in since their marriage and used it during Irene's New York visits. While she was in California, Frank shared bachelor quarters at his club with Irene's brother Charles. Irene later said it was a lonely time for her, despite the fact that her mother shared her Hollywood home. When asked if she had any regrets, Irene always mentioned the time she missed with her husband.

Irene's on-screen roles paralleled her off-screen loneliness, beginning with the 1932 tearjerker <u>Symphony of Six Million</u>. Irene played a crippled teacher who led a corrupted doctor back to the ghettos to practice. The Fannie Hurst melodrama was followed up by another Hurst soap opera, <u>Back Street</u>. Irene was loaned to Universal for the film, which cast her as a kept woman. It established her as a star. <u>Back Street</u> premiered at the Mayfair Theatre on August 28, 1932 and broke the studio's box office record, previously held by <u>All Quiet on the Western Front</u>.

RKO delayed the release of <u>Thirteen Women</u> to take advantage of Irene's success. Although second billed to leading man Ricardo Cortez, the studio rationalized that Irene's new popularity could easily carry the pseudo-mystery. Irene played one of the women who were stalked by former schoolmate Myrna Loy. The film premiered at the Roxy Theatre on October 14, 1932. <u>No Other Woman</u> further established Irene as the queen of the soap operas, opening at the Roxy Theatre on January 29, 1933. The story showed how money corrupted a steelworker and his wife.

Irene's services were lent to MGM for The Secret of Madame Blanche, a Madame X-style melodrama about a chorus girl turned brothel owner, whose identity was a secret from her son.

After proving her adeptness at martyrs, Irene embarked on a series of more headstrong, independent roles. Although she was no longer the victim, her characters continued to do the right thing in times of trouble. Ann Harding and Katharine Hepburn turned down The Silver Cord, which Irene made for RKO in 1933. The Silver Cord allowed Irene to play an intelligent career woman who took an active stand against her possessive mother-in-law to save her marriage. The film premiered at Radio City Music Hall on May 4, 1933. Ann Vickers (RKO, 1933) concerned an overly ambitious woman involved in social work reform, who learned career was not everything. If I Were Free was essentially a love triangle, with Irene falling for a married lawyer and clashing with his wife over his affections. It opened at Radio City Music Hall on January 4, 1934. This Man is Mine also had Irene involved in an unhappy marriage. Although the film was played as a drama, there were elements of slapstick, with Irene cracking a picture over the head of her philandering husband, played by Ralph Bellamy. The Age of Innocence (RKO, 1934) cast Irene as a divorcee attracted to her cousin's fiance. Always the lady, Irene returned to Europe so not to break up the couple.

By 1933, musicals were having a resurgence of popularity. Irene was mentioned to co-star with Jeanette MacDonald and Lawrence Tibbett in The Merry Widow, however by the time the film was released in 1934, Irene and Tibbett had been replaced by Una Merkel and Maurice Chevalier. Irene and Laurence Olivier were supposed to be teamed in a feature for RKO in the early 1930s, but the film never progressed beyond wardrobe fittings. In September, 1933, two other projects were announced: a musical called Frivolous Sal and an untitled film with Francis Lederer. Neither project developed.

RKO finally allowed Irene to vocalize in Stingaree in 1934. Part adventure, part romance, Stingaree reunited Irene with her Cimarron co-star Richard Dix in a tale about an Australian Robin Hood. Irene continued her musical phase with Sweet Adeline in 1935. On loan from RKO, the Warner Bros. film gave Irene her first opportunity to perform Jerome Kern songs on film. They included "Why Was I Born?" and "Don't Ever Leave Me."

Although Roberta is often remembered today for the dancing wizardry of Fred Astaire and Ginger Rogers, it was Irene who had top billing in the film. As the exiled White Russian princess, she introduced Jerome Kern's "Lovely to Look At," which became a best seller for her. The song, recorded on the Brunswick label in April, 1935, climbed to number twenty on Billboard's popular song chart in June.

Following Roberta, Irene left the security of RKO to pursue her own projects. Her motives were both financial and philosophical. She wanted to be able to choose roles to her liking without being forced to make four films a year at the studio's insistence. The decision may not have been one-sided, as the studio was slowly replacing its older actresses, like Ann Harding and Constance Bennett, with younger stars like Katharine Hepburn and Ginger Rogers.

Before Irene's departure, RKO planned to star her in <u>The Mad Miss Manton</u>, but Barbara Stanwyck ended up playing in the screwball comedy when it was released in 1937. Other commitments kept Irene from starring in <u>Follow the Fleet</u> with Fred Astaire and Ginger Rogers at RKO in 1936. Irene's intended role went to Harriet Hilliard. Paramount offered <u>Enter Madame</u> and <u>Peter Ibbetson</u> in 1935, but Irene turned down both films. Elissa Landi took over in <u>Enter Madame</u>; Ann Harding accepted <u>Peter Ibbetson</u>. RKO tried to work out a deal involving a trade with Paramount, who owned the rights to a film Ann Harding wanted to make. In it, Paramount would borrow the services of Harding and Irene for <u>The Old Maid</u>, in exchange for the rights to <u>The Indestructible Mrs. Talbot</u>. Irene did not proceed with negotiations. <u>The Indestructible Mrs. Talbot</u> became <u>The Lady Consents</u> (RKO, 1936), with Ann Harding in the title role. <u>The Old Maid</u> was filmed with Bette Davis and Miriam Hopkins by Warner Bros. in 1939.

Irene began her free-lance career by accepting a short-term contract at Universal. She later expanded her horizons with a picture-a-year deal with Columbia, Paramount, and RKO.

Although Universal's main reason for hiring Irene was for an upcoming screen version of <u>Show Boat</u>, she ended up being cast in <u>Magnificent Obsession</u> first. Released in 1935, the film was a typical weeper, with playboy Robert Taylor redeeming himself by picture's end to find happiness with Irene. Although Taylor was under contract at MGM, he had played mostly mannequin roles. Irene was responsible for him being cast in <u>Magnificent Obsession</u>, which proved to be the turning point in his career.

<u>Show Boat</u> came to the screen in 1936, gathering a cast who had experience with their roles, as most had played their parts on Broadway or on tour. Irene reprised her role as Magnolia, with Allan Jones as Gaylord Ravenal. Jerome Kern wrote three new songs for the film, including "Gallavantin' Around," which was performed by Irene in blackface. The number, and a comic shuffle she did during "Can't Help Lovin' Dat Man," gave audiences a jolt. Used to seeing Irene in prim and proper roles, they were suddenly aware that her talents included comedy.

The studios were already aware of Irene's diverse abilities. In 1935, Columbia offered Irene the title role in a comedy, <u>Theodora Goes Wild</u>. Although she agreed that a comedy would be a refreshing change of pace, she found the script too brash and too big a departure from her usual screen roles. Her reluctance became more intense as the shooting date grew closer. Besides, she had her heart set on playing Madame Curie, which Universal had promised her. Irene and Frank went on a European vacation to escape <u>Theodora Goes Wild</u> and meet with Curie's daughter Eve about the upcoming biographical picture. When Irene returned, Theodora was still waiting. Never temperamental, when Irene learned Columbia mogul Harry Cohn had put her on salary suspension, she gave in and appeared in the film. Theodora Goes Wild centered on a prim New England Sunday school teacher who wrote a scandalous best seller, then tried to live up to her reputation. The public went wild over Theodora Goes Wild and Irene was heralded as the latest comic find, joining the burgeoning ranks of Carole Lombard, Jean Arthur, and Claudette Colbert. Irene received her second Oscar nomination for Theodora Goes Wild, but lost to Luise Rainer for The Great Ziegfeld.

After announcing John Boles as a possible candidate to play Pierre Curie in Madame Curie, Universal postponed the film. They later sold the rights to MGM, who wanted the story for Greta Garbo. Instead, MGM filmed Madame Curie in 1943 with Greer Garson and Walter Pidgeon. Irene said losing the film was one of her biggest disappointments. She turned down Sister Carrie, fearing the Theodore Dreiser novel would have to be censored. Ginger Rogers was also offered the lead before RKO canceled the film in 1941. The story was finally filmed by Paramount as Carrie with Jennifer Jones in 1952.

Frank gave up his New York practice in 1936 to join his wife in California. At first, he became involved in her career, helping her agent Charles Feldman. Then he developed his own business interests, including investments in California and Nevada real estate. The Griffins had a home built in Holmby Hills, a Beverly Hills suburb. Designed by architect Paul Williams, the house boasted a hidden staircase, which provided the Griffins with a secret route to their bedroom, to freshen up if guests dropped in unexpectedly.

Further changes came when the Griffins adopted a little girl in December, 1936. Although Irene expressed a preference for the name Joan, they called her Mary Frances, nicknamed Missy. She had been known as Anna Mary Bush when she resided at the New York Foundling Home. On March 15, 1938, the Griffins signed the final adoption papers. Although Missy lived with Irene and Frank for over a year before the adoption, Irene claimed she kept proceedings a secret, even from her closest friends, until the matter had been finalized. She told McCall's, "I'm superstitious about talking about good things until they happen" (B-28). Irene insisted she did not want to spoil her daughter, but presents poured in, including a lullaby written by Jerome Kern and a pair of tap shoes from Fred Astaire. There has been some discrepancy about Mary Frances's age, with the New York Times claiming she was four at the time of the final adoption in 1938 and other sources saying she was eleven months old when she came to live with the Griffins, making her born in early 1936.

Irene had bad memories of filming High, Wide and Handsome (Paramount, 1937), as her mother died during the shooting. Adelaide, then sixty, continued to live with Irene and Frank in their new home. After returning from a shopping trip, she went into a coma and died of a cerebral

Dr. Francis Griffin joined his wife in California in 1936. (Author's collection)

hemorrhage on December 17, 1936. Mary Frances had come to live with the Griffins just a few weeks before her grandmother's death. Irene said her new daughter helped her get over the loss.

High, Wide and Handsome centered on the founding of the Tidewater Oil Company. Directed by Rouben Mamoulian, the musical epic co-starred Randolph Scott. Once again, Irene sang the music of Jerome Kern and Oscar Hammerstein II. High, Wide and Handsome opened at New York's Astor Theatre on July 21, 1937. When she viewed the film on television, years after its release, Irene admitted that it was not as bad as she remembered.

Irene returned to comedy with The Awful Truth (Columbia, 1937). Director Leo McCarey enjoyed improvising, so much of the film was made up as the crew shot it. Irene admitted that the technique scared her and co-star Cary Grant at first, but they soon got used to it. The Awful Truth was the comic tale of a husband and wife who divorced after a misunderstanding, then found they could not live without each other. Like Theodora, it contained screwball bits which played against Irene's image, like her raucous attempts to embarrass Grant in front of his new fiancee and a mock striptease. The Awful Truth earned Irene a third Academy Award nomination, but she lost to Luise Rainer for The Good Earth.

When Ann Sothern bailed out of Joy of Living (RKO, 1938), Irene was cast as the musical comedy star who was rescued from her parasitic family by a free-thinking bon vivant, played by Douglas Fairbanks, Jr. John Boles was first mentioned for the role. The script allowed Irene to sing several Jerome Kern songs, including "What's Good About Good Night?" Kern planned to write a complete score for the film, but had a heart attack before production began. Joy of Living marked Irene's last film with Kern, who died in 1945.

Columbia offered Irene the title role in The Elizabeth Blackwell Story in 1938. The story concerned a British woman who defied convention by coming to the United States to study at the New York Medical School at Geneva. Although Irene was disappointed when the film was canceled, she was more upset about losing a part in another film released by Columbia in 1938: Holiday. According to film historian Clive Hirschhorn, Columbia mogul Harry Cohn wanted to cast Irene in the leading role, but director George Cukor insisted on hiring Katharine Hepburn, who had understudied the role on Broadway (B-177). Irene was later quoted as saying she cried her eyes out after losing the part.

Irene was reunited with director Leo McCarey in Love Affair (RKO, 1939). Still a strong believer in improvisation, McCarey encouraged Irene and co-star Charles Boyer to help build the picture. Love Affair was the story of a shipboard romance between an artist and a singer. Both learned that love was more important than material things. Irene often said Love Affair was one of her favorite films, not only because it was so well done, but because she had such a good time making it. She received her fourth Oscar nomination, but lost to Vivien Leigh in *Gone with the Wind*.

Throughout the 1930s and '40s, Irene made many appearances on radio, discussing her career, performing musical selections, and recreating her film roles in condensed adaptations. She was a frequent guest on *The Lux Radio Theatre*, *The Gulf Screen Guild Theater*, *Cavalcade of America*, and *The Family Theatre*. Although she once told the *New York Times* that she disliked the medium and the precision it involved (B-206), *The New Movie Magazine* claimed she made anonymous singing appearances on several programs because she liked to keep in practice (B-433).

Invitation to Happiness marked Irene's first screen pairing with Fred MacMurray. Produced by Paramount in 1939, the film concerned a society woman and a prizefighter. Trying to cash in on the success of *Love Affair*, Universal reunited Irene and Charles Boyer in *When Tomorrow Comes* (1939). Although the film garnered good reviews, critics were quick to point out the similarity in the stories. Instead of an artist, Boyer was cast as a musician in this tale of mismatched lovers.

A third Boyer pairing almost occurred in 1940, when Irene was offered the lead in *All This and Heaven Too*. However, veteran Warner Bros. star Bette Davis returned from suspension and took over the role. Davis also was cast in the lead in *Now, Voyager* (Warner Bros., 1942), although mogul Jack Warner wanted Irene. Columbia offered Irene the lead in a remake of *The Front Page*, but she turned it down. Claudette Colbert, Ginger Rogers, Carole Lombard, Margaret Sullavan, and Jean Arthur could not see potential in the script either and the role in the retitled *His Girl Friday* went to Rosalind Russell.

Broadway also beckoned in 1940. Although Moss Hart, Ira Gershwin, and Kurt Weill had written the musical *Lady in the Dark* with Gertrude Lawrence in mind, they had some trouble getting her to sign a contract. Fed up with Lawrence's leading them along, they offered the role of the troubled magazine editor to Irene. She turned it down, but coming close to losing the part was the push Lawrence needed. She signed the contract and *Lady in the Dark*, which ran for 462 performances on Broadway, became one of the highlights of her career.

My Favorite Wife (RKO, 1940) was supposed to reunite the *Awful Truth* trio, however, Leo McCarey was seriously injured in a car accident before shooting began. Although still billed as producer, and a definite force on set, McCarey's improvisational techniques were abandoned when Garson Kanin took over as director. Based on Alfred Lord Tennyson's poem "Enoch Arden," *My Favorite Wife* concerned a woman who returned home after being shipwrecked for seven years, only to find that her husband had remarried. Irene, Grant, and Randolph Scott played it for hilarity and the film was a big success. Irene and Frank traveled to Louisville for the world premiere, which coincided with the Kentucky Derby. The film opened at Radio City Music Hall on May 4, 1940.

Irene, Grant, and Kanin discussed a second collaboration. In <u>Together Again!</u>, a book about famous screen teams, Kanin recalled bringing a story idea to the actors for another film. Although Irene and Grant liked it, Kanin was drafted before the project got off the ground (B-245).

In November, 1940, Irene joined agent Charles Feldman and his clients Charles Boyer, Ronald Colman, Lewis Milestone, and Anatole Litvak in forming Group Productions. The company planned to make films at 20th Century-Fox with money supplied by the studio. It would not only give the actors and directors more control of their films, but would strengthen the studio's star roster and allow 20th Century-Fox to trade talent with other studios. The major participants planned to collect a minimal salary, plus a percentage of the films' profits.

A clip from <u>Cimarron</u> was utilized in <u>Land of Liberty</u>, a patriotic compilation of scenes, put together to tell the history of the United States. First shown at the New York World's Fair and the San Francisco Exposition in 1939, the film was re-edited by Cecil B. DeMille and given a national release in 1941. <u>Land of Liberty</u> was a cooperative effort, with all the studios contributing footage. The final product, released by MGM, donated all profits to war emergency welfare work.

After two comedies, critics and audiences were not sure what to think when Irene and Cary Grant were paired in a drama. Told in a series of flashbacks, <u>Penny Serenade</u> (Columbia, 1941) was a serious story about a childless couple who adopted a baby, and the disintegration of their marriage when the child died. Although the basic plot was a tearjerker, Irene and Grant infused humor in many scenes, making the film more realistic. Irene often called <u>Penny Serenade</u> one of her favorite films, saying it reminded her of her own adopted daughter.

Two disappointing comedies followed. <u>Unfinished Business</u> (Universal, 1941) cast Irene as a singer who loved Preston Foster, but married his brother, Robert Montgomery, for spite. <u>Lady in a Jam</u> (Universal, 1942) featured Irene as a dizzy spendthrift who chased psychiatrist Patric Knowles. Although both films were directed by Gregory La Cava, who had helmed Irene in the serious <u>Symphony of Six Million</u> and Carole Lombard and William Powell in the screwball <u>My Man Godfrey</u>, neither <u>Unfinished Business</u> nor <u>Lady in a Jam</u> proved to be a classic.

Irene concentrated on her musical career in 1941, recording an album of Jerome Kern songs, which included "Smoke Gets in Your Eyes" from <u>Roberta</u> and "Why Was I Born?" from <u>Sweet Adeline</u>. She took time out from her film responsibilities to appear with the Chicago Symphony Orchestra during the 1941-42 season. She also was asked to perform with the Philadelphia Symphony.

During World War II, Irene was active selling war bonds and entertaining soldiers. She was one of the charter members of the Hollywood Victory Committee, which organized the film industry's efforts to entertain the troops. Irene appeared in a USO show in 1941 at the Hollywood Bowl and several war bond rallies around the country. She was part of a celebrity bond tour called "Stars Over America," the goal of which was to boost war bond sales over the billion-dollar mark. Among the participants were Bette Davis, Joan Crawford, James Cagney, Margaret Sullavan, Janet Gaynor, Alice Faye, Nelson Eddy, Dorothy Lamour, Henry Fonda, Greer Garson, and Walter Pidgeon. She appeared on several broadcasts on the Armed Forces Radio Network, which were heard by servicemen around the globe. Clips of Irene at a U.S.O. show were used in the morale-boosting film <u>Follow the Boys</u> (Universal, 1944) and in the short <u>Show Business at War</u> (20th Century-Fox, 1943). She spent her spare time visiting hospitalized soldiers and volunteering at the Hollywood Canteen. On September 9, 1942, the U.S. Treasury Department awarded her with a certificate for her work with the National War Savings Program.

Although it was announced that Irene would have a leading role in <u>Tales of Manhattan</u> (20th Century-Fox, 1942), she was not in the finished film. <u>The New York Times</u> reported that her character was to have been married to Thomas Mitchell, while having an affair with Charles Boyer (B-128). The role went to Rita Hayworth, who was both younger and less expensive to employ than Irene. Ernst Lubitsch planned a comedy/fantasy for Irene and Charles Boyer in 1943, but it was put on hold when Lubitsch began working on something more timely about the WACs. The story intended for Irene and Boyer later was used as the basis for <u>That Lady in Ermine</u> (20th Century-Fox, 1948), which starred Betty Grable and Douglas Fairbanks, Jr.

Like many stars of the era, Irene's likeness was used in a series of endorsements at the behest of the studio. From the 1930s through the 1950s, her face appeared in ads touting a variety of products, including Lux soap, Royal Crown cola, Elizabeth Arden makeup, U.S. Savings Bonds, and Rheingold Extra Dry lager beer. Despite the commercialism, her image was still that of the great lady. Movie magazine writers complained that, while Irene seemed like a very sweet woman, she was not good copy. When other stars were quoted about their latest romances, Irene was pictured modeling hats or giving gardening tips. While other actresses' contracts demanded elaborate dressing rooms and special treatment, Irene only requested choice of director.

In 1943 producer William Perlberg was searching for an actress to play the leading role in <u>The Song of Bernadette</u> for 20th Century-Fox. He told Louella Parsons, "Irene Dunne, whose life off the screen has always been above reproach and who is a devout Catholic, has appeared in too many sophisticated comedies and matrimonial satires. A young Irene yet to be discovered would be perfect" (B-254). Jennifer Jones ended up being cast in the role.

When Myrna Loy married John Hertz, Jr. in 1942, she retired from the screen and moved to New York. Irene was the first choice to replace her in the <u>Thin Man</u> series with William Powell. Like Loy, Irene's screen persona was the perfect wife. Although Loy claimed the publicity about

Irene replacing her was strictly to lure Loy back to MGM, the studio signed Irene to a contract in 1942. In addition to a planned Thin Man film, Irene's contract provided that she would star in The White Cliffs of Dover and Gaslight. According to Loy, there was an uproar from Thin Man fans and MGM abandoned its plans to team Irene with William Powell. In the end, Loy returned for The Thin Man Goes Home in 1944.

MGM, long known for its lavish musicals and big-budget productions, seemed an appropriate place for Irene, as mogul Louis B. Mayer admired women who were well-bred and refined. Stars like Norma Shearer, Myrna Loy, Katharine Hepburn, and Greer Garson had long been associated with the studio. Despite the original announcement, the first film Irene made was A Guy Named Joe (MGM, 1943). She played a ferry command pilot who was in love with a flier, played by Spencer Tracy. When Tracy was killed, Irene became interested in a young cadet, played by Van Johnson. During the filming, Johnson was seriously injured in a car accident. MGM wanted to recast the role and refilm Johnson's scenes. However, Tracy insisted they postpone filming until the actor recovered. In exchange, Tracy promised to stop bothering Irene, who had complained to Louis B. Mayer about Tracy's impropriety, variously reported as teasing, insulting, or flirting.

While Irene was waiting for Johnson to recover so they could finish A Guy Named Joe, she began work on The White Cliffs of Dover. Primarily a piece of propaganda to promote good feelings between the United States and Great Britain at the dawning of World War II, the film was the sentimental tale of a woman who lost her husband and son in battle. Irene dismissed the criticism, saying, "I don't think it smacks of propaganda, but if it does then I'm glad. I feel everything possible should be done to cement the friendship between two nations that are most alike and speak the same language" (B-386). The White Cliffs of Dover opened at Radio City Music Hall on May 10, 1944.

Gaslight was an on-again, off-again project for Irene. Columbia originally bought the rights to the play Angel Street, which became the film Gaslight, with her in mind. Columbia then sold the rights to MGM, who wanted it for Hedy Lamarr. Although Gaslight was announced as one of Irene's initial ventures at MGM, the studio ended up casting Ingrid Bergman in the film, which was released in 1944. In a move to trim the studio budget, Louis B. Mayer chose not to renew Irene's contract after her two films. MGM already had Greer Garson on the lot, who played similar roles. With a ten-year age difference, Garson seemed the better investment for the studio. Ironically, she starred in Irene's coveted role of Madame Curie for MGM in 1943.

Irene and Charles Boyer were reunited for the final time on screen in Together Again (Columbia, 1944), a light, romantic comedy about a widow and a sculptor. Over 21 (Columbia, 1945) cast Irene as a screenwriter, forced to live in barracks when her newspaper columnist husband enlisted.

Although RKO wanted Bing Crosby and Ingrid Bergman to star in The Bells of St. Mary's in 1946, Irene almost got involved in the film. Producer David O. Selznick, who had been production head at RKO from 1931 to 1933, owned Bergman's contract. He insisted that she refuse to make the film until his salary demands were met. Irene later said that Bergman became ill before filming began, putting Irene in the running for the role again. "I remember going upstairs and taking a towel and putting it over my head to see how I would look as a nun," Irene recalled, "But Ingrid got well" (B-382).

Irene returned to lush, big-budget productions with Anna and the King of Siam (20th Century-Fox, 1946). It was one of the first post-war films to have the tremendous sets and costumes of pre-war days. Irene played Anna Owens, an English governess who traveled to Siam to teach western manners to the barbaric king and his family. The film premiered at Radio City Music Hall on June 20, 1946. Irene and co-star Rex Harrison placed their foot and hand prints at Grauman's Chinese Theatre in Hollywood on July 8, 1946.

Although Irene never made it to the screen as the Thin Man's Nora Charles, she finally got to play opposite William Powell in Warner Bros.'s Life with Father in 1947. Based on the long-running play, the plot concerned the Victorian Day family, headed by the cantankerous Clarence, who refused to be baptized. Mary Pickford had been tested for Vinnie Day, but director Michael Curtiz did not want to use her. He repeatedly asked Irene to play the role, but she refused. Shortly before filming began, Irene changed her mind, although she still disliked the trickery her character employed to get her husband baptized. It was Irene's only full-length color film.

Irene received her fifth and final Oscar nomination for I Remember Mama (RKO, 1948). She lost to Jane Wyman for Johnny Belinda. The role of the Norwegian immigrant had been offered to Greta Garbo, and Irene was also reluctant to take it. For the first time, she appeared on screen in a less-than-glamorous fashion, in worn dresses and with her hair in a severe braid. However, in the end, Irene decided that the homespun story of an immigrant family in San Francisco was for her. Through the years, she called I Remember Mama one of her favorite films.

In the late 1940s, Irene began slowing down, making only one film a year. Quality roles for women her age were becoming less frequent. Irene was offered the replacement lead in the Broadway production of Goodbye, My Fancy, but turned it down. She continued her radio work and increased her involvement with charitable organizations, like the American Heart Association and the American Cancer Society. In 1949 Irene was named campaign vice chairman for the American Red Cross. She appeared in a two-minute film entitled Irene Dunne American Red Cross Fund Appeal, which ran in thirteen thousand movie theatres across the country.

Politics became more important in those post-war years. Although a staunch Republican, Irene was active with several non-partisan groups that promoted freedom. In 1947, she was one of many stars who banded together to speak out in favor of the First Amendment, following the House Un-American Activities Committee's investigation into alleged Communist activity in Hollywood. Irene participated in a broadcast entitled <u>Hollywood Fights Back</u>, with stars in New York, Hollywood, and Washington, D.C. joining forces to restore the movie industry's reputation.

In 1949, Irene donated her services to help the Christophers, a non-sectarian movement with anti-totalitarian and anti-Communist aims. Founded by Maryknoll priest Father James Keller in 1945, the Christophers preached that citizens should put their moral concepts to work in society. On November 30, 1949, Irene filmed a thirty-minute short entitled <u>You Can Change the World</u>. Directed by Leo McCarey, and starring Loretta Young, William Holden, Paul Douglas, Bob Hope, Ann Blyth, Jack Benny, and Rochester, the film was the first in a planned series of thirty shorts. Two hundred copies of the film were made available, free of charge, to interested groups around the country. The additional twenty-nine films were scheduled to be made as soon as the Christophers acquired enough donations to finance them. By 1956, sixteen films had been produced, including <u>The Story of Two Men</u>, which was introduced by Irene. <u>You Can Change the World</u> was released to television in 1952. During the 1950s Irene appeared on the group's syndicated television program <u>The Christophers</u> in segments promoting law and education.

The late 1940s also began a time of reflection, as Irene was honored by many organizations for her exemplary behavior on and off screen. Her alma mater, the Chicago Musical College, gave her an honorary degree of Doctor of Music on June 14, 1945. Irene, Frank, and Mary Frances traveled to South Bend, Indiana, in 1949 when the University of Notre Dame presented her with the Laetare Medal, the highest honor bestowed upon a Catholic lay person.

In 1949, Irene was one of four honorees chosen by the National Conference of Christians and Jews for their contributions to good relations among faiths. During the luncheon at the Waldorf-Astoria, when asked if America was perfect, Irene recalled her role as a Norwegian immigrant in <u>I Remember Mama</u>. She said, "When we have learned to love our neighbor, not just ourselves, no matter where he comes from, then America will be perfect" ("Award for Religious Amity." <u>New York Herald Tribune</u>. February 5, 1949.). Other recipients were Richard Rodgers, Oscar Hammerstein II, and RKO president Ned E. Depinet.

Mount St. Mary's College for Women gave Irene an honorary degree of Doctor of Laws on June 5, 1949. The Los Angeles college awarded the degree in recognition of her work with cancer research organizations and "courageous fidelity to Catholic principles in public and private life."

In the fall of 1949, Irene was announced as one of six rotating stars of the radio series <u>Prudential Family Hour of Stars</u>. She opened the season on October 2, recreating her <u>Love Affair</u> performance. The other stars who shared the series were Loretta Young, Jane Wyman, Ronald Colman,

Dana Andrews, and Kirk Douglas. Despite the publicity, the rotating stars soon were replaced. Irene appeared in only one additional episode.

Everyone in Hollywood seemed intent to get Irene back to the screen. On September 23, 1949, columnist Hedda Hopper announced that producer Gayle Titterman had come up with an ideal project for Irene. Entitled *My Dear Lady*, the story dealt with Anna Ella Carroll, an unofficial member of Abraham Lincoln's Cabinet during the Civil War. Carroll's efforts to help shorten the length of the war were written into the Congressional Record. Hopper pointed out that the story also had a "charming romance" running through it. Although the film was not made, Hopper's description made it sound much more promising than the three projects Irene chose to complete her film career.

Never a Dull Moment (RKO, 1950) reunited Irene with Fred MacMurray in a story about a mismatched couple out west. Irene played a sophisticated songwriter who married a widowed rancher with two children. Although mostly a light comedy, the film gave her a chance to sing three songs. Critics were less than thrilled with the film, which they compared to *The Egg and I*, a hit 1947 country/city clash starring MacMurray and Claudette Colbert.

While *I Remember Mama* had been Irene's first departure from glamour, *The Mudlark* (20th Century-Fox, 1950) was really a stretch. Playing the role of Queen Victoria, Irene was required to wear extensive makeup and padding, rendering her almost unrecognizable. There was a great controversy when she was cast, with British organizations outraged that an American actress would play the monarch. By the time the film was released in 1950, the brouhaha had died down and the film was given a Command Performance for the royal family.

Irene's final film was *It Grows on Trees* (Universal, 1952). While she admitted the idea of a housewife finding dollar bills growing in her backyard was "cute," Irene regretted that the picture did not have a more noted director or leading man. With the light touch of a Leo McCarey or a Tay Garnett, or with the comic talents of a Cary Grant, *It Grows on Trees* might have risen above its mediocrity. Instead, it was a low-budget entry that might have done better as a half-hour TV show than a full-length film. It was an unfitting curtain for a stellar screen career.

But Irene was branching out into other areas even as she concluded her big screen appearances. In August, 1951, she signed a contract with the Frederic Ziv Company to co-star in a radio series with Fred MacMurray. *Bright Star* cast her as the editor/publisher of a small town newspaper, with MacMurray as her chief reporter. The comedy/drama was recorded and syndicated in 1952.

On January 23, 1952, Irene signed a contract to host twenty-six episodes of *Spotlight Theatre*, a television anthology series. The title changed to *Schlitz Playhouse of Stars*. Irene hosted the show from May 30 to November 21, 1952. She appeared in a prologue, introducing the episode and giving the viewer a hint of its flavor. She returned to close the show. Although other movie star hosts, like Loretta Young, Jane Wyman, and Robert Montgomery, occasionally acted in their series, Irene appeared only in the openings and closings. Throughout her association with <u>Schlitz Playhouse of Stars</u>, critics said the brief skits were a waste of her talents. Although several press reports claimed Irene left due to pressure from her fans, outraged that their idol would appear on a program sponsored by a brewery, her contract stipulated twenty-six episodes.

Throughout the 1950s Irene made television appearances. Although most were episodes of dramatic anthologies, like <u>The Loretta Young Show</u>, <u>The June Allyson Show</u>, and <u>Ford Television Theatre</u>, she dabbled in comedy and variety with <u>The Jack Benny Show</u>, <u>The Colgate Comedy Hour</u>, and <u>The Perry Como Show</u>. She even did a few whimsical turns, christening the Mark Twain paddlewheeler on <u>Dateline Disneyland</u> and appearing as a mystery guest on <u>What's My Line?</u>.

Irene continued to receive film offers. She turned down a leading role in <u>The Swan</u> (MGM, 1956), as well as in the musical <u>Gigi</u> (MGM, 1958). She continued to be a voting member of the Academy of Motion Picture Arts and Sciences, and presented Oscars at the 1954 and 1959 ceremonies.

During this time, Irene became more active in politics. She was a member of the delegation from California at the National Republican Convention in 1948. She actively campaigned for Presidential candidates Thomas Dewey in 1948 and Dwight Eisenhower in 1952 and 1956. In 1951, she was named a member of the Defense Advisory Committee to advise the State Department on welfare matters in the women's services. The committee was made up of women from all walks of life. In 1956 Irene and Charles H. Percy, president of Bell and Howell, coordinated a televised "surprise party" for President Eisenhower. The all-star cast included James Stewart, Helen Hayes, Nat King Cole, and Fred Waring.

On August 9, 1957, President Eisenhower nominated a ten-member delegation to represent the United States at the next session of the United Nations. Irene was appointed an alternate representative. At the time, she called the appointment the highlight of her career. The 1957 session began September 17, 1957. Irene first addressed the General Assembly on October 4, announcing the United States' financial pledges for the U.N. refugee relief programs. She was assigned to the U.N. Trusteeship Committee, which tried to establish better relations with South Africa. Irene told the <u>New York Herald Tribune</u>, "I wish every woman I know could have this experience. It's tremendously broadening and I'm trying to get as much out of it as I can" (B-216).

The 1950s were also a time of honors. Irene's involvement with the Catholic Church was rewarded with the presentation of the Lateran Cross in 1951. She received the Award of Merit from the Sister Elizabeth Kenny Foundation in 1953 for her efforts raising money to fight polio. The

In 1957, Irene Dunne served as an alternate delegate to the United Nations. (Author's collection)

National Council of Catholic Youth gave her the Pro Deo Juventute Award in 1957. She received an honorary Doctor of Laws from the University of Notre Dame in 1958. She was also named Indiana Woman of the Year by the Indianapolis alumnae chapter of Theta Sigma Phi, a sorority now known as Women in Communication.

For many years Irene was an active fundraiser for Saint John's Hospital and Health Center in Santa Monica. In 1951, she was elected president of the Saint John's Hospital Foundation. She served on the board until 1966, and even then, continued to be involved with the developmental committee. She and her husband established the Irene Dunne-Francis D. Griffin Foundation to benefit the hospital.

In 1958, Irene wrote a letter to George Rosenberg and Bob Coryell, urging them to produce a television special to benefit Saint John's building fund. The special did not materialize, but one of the producers heard a record of How the West Was Won and decided to make the story into a film, which would serve as a fundraiser for Saint John's. Irene procured most of the talent, convincing the actors to work for the minimum union wage and to accept equal billing. She kept silent about the project for a long time, fearing she would be unable to pull it off. Among those stars whose talents she borrowed were James Stewart, Henry Fonda, Gregory Peck, Debbie Reynolds, and John Wayne. Clark Gable and Gary Cooper both committed to the project, but died before the film was produced. How the West Was Won opened on February 20, 1963, with a gala premiere which benefited Saint John's building fund. Additionally, ten percent of the world gross of the film went to the hospital. By November 30, 1963, the film had grossed $17 million. In 1985 the hospital honored Irene by erecting a statue of her in a garden called Foundation Court.

In addition to her charity work, Irene spent the early 1960s making occasional television appearances. She was one of many celebrities on hand to celebrate former First Lady Eleanor Roosevelt's seventy-sixth birthday with Eleanor Roosevelt's Diamond Jubilee Plus One. Irene also appeared on the anthologies Frontier Circus, G.E. Theatre, and Saints and Sinners. Harcourt Brace approached her about writing her memoirs, but her husband discouraged her, teasing her that no one wanted to read about her grandmother.

By then, Irene herself was a grandmother. After attending Manhattanville College, Mary Frances married Richard Lee Shinnick in the late 1950s. The Shinnicks settled in Beverly Hills and had two children: Mark, born in 1958, and Ann Marie, born in 1959. Irene was close to her grandchildren, finding time to do the simple things she missed with Mary Frances, like taking them swimming or to movies.

After a long illness, Frank died of a heart ailment on October 15, 1965. He was seventy-nine. In addition to his real estate holdings, he was on the advisory board of the Bank of America, and was a director of the Beverly Wilshire Hotel and the Griffin Wellpoint Corporation. After her husband's death, Irene took over his business interests, moving the office into her home.

Although Irene had been absent from the social scene for years, preferring to spend time with her husband, she began to appear sporadically at Hollywood functions. In 1965, she became the first woman to be named to the board of directors of Technicolor, Inc. She presented the Jean Hersholt Humanitarian Award to George Bagnall at the Academy Awards ceremony on April 10, 1967. When asked about her husband's death, she told TV Radio Mirror, "I believe my staying in the atmosphere of our long happiness has helped. That, and my friends, and keeping very busy" (B-400).

In 1967, Ronald Reagan, then governor of California, appointed Irene to the board of the California Arts Commission (CAC). Established by the State Legislature in 1964, the CAC fostered the growth of the arts in communities. The largest project undertaken during Irene's three-year tenure was an exhibit called "Dimension." Consisting of thirty pieces of sculpture on loan from California museums and galleries, the exhibit was the first traveling "gallery" geared to the handicapped. The exhibit encouraged both blind and sighted patrons to touch the sculptures; signs, maps, and programs were all printed in Braille. "Dimension" opened at San Francisco's M.H. de Young Memorial Museum on January 12, 1970 and traveled to Los Angeles, Sacramento, San Diego, Fresno, and Long Beach over the next eleven months. Irene was on hand for the opening. She also recorded a talking book about the exhibit, enabling the blind to get a deeper understanding of the sculpture.

Awards continued to pour in. In 1965, Irene became the first woman to receive the Bellarmine College Medal, honoring her for her contribution to the arts, as well as her civic and philanthropic activities. She was one of four film greats honored by the fraternity Delta Kappa Alpha in 1967. She received the Golden Eve Award for repeatedly being nominated as one of Southern California's best dressed women. In 1968, she was named one of Colorado's Women of Achievement.

Irene's public appearances became less frequent during the 1970s. She was seen occasionally at screenings and at the funerals of her contemporaries. She made it her business to attend Mass daily. She told TV Radio Mirror, "A Mass takes 25 minutes and it's no sacrifice for me to give that much time to say, 'Praise you, my Lord.' I'm just grateful that I'm well enough to go" (B-400). She donated the altar of St. Teresa in Hollywood's Church of the Blessed Sacrament.

Irene was still receiving offers in 1972, but she told film historian John Kobal that she was busy with other things. "I think for an old person who's had the success I have to start playing second- or third-rate parts...I just wouldn't like that," she said (B-250). She was offered the role of the aging designer in a Broadway revival of Roberta, a project she quickly dismissed. Producer Ross Hunter tried to lure her out of retirement in 1977 by offering her a role in a planned NBC miniseries entitled *Story of a House*. Irene refused the role; the miniseries was never produced.

Irene must hold a record for the number of films which have been remade, a comment on her ability to recognize a lasting story. Among the movies which were filmed again were: *Cimarron*, *Back Street*, *Roberta* (*Lovely to Look At*), *Magnificent Obsession*, *Show Boat*, *The Awful Truth* (*Let's Do It Again*), *Love Affair* (*An Affair to Remember*), *When Tomorrow Comes* (*Interlude*), *My Favorite Wife* (*Move Over Darling*), *A Guy Named Joe* (*Always*), and *Anna and the King of Siam* (*The King and I*). Unfortunately, the proliferation of remakes kept many of Irene's films from being shown on television or in revivals. The 1970s changed that, bringing Irene a new legion of fans. The Los Angeles County Museum and the California Palace of the Legion of Honor hosted the first Irene Dunne film retrospective in November, 1970. Irene was on hand to answer questions, following a screening of *Roberta*.

The Los Angeles International Film Exposition (Filmex) was the next group to honor Irene, on March 23, 1975. Coordinated by film historian David Chierichetti and moderated by Roddy McDowall, the impressive five-hour program included clips from fifteen films and two television shows, as well as a discussion period. Filmex even paid for a new print of *Love Affair* to be struck from the Museum of Modern Art's negative, making the film accessible for the first time in many years.

Irene traveled to Washington, D.C. in 1977 to help the American Film Institute celebrate its tenth anniversary. After screening clips from *Roberta* and *My Favorite Wife*, as well as the complete *Love Affair*, Irene answered questions from the audience. In turn, the American Film Institute honored Irene in Los Angeles on August 25, 1979. Once again, Irene was on hand to answer questions about her career, following a screening of *Love Affair* and clips from *The Awful Truth*.

The National Art Association honored Irene with a dinner, which was held at the Beverly Wilshire Hotel's Grand Ballroom on May 18, 1985. In addition to film clips highlighting Irene's career, John Raitt performed musical selections.

A further tribute came in 1985 when Irene was selected as one of the recipients of the annual Kennedy Center Honors. The medal, suspended on a rainbow striped ribbon, was awarded to performing artists for their contributions to the arts and humanities. Irene was thrilled to be chosen, saying, "There I'll be with my favorite comedian (Bob Hope), my favorite opera singer (Beverly Sills) and the two fellows who wrote my favorite show of all (Frederick Loewe and Alan Jay Lerner of *My Fair Lady*)" (B-47). The two-day festivities included a dinner at the State Department, a reception at the White House, and a performance at Kennedy Center. Irene attended the dinner, but was plagued by back trouble. She ended up in Georgetown Hospital when pain medication made her ill. She missed the stage tribute, in which Fredericka von Stade performed "You Are Love" and "Smoke Gets in Your Eyes." Irene's biographical segment was narrated by her old friend James Stewart, who called her "an authentic American thoroughbred."

At the time of this writing, Irene is the only Kennedy Center Honors recipient who did not attend the program in which they were honored. There have been rumors that she was adamant about her fans remembering her as she looked at the height of her fame and therefore did not attend the televised ceremony. However, it seems unlikely that she would have traveled to Washington for the dinner, which was highly photographed, and then avoided the tribute itself.

The Los Angeles County Museum of Art honored Irene with a two-day film festival in December, 1986. Billed as "The Best of Irene Dunne," the tribute ran <u>Back Street</u>, <u>Magnificent Obsession</u>, <u>Roberta</u>, and <u>Sweet Adeline</u>. Unlike the previous career retrospectives, Irene was not present. By 1983, a back accident had robbed her of her daily Mass, a condition she called "the extreme sacrifice." She declined an invitation to appear as guest of honor at a special performance of <u>Roberta</u>, which was a fundraiser for the Cincinnati Opera.

Despite her failing health, Irene was still quick to act for charity. Actress Joan Leslie recalled an incident involving St. Anne's Home for Unwed Mothers. When St. Anne's wanted to present its Angel Award to Irene for her artistic and civic achievements, she was forced to decline because of her health. However, she was instrumental in getting an invitation to Nancy Reagan, giving Leslie instructions about how to write to the First Lady, then mailing the invitation for Leslie, to an inside White House address so that it would get immediate attention from Reagan's secretary. Leslie said, "I'm sure very few close friends of the Reagans had that privilege given to them."

Irene died of heart failure in her Holmby Hills home on September 4, 1990. She had been suffering from an irregular heartbeat for over a year and had been attended by private nurses. She was survived by her daughter, now Mary Frances Gage, grandchildren Ann and Mark Shinnick, a great-granddaughter, and a niece. Irene requested that memorial donations be sent to Saint John's Hospital.

Although publicity about Irene had been scant during her last years, her death brought a rush of fond memories. Longtime friend Ronald Reagan was quoted as saying, "Losing her is like losing a member of the family. More than just a Hollywood legend, Irene was one of the world's most celebrated movie stars because of her great talent, which thrilled her millions of fans" (B-232).

On September 8, 1990, Irene was buried beside her husband at Calvary Cemetery after a Mass at the cemetery's mausoleum chapel. She had requested that her funeral be very private. The only celebrity in attendance was Loretta Young. Even Ronald Reagan was turned away when he called to request an invitation to the funeral.

A month after Irene's death, the <u>Los Angeles Times</u>

announced that her home at 461 North Faring Road was for sale. The one-acre estate, which included a six thousand square-foot French colonial house with four bedroom suites and three servants' rooms, was listed at $6.9 million. Ironically, one of the realtors was William Bakewell who had acted with Irene in Back Street in 1932 (B-367).

Several months before Irene's death, the author queried many of the actress' friends and colleagues for reminiscences. Everyone agreed that she deserved to be called "The First Lady of Hollywood," for she not only built a solid career on playing noble characters, but carried the same grace and humanity into her personal life.

Although Joan Leslie had a bit part in Love Affair and guested on Schlitz Playhouse of Stars, she regretted never getting the opportunity to work directly with Irene. Leslie recalled how Irene's screen appearances inspired Leslie and her sisters to be actresses. She said, "Her gentility, refinement - gorgeous sense of humor - lovely singing voice - we could always point to her outstanding example as a woman and a star....Always the lady - charming and fun." Leslie continued, "I hope that her career was not hard for her. I hope she looks back with lots of pride on what she did. She should."

Joseph Cotten recalled working with Irene in a Lux Radio Theatre version of Penny Serenade. Although it was their only collaboration, they continued to see each other socially through the years. Cotten concluded, "I admire Miss Dunne enormously as an actress and as a person." Perry Como remembered her as a very lovely, gracious lady when she appeared on his 1950s variety show. Back Street co-star William Bakewell said, "She was a darling and a lady of quality in every sense of the words."

Roddy McDowall penned a moving tribute, calling Irene "one of the most unique and remarkable of actresses." He said, "I always counted myself wildly fortunate to play her son in The White Cliffs of Dover, an experience which ranks as one of the most special in my entire career. It was a rapture to work with her and my friendship with her since 1944 has always been one of the jewels in my life." McDowall confessed that he "lost his heart" to Irene after seeing her in his first feature film, Roberta. "Her elegance, wit, charm, and grace set her apart from anyone else," he said. "Her obvious culture, coupled with delicious naughtiness, make her comedies quite unique and her particular star charisma, wedded with her special sense of humanity, have made her dramatic appearances deeply moving."

Ralph Bellamy had similar feelings. He wrote, "I had the pleasure of making three pictures with Irene. It was like a three-layered cake with candles" He continued, "She was a delight to work with - on and off camera, truly a professional, extremely talented, and socially attractive and beautiful. I carry a fund of lasting memories of her."

Although longtime friend James Stewart never worked with Irene, he was delighted to hear that a book was being written about her career. "She is the best," he wrote, "Up there in a class by herself." With her films being discovered by a new generation, thanks to cable television and videotape, hopefully she will always be remembered that way.

Plays and Personal Appearances

This chapter features plays and personal appearances made by Irene Dunne. Each entry includes cities played, performance dates, credits, synopsis, and a brief note about Miss Dunne's participation. The spelling of "Dunn" or "Dunne" is as it appeared in the program or reviews. As it is impossible to chronicle all of the appearances Miss Dunne made during World War II and on behalf of the many charities she supported, only a sampling of those public appearances are given.

P-1   <u>A Midsummer Night's Dream</u>   grammar school play
City played: Madison, IN (5.29.13 and 6.2.13, Madison Grammar School).

Play: William Shakespeare. Pianist: Helen Leland.

CAST: Hayden Bear (Theseus, Duke of Venice), Alfred Donat (Egeus), Cecil Sailar (Lysander), Robert Caplinger (Demetrius), Leona Bondurant (Hermia), Juanita Schmidt (Helena), Bessie Thacker (Hippolyta), Virginia Tevis (Titania), Philip Francisco Stapp (Queen's page), Louis McIntyre (Oberon), Harold McKenna (Puck), Tena Higgins (Moth), Hazel Augustin (Peasblossom), Irene Dunn (Mustardseed), Lenora Loth (Cobuleb), Eleanor Tevis (Butterfly), Marie Vaughn (Moonbeam), Cleone McKay (Starlight), Harry Horton (Nick Bottom), Ruth Hanna, Nellie Taylor, Earl Turner, Wenonah Paden, Morris Strother, Nathan Schad (Fairies).

See also B-461

NOTES: <u>A Midsummer Night's Dream</u> marked Irene Dunn's stage debut. Admission was $1.75.

P-2   <u>St. Cecelia</u>   benefit performance
Cities played: Madison, IN and Milton, KY.

30   Irene Dunne

NOTES: <u>St. Cecelia</u> was staged as a benefit for the King's Daughters Hospital in Madison. It was so successful, residents in Milton asked for a performance. The show was Irene Dunn's first road experience.

P-3   <u>Irene</u>   touring company
City played: Chicago (beginning 11.20, Garrick Theatre).

Producer: Vanderbilt Producing Co. Director: Edward Royce. Libretto: James Montgomery. Music: Harry Tierney. Lyrics: Joe McCarthy.

CAST: Helen Shipman (Irene O'Dare), Jeanette MacDonald (Eleanor Worth), John B. Litel (Donald Marshall), C. Bailey Hick (Robert Harrison), Henry Coote (J.P. Bowden), George P. Collins (Lawrence Hadley), George Clayton Mantell (Clarkson), Sydney Reynolds (Helen Cheston), Erica Mackay (Jane Gilmour), Dorothy La Mar (Mrs. Marshall), Flo Irwin (Mrs. O'Dare), Lillian Cameron (Mrs. Cheston), Jere Delaney (Madame Lucy), Irene Dunne (Chorus).

SYNOPSIS: Shop girl Irene O'Dare meets wealthy Donald Marshall when he rescues her from an unpleasant situation at his familial home. Donald gets Irene a job as a model for a ladies' tailor. Irene's mother is suspicious of his attentions because of the class difference. Irene is a hit at a Long Island party, where she models an elaborate wardrobe, sings, and dances. Despite Mrs. O'Dare's initial objections, Donald proposes to Irene and they live happily ever after.

See also B-120, B-146, B-154, B-197, B-225, B-232, B-244, B-247, B-444

NOTES: Although many reports claimed that Irene Dunne played the title role in the Chicago production of <u>Irene</u> in 1920, <u>Variety</u> hailed Helen Shipman as the company's leading lady. According to an article entitled "<u>Irene</u> Knockout," "Helen Shipman in the lead was proclaimed by all critics a sensational find" (<u>Variety</u>, December 10, 1920). It is more likely that Irene Dunne appeared in the chorus of the show, as a few of her biographies noted. The production moved to Chicago's Studebaker Theatre in March, 1921. Most of the cast moved with the musical, but Irene Dunne was not listed in the program. <u>Modern Screen</u> claimed that Irene played four performances on Broadway before embarking on the tour, replacing leading lady Patti Harrold in the title role at New York's Vanderbilt Theatre. <u>Modern Screen</u> also reported that the <u>Irene</u> tour lasted twenty weeks and included dates in New Jersey, Pennsylvania, and West Virginia (B-197).

P-4   <u>The Clinging Vine</u>   original Broadway cast, replacement on tour

Cities played: Hartford, CT (beginning 11.30.22, Parson's Theatre), New York (188 performances beginning 12.25.22, Knickerbocker Theatre), Cleveland, OH (1.24, Baker Theatre).

BROADWAY PRODUCTION:
Producer: Henry W. Savage. Director: Ira Hards. Choreographer: Julian Alfred. Libretto: Zelda Sears. Lyrics: Zelda Sears. Music: Harold Levy. Costumes: Peggy Hoyt.

CAST: Irene Dunne (Tessie), Nathaniel Wagner (Plummer), Royal Hallee (Billings), Charles Schofield (Titus M. Tutewiler), Christian Holtum (Bill), Bradford Hunt (Smith), Roy Marvin (Brown), William Rogers (Jones), Peggy Wood (Antoinette Allen), Josephine Adair (Mildred Mayo), Eleanor Dawn (Janet Milton), James C. Marlowe (Francis Milton), Raymond Crane (Randolph Mayo), Jane Arrol (Jane), Jean Ferguson (Jean), Margery Wall (Margery), Rosa Vera (Rosa), Helen Hipkins (Helen), Louise Scheerer (Louise), Eleanor Livingston (Eleanor), Virginia Clark (Virginia), Florence McGuire (Florence), Victoria White (Victoria), Louise Galloway (Mrs. Anthony Allen), Reginald Pasch (Vacarescou), Joyce White (Agnes), William C. Gordon (Bascom), Charles Derickson (Jimmy Manning).

SYNOPSIS: Antoinette Evans is an efficient executive in an Omaha paint firm who kowtows to no man. When she is called east on business, she visits her grandmother, Mrs. Anthony Allen. Grandma advises her to pretend to be a "clinging vine" in order to hook a husband. Antoinette puts on a good act, winning the admiration of a score of suitors. She falls in love with Jimmy Manning, a poor inventor. Antoinette beats her suitors in a real estate deal and takes her fortune back to Omaha and Jimmy.

REVIEWS:
Variety, 12.8.22: "The Clinging Vine is the unusual in musical offerings;...it is more of a comedy with music than a musical comedy. It has a definite plot that is well worked out and put over with the assistance of some exceedingly clever comedy lines. The musical numbers are catchy and clever..."

New York American, 12.26.22: "A delightfully amusing little show....some of the ditties tinkle and cavort and undeniably 'get you.'"

Variety, 1.5.23: "The Clinging Vine will attract the public. It is a charming story Zelda Sears has evolved. The tuneful and catchy score of Harold Levy and the really clever performance with Peggy Wood in the titular role will get the business."

32   Irene Dunne

See also F-40, B-65, B-133, B-154, B-268, B-302

NOTES: During the show's run, Irene Dunne pursued her musical studies. Her role of Tessie was only onstage for about four minutes during the musical's first act. Irene wrote playwright Zelda Sears a note, thanking her for Tessie's brevity, allowing Irene to have time for her daily studies. The note was well-circulated and brought Irene to the attention of many important figures in the world of musical comedy. Irene also acted as leading lady Peggy Wood's understudy. During a tour of <u>The Clinging Vine</u>, Wood came down with laryngitis, and Irene was called to Cleveland to replace her. As Tessie, Irene sang "A Little Bit of Paint;" as Antoinette, she sang "A Little Bit of Paint," "Once Upon a Time," "Age of Innocence," "Homemade Happiness," and "Serenade."

P-5   <u>Lollipop</u>   Broadway replacement
      City played: New York (1924, Knickerbocker Theatre).

      Producer: Henry W. Savage. Director: Ira Hards. Choreographers: Bert French, John Tiller, and Mary Read. Libretto: Zelda Sears. Lyrics: Zelda Sears and Walter DeLeon. Music: Vincent Youmans.

      CAST: Irene Dunne (Virginia), Leonard Ceiley (Don Carlos), Adora Andrews (Mrs. Mason), Aline McGill (Tessie), Nick Long, Jr. (Omar K. Garrity), Virginia Smith (Petunia), Ada-May (Laura Lamb), A Dark Secret (Rufus), Gus Shy (George Jones), Harry Puck (Bill Geohagen), Amelia Gardner (Mrs. Garrity), Florence Webber (Helene), Addison Fowler, Florenz Tamara (Specialty dancers), Mark Smith (Parkinson), William C. Gordon (Lindsay), Leonard St. Leo (Pan), Muriel Marlowe, Ethel Helliwell, Connie Aldis, Florence McCabe, Vera Longren, Elsie Holt, Ethel Fraser, Pat Fraser, Alice Wright, Doris Carter, Veronica Preston, Edith Morgan (John Tiller's Dancing Lollipops), Evelyn Kindler, Guerida Crawford, Nerene Swinton, Katherine Huth, Maude Troup, Carol Joyce, Ruth Tester, Elizabeth Childs, Lucille Constante, Mary Jayne, Eleanor Livingston, Katherine Odell (Dancing girls), Bobby Culbertson, George Rand, Walter Crisham, Harold Raymond, Charles Townsend, Carl Judd (Dancing boys), Elsa Gray, Louise Scheerer, Royal Halee, Charles King (Special singing quartette).

SYNOPSIS: Laura Lamb is nicknamed "Lollipop" at the orphanage where she lives. She is adopted by wealthy Mrs. Garrity, but the nickname sticks. Lollipop meets an attractive plumber. She is accused of stealing Mrs. Garrity's purse, but proves her innocence at a masked costume ball.

NOTES: Irene Dunne replaced Gloria Dawn as Virginia during the musical's Broadway run. Irene sang "Love in a Cottage,"

Plays and Personal Appearances   33

"When We Are Married," and "Deep in My Heart." A five-year agreement signed by the Producing Managers' Association and the Actors' Equity Association expired on May 31, 1924. Several producers, including Henry W. Savage, demanded better terms with their actors. When no settlement was reached, Lollipop closed. Cast from March 17, 1924.

P-6 The City Chap   original Broadway cast
Cities played: Philadelphia (opened 9.29.25, Garrick Theatre), New York (72 performances beginning 10.26.25, Liberty Theatre).

Producer: Charles Dillingham. Director: R.H. Burnside. Choreographer: David Bennett. Libretto: James Montgomery. Based on the play The Fortune Hunter by Winchell Smith. Lyrics: Anne Caldwell. Music: Jerome Kern. Musical director: Victor Baravalle. Orchestrations: Robert Russell Bennett. Costumes: James Reynolds. Sets: James Reynolds.

CAST: Fred Lennox (Robbins), Irene Dunn (Grace Bartlett), John Rutherford (Stephen Kellogg), Richard "Skeet" Gallagher (Nat Duncan), Robert O'Connor (Pete), Eddie Girard (Watty), Phyllis Cleveland (Betty Graham), Francis X. Donegan (Tracey Tanner), Mary Jane (Angie), Frank Doane (Blinkey Lockwood), Ina Williams (Josie Lockwood), Hansford Wilson (Roland Barnett), Eddie Girard (Sam Graham), George Raft (George Spelvin), Helyn Eby Rock (Miss Sperry), Pearl Eaton (Pearl), Betty Compton (Betty), Beth Meakins, Blossom Vreeland, Constance Brown, Ona Hamilton, Danzie Goodell, Mary Pierce, Jeanne Edwards, Frisco De Vere, Jerry Markham, Betty Winslow, Katherine Kohler, Nickie Pitell, Mildred Sinclair, Betty Block, Jane Lane, Lucy Monroe, Katherine Burnside, Ursula Dale, Margaret Morris, Kathleen Errol, Beatrice Hughes, Myrtle Cox, Rita Farrell, Mildred Lunnay (Ladies of the ensemble), Al Watson, Hal Stevens, J. Hughes, Alfred Hale, Ward Arnold, Wallace Jackson, Milton Halpern, Hal Hennessey (Gentlemen of the ensemble), Eugene Revere, Charles Abbe, Marjorie Moss and Georges Fontana, George Olsen and His Orchestra, the Mound City Blue Blowers.

SYNOPSIS: Broke and discouraged, Nat Duncan travels from New York to the small town of Radford, intending to impress Josie Lockwood, the banker's daughter, with his city ways. Instead, Nat falls in love with Betty Graham, the druggist's daughter. Nat finally weds Betty, after opening a jazz tearoom at the drugstore and becoming an entrepreneur of sorts.

REVIEWS:
Variety, 9.30.25: "Honors for the women must be divided by [Phyllis] Cleveland with Irene Dunn as the small-town belle. This girl has a great personality, can dance like a streak and knows how to handle her voice. Her duet number

with [Skeet] Gallagher, 'Walking Home with Josie,' looks like the best song bet in the show."

New York Sun, 10.27.25: "A highly efficient, zestful and polished musical comedy....it is excellent, if extremely conventional entertainment."

New York Times, 10.27.25: "The idle rich were handsomely represented in town and country in Irene Dunn, John Rutherford and a personable chorus..."

Variety, 10.28.25: "But **The City Chap** will still not rank with the biggest and the best unless some tall rewriting can be done to shift the ballast so that more than two slender [Skeet] Gallagher shoulders are called on to tote it through the plot."

New York Daily News, 10.29.25: "If this isn't good, I don't know musical shows."

NOTES: This was Irene Dunn's first association with composer Jerome Kern. She sang "Walking Home with Josie." Richard "Skeet" Gallagher later became known as Skeets Gallagher.

P-7 **Sweetheart Time** Broadway replacement
City played: New York (beginning 3.8.26, Imperial Theatre).

Producers: James La Penner and Edward A. Miller. Director: William Collier. Choreographer: Larry Ceballos. Libretto: Harry B. Smith. Based on the play **Never Say Die**. Lyrics: Ballard Macdonald and Irving Caesar. Music: Walter Donaldson and Joseph Meyer. Costumes: Charles LeMaire and Boue Soeurs.

CAST: Irene Dunne (Violet Stevenson), Eddie Buzzell (Dion Woodbury), Starke Patterson (Jeffries), Laine Blaire (Nina), Jackie Hulbert (Marian Stevenson), Barnett Greenwood (Roy Henderson), Jean Newcombe (Mrs. Stevenson), James S. Barrett (Dr. Ralph Galesby), Fred Leslie (Lord Hector Raybrook), W.J. McCarthy (Griggs), John Sheehan (Detective James), M. Marcel Rousseau (Alphonse), Dorothy Brown (Cleopatra McNulty/Dorothy), Bob Callahan (Waiter), Dorothy Van Alst (Dorothy), Betty Wright (Betty), Bessie Kademova (Bessie), Bobbie Breslaw (Bobbie), Mary Hoover, Aida Winston, Dorothy Fitzgibbons, Ann Hardman, Neida Snow, Beverley Maude, Loretta Rehm, Adele Hart, Alice Monroe, Nellie McCarthy, Peggy Thayer, Millicent Olson, Adele Sinclair (Young ladies of the ensemble).

SYNOPSIS: Nervous Dion Woodbury meets Violet Stevenson and falls in love immediatly. However, Violet is about to marry Lord Raybrook for his money. Believing he is about to die, Dion proposes to Violet and offers to leave her at the altar, freeing her to chose a husband for love after his death. Violet agrees and Dion disappears after the wedding. Violet is convinced there is something in prayer when he returns a year later, completely cured.

See also B-141, B-413

NOTES: Irene Dunne replaced Genevieve Tobin as Violet on March 8, 1926, two months after the musical opened on Broadway. Irene sang "Sweetheart Time" and "Girl in Your Arms." Cast from May 10, 1926.

P-8 St. Louis Municipal Opera   summer season
City played: St. Louis (Municipal Theatre, 5.31.26-8.22.26).

Producer: Municipal Theatre Association of St. Louis.

CAST: Dorothy Maynard, Irene Dunne, Bernice Mershon, Maude Gray, Thomas Conkey, Robinson Newbold, Edward Molitore, Detmar Poppen, William McCarthy, Roland Woodruff.

Eileen   5.31.26-6.6.26
Irene Dunne played Lady Maude Eastbrook.

The Red Mill   6.7.26-6.13.26
Irene Dunne was Bertha, the Bergomaster's sister.

The Chocolate Soldier   6.14.26-6.20.26
Irene Dunne was not listed in program.

The Spring Maid   6.21.26-6.27.26
Irene Dunne essayed the title role, Annamirl, who was known as "The Spring Maid."

The Pink Lady   6.28.26-7.4.26
Irene Dunne portrayed Angele.

Il Trovatore   7.5.26-7.11.26
Irene Dunne was not listed in program.

Sweethearts   7.12.26-7.18.26
Irene Dunne was Liane, a milliner.

Iolanthe   7.19.26-7.25.26
Irene Dunne played the title role.

Count of Luxembourg   7.26.26-8.1.26
Irene Dunne was cast as Juliette, a model.

Woodland   8.2.26-8.8.26
Irene Dunne portrayed Miss Jennie Wren.

Fra Diavolo   8.9.26-8.15.26
Irene Dunne was not listed in program.

36   Irene Dunne

>Babes in Toyland   8.16.26-8.22.26
>Irene Dunne was not listed in program.

See also B-64, B-397

NOTES: The St. Louis Municipal Opera (the MUNY) is one of the oldest summer theatres in the United States, having presented its first season in 1919. Located in Forest Park, the outdoor theatre hosted a variety of stars through the years, including Ethel Merman, Bob Hope, and Cary Grant. Irene Dunne made her Municipal Theatre debut in Eileen, which opened May 31, 1926. The ten-member company played the majority of the leading roles during the twelve-week season. They were joined by Metropolitan Opera stars Frances Peralta, Marion Telva, James Wolfe, Greek Evans, and Judson House for Il Trovatore. The performances included a ninety-six-member chorus and a fifty-piece orchestra. According to the MUNY's files, Irene's contract was for the 1926 summer season, however her name was not listed in the programs for all the shows. It is not known whether she was in the chorus of those productions. Irene later told the St. Louis Globe-Democrat that the engagement was "one of the most valuable, and at the same time, one of the hardest experiences I've ever had" (Magazine section. February 23, 1930. p. 14.).

P-9   Light Opera Company
      City played: Atlanta (1926).

NOTE: Irene Dunne performed the music of Gilbert and Sullivan with a group of young singers from the Metropolitan Opera. The Atlanta Historical Society could find no further details.

P-10 Yours Truly   original Broadway cast
      Cities played: Detroit, Pittsburgh, New York (127 performances beginning 1.25.27, Shubert Theatre).

   Producer: Gene Buck. Directors: Gene Buck and Paul Dickey. Choreographer: Ralph Reader. Libretto: Clyde North. Music: Raymond Hubbell. Lyrics: Anne Caldwell. Musical director: Raymond Hubbell. Sets: Josef Urban. Costumes: Mabel E. Johnston.

   CAST: Jack Squires (Shuffling Bill), Jack Stanley (Joey Ling), John Kearney (Mac), David Herblin (Phil), Edgar Nelson (Mike), Irene Dunne (Diana), Theodore Babcock (J.P. Stillwell), Leon Errol (Truly), Vic Casmore (Bonzolino), Audrey Berry (Ruth), Ina Williams (Scats), Marion Harris (Mary Stillwell), David Herblin (Bandit), Harry Kelly (Dinty Moore), Greek Evans (Chang), Geneva Mitchell (Who's This), Anastasia Reilly (What's Her Name), Hilda Ferguson (A bowery rose), Lotta Fanning (Tillie Dupont), Joy Sutphen (Minnie Fletcher), Earl Van Horn (Old "Pop"), Inez Van Horn (Cynthia Jones), Harry Long (Tom), Ronald Wyse

Plays and Personal Appearances   37

(Abe Levy), Charles Wheeler (Wing Sing), Aida DeMaris (Paquita), Jimmie McCallion (Jimmie), Herbert Schwartz (Herbert), the John Teller Girls.

SYNOPSIS: Wealthy Mary Stillwell becomes a social worker and nightclub singer, despite the objections of her millionaire father. He tries to bring her back home, following Mary to Chinatown where she is involved with a narcotics cop, disguised as a crook. Stillwell is shanghaied, but all ends happily with a party at the Stillwell mansion.

REVIEWS:
New York Herald Tribune, 1.26.27: "One of the best and biggest of the boy and girl shows....tensely populated by scores of song and dance dervishes...[it] treads the usual path of elaborate musical comedy and discovers no ideas that are new."

Billboard, 2.5.27: "The principal decoration of the show is left to Irene Dunn [sic], who is capable of far more..."

Variety, 2.9.27: "With the rep of a comedy show and the reaction of the song hits as they circulate, the Shubert may be holding a smash at last, even at the $5.50 top."

NOTES: Although Irene Dunne played the role of Diana when the musical opened on Broadway, two months later she replaced leading lady Marion Harris as Mary Stillwell. As Mary, her songs included "Look at the World and Smile" and "Somebody Else."

P-11 She's My Baby   original Broadway cast
Cities played: Washington, D.C. (week of 12.12.28, National Theatre), New York (nine weeks beginning 1.3.28, Globe Theatre).

Producer: Charles Dillingham. Director: Edward Royce. Choreographer: Mary Read. Libretto: Guy Bolton, Bert Kalmar, and Harry Ruby. Lyrics: Lorenz Hart. Music: Richard Rodgers.

CAST: William McCarthy (Stage manager), Margaret Hart (Pianist), Nick Long, Jr. (Dance director), Pearl Eaton (Pearl), Joan Clement (Joan), Phyllis Rae (Phyllis), William Frawley (Meadows), Ula Sharon (Josie), Irene Dunne (Polly), Jack Whiting (Bob Martin), Beatrice Lillie (Tilly), Clifton Webb (Clyde Parker), Frank Doane (Mr. Hemingway), William McCarthy (Policeman), Geraldine Fitzgerald (Nursemaid), Peggy Sowden, Lily Reilly, Grace Holt, Hilda Winstanley, Doris Waterworth, May Cornes, Iris Smith, Elsie Holt (John Tiller's Lillie Cocktails), Cleo Cullen, Peggy Cunningham, Evelyn Dehkes, Teddy Denton, Geraldine Fitzgerald, Violet Hanbury, Muriel Hayman, Catherine NaVarro, Blanche O'Donohoe, Anna Riley, Georgie

Sewell, Hazel Webb, Vivian Wilson, Dorothy Wyatt, Norma Taylor, Topsy Humphries, Jill Williams (Ladies of the ensemble), Robert Spencer, James H. Beattie, Malcolm Duffield, Alfred Hale, Glenn McComas, William Sholar, Jr., Robert Vreeland, Ward Tallmon (Gentlemen of the ensemble).

SYNOPSIS: Bob Martin must pretend to have a wife and child in order to get his uncle Hemingway to loan him two hundred thousand dollars. Tilly, the maid, masquerades as the wife, and a baby is borrowed from a neighbor in order to pull off the ruse.

REVIEWS:
Variety, 12.21.27: "In for a while, but never a smash."

New York Herald Tribune, 1.3.28: "A wonderwork of inanity....'You're What I Need' [is] a tricky ballad delivered effectively by Miss Irene Dunne and Mr. Jack Whiting."

New York Sun, 1.4.28: "Without the blessed mimicry of [Beatrice Lillie] to give it occassional gas...it would show signs of famine."

New York Times: 1.4.28: "In addition to Jack Whiting and Irene Dunne the singers include a charming quartet of well-planned young ladies."

Variety, 1.11.28: "Miss Dunne sings nicely."

Billboard, 1.14.28: "Miss Dunne sings and acts prettily in her typically Polly role."

See also B-376

NOTES: Irene Dunne sang "You're What I Need" and "If I Were You." The musical marked Irene's first association with Richard Rodgers, who musicalized two of her films.

P-12 **Luckee Girl** original Broadway cast
City played: New York (81 performances beginning 9.16.28, Casino Theatre).

Producers: The Shuberts. Director: Lew Morton. Choreographer: Harry Puck. Libretto: Gertrude Purcell. Based on the French musical Un Bon Garcon by Andre Barde and Maurice Yvain. Songs: Maurice Yvain, Maurie Rubens, Max Lief, and Nathaniel Lief. Sets: Watson Barrett.

CAST: Irene Dunne (Arlette), Flo Perry (Colette), Clifford Smith (Man), Irving Fisher (Lucien DeGravere), Lou Powers (Tampon), Gertrude McGushion (Lulu), Dorothy McGushion (Lili), Dorothy Barber (Celina), Frank Lalor (Pontaves), Billy House

Plays and Personal Appearances   39

(Hercules), Doris Vinton (Camille), Josephine Drake (Mme. Falloux), Clifford Smith (Jean), Harry Puck (Paul Pechard), Loraine Welmar (Mme. Pontaves), Harold Vizard (DeGravere).

SYNOPSIS: Arlette is upset to learn her boyfriend Lucien is betrothed to a girl in his hometown. When Lucien leaves Paris, Arlette enlists the help of Hercules, the comic waiter, to catch him. She finds Lucien and convinces him to marry her instead of the country girl.

REVIEWS:
New York Herald Tribune, 9.17.28: "No records for novelty were shattered anywhere in the course of its progress....the heroine was Irene Dunne, a cool, pleasantly detached young lady."

New York Times, 9.17.28: "Irene Dunne is far from being the least attractive participant in the entertainment."

New York Post, 9.19.28: "A routine musical comedy...[it] bored me to tears....Irene Dunne is way out ahead of most leading ladies; charming voice, unusually lovely face and a bright, guileless clarity which was not without dignity too."

Variety, 9.26.28: "The people save Luckee Girl. The cast not only sustains the tempo, but more than offsets the deficiencies of their assignments. [Irene] Dunne in the femme lead is worthier of better things..."

Billboard, 9.29.28: "The balance of the honors are divided between Irene Dunne and Doris Vinton. The former is a charming ingenue who possesses a captivating personality and a sweet voice. She deserves watching."

See also B-337

NOTE: Irene Dunne sang "A Flat in Montmartre" and "I Love You So."

P-13   Show Boat   national tour 1929-30
Cities played: Boston (6.1.29-6.15.29, Colonial Theatre), Newark (9.23.29-9.29.29, Shubert Theatre), Chicago (16 weeks beginning 10.1.29, Illinois Theatre), St. Louis (1.20.30-1.26.30, American Theatre), Milwaukee (1.27.30-2.2.30, Davidson Theatre), Detroit (2.3.30-2.9.30, Wilson Theatre), Cleveland (2.10.30-2.16.30, Ohio Theatre), Pittsburgh (2.17.30-2.23.30, Nixon Theatre), Washington (2.24.30-3.2.30, National Theatre), Baltimore (3.3.30-3.9.30, Ford's Theatre).

Producer: Florenz Ziegfeld. Director: Zeke Colvan. Libretto: Oscar Hammerstein II. Based on the novel by Edna Ferber. Music: Jerome Kern. Lyrics: Oscar

Hammerstein II. Musical director: George Hirst. Sets: Joseph Urban. Costumes: John Harkrider.

CHICAGO PRODUCTION:
CAST: Irene Dunn (Magnolia), Allan Campbell (Windy), Charles Ellis (Steve), Bert Chapman (Pete), Aunt Jemima (Queenie), Edna May Oliver (Parthy Ann Hawks), Charles Winninger (Cap'n Andy), Eva Puck (Ellie), Sammy White (Frank), Francis X. Mahoney (Rubber Face), Margaret Carlisle (Julie), Howard Marsh (Gaylord Ravenal), Thomas Gunn (Vallon), Jules Bledsoe (Joe), Phil Sheridan (Faro dealer/gambler), Jack Daley (Backwoodsman), Phil Sheridan (Jeb), Dorothy Denese (La Belle Fatima), Annie Hart (Landlady), Edna Hagen (Kim as a child), Irene Dunn (Kim as an adult), Robert Farley (Jake the piano player), Jack Daley (Jim).

SYNOPSIS: Gaylord Ravenal is a gambler who falls in love with Magnolia Hawks, the daughter of a showboat captain. Magnolia marries Ravenal and they have a daughter Kim. However, he finds he cannot mend his gambling ways. He abandons his family, leaving Magnolia to support Kim. With the help of Julie, a mulatto singer who worked on the showboat, Magnolia lands a singing job. She becomes a star and is eventually reunited with Ravenal, thanks to her daughter.

REVIEWS:
Newark Evening News, 9.24.29: "Girlish and winsome is Miss Dunn as Magnolia in the earlier scenes. In the later episodes she so depicts the forlornness of the abandoned wife as to excite sympathy for her."

Chicago Tribune, 10.2.29: "As to the performance, it is much as when I saw the diversion in New York....Miss Norma Terriss [sic], who was Magnolia (and Kim) down there,...is gone; and I prefer [Irene] Dunn, who now has the roles."

St. Louis Daily Globe-Democrat, 1.21.30: "Irene Dunne is a favorite in St. Louis. And deserves to be. Her childish eagerness as the young Magnolia anxious to pierce the mysteries of life; her do-or-die efforts to be an actress; her womanly grace as the pampered wife in the Chicago of the World's Fair time, her pitiful figure as the abandoned Magnolia - these were characterizations that created in the ensemble the real character of Magnolia of Edna Ferber's novel. Her voice charms, and charming and personable she can also dance."

Milwaukee Journal, 1.28.30: "Irene Dunne is the Magnolia and Margaret Carlisle the Julie. Both can be warmly sentimental and appealing as these charmingly old fashioned heroines and both make the most of it. Both can sing and do....Incidentally, both Miss Dunne and Miss Carlisle are something special to look at."

Irene Dunne starred as Magnolia in the 1929-30 tour of *Show Boat*. (Wisconsin Center for Film and Theater Research)

Detroit News, 2.4.30: "Miss Dunne makes a charming figure of soprano femininity as Magnolia..."

Detroit Times, 2.4.30: "...Irene Dunne as Magnolia is quite as lovely as [the creator of the role] Norma Terris and an even finer vocalist."

Cleveland Plain Dealer, 2.11.30: "Irene Dunne, who plays Magnolia, is I think, better than Norma Terris..."

Pittsburgh Post-Gazette, 2.18.30: "Irene Dunne...is an acquisition vocally and personably. She showed a plushed [sic] soprano voice to advantage."

Pittsburgh Press, 2.18.30: "Miss Irene Dunne has stepped into the Norma Terris character of Magnolia and she carries on a sterling role with splendid effect..."

Pittsburgh Sun-Telegraph, 2.18.30: "The hero, Gaylord Ravenal, is now sung by Howard Marsh, and the heroine Magnolia, as well as the grown Kim, by Irene Dunne. This pair incorporates the charm and tenderness that are needed to make them credible....Miss Dunne was particularly happy in the third act of 'The Parson's Bride.'"

Evening Star [Washington, D.C.], 2.25.30: "...the somber croonings of Helen Morgan are no more, nor the graces that were Norma Terris', but in their place Margaret Carlisle as the unfortunate Julie and Irene Dunne as Magnolia suffer nothing at all from comparison. They are, in fact, the embodiment of what they should be."

Washington Post, 2.25.30: "Irene Dunne, in the twin roles of Magnolia and as Magnolia's daughter Kim, gives a finished performance in both roles, one of them tremendously exacting."

Baltimore Morning Sun, 4.10.30: "The question naturally arises, is Show Boat now at Ford's the same production which ran so long in New York?...Norma Terriss [sic] has been replaced by Irene Dunne, who...is a gifted singer, dancer and actress."

See also B-21, B-44, B-45, B-123, B-188, B-232, B-246, B-252, B-357, B-397, B-433, B-492

NOTES: Two days after the Broadway production of Show Boat closed, the major players went to Boston to reprise their roles, beginning May 6, 1929 at the Colonial Theatre. When the theatre season ended, several actors abandoned their roles to make films. Irene Dunne replaced Norma Terris as Magnolia and Kim on June 1, 1929. According to Henry F. Scannell of the Boston Public Library, the production was not re-reviewed. Irene allegedly won the part in Show Boat after meeting producer Florenz Ziegfeld in an elevator. Early in the tour, Irene's name was

Plays and Personal Appearances   43

spelled "Dunn." However, she was listed as "Irene Dunne" in a program from the second week of the Chicago run and in all cities later in the tour. During the musical's Baltimore engagement, scouts from RKO discovered Irene and signed her for <u>Leathernecking</u>. Irene sang "Make Believe," "Can't Help Lovin' Dat Man," "You Are Love," and "Why Do I Love You?"

P-14 <u>U.S.O. Show</u>   charity benefit
      City played: Hollywood (6.29.41, Hollywood Bowl).

Producers: Harry M. Warner and Charles Vanda. Director (finale): Mike Marco. Musical directors: Leon Leonardi, Lud Gluskin, and Meredith Willson. Talent coordinator: Edward Arnold. Chairman: Harry Maizlish. Publicity director: Jerry Hoffman.

CAST: Bob Burns, Connie Boswell, Dick Powell, Irene Dunne, Judy Garland, Orson Welles, Frances Langford, Gene Autry, George Burns and Gracie Allen, Fannie Brice, Cary Grant, Charles Boyer, Frank Morgan, Nelson Eddy, Rosalind Russell, Leo Carrillo, the Nicholas Brothers, Lowe, Stanley and Hite, Virginia O'Brien, Fanchonettes, Ada Broadbent Ballet, Rufe Davis, Edward G. Robinson, Norma Shearer, Jackie Cooper, Tyrone Power, Bette Davis, Lionel Barrymore, John Barrymore, Loretta Young, Hanley Stafford, John Conte, Jane Withers, Hattie McDaniel, Robert Taylor, Barbara Stanwyck, Thomas E. Dewey, Rogers Dancers.

REVIEW:
<u>Variety</u>, 7.2.41: "Handicapped by poor material and improper spotting were Fannie Brice, Nelson Eddy, Cary Grant, Rosalind Russell, Charles Boyer, Irene Dunne, Frank Morgan."

See also R-20, B-125, B-453

NOTES: The show was staged for the benefit of the United Service Organization, raising money for entertainment, recreation, and religious services for soldiers in army camps. Ticket prices ranged from $.50 to $10, with the program raising $23,675 in paid admissions. The show was broadcast over CBS.

P-15 <u>Chicago Symphony Concert</u>
      City played: Chicago (1941-42 season).

NOTE: Despite the fact that the concert was mentioned in many periodicals, the Chicago Symphony Orchestra could not find any reference to Irene Dunne appearing as a guest artist during the 1941-42 season.

P-16 <u>Red Cross Fund Drive</u>   charity benefit
      City played: Los Angeles (1.19.42).

44   Irene Dunne

    CAST: Irene Dunne, Patric Knowles, Bob Hope, George Brent, others.

See also B-352

P-17   **War Bond Rally**   charity benefit
City played: Hartford (7.31.42, Yale Bowl).

    CAST: Irene Dunne, Ed Wynn, Carol Bruce, Bert Lytell, Lucy Monroe, Bob Maurice.

See also B-335

NOTES: The war bond rally marked the conclusion of the Treasury Department's nation-wide, month-long campaign to sell a billion dollars in bonds through retail trade outlets. Carol Bruce was the singer who performed with Ben Bernie's Orchestra, rather than the actress of the same name.

P-18   **Stars Over America**   war bond tour
(September, 1942).

    CAST: Bud Abbott, Walter Abel, Edward Arnold, Wallace Beery, Ralph Bellamy, Joan Bennett, James Cagney, Leo Carrillo, Claudette Colbert, Ronald Colman, Lou Costello, Joan Crawford, Bing Crosby, Bette Davis, Laraine Day, Andy Devine, Irene Dunne, Nelson Eddy, Alice Faye, Henry Fonda, Greer Garson, Janet Gaynor, Virginia Gilmore, Paulette Goddard, Miriam Hopkins, Hedy Lamarr, Dorothy Lamour, Charles Laughton, Joan Leslie, Herbert Marshall, Thomas Mitchell, Dennis Morgan, Walter Pidgeon, Ann Rutherford, Martha Scott, Norma Shearer, Dinah Shore, Ginny Simms, Alexis Smith, Margaret Sullavan, Gene Tierney, Franchot Tone, Jane Wyman, Robert Young, Vera Zorina.

See also B-254, B-298, B-299, B-308, B-396

NOTES: Celebrities banded together to boost war bond sales over the billion-dollar mark in **Stars Over America**, a nationwide bond tour, which was launched on the steps of the U.S. Treasury on August 31, 1942. Among those stars at the opening in Washington were Irene Dunne, Bing Crosby, Greer Garson, and James Cagney. Although the drive did not begin until noon, the crowd began lining up at 7:30 A.M. They bought over a million dollars' worth of bonds from the stars in one day. Planning to cover three hundred cities in thirty days, the celebrities disbursed after the Washington junket. They all traveled by railroad because of a "no publicity" rule on the commercial airlines. Since the stars were not being paid for their time or effort, many felt the ensuing publicity from the bond drive was the only perk. **Variety** reported, "Many of the pic crowd felt that when they were just junketing they wanted no publicity, but that they were entitled to a few paragraphs when they flew in

Plays and Personal Appearances   45

the interests of the war efforts ("'No Publicity' Key to Filmers' Nix of Sky in Bond Drive." <u>Variety</u>. September 2, 1942.).

P-19 <u>War Bond Rally</u>   charity benefit
City played: New York (9.8.42, Times Square).

CAST: Irene Dunne, Will Osborne and his band, Liu Liang-mo, Max A. Cohen.

See also B-68

NOTES: Miss Lee Yachine, Chinese aviator, presented Irene Dunne with a goodluck token. The war bond rally was held in cooperation with Chinese groups. Irene urged the crowd to put nails in the coffins of Hitler, Hirohito, and Mussolini by purchasing war bonds at the Times Square rally. The rally was part of the Treasury Department's September billion-dollar drive.

P-20 <u>Film Junket</u>
Places played: Rio de Janeiro, Brazil; Punta del Este, Uruguay; South American countries (spring, 1951).

CAST: Irene Dunne, Fred MacMurray, Robert Cummings, Joan Fontaine, June Haver, Rhonda Fleming, Evelyn Keyes, Wendell Corey, Harry Crocker, Errol Flynn, Patricia Neal.

See also B-122

NOTES: This junket was sponsored by the State Department to promote good relations between the United States and South American countries and renew interest in American-made movies. The celebrities attended film festivals in Rio de Janeiro and Punta del Este.

P-21 <u>Jack Benny's 63rd Birthday Dinner</u>   charity benefit
City played: Beverly Hills (1957, Beverly Hilton Hotel).

CAST: George Jessel, Goodwin Knight, Irene Dunne, Deborah Kerr, Admiral J.B. Pearson, Jr., Dean Martin, Frank Sinatra, Tony Martin, Ronald Reagan, George Burns, Bob Hope, Art Linkletter, Jack Benny.

See also B-110

NOTES: Celebrities gathered to honor Jack Benny's sixty-third birthday at this $100-a-plate dinner given by the Friars Club. Irene Dunne turned comedienne for the evening to roast her longtime friend in this benefit for the Heart Fund.

P-22 <u>Conference on Family Security</u>   speaker

46   Irene Dunne

    City played: Anaheim, CA (1.9.59, Disneyland).

See also B-93

NOTE: Irene Dunne gave a speech entitled "Freedom Is Responsibility" at the conference, which was sponsored by the Insurance Company of North America.

P-23 <u>Ken Murray's Hollywood</u>   filmed Broadway appearance
    City played: New York (beginning 5.10.65, John Golden Theatre).

    Producers: Alexander H. Cohen and Arthur Whitelaw. Musical director: Armin Hoffman. Lighting: Ralph Alswang.

    CAST: Ken Murray, Armin Hoffman (Pianist).

NOTES: Irene Dunne was one of the many celebrities shown in this collection of candid home movies filmed by actor/raconteur Ken Murray, who had co-starred with her in <u>Leathernecking</u>. The show was divided into six segments: "Prelude by Armin Hoffman," "Hollywood's Number One Movie Fan Ken Murray," "Hollywood Family Album," "San Simeon," "Backstage with <u>Bill and Coo</u>," and "Hollywood Thirty Years Later." Murray, whose film <u>Bill and Coo</u> won an honorary Academy Award in 1947, often appeared on television with his vintage Hollywood home movies. A clip of Irene was also seen in Murray's television special <u>Hollywood without Makeup</u> (T-27).

P-24 <u>Los Angeles County Museum Tribute</u>
    City played: Los Angeles (11.70).

See also A-62

NOTES: Sponsored by the Los Angeles County Museum and the California Palace of the Legion of Honor, Irene Dunne's career was given a retrospective. Following the film clips, Irene answered questions posed by the audience.

P-25 <u>Filmex Tribute</u>
    City played: Century City, CA (3.23.75, Plitt Theatre).

See also A-64, B-49, B-80, B-81, B-213, B-226, B-455

NOTES: Irene Dunne was honored at a five-hour tribute by the Los Angeles International Film Exposition. The program included clips from fifteen films and two TV shows, as well as a screening of <u>Love Affair</u>. Roddy McDowall moderated the program, which was coordinated by David Chierichetti. Irene took part in a twenty-five-minute discussion period following the clips and sang "Wishing (Will Make It So)" as she left the tribute.

Plays and Personal Appearances   47

P-26   *Irene Dunne in Person with Love Affair*
       City played: Washington, D.C. (11.7.77, Eisenhower Theatre).

See also B-12, B-328, B-349

NOTES: To celebrate the American Film Institute's tenth anniversary, Irene Dunne appeared at a screening of *Love Affair* in Washington, D.C. In addition to answering questions about her films, Irene shared clips from *Roberta* and *My Favorite Wife*. Irene was quoted in the program, saying, "*Love Affair* is my favorite of all my films not only because it was so well done, but also because we had such a good time making it." The question-and-answer session was given a lot of press after Edward Smith asked her to autograph his 78 record album.

P-27   *American Film Institute Tribute*
       City played: Los Angeles (8.25.79, San Gabriel Civic Auditorium).

See also A-65, B-382

NOTES: Irene Dunne was saluted in "Best Remaning Seats," the third in a series of tributes which honored people and movie palaces from the golden age of films. Irene's tribute included a screening of *Love Affair*, film clips from *The Awful Truth*, and a question-and-answer session.

Filmography

This chapter lists credits, synopses, and reviews for all of Irene Dunne's films. Features are listed in chronological order, according to their release date. They are identified by the letter "F." Shorts are listed after the features and have the prefix "FS." All films are in black and white unless noted.

FEATURES:
F-1   Leathernecking   (RKO, 1930)   81 minutes   Black and white and color

Associate producer: Louis Sarecky. Director: Edward Cline. Assistant director: Frederick Fleck. Choreographer: Pearl Eaton. Screenplay: Alfred Jackson and Jane Murfin. Based on the musical Present Arms by Herbert Fields, Richard Rodgers, and Lorenz Hart. Songs: Richard Rodgers, Lorenz Hart, Sidney Clare, Oscar Levant, Benny Davis, and Harry Akst. Music: Oscar Levant. Musical director: Victor Baravalle. Photography: J. Roy Hunt. Art director: Max Ree. Sound: John Tribby.

CAST: Irene Dunne (Delphine Witherspoon), Ken Murray (Frank), Louise Fazenda (Hortense), Ned Sparks (Sparks), Lilyan Tashman (Edna), Eddie Foy, Jr. (Chick Evans), Benny Rubin (Stein), Rita Le Roy (Fortuneteller), Fred Santley (Douglas), William von Brinken (Richter), Carl Gerrard (Colonel), Werther Weidler, Wolfgang Weidler (Richter's sons).

SYNOPSIS: Marine private Chick Evans steals his captain's uniform and distinguished service medal in order to attend a party at the home of socialite Delphine Witherspoon. The ruse gets Chick an invitation, but things go awry when his buddies crash the party and accidentally expose him. When Delphine learns Chick's true rank, she denounces him. However, Delphine's friend Edna realizes that Chick loves Delphine. Edna maneuvers the mismatched lovers onto her yacht. Chick arranges with the captain to fake a shipwreck. When a real storm breaks out, Chick and Delphine are stranded on a deserted island. When they return, Chick is tossed in the brig and Delphine refuses to see him. She changes her mind when a fortuneteller warns her that Chick is about to be shot for desertion. Delphine hurries to his rescue. When she learns Chick has been retroactively promoted to captain for his bravery during a recent campaign, Delphine and Chick reconcile.

REVIEWS:
New York Times, 9.13.30: "The film's chief virtue is its failure to take itself seriously, and in so doing frolics along to a slapstick beat..."

Variety, 9.17.30: "Balances are all wrong. What, for example, is the idea of casting a charming romantic actress like Irene Dunne opposite a comedian like Eddie Foy, Jr...."

See also B-178, B-188, B-200, B-238, B-255, B-357, B-378

NOTES: Leathernecking marked Irene Dunne's screen debut. Although the film was based on the 1928 Broadway musical Present Arms, the majority of the songs were cut before its release. Most of the movie was shot in black and white, however, the last twenty minutes were filmed in color. Leathernecking opened at New York's Globe Theatre on September 12, 1930. In Great Britain, the title remained Present Arms.

F-2   Cimarron   (RKO, 1931)   131 minutes

Producer: William LeBaron. Associate producer: Louis Sarecky. Director: Wesley Ruggles. Assistant director: Doran Cox. Screenplay: Howard Estabrook. Based on the novel by Edna Ferber. Editor: William Hamilton. Photography: Edward Cronjager. Art director: Max Ree. Costumes: Max Ree. Sound: Clem Portman. Special effects: Lloyd Knechtel.

CAST: Richard Dix (Yancey Cravat), Irene Dunne (Sabra Cravat), Estelle Taylor (Dixie Lee), Nance O'Neil (Felice Venable), William Collier, Jr. (The Kid), Rosco Ates (Jesse Rickey), George E. Stone (Sol Levy), Stanley Fields (Lon Yountis), Robert McWade (Louis Heffner), Edna May Oliver (Mrs. Tracy Wyatt), Frank Darien (Mr. Bixley), Eugene Jackson (Isaiah), Dolores Brown (Ruby Big Elk, adult), Gloria Vonic (Ruby Big Elk, child), Otto Hoffman (Murch Rankin), William Orlamond (Grat Gotch), Frank Beal (Louis Venable), Nancy Dover (Donna Cravat, adult), Helen Parrish (Donna Cravat, child), Donald Dillaway (Cim Cravat, adult), Junior Johnson (Cim Cravat, child), Douglas Scott (Cim Cravat, toddler), Reginald Streeter (Yancey Cravat, II), Lois Jane Campbell (Felice Cravat), Ann Lee (Aunt Cassandra), Tyrone Brereton (Dabney

Venable), Lillian Lane (Cousin Bella), Henry Roquemore (Jonett Goforth), Nell Craig (Arminta Greenwood), Robert McKenzie (Pat Leary), Clara Hunt (Indian girl), Bob Kortman (Killer), Dennis O'Keefe (Extra), William Janney (Worker).

SYNOPSIS: Yancey Cravat, a lawyer and editor, joins the Oklahoma Land Rush of 1889 to stake out a claim. Dixie Lee, a fellow pioneer with a shady reputation, feigns injury and, when Yancey stops to help her, she claims the land he wanted. Undaunted, Yancey takes his family to the Oklahoma territory, where he starts a crusading newspaper. Although his wife Sabra initially wants to return to Kansas, she soon gets used to Osage. Yancey stands up for his principles, defending the town from bandits, but refusing to take a reward, and championing Indian rights. The opening of the Cherokee Strip causes another land rush. Yancey's wanderlust returns and he leaves Osage. In his absence, Sabra operates the newspaper. After five years, Yancey comes back, having served in the Spanish-American War. He rushes to Dixie's defense when she is charged with prostitution, believing everyone should have a fair trial. By 1907, Yancey is weighing a political career. However, he refuses to compromise on his belief in Indian citizenship, causing him to lose a corrupt backer. Yancey is called to adventure again, leaving Sabra to run the newspaper. By 1929, she has reconsidered her thoughts on Indian citizenship and runs her husband's editorial on the subject in the newspaper's fortieth anniversary issue. Sabra is elected to Congress in 1930. Although she initially protested her son's involvement with an Indian woman, Sabra is proud of Cim's marriage. En route to the unveiling of a statue honoring Oklahoma pioneers, Sabra meets Yancey, who has been injured in an oil field accident, saving the lives of other workers. He dies in his wife's arms, but his spirit is preserved in the statue.

REVIEWS:
New York Times, 1.27.31: "Irene Dunne is excellent as Sabra."

Variety, 1.28.31: "Miss Dunne does nicely enough in a role of a loving wife and mother, which does not permit her to be much else. What she later accomplishes in a political way is suggested rather than acted."

Outlook, 2.11.31: "Edna Ferber's story of the settling of Oklahoma has been done into an exciting and completely satisfying film....Irene Dunne does admirably as Sabra..."

The New Statesman and Nation, 3.14.31: "Cimarron is worth seeing for a few moments of first-rate spectacle, which become merged in a mess of moralizing, elevating in itself, but tiresome to listen to. Probably, however, the film is better than it sounds."

Saturday Review, 3.14.31: "If the second half of *Cimarron*...had matched the first, this picture would be a remarkable one....Irene Dunne, as Yancey's wife Sabra, starts none too well, but later, as the conventional woman, materially helps the director to upset the picture's balance."

Photoplay, 4.31: "I've seen [*Cimarron*] three times and got the same thrill everytime....It...starts Irene Dunne off as one of our greatest screen artists."

See also F-29, R-23, R-55, A-6, B-25, B-29, B-84, B-167, B-175, B-213, B-238, B-277, B-279, B-351, B-353, B-361, B-383, B-401, B-435, B-439, B-450, B-474, B-479

NOTES: *Cimarron* cost $1,433,000 to produce, the largest budget RKO had committed to a film at that time. The studio purchased the rights to the bestselling novel of 1931 for leading man Richard Dix, whom they had under contract. With only one film credit behind her, and an unsuccessful film at that, Irene Dunne was far from the first choice to play Sabra Cravat. Already cast as Sabra, Fay Bainter lost favor with producer William LeBaron and left the film. Irene convinced RKO makeup expert Ern Westmore and photographer Ernest Bracken to work with her one Saturday in an effort to win the role. Westmore aged her forty years, while Bracken captured the results on film. After seeing the pictures, LeBaron ordered a screen test. Dix had seen Irene on stage and thought she could play the role. He made the test with Irene and helped convince director Wesley Ruggles that she was the right choice.

Cimarron opened at New York's Globe Theatre on January 26, 1931. Irene Dunne sang "Who Are You at Home." The film was a landmark in cinema history, becoming the only western to win the Academy Award for Best Picture until 1991's *Dances with Wolves*. *Cimarron* also won Oscars for Best Film Best Adaptation and Best Set Decoration. Despite three Academy Awards and four nominations, including Dix and Ruggles, the film lost more than half a million dollars during its initial release. Irene received her first Best Actress Academy Award nomination for *Cimarron*, but lost to Marie Dressler for *Min and Bill*. *Cimarron* was remade by MGM in 1960, starring Glenn Ford and Maria Schell. The 1931 version was withheld from television and revivals for many years because of the remake. Although *Cimarron* was one of Irene's favorite films for many years, she deemed it "awfully hammy" after a 1975 viewing (B-213).

F-3   *Bachelor Apartment*   (RKO, 1931)   77 minutes

    Producer: William LeBaron. Associate producer: Henry Hobart. Director: Lowell Sherman. Screenplay: J. Walter Ruben. Based on a story by John Howard Lawson. Editor: Marie Halvey. Photography: Leo Tover. Costumes: Max Ree. Sets: Max Ree.

Sound: Clem Portman.

CAST: Lowell Sherman (Wayne Carter), Irene Dunne (Helene Andrews), Mae Murray (Agatha Carraway), Norman Kerry (Lee Graham), Claudia Dell (Lita Andrews), Ivan Lebedeff (Pete de Moneau), Noel Francis (Janet Reynolds), Roberta Gale, Arline Judge (Whoopee girls), Purnell Pratt (Henry Carraway), Charles Coleman (Rollins, the butler), Kitty Kelly (Miss Clark), Bess Flowers (Charlotte), Arthur Housman (Tippler), Florence Roberts (Mrs. Halloran), Boston Winston (Brown), Lee Phelps (Traffic cop).

SYNOPSIS: Although Agatha Carraway is married, she wants to resume her affair with her former boyfriend, wealthy bachelor Wayne Carter. Despite his reputation as a playboy, Carter refuses, as her husband is also a friend. Carter admits to his butler, Rollins, that he is tiring of the fast life; Rollins advises him to find a "good" woman. Instead, Carter picks up Janet Reynolds during a traffic tie-up and brings her back to his apartment for lunch. Meanwhile unemployed sisters Helene and Lita Andrews dream of being rich. Lita, a chorus girl, thinks she can make a fast buck by dating wealthy men. Helene, a stenographer, warns that Lita will get hurt. Lita leaves for a date at Carter's apartment. When a telegram arrives, offering Lita a job in a revue if she can be at the rehearsal that afternoon, Helene goes to Carter's apartment to retrieve her sister. Although Carter denies that Lita is there, Helene searches the apartment. When she finds Janet instead, Helene apologizes. Intrigued by Helene's morality, Carter invites her to dinner, but she refuses. After finding Lita lunching with Rollins, Carter learns Helene is a stenographer. He hires her and promises to keep things strictly professional. While working at Carter's home one afternoon, Helene gets a taste of his lifestyle. Agatha returns to convince him to renew their affair. Meanwhile, Agatha's husband asks Carter's help in locating Agatha's lover, as he bought a gun to shoot him. Embarrassed that Helene saw everything, Carter stays away from the office for a week. Upon his return, he confesses that he loves Helene and invites her to dinner. When Carter gets home, he finds Agatha in his bed, refusing to leave. Helene sees her and jumps to the wrong conclusion. Carraway arrives and threatens to shoot Carter. Helene saves Carter by donning a robe, implying that she is the only woman in the apartment. Agatha finally leaves, vowing never to see Carter again. Despite Helene's similar feelings, she enlists Carter's help when Lita does not come home after a night on the town. They discover Lita eloped, marrying for love, not money. Carter reads Helene a letter from Agatha, admitting she was chasing him and telling him she has gone back to her husband. Helene forgives Carter and they kiss.

REVIEWS:
New York Times, 5.16.31: "Miss Dunne is competent as

54   Irene Dunne

Helene."

Variety, 5.20.31: "Irene Dunne is best and offers the only real attempt at acting, but [Lowell] Sherman's direction nullifies any hope for the cast to show to advantage."

British Monthly Film Bulletin, 5.81: "... a relatively unglamorised [sic] Irene Dunne seems already to have mastered the register of unfussy romanticism familiar from her later Thirties work..."

See also B-238

NOTES: Film historian Gilbert Adair noted that the structure of Bachelor Apartment was very much like a three-act play, although the screen credits do not indicate that the story had its origins on the stage ("Retrospective." British Monthly Film Bulletin. May, 1981.). Leading man Lowell Sherman also directed the film.

F-4   The Great Lover   (MGM, 1931)   79 minutes

Director: Harry Beaumont. Screenplay: Gene Markey and Edgar Allan Woolf. Based on the play by Leo Ditrichstein, Frederick Hatton, and Fanny Hatton. Editor: Helen Warne. Photography: Merritt B. Gerstad. Art director: Cedric Gibbons. Costumes: Rene Hubert. Sound: Douglas Shearer.

CAST: Adolphe Menjou (Jean Paurel), Irene Dunne (Diana Page), Ernest Torrence (Potter), Neil Hamilton (Carlo Joneno [Carl Jones]), Baclanova (Mme. Savarova), Cliff Edwards (Finny), Hale Hamilton (Stapleton), Rosco Ates (Rosco), Herman Bing (Losseck), Else Jansen (Mme. Neumann Baumbach).

SYNOPSIS: Jean Paurel is a temperamental baritone Casanova. He meets Diana Page, an aspiring singer, and arranges an audition for her. At the opera house, Diana runs into her former boyfriend Carl Jones, now known as Carlo Joneno and Jean's understudy. Diana refuses to marry Carlo and give up her career. Jean soon falls in love with Diana. Despite others' protests that she is not ready for an opera career, Jean insists that she sing opposite him in Don Giovanni. He coaches her and, out of gratitude, Diana agrees to marry him. Despite a strained voice, Jean performs the first act of the opera. When he hears that Diana and Carlo love each other, he loses his voice, forcing Carlo to go on in the second act. Diana makes a successful debut, but cannot find happiness. She feels guilty when Jean permanently loses his voice. She must decide whether to go through with the marriage or admit to her mentor that she really loves Carlo. After their success, Carlo insists that she stay in New York to perform with him; Jean wants to marry her and take her to Europe. When Jean sees how much the young singers love each other, he sacrifices his own happiness so that Diana can wed Carlo. Jean reluctantly returns to his playboy ways.

REVIEWS:
New York Times, 8.24.31: "Neither Neil Hamilton,...nor Miss Dunne does much to help the success of the film, but in justice to them it should be stated that their lines are often poorly written."

Variety, 8.25.31: "Irene Dunne makes a charming figure as leading woman, and contributes several songs necessary to the action. Part calls for quiet and persuasive grace, which this young actress possesses abundantly."

See also B-100

NOTES: Although Irene Dunne was noticed by RKO because of her vocal talents, it was during a loan-out to MGM that she got her first opportunity to sing on screen. The Great Lover allowed her to perform an aria, "I Love Thee Now," "The Waltz" from Romeo and Juliet, and excerpts from Don Giovanni. The original 1915 play ran for 245 performances and starred playwright Leo Ditrichstein.

F-5   Consolation Marriage   (RKO, 1931)   82 minutes

Producer: William LeBaron. Associate producer: Myles Connolly. Director: Paul Sloane. Screenplay: Humphrey Pearson. Based on a story by William Cunningham. Song: Myles Connolly and Max Steiner. Musical director: Max Steiner. Editor: Archie Marshek. Photography: J. Roy Hunt. Costumes: Max Ree. Sets: Max Ree.

CAST: Irene Dunne (Mary Brown), Pat O'Brien (Steve Rollo Porter), Myrna Loy (Elaine), John Halliday (Jeff), Matt Moore (The Colonel), Lester Vail (Aubrey), Wilson Benge (Butler), Pauline Stevens (Baby).

SYNOPSIS: Reporter Steve Rollo Porter travels to London to marry his childhood girlfriend Elaine. Devastated when Elaine tells him that she has married someone else, Steve returns to New York. Meanwhile, Mary Brown encourages her boyfriend Aubrey, a pianist, to marry wealthy Mrs. Simpson to help his career. Mary and Steve meet in a speakeasy and learn both are still carrying a torch for their former loves. They become friends right away and decide to marry. They agree to divorce if either should become bored with the arrangement or if their lost lovers return. When Elaine and her husband divorce, she contacts Steve, wanting to renew their romance. Steve intends to go to London to see her, but cancels his plans when he learns Mary is pregnant. A year later, Elaine comes to New York and contacts Steve again. Mary is sure she has lost Steve, so when the newly-separated Aubrey invites her to Vienna, she agrees to

Off-screen friends Irene Dunne and Pat O'Brien appeared in a story about a marriage of convenience with *Consolation Marriage* (RKO, 1931). (Author's collection)

go. Although she is reluctant to leave her baby, she wants to hurt Steve before he can hurt her. Mary immediatly regrets her decision and returns home, realizing she has learned to love Steve. Aware of how well suited the Porters are, Steve's boss invites Elaine to their house, hoping Steve will make the right decision. Mary sees Elaine is shallow, but encourages Steve to pursue her. After a kiss, Steve realizes he no longer loves Elaine. He confesses to Mary that he loves her, but insists that she still be allowed to pursue Aubrey if he returns. Elaine tells him the truth and they embrace, ready to start their marriage again.

REVIEWS:
New York Times, 10.30.31: "Miss Dunne's performance is capable, almost as good as her portrayal in 'Cimarron.'"

Motion Picture, 10.31: "It has suspense and sparkling dialogue."

Variety, 11.3.31: "Excepting for a few moments that show need of more care in lighting or making up the eyes, Irene Dunne looks well in her first star role. As far as her performance is concerned, she does as well as she did in 'Cimarron.' Her work opposite [Richard] Dix in that talker established her as a player. She upholds that rank."

Photoplay, 3.32: "Don't miss this truly sophisticated 1931 movie!"

See also B-238, B-334, B-363

NOTES: In Great Britain, Consolation Marriage was released as Married in Haste. Irene Dunne sang "Devotion." Although the story was set in New York, Irene and Pat O'Brien were sent on location to San Francisco to film a scene at the aquarium, as the studio deemed it too expensive to recreate the giant fish tanks. Irene and O'Brien were friends off screen. Irene was godmother to his adopted son Terry.

F-6 Symphony of Six Million (RKO, 1932) 94 minutes

Executive producer: David O. Selznick. Associate producer: Pandro S. Berman. Director: Gregory La Cava. Screenplay: Bernard Schubert, J. Walter Ruben, and James Seymour. Based on the novel by Fannie Hurst. Music: Max Steiner. Editor: Archie F. Marshek. Photography: Leo Tover. Art director: Carroll Clark. Sound: George Ellis.

CAST: Irene Dunne (Jessica), Ricardo Cortez (Dr. Felix Klauber), Gregory Ratoff (Meyer Klauber), Anna Appel (Hannah Klauber), Lita Chevret (Birdie Klauber), Noel Madison (Magnus Klauber), Helen Freeman (Miss Spencer), Julie Haydon (Nurse/receptionist), Josephine

Whittell (Mrs. Gifford), Oscar Apfel (Doctor), Harold Goodwin (Intern), John St. Polis (Dr. Schifflen), Eddie Phillips (Birdie's husband), Lester Lee (Felix, child).

SYNOPSIS: Felix Klauber is an intelligent Jewish boy who shows concern for the sick and disabled at a young age. He dreams of becoming a surgeon. Felix grows up and becomes a doctor, devoting his life to helping his neighbors in the ghetto. He dates his childhood friend Jessica, a crippled teacher in a school for the blind. With prodding from her son Magnus, Felix's mother urges Felix to move his practice uptown to better the family's existence. Despite his convictions, Felix moves to Park Avenue. He begins neglecting the clinic and his family, giving them money rather than his time. Although he becomes rich and famous, Felix feels guilty for catering to the whims of his wealthy patients. He vows to return to the ghetto, but Magnus makes him feel guilty about supporting the family. Jessica is angry when Felix does not operate on one of her pupils and the child dies. She tells off Felix, claiming he has lost his ideals. When Felix's father Meyer develops a brain tumor, the family demands that Felix operate. Meyer dies during surgery. Devastated, Felix gives up his practice. Returning to the ghetto, he learns that Jessica's spine has weakened, confining her to a wheelchair. She convinces him to perform risky corrective surgery. After the successful operation, Felix regains his confidence and his sense of values. He returns to his neighborhood practice, vowing to help the poor.

REVIEWS:
New York Times, 4.15.32: "[Ricardo] Cortez is capable and likewise Miss Dunne."

Variety, 4.19.32: "Irene Dunne is meaningless, appearing but seldom and then always in forced and unreal situations."

Screen Book, 7.32: "Deeply human and moving story with excellent dramatic acting by Ricardo Cortez and Irene Dunne."

British Monthly Film Bulletin, 1.77: "Ricardo Cortez and Irene Dunne give wan, perfunctory performances; the only character with any claim to individuality is Gregory Ratoff's Jewish poppa..."

See also B-87, B-167, B-175, B-238, B-383

NOTES: The first of Irene Dunne's many "weepers," the film cost RKO $270,000 to produce. It marked the first time an elaborate surgical procedure was filmed. The music for Symphony of Six Million was Max Steiner's first complete score. He went on to write music for many films, including Gone with the Wind. In Great Britain, Symphony of Six Million was released as Melody of Life.

Filmography   59

F-7   Back Street   (Universal, 1932)   89 minutes

Producer: Carl Laemmle, Jr. Associate producer: E.M. Asher. Director: John M. Stahl. Assistant director: Scott R. Beal. Screenplay: Gladys Lehman and Lynn Starling. Based on the novel by Fannie Hurst. Editor: Milton Carruth. Photography: Karl Freund. Art director: Charles D. Hall. Costumes: Vera. Sound: C. Roy Hunter.

CAST: Irene Dunne (Ray Schmidt), John Boles (Walter Saxel), June Clyde (Freda Schmidt), George Meeker (Kurt Shendler), ZaSu Pitts (Mrs. Dole), Shirley Grey (Francine), Doris Lloyd (Mrs. Saxel), William Bakewell (Richard Saxel), Arletta Duncan (Beth Saxel), Maude Turner Gordon (Mrs. Saxel, Sr.), Walter Catlett (Bakeless), James Donlan (Prothero), Paul Weigel (Mr. Schmidt), Jane Darwell (Mrs. Schmidt), Robert McWade (Uncle Felix), Paul Fix (Hugo Hack), Russell Hopton, Gene Morgan, James Flavin (Reporters), James Farley (Conductor), Bob Burns (Streetcar conductor), Rolfe Sedan (Croupier), Grace Hayle (Lady in street), Jack Chefe (Onlooker), Mahlon Hamilton, Virginia Pearson, Caryl Lincoln, Beulah Hutton, Rosalie Roy, Tom Karrigan, Rose Dione.

SYNOPSIS: Ray Schmidt is the independent daughter of a middle-class German family living in Cincinnati at the turn of the century. Although her step-mother criticizes her running around, it is clear that Ray is still a virgin. Ray's father encourages her to marry Kurt Shendler, the owner of a bicycle shop. Despite Kurt's promise in the fledgling automobile business, Ray refuses. She meets Walter Saxel, a young banker, and immediatly is attracted. Despite the fact that Walter is engaged, he continues to date Ray. Hoping to break his engagement, he asks Ray to meet him and his mother at a concert in the park. On her way to the concert, Ray is delayed by the histrionics of her sister, who threatens to kill herself if Ray does not help her keep her boyfriend from leaving town. When Ray arrives at the concert, Walter and his mother are gone. Five years later, Ray and Walter meet in New York. He is now a wealthy banker and the father of two. He confesses that he still loves Ray and sets her up in an apartment. Ray quits her job, spending every moment waiting for Walter's visits. She is crushed when she cannot go with him on a business trip to Europe. When he returns, she begs him to give her a baby to cure her loneliness. Walter refuses, reminding her that she is only his mistress. Kurt, now a successful automobile manufacturer, proposes to Ray again. She breaks up with Walter and returns to Cincinnati to marry Kurt. Walter follows her and begs her to return to him. She capitulates. Twenty-five years later, Walter and his family sail for Europe; this time Ray is with them. Walter's children recognize her as their father's mistress. In Paris, Walter's son Richard confronts her and tells her to get out of their lives. Walter tries to explain, but Richard storms out. The next day Walter has a stroke. On his deathbed, he asks Richard to call Ray so Walter can say goodbye. He dies during the phone call. Richard visits Ray, offering to provide for her as his father wished. Ray dies, wondering how her life would have differed if she had met Walter's mother at the concert.

REVIEWS:
New York Times, 8.29.32: "[John] Boles is handsome and Miss Dunne is attractive, but the dialogue in this film is a handicap to both of them....Miss Dunne does well enough considering the wobbly character she plays."

Variety, 8.30.32: "Miss Dunne is excellent as Ray Schmidt. She is the personification of 'a real woman,' an excellent casting assignment for this sort of role."

Motion Picture, 10.32: "The director knows his heart strings, and both Irene Dunne, as the woman who gave so generously, and John Boles, as the man who forfeited the privilege of protecting the woman he loved, rise above their usual excellent level of performance."

See also A-69, B-7, B-116, B-151, B-166, B-175, B-179, B-235, B-249, B-290, B-320, B-327, B-347, B-351, B-364, B-367, B-394, B-395, B-408, B-440, B-447

NOTES: Back Street was Irene Dunne's second film based on a Fannie Hurst novel. The movie premiered at New York's Mayfair Theatre on August 28, 1932. According to The RKO Gals, Irene Dunne considered Back Street's message as trash, although she enjoyed working with director John Stahl (B-343). The film established her as the first lady of screen soap operas. Back Street was rereleased in 1935. The film was remade by Universal in 1941 with Margaret Sullavan and Charles Boyer, and in 1961 with Susan Hayward and John Gavin. The second remake was eighteen minutes longer than the previous movies and was filmed in color. Ironically, Irene's daughter Mary Frances Griffin played the small part of a nurse in the 1961 version.

F-8   Thirteen Women   (RKO, 1932)   73 minutes

Executive producer: David O. Selznick. Director: George Archainbaud. Screenplay: Bartlett Cormack and Samuel Ornitz. Based on the novel by Tiffany Thayer. Musical director: Max Steiner. Editor: Charles J. Kimball. Photography: Leo Tover. Art director: Carroll Clark. Sound: Hugh McDowell.

CAST: Ricardo Cortez (Sergeant Barry Clive), Irene Dunne (Laura Stanhope), Myrna Loy (Ursula Georgi), Jill Esmond (Jo Turner), Florence Eldridge (Grace Coombs), Kay Johnson (Helen Dawson Fry), Julie Haydon (Mary), Harriet Hagman (May Raskob), Mary Duncan (June

Raskob), Peg Entwistle (Hazel), Marjorie Gateson (Martha), Elsie Prescott (Nan), Wally Albright (Bobby Stanhope), C. Henry Gordon (Swami Yogadachi), Ed Pawley (Burns), Blanche Frederici (Miss Kirsten), Phyllis Fraser (Twelfth woman), Betty Furness (Thirteenth woman), Audrey Scott, Aloha Porter (Equestriennes), Clayton Behee, Eddie Viera, Eddie DeComa, Buster Bartell (Trapeze acts), Teddy Mangean (Wire walker), Cliff Herbert (Circus act), Lee Phelps (Conductor), Edward LeSaint (Police chief), Lloyd Ingraham (Inspector), Mitchell Harris (Detective), Leon Ames, Kenneth Thomson, Clarence Geldert, Violet Seaton, Louis Natheaux, Oscar Smith, Allan Pomeroy.

SYNOPSIS: Years after being the victim of prejudice in a finishing school sorority, Ursula Georgi, a half Javanese/half Hindu woman, vows to get revenge. Ursula enlists the help of Swami Yogadachi to scare her former classmates with terrifying horoscopes, believing the power of suggestion will make the predictions come true. When the swami refuses to go along with her scheme, she signs his name to her predictions, then watches as her classmates commit murder and suicide. Laura Stanhope urges her friends to ignore the predictions and organizes a reunion. Grace Coombs argues that they will know the fortunes are true if the swami dies before July 1, as he predicted. After the swami sees a dire ending for Ursula, she pushes him in front of a train, reinforcing the predictions. Laura refuses to give in to the horoscope, although she fears for her son Bobby's life. When Bobby receives poisoned candy, Laura enlists the help of Sergeant Barry Clive. He realizes the swami must have an accomplice and soon suspects Ursula. Meanwhile, with the help of Laura's chauffeur, Ursula tries to kill Bobby with a bomb in his ball. Clive realizes Ursula is the killer and convinces Laura to go to New York. Despite the swami's prediction that Ursula will die in a train accident, Ursula heads for New York too. She confronts Laura on the train and hypnotizes her. When Ursula enters Bobby's compartment, Clive goes after her. Ursula jumps off the train, fulfilling the swami's prediction.

REVIEWS:
New York Times, 10.15.32: "Irene Dunne and Jill Esmond are the two quite sane women among the thirteen."

Variety, 10.18.32: "The featured players are Irene Dunne and Ricardo Cortez, neither of whom had much to do."

See also B-35, B-238, B-251, B-350, B-363

NOTES: Thirteen Women was based on the 1930 novel by Tiffany Thayer. The movie opened at New York's Roxy Theatre on October 14, 1932. Although Irene Dunne received second billing, RKO held up its release to cash in on the publicity of Back Street. According to American Movie Classics cable network host Bob Dorian, the producer of <u>Thirteen Women</u> hired an astrologer to make up charts for the stars of the film since the plot involved astrology. Irene Dunne, a devout Catholic, did not believe in astrology so she bet the other actresses that none of the predictions would come true. The ladies agreed to meet in five years to find out the results. Unfortunately, Dorian reported, no one seemed to have kept a record of whether or not the actresses met. Peg Entwistle, who played Hazel, gained notoriety for commiting suicide by jumping off the thirteenth letter of the Hollywoodland sign in 1932.

F-9 <u>No Other Woman</u>   (RKO, 1933)   58 minutes

Executive producer: David O. Selznick. Director: J. Walter Ruben. Assistant director: James Anderson. Screenplay: Wanda Tuchock and Bernard Schubert. Based on the play <u>Just a Woman</u> by Eugene Walter. Musical director: Max Steiner. Editor: William Hamilton. Photography: Edward Cronjager. Sound: Clem Portman. Transitional effects: Slavko Vorkapich.

CAST: Irene Dunne (Anna Stanley), Charles Bickford (Jim Stanley), J. Carroll Naish (Bonelli), Eric Linden (Joe Lacovia), Gwili Andre (Margot Von Dearing), Buster Miles (Bobbie Stanley), Lelia Bennett (Susie), Christian Rub (Eli), Hilda Vaughn (Miss LeRoy), Brooks Benedict (Chauffeur), Joseph E. Bernard (Frank, the butler), Frederick Burton (Anderson), Theodore Von Eltz (Sutherland), Edwin Stanley (Judge).

SYNOPSIS: Jim Stanley works in a Pennsylvania steel mill. His girlfriend Anna urges him to save his money so he can better himself. After they marry, Anna takes in boarders and saves money, hoping for a chance to get out of the steel town. When office worker Joe Lacovia shows Anna a dye he created from mill waste, Anna urges him to start his own business with Jim as a partner. Jim dislikes the idea and goes on a drinking binge. He returns repentant and agrees to invest in the dye company. In a few years, business booms and the Stanleys are living in a Pittsburgh mansion. They have a son Bobbie. During a business trip to New York, Jim meets Margot Von Dearing and begins an affair with her. She pressures him to divorce Anna and marry her. Anna overhears gossip about Jim's affair and confronts him. She insists it is just a fling and he will return to his wife and child. Anna vows not to give him a divorce so he sues her for adultery. Jim and paid witnesses lie during the divorce trial. Jim's lawyer accuses Anna of wanting Jim's money and demands full custody of Bobbie. Desperate to keep her son, Anna agrees to Jim's charges of adultery and claims Jim is not Bobbie's father. Jim admits he committed perjury and withdraws the divorce. While Jim is serving a year in prison for perjury, the business collapses. When he gets out of jail, he returns to the mill and reunites with his wife and son.

REVIEWS:
New York Times, 1.30.33: "Miss Dunne's role is a thankless one, but she is attractive and sincere in the acting of it."

Variety, 1.31.33: "Irene Dunne as the simple and ambitious housewife interprets her role during most of the running time in a manner which commands sympathy."

See also B-238, B-427

NOTES: No Other Woman premiered at New York's Roxy Theatre on January 29, 1933. The play on which it was based, Just a Woman, ran for 136 performances in 1916.

F-10   The Secret of Madame Blanche   (MGM, 1933)
       83 minutes

   Director: Charles Brabin. Screenplay: Frances Goodrich and Albert Hackett. Based on the play The Lady by Martin Brown. Music: Dr. William Axt. Editor: Blanche Sewell. Photography: Merritt B. Gerstad. Art director: Cedric Gibbons. Costumes: Adrian. Sound: Douglas Shearer.

   CAST: Irene Dunne (Sally Sanders), Lionel Atwill (Aubrey St. John), Phillips Holmes (Leonard St. John), Una Merkel (Ella), Douglas Walton (Leonard St. John, Jr.), C. Henry Gordon (State's attorney), Jean Parker (Eloise), Mitchell Lewis (Duval).

SYNOPSIS: American chorus girl Sally Sanders meets British aristocrat Leonard St. John. Realizing that his usual playboy line will not work with Sally, Leonard marries her. Untrained for anything but gambling, Leonard must rely on the support of his father Aubrey. Because of the class difference between Sally and Leonard, Aubrey disapproves of the marriage and cuts off his support. Leonard goes broke in Monte Carlo as Sally learns she is pregnant. Desperate, Leonard agrees to leave Sally if his father will give her some money. Leonard commits suicide, realizing he cannot live without her. Sally gives birth to Leonard, Jr. and gets a job singing in a seedy cafe. Aubrey hires a private detective to find her when he learns he has a grandson. He claims Sally is an unfit mother and gains custody of Leonard, Jr. Aubrey refuses to let Sally see her son. Eighteen years pass. Sally, now known as Madame Blanche, operates a cafe and bordello in Paris. Leonard, Jr. is stationed in France during World War I. He takes Eloise Duval to the brothel and gets involved in a drunken brawl. Sally recognizes her son and tries to discourage his wild behavior without revealing her identity. Eloise's father tries to kill Leonard at the brothel, but Leonard shoots him. Sally provides an alibi to protect her son and confesses to the murder. In court, Sally claims the killing was self defense. The state's attorney reveals that Sally is Leonard's mother and Leonard confesses to the murder. He denounces his grandfather's ideas and makes up with Sally. They plan a trip to America after Leonard is released from prison. Leonard vows to study and make a new life for himself.

REVIEWS:
New York Times, 2.4.33: "...Miss Dunne gives quite [an] appealing and sincere performance....Miss Dunne is ingratiating both as a young woman and as the mother of twenty years later. She makes most of her scenes convincing."

Variety, 2.7.33: "Miss Dunne, moving through most of a normal lifetime as the action progresses from the 1890s to wartime, is at all times excellent. She is as much the picture as any part of it. That she will increase her following, a deserved due, is certain after 'Secrets' [sic] gets into circulation....Miss Dunne does a complete finale number with her show and later on sings at the piano in cheap Paris cafes. More of this sort of thing could be stood, especially if the singing is in as capable hands as Miss Dunne's."

See also T-7, A-70, B-35, B-39, B-100, B-270, B-283, B-289, B-306

NOTES: The working title of The Secret of Madame Blanche was The Lady, as it was based on the 1923 play of the same name. Mary Nash starred in the Broadway production, which ran for 85 performances. In The Secret of Madame Blanche, Irene Dunne sang "If Love Were All," "Tempting Kisses," and a suggestive music hall number. Despite the fact that her character ended up running a brothel, Irene did not express displeasure with the film in later years, as she did after playing a mistress in Back Street. The Secret of Madame Blanche was one of a series of films in the early days of talking pictures, which focused on women sacrificing everything in a male-dominated world. Other films of this genre include Madame X (MGM, 1929) with Ruth Chatterton and The Sin of Madelon Claudet (MGM, 1931) with Helen Hayes.

F-11   The Silver Cord   (RKO, 1933)   74 minutes

Executive producer: Merian C. Cooper. Producer: Pandro S. Berman. Director: John Cromwell. Screenplay: Jane Murfin. Based on the play by Sidney Howard. Musical director: Max Steiner. Editor: George Nicholls, Jr. Photography: Charles Rosher. Sets: Van Nest Polglase. Sound: Clem Portman.

CAST: Irene Dunne (Christina Phelps), Joel McCrea (David Phelps), Frances Dee (Hester), Eric Linden

(Robert Phelps), Laura Hope Crews (Mrs. Phelps), Helen Cromwell (Delia), Gustav von Seyffertiz, Reginald Pasch, Perry Ivins.

SYNOPSIS: Architect David Phelps and research biologist Christina Phelps are American newlyweds living in Heidelberg. Christina is an independent woman who feels she can juggle career and family, and encourages her husband to do the same. When David receives an offer from a New York architectural firm, the couple returns to the United States. Before David starts his new job, they stop to visit his mother. Mrs. Phelps is possessive and over-protective. She alienates her new daughter-in-law by putting David and Christina in separate bedrooms, urging Christina to quit her job, being less than enthusiastic over Christina's pregnancy, and offering David a position constructing a near-by housing development. Although Christina promises not to come between David and his mother, she is forced to take sides when Mrs. Phelps encourages her younger son Robert to break his engagement to Hester. Christina knows that if David allows his mother to control Robert's life, Mrs. Phelps will eventually break up their marriage too. David refuses to take a stand, but saves Hester's life when she nearly drowns, trying to commit suicide in the frozen pond. The next morning, Christina gives David an ultimatum: choose between being a son or a husband. Mrs. Phelps confesses that she found the romance she lacked in her marriage in motherhood. She begs David to go on a European trip with her and Robert. Despite his mother's pleas, David goes with his wife. In the car, Christina assures him that someday his mother will understand, although she may not admit it.

REVIEWS:
New York Times, 5.5.33: "Irene Dunne acts commendably, but here and there the lengthy dialogue is too much for her..."

Variety, 5.9.33: "Equally as good [as Laura Hope Crews], though with less opportunity, is Miss Dunne's clear visioned scientist..."

New Outlook, 6.33: ""Eric Linden and Joel McCrea, as the sons, and Irene Dunne, as the wife of the elder one, turn in performances of merit."

Motion Picture, 7.33: "There is too much talking for the average moviegoer's taste and the action is confined to drawing-rooms....Performances, dialogue and direction are brilliant....Irene Dunne and Frances Dee [are] the girls whose love is stifled in this powerful Silver Cord."

See also B-18, B-238, B-272, B-295, B-306, B-383, B-407

NOTES: The Silver Cord opened at Radio City Music Hall on May 4, 1933. Although Irene Dunne had been given the role

66   Irene Dunne

to reward her for her consistently high returns at the box office, both Katharine Hepburn and Ann Harding had been offered the part first. <u>The Silver Cord</u> opened on Broadway in 1926 and ran for 130 performances. Margalo Gillmore played the role Irene essayed on screen. Laura Hope Crews originated the role of the possessive mother on stage. Frances Dee and Joel McCrea met during the filming of <u>The Silver Cord</u> and married in 1933.

F-12 <u>Ann Vickers</u>   (RKO, 1933)   72 minutes

> Executive producer: Merian C. Cooper. Producer: Pandro S. Berman. Director: John Cromwell. Screenplay: Jane Murfin. Based on the novel by Sinclair Lewis. Musical director: Max Steiner. Editor: George Nicholls, Jr. Photography: David Abel and Edward Cronjager. Art directors: Van Nest Polglase and Charles Kirk. Sound: Paul F. Wiser.
>
> CAST: Irene Dunne (Ann Vickers), Walter Huston (Barney Dolphin), Conrad Nagel (Lindsey Atwell), Bruce Cabot (Captain Lafe Resnick), Edna May Oliver (Dr. Malvina Wormser), Mitchell Lewis (Captain Waldo), Sam Hardy (Russell Spaulding), Murray Kinnell (Dr. Slenk), Helen Eby-Rock (Kitty Cognac), Gertrude Michael (Mona Dolphin), J. Carroll Naish (Dr. Sorrell), Sarah Padden (Lil), Reginald Barlow (Chaplain), Rafaella Ottiano (Feldermus), Irving Bacon (Waiter), Geneva Mitchell (Leah Burbaum), Mary Foy (Matron), Frederic Santley (Sam, reform assistant), Wally Albright (Mischau), Edwin Maxwell (Defense attorney), Larry Steers (Prosecutor), Arthur Hoyt (Mr. Penny), Jane Darwell (Mrs. Gates),

SYNOPSIS: Dedicated social worker Ann Vickers spurns the advances of Russell Spaulding, claiming her career is more important than love. Despite her valiant words, she meets Captain Lafe Resnick at a settlement house dance. Lafe confesses that he is scared to go overseas to fight World War I and proposes during their first dance. Ann is quickly swept off her feet and has an affair with him before he ships out. Pregnant with Lafe's child, Ann finds he is not the knight in shining armour that she thought. When she tells him of her pregnancy, his lack of enthusiasm makes Ann resolve to go back to her career and raise their daughter alone. Ann loses the baby and goes to work at Copperhead Gap prison. She is horrified to learn that the guards use brutality to keep the prisoners in line. When she vows to change things, prison officials try to blackmail her into resigning. Undaunted, Ann writes a best selling book on prison reform, which leads to her being appointed head of a women's detention home. Despite her success, Ann is lonely. She meets Barney Dolphin, a prominent judge whose wife is cheating on him. Dolphin's wife refuses to give him a divorce. He has an affair with Ann, which leads to the birth of an illegitimate son. Dolphin is indicted for taking stock tips from criminals. When he faces jail, his wife agrees to a divorce. The prison board asks for Ann's resignation because of her private life. While Dolphin is in jail, Ann supports herself and their child by writing articles on prison reform. After serving three years, Dolphin is pardoned. Ann gladly gives up her career for her husband, finally realizing that work is not everything.

REVIEWS:
New York Times, 9.29.33: "Irene Dunne, who gives quite a commendable portrayal as Ann, and several of the other players speak some of [Sinclair] Lewis's own lines without the desired spontaneity, as though they were struggling with several of the lengthy speeches....Miss Dunne...acquits herself favorably."

Variety, 10.3.33: "Star gives fine performance. She is sincere and believable except that so handsome and fascinating a warden for a woman's prison is a bit beyond probablity."

New Yorker, 10.7.33: "Irene Dunne, as Ann, and Walter Huston, as the judge, manage to pick the thing up considerably by their intelligent acting, and the film is good entertainment without being in any way provocative."

See also B-238, B-261, B-306, B-383, B-402

NOTES: Sinclair Lewis's controversial novel came to the screen, despite the taboo subjects it touched on: premarital sex, illegitimacy, corrupt law. The Dame in the Kimono, a book chronicling Hollywood censorship, claimed that the censorship board sometimes allowed things to slip by if the stars or directors had sterling reputations. Authors Leonard J. Leff and Jerold L. Simmons said that by using Irene Dunne and director John Cromwell, RKO was assuring the censors that the film would be handled tastefully (B-261). Time remarked that Cromwell directed "with almost too much dignity" ("The New Pictures." October 9, 1933.). The New Yorker noted that the film eliminated several major points from the book, including the religious differences of the captain and the judge ("Vickers Vapor Rub." October 7, 1933.). Today the film would probably get a "G" rating, for the sex and violence is all implied.

F-13 If I Were Free (RKO, 1933) 66 minutes

Executive producer: Merian C. Cooper. Associate producer: Kenneth MacGowan. Director: Elliott Nugent. Screenplay: Dwight Taylor. Based on the play Behold, We Live by John Van Druten. Musical director: Max Steiner. Editor: Arthur Roberts. Photography: Edward Cronjager. Art directors: Van Nest Polglase and Charles Kirk. Sound: George D. Ellis.

CAST: Irene Dunne (Sarah Cazenove), Clive Brook (Gordon Evers), Nils Asther (Tono Cazenove), Henry Stephenson (Hector Stribling), Vivian Tobin (Jewel Stribling), Laura Hope Crews (Dame Evers), Tempe Pigott (Mrs. Gill), Lorraine MacLean (Katherine Evers), Halliwell Hobbes (Evers's butler), Mario Dominci.

SYNOPSIS: Sarah Cazenove's cheating husband Tono threatens to shoot her when she refuses to go to Cannes with him and his mistress. At a party, Sarah meets Gordon Evers, a wealthy lawyer who is also unhappily married. After Tono encourages her to go out with Gordon, she tries to commit suicide. Gordon stops her, encouraging her to move to London and start a new life. Sarah divorces Tono and opens an interior decorating business. Katherine Evers refuses to give Gordon a divorce, but he continues to see Sarah. When Gordon's friend tells her that the relationship is hurting his career, she reluctantly breaks up with Gordon. Meanwhile, Gordon learns a bullet in his lung, an injury sustained in World War I, must be removed. He decides to go through with the risky surgery without telling Sarah. When she learns of Gordon's condition, she returns to his side. Gordon's mother urges Katherine to give in about the divorce, allowing Gordon and Sarah to marry. Katherine relinquishes, and Gordon and Sarah reconcile after his successful surgery.

REVIEWS:
New York Times, 1.5.34: "Considering the limited possiblities of her role, Miss Dunne does remarkably well."

Variety, 1.9.34: "Performances by the cast of four, Irene Dunne, Clive Brook, Nils Asther and Henry Stephenson, who virtually carry it alone, are far superior to the subject. Miss Dunne and Brook, by the capable manner in which they play, hold it together. Less skilled performers would have made 'If I Were Free' much less acceptable screen fare."

Newsweek, 1.13.34: "Grown-up dialogue and situations which conceivably could occur in real life make this RKO offering a movie out of the ordinary. Irene Dunne and Clive Brook convincingly depict two people unhappily married - not to each other."

See also B-35, B-238, B-473

NOTES: The film was released in Great Britain as Behold We Live. Irene Dunne sang "Early Rising" and a German song.

F-14   This Man Is Mine   (RKO, 1934)   76 minutes

Producer: Pandro S. Berman. Director: John Cromwell. Screenplay: Jane Murfin. Based on the play Love Flies in the Window by Anne Morrison Chapin. Musical director: Max Steiner. Editor:

William Morgan. Photography: David Abel. Art directors: Van Nest Polglase and Carroll Clark.

CAST: Irene Dunne (Tony Dunlap), Constance Cummings (Francesca Harper), Ralph Bellamy (Jim Dunlap), Kay Johnson (Bee McCrea), Charles Starrett (Jud McCrea), Sidney Blackmer (Mort Holmes), Vivian Tobin (Rita), Louis Mason (Slim).

SYNOPSIS: Tony Dunlap is an artist whose mother ran off with another man. She regrets that her father let the tragedy ruin his painting career, vowing the same will not happen to her. Tony's husband Jim confesses that he was in love with Francesca Harper before he met Tony, but Fran eloped with someone else. Tony insists that she knows Jim loves her, not Fran. When Fran gets a divorce, she returns to town. Although she knows that Jim is happily married, she flirts outrageously with him. Jim's old feelings soon return and he asks Tony for a divorce. She insists they wait six months before filing. Meanwhile, Tony spies Fran kissing Mort Holmes and concludes that Fran is using Jim. Jim sees Fran and Mort and jumps to the opposite conclusion, that Fran is using Mort to make Jim jealous. Jim demands a quick divorce so he can marry Fran. Tony agrees, threatening to name Fran as corespondent and sue her for a million dollars for alienation. Afraid of the publicity, Fran breaks up with Jim and elopes with Mort. Tony and Jim fight, then reconcile.

REVIEWS:
New York Times, 4.13.34: "Irene Dunne does very well by the role of Tony."

Variety, 4.17.34: "As a starring vehicle for Irene Dunne the picture is not precisely what a star might order. It would be unfair to state that Miss Dunne is secondary to other characters, but the fact is that the three feminine roles are of about equal importance....Miss Dunne is never negative or passive and she mixes a nice reasonableness with an understandable yen for getting even."

Film Fun, 7.34: "What this one lacks in action is more than replenished by sophisticated dialog [sic] and well-placed laughs."

See also B-1, B-35, B-113, B-186, B-238, B-295, B-472

NOTES: The working title of This Man Is Mine was Transient Love. It marked the first of Irene Dunne's three screen appearances with Ralph Bellamy. Irene sang "When Apples Grow on a Lilac Tree." Despite the film's serious tone, a scene near the end, with Irene smashing a painting over Bellamy's head, bordered on slapstick.

F-15 Stingaree (RKO, 1934) 76 minutes

Producer: Pandro S. Berman. Director: William A. Wellman. Screenplay: Becky Gardiner. Based on the stories of E.W. Hornung. Songs: Gus Kahn, W. Franke Harling, Gounod, Flotow, Edward Eliscu, and Max Steiner. Musical director: Max Steiner. Editor: James B. Borley. Photography: James Van Tree.

CAST: Irene Dunne (Hilda Bouverie), Richard Dix (Stingaree), Mary Boland (Mrs. Clarkson), Conway Tearle (Sir Julian Kent), Andy Devine (Howie), Henry Stephenson (Mr. Clarkson), Una O'Connor (Annie), George Barraud (Inspector Radford), Reginald Owen (Governor-general), Snub Pollard (Victor), Billy Bevan, Robert Greig.

SYNOPSIS: Hilda Bouverie, a maid for the wealthy Clarksons, dreams of becoming an opera singer. She hopes that composer Sir Julian Kent will discover her when he comes to test Mrs. Clarkson's voice. Stingaree, a highway bandit, kidnaps Kent and poses as the composer in order to gain entrance to the wealthy home. Stingaree arrives at the Clarksons', but finds Hilda is the only one there. He is charmed by her audition and promises to help her get started on a musical career. She becomes infatuated with him. When Stingaree's identity is revealed, he kidnaps Hilda and takes her to his hideout, planning to have her audition for Kent. Instead, he finds Kent has escaped. Determined to help Hilda, Stingaree dresses her in stolen clothes and escorts her to a party given for Kent. At gunpoint, Stingaree forces Kent to listen to Hilda sing. Despite the circumstances, Kent is impressed by Hilda's voice and offers to take her to London to train her. When Stingaree is shot and imprisoned, Hilda is reluctant to leave, however he insists she put her career first. Hilda becomes a famous singer, but she misses Stingaree. She turns down a proposal from her mentor, Kent, and returns to Australia for a gala to be attended by the governor-general. Stingaree escapes from prison and disguises himself as the governor-general, replacing the dignitary in his box. Hilda gives a stellar performance, then confesses to the hunted Stingaree that her career means nothing to her. They run off for a life in the bush country.

REVIEWS:
New York Times, 5.18.34: "Miss Dunne gives a charming performance and she sings several songs very agreeably."

Variety, 5.22.34: "Radio probably realized that the horse operas have done much to rub the bloom of youth from hard riding and gives it mostly to Miss Dunne, who plays competently and sings better. The song 'Tonight Is Mine' is the chief musical number though excerpts from 'Faust' and 'Martha' are introduced as parts of the mimic stage performance. Musically Miss Dunne rises above her dramatic work, since the authors have given her small opportunity, and she wisely does not attempt to steam it up."

Harrison's Reports, 5.19.34: "Irene Dunne sings songs of the operatic as well as the ballad type, and she does so well; and since the music is made part of the plot the action does not slow up at any time."

See also S-7, B-84, B-238, B-271, B-353

NOTES: *Stingaree* reunited Irene Dunne with her *Cimarron* co-star Richard Dix. Songs were "Stingaree's Ballad," "Tonight Is Mine," "I Wish I Were a Fisherman," "Once You're Mine," and excerpts from *Faust* and *Martha*.

F-16 The Age of Innocence   (RKO, 1934)   81 minutes

Executive producer: Pandro S. Berman. Director: Philip Moeller. Associate director: James Loring. Screenplay: Sarah Y. Mason and Victor Heerman. Based on the novel by Edith Wharton and the play by Margaret A. Barnes. Music: Max Steiner. Editor: George Hively. Photography: James Van Tree. Art directors: Van Nest Polglase and Al Herman. Costumes: Walter Plunkett. Sound: John L. Case.

CAST: Irene Dunne (Countess Ellen Olenska), John Boles (Newland Archer), Lionel Atwill (Julius Beaufort), Laura Hope Crews (Mrs. Welland), Helen Westley (Granny Mingott), Julie Haydon (May Welland), Herbert Yost (Mr. Welland), Theresa Maxwell Conover (Mrs. Archer), Edith Van Clive (Janey Archer), Leonard Carey (Butler).

SYNOPSIS: Lawyer Newland Archer is engaged to socialite May Welland. May's cousin, Ellen Olenska, is about to be divorced from a Polish count, causing her to be ostracized from New York society. Ellen's grandmother forces her to mingle with the New York elite by throwing a ball in her honor. Ellen renews her acquaintance with Newland, on whom she had a crush when she was young. Newland is newly attracted to Ellen, despite his engagement. Julius Beaufort, a married businessman, also woos her. Newland wins Ellen's divorce suit, but feels bound to marry May. After his honeymoon, Newland meets Ellen again and finds he still loves her. He decides to leave May and go away with Ellen. However, when Ellen learns her cousin is going to have a baby, Ellen exiles herself to Europe, forcing Newland to return to his wife.

REVIEWS:
Harrison's Reports, 9.22.34: "Excellent adult fare....Irene Dunne and John Boles have never been seen to better advantage. It is filled with human interest and has fine comedy situations."

New York Times, 10.19.34: "Miss Dunne is more effective [than John Boles], possibly, but it requires a more profoundly moving skill than hers to etch the tragedy

72   Irene Dunne

brilliantly against the background."

Variety, 10.23.34: "John Boles and Irene Dunne are paired above the title, latter as the divorcee giving a more impressive performance than Boles."

Film Fun, 12.34: "Irene Dunne and John Boles find themselves still torn between screen love and screen duty....Picture has more than its quota of charm, and should appeal especially to the family trade."

See also B-238

NOTES: The Age of Innocence reunited Irene Dunne with John Boles, in hopes of recapturing their success in Back Street. The Age of Innocence first was offered to Katharine Hepburn, but she turned it down. The film was based on Edith Wharton's 1920 Pulitzer-Prize-winning novel and the 1928 play by Margaret Ayer Barnes. The stage version ran 209 performances and starred Katharine Cornell.

F-17   **Sweet Adeline**   (Warner Bros., 1935)   87 minutes

Producer: Edward Chodorov. Director: Mervyn LeRoy. Choreographer: Bobby Connolly. Screenplay: Erwin S. Gelsey. Based on the musical by Jerome Kern, Oscar Hammerstein II, Harry Armstrong, and Dick Gerard. Songs: Jerome Kern and Oscar Hammerstein II. Orchestral arrangements: Ray Heindorf. Musical director: Leo F. Forbstein. Editor: Ralph Dawson. Photography: Sol Polito. Art director: Robert Haas. Costumes: Orry-Kelly.

CAST: Irene Dunne (Adeline Schmidt), Donald Woods (Sid Barnett), Ned Sparks (Dan Herzig), Hugh Herbert (Rupert Rockingham), Winifred Shaw (Elysia), Louis Calhern (Major James Day), Nydia Westman (Nellie Schmidt), Joseph Cawthorn (Oscar Schmidt), Dorothy Dare (Dot, the band leader), Phil Regan (Juvenile), Noah Beery, Sr. (Sultan), Don Alvarado (Renaldo), Martin Garralaga (Dark young man), Emmett Vogan (Captain), Howard Dickinson (Civilian), Eddie Shubert (Eddie), Nick Copeland (Prop man), Ferdinand Munier (General Hawks), William V. Mong (Cobbler, a spy), Johnny Eppelite (Young Jolson), Mary Treen (Girl), Milton Kibbee (Stagehand), Joseph Bernard (Waiter), Charles Hickman (Manx), Howard H. Mitchell (Bartender), Landers Stevens, William Arnold (Men), David Newell (Young man), Evelyn Wynans (Woman), Harry Tyler (Louise), Jack Mulhall (Bob).

SYNOPSIS: Composer Sid Barnett and Spanish-American War Army major James Day vie for the attentions of Adeline Schmidt, an aspiring singer who works in her father's beer garden. Adeline's father dislikes show business, therefore encourages Adeline to date the major. Impressario Rupert

Rockingham casts his girlfriend Elysia in Sid's operetta, despite Sid's insistence that Adeline play the role. They have a fight when Adeline refuses the part, knowing it will hurt her father. Sid tricks Adeline into auditioning before the company. The major offers to back the show if Adeline stars, much to Sid's dismay. Sid is jealous when Adeline continues to date the major. Sid tries to make her jealous by going out with Elysia, but it does not work. Expecting a proposal, Adeline is hurt when the major asks her to be his mistress. Although she is ready to quit the show on opening night, Sid convinces her to stay. Mr. Schmidt is proud of Adeline, despite his initial objections to show business. During the show, Rupert, a member of the secret service, arrests Elysia as a spy, but lets her finish the performance, unaware that she wants to kill Adeline for stealing her role. During a musical number in a swing, Elysia cuts the ropes, sending Adeline crashing to the floor. Elysia is arrested for spying and attempted murder. The show closes while Adeline recovers. Sid writes a new autobiographical show about the beer garden, which ends with Adeline and Sid in an embrace.

REVIEWS:
New York Times, 1.7.35: "Chiefly [the film] permits the amiable film-goer [sic] to hear Irene Dunne adjusting her cool and pleasant soprano to such memorable romantic songs as 'Here Am I,' 'Don't Ever Leave Me,' 'Why Was I Born?' 'Twas Not So Long Ago' and 'We Were So Very Young.'...Since Miss Dunne possesses the handsome and aloof manner of the assured metropolitan, it is a little disconcerting to find her enrolled as the innocent maid of the fable."

Variety, 1.8.35: "Miss Dunne, in fine voice, is comely as Adeline, and effective, also, despite that she's not suited to torch songs. They didn't make it a cinch for her, either, in doing such things as requiring her to sing a number after reading a lyric sheet once."

Film Fun, 3.35: "Pleasing musical concerning a beer garden warbler who becomes a stage star. Irene Dunn [sic] has the leading role, but Hugh Herbert steals the picture with a swell brand of comedy."

See also R-84, D-6, D-10, D-13, D-18, D-20, D-21, D-22, D-26, A-69, A-70, B-172, B-178, B-180, B-229, B-326, B-390, B-432, B-440

NOTES: Sweet Adeline marked Irene Dunne's first Jerome Kern musical on screen. She became the film singer most identified with his music, starring in Sweet Adeline, Roberta, Show Boat, High, Wide and Handsome, and Joy of Living. In Sweet Adeline, Irene sang "Here Am I," "We Were So Young," "Why Was I Born?," "Lonely Feet," and "Don't Ever Leave Me." Helen Morgan, Irene's Show Boat co-star, originated the role of Adeline on Broadway in 1929. Although most of the Broadway score was retained, Kern wrote two new songs for the film: "Lonely Feet" and "We Were So Young."

F-18 Roberta (RKO, 1935) 105 minutes

Producer: Pandro S. Berman. Director: William A. Seiter. Choreographers: Fred Astaire and Hermes Pan. Screenplay: Jane Murfin, Sam Mintz, Glenn Tryon, and Alan Scott. Based on the novel Gowns by Roberta by Alice Duer Miller and the musical Roberta by Jerome Kern and Otto Harbach. Songs: Jerome Kern, Otto Harbach, Bernard Dougall, Oscar Hammerstein II, Dorothy Fields, and Jimmy McHugh. Musical director: Max Steiner. Editor: William Hamilton. Photography: Edward Cronjager. Art directors: Van Nest Polglase and Carroll Clark. Costumes: Bernard Newman. Sets: Thomas K. Little. Sound: John Tribby.

CAST: Irene Dunne (Stephanie), Fred Astaire (Huck Haines), Ginger Rogers (Countess Scharwenka [Lizzie Gatz]), Randolph Scott (John Kent), Helen Westley (Roberta [Aunt Minnie]), Victor Varconi (Ladislaw), Claire Dodd (Sophie), Luis Alberni (Voyda), Ferdinand Munier (Lord Delves), Torben Meyer (Albert), Adrian Rosley (Professor), Bodil Rosing (Fernando), Lucille Ball, Jane Hamilton, Margaret McChrystal, Kay Sutton, Maxine Jennings, Virginia Reid, Lorna Low, Lorraine DeSart, Wanda Perry, Diane Cook, Virginia Carroll, Betty Dumbries, Donna Roberts (Mannequins), Mike Tellegen, Sam Savitsky (Cossacks), Zena Savine (Woman), Johnny "Candy" Candido, Muzzy Marcellino, Gene Sheldon, Howard Lally, William Carey, Paul McLarind, Hal Bown, Charles Sharpe, Ivan Dow, Phil Cuthbert, Delmon Davis, William Dunn (Orchestra), Judith Vosselli, Rita Gould (Bits), Mary Forbes (Mrs. Teal), William B. Davidson (Purser), Grace Hayle (Reporter), Dale Van Sickel (Dance extra).

SYNOPSIS: Football player John Kent travels to Paris with his friend Huck's band. Before they start to work, the band is fired over a misunderstanding. Pressed for money, John decides to visit his Aunt Minnie, who is known as the famous dressmaker Roberta. At the couturiere's, John meets Stephanie, a White Russian princess who has worked as a designer at Roberta's salon since the revolution. John sets out to acquire European culture to impress his fiancee Sophie. Huck runs into his old girlfriend Lizzie Gatz, who is passing herself off as a Polish countess. She gets the band a job and renews her romance with Huck. When Aunt Minnie dies, John inherits the dress shop. He and Stephanie become partners in the salon and fall in love. In hopes of breaking John's engagement to Sophie, Huck persuades Stephanie to sell Sophie a dress John dislikes. John breaks up with Sophie and gets drunk. He and Stephanie quarrel over the dress and she quits. Huck tries to run the salon with disasterous results. He convinces Stephanie to return to the shop. They stage an elaborate musical fashion show, and John and Stephanie reconcile.

REVIEWS:
Variety, 3.13.35: "Irene Dunne looks like a million and sings like just as much. Her voice registers better here than in previous films in which she has warbled."

Time, 3.18.35: "[Helen Westley's] assistant, the Russian princess whose chief function is to put her to sleep with sentimental lullabies every afternoon, is Irene Dunne....[The songs, Westley, Dunne, and Randloph Scott], in addition to a series of handsome modernistic interiors and a fashion show..., can be listed among the advantages of the picture. But the most pleasant moments in Roberta arrive when Fred Astaire and Ginger Rogers turn the story upside down and dance on it."

Liberty, 3.30.35: "...aided by lovely Irene Dunne and Randy Scott, late of the horse operas, as the more conventionally romantic pair, the film becomes an item for the 'must' list of every amusement seeker."

Stage, 4.35: "Irene Dunne hasn't the nostalgic wistfulness of [original Broadway cast member] Tamara, but she has a very lovely voice..."

New York Times, 5.8.35: "For the liquid sentimental songs like 'Lovely to Look At,' 'Yesterday' [sic] and 'Touch of Your Hand' there is the cool soprano of Irene Dunne."

The New Statesman and Nation, 6.8.35: "It may be unfair to Miss Dunne to class her part of the film, singing and all, as subsidiary; but it seemed essential only to the plot (which is naturally negligible) to hear her entertain a group of reverently homesick White Russians with a song about smoke, or snow, or something, getting into their eyes. Her French, too, is so bad it startles the rest of the cast..."

See also R-1, R-85, T-3, T-30, D-2, D-4, D-10, D-16, D-17, D-19, D-21, D-22, D-23, D-27, D-28, D-29, D-30, D-31, D-32, A-62, A-69, A-70, S-1, B-2, B-12, B-61, B-76, B-143, B-148, B-149, B-156, B-162, B-172, B-178, B-187, B-238, B-249, B-264, B-276, B-278, B-290, B-295, B-301, B-322, B-339, B-366, B-440, B-443, B-465

NOTES: Irene Dunne was cast in Roberta as box office insurance, as RKO was not certain that Fred Astaire and Ginger Rogers could carry a film of that magnitude by themselves. It was initially announced that Jerome Kern would compose a new score for the movie, which was based on the 1933 Broadway musical and Alice Duer Miller's book. In the end, only two songs were added to the film: "I Won't Dance," which was performed by Astaire and Rogers, and "Lovely to Look At," which was sung by Irene. Further

76   Irene Dunne

revisions were made in the Broadway script when characters were combined to build up the parts played by Astaire and Rogers. Despite Irene's top billing and laudatory notices, critics and film historians focused on the contributions of Astaire and Rogers.

<u>Roberta</u> cost $750,000 to film, about one third of which was spent on the principals' salaries. Other costly expenditures included the elaborate wardrobe. One of Irene's furs cost six thousand dollars. According to <u>Liberty</u>, Irene was followed around the RKO lot by a fireman while she wore one highly flammable costume. It seems Miriam Hopkins had a gown catch fire recently (Beverly Hills. "Rhythm, Romance, Realism." <u>Liberty</u>. March 30, 1935.).

<u>Roberta</u> premiered at Radio City Music Hall on March 7, 1935. Irene sang "Russian Song," "Yesterdays," "Smoke Gets in Your Eyes," and "Lovely to Look At." For many years, <u>Roberta</u> was withheld from television because of the 1952 remake, <u>Lovely to Look At</u>. Released by MGM, the film starred Kathryn Grayson and Howard Keel in the roles played by Irene and Randolph Scott. <u>Roberta</u> was the last film Irene made under her initial RKO contract. When asked about the film in later years, Irene said she was surprised at how well it held up. Although she admitted the plot was silly, she praised <u>Roberta's</u> entertainment value (B-250).

F-19   <u>Magnificent Obsession</u>   (Universal, 1935)
       112 minutes

Producer: John M. Stahl. Associate producer: E.M. Asher. Director: John M. Stahl. Screenplay: George O'Neil, Sarah Y. Mason, and Victor Heerman. Based on the novel by Lloyd C. Douglas. Musical director: Franz Waxman. Editor: Milton Carruth. Photography: John J. Mescall and John P. Fulton. Art director: Charles D. Hall. Costumes: Vera West. Sound: Gilbert Kurland.

CAST: Irene Dunne (Helen Hudson), Robert Taylor (Robert Merrick), Sara Haden (Nancy Ashford), Charles Butterworth (Tommy Masterson), Betty Furness (Joyce Hudson), Henry Armetta (Tony), Arthur Hoyt (Perry), Gilbert Emery (Dr. Ramsey), Marion Clayton (Amy), Arthur Treacher (Horace), Ralph Morgan (Randolph), Inez Courtney, Georgette Rhodes, Helen Brown, Joyce Compton, Norma Drew (Nurses), Alan Davis (Dr. Justin), Craufurd Kent (Dr. Thomas), Edward Earle (Dr. Miller), Lowell Durham (Junior Masterson), Sumner Getchell (Jimmy), Walter Walker (Nicholas Merrick), William Arnold (Chief inspector), Leah Winslow, Ethel Sykes (Women on boat), Sherry Hall, Allen Connor, William Worthington, Louis LaVoie (Men on boat), Oscar Rudolph (Western Union boy), Eddy Chandler (Mechanic), Mickey Daniels (Billy, boy in Ford), Beryl Mercer

(Mrs. Eden), Sidney Bracey (Butler), Alice Ardell (Maid), Cora Sue Collins (Girl in park), Roy Brown, Gretta Gould, Frank Mayo, John M. Saint Polis, George Hackathorne, Beth Hazelton (Ex-patients), Sid Marion (Sword swallower), Frank Reicher (Dr. Rochard), Leonard Mudie (Dr. Bardendreght), Arnold Korff, William Stack, Frederic Roland, Fredrik Vogeding, Theodor Von Eltz (Doctors), Rollo Lloyd (Tramp), Charles Coleman (Butler), Purnell Pratt (Hastings the attorney), Walter Miller (Chauffeur), Lucien Littlefield (Breezy), Gino Corrado (Antoine), Vance Carroll, Henry Hale, Ray Johnson, Louis Natheau, Jack Hatfield, Gladden James, Donald Kerr (Reporters), Frank Maye (John Stone).

SYNOPSIS: Helen Hudson's husband dies of a heart attack because the hospital's pulmotor resuscitator is being used on Robert Merrick, a drunken playboy. After her husband's death, Helen discovers Dr. Hudson's many philanthropic and charitable efforts and she vows to hate Robert. Robert feels guilty that he was saved and the doctor was not, but continues his devil-may-care lifestyle. After a drunken binge, Robert hears of Dr. Hudson's good works and religious influence. Randolph, a stonecutter, encourages Robert to adopt Dr. Hudson's philosophy of anonymously helping people. Trying it out, Robert feels rewarded when he meets Helen. His flirtation angers her and she flees the car. As she's getting out, she is run down by another speeding auto and blinded. Robert watches Helen struggling with Braille, feeling guilty about the accident. Learning she is nearly broke, he arranges for Helen to be supported and consults with a series of specialists about surgery to restore her sight. Helen does not recognize his voice and finds herself falling in love with him. Although the doctors refuse to operate, they tell her that her sight may return eventually. Robert confesses his identity and proposes, but Helen refuses because of her blindness. She flees to Virginia without telling anyone. After studying abroad for six years, Robert returns to the United States as an esteemed surgeon. Through Randolph, he locates Helen and learns her condition has deteriorated. Robert performs a dangerous operation and restores her sight. Helen awakens to find that he not only has brought back her vision, he has adopted the charitable ways of Dr. Hudson.

REVIEWS:
New York Times, 12.31.35: "Miss Dunne rises to what probably should be respectfully referred to as dramatic heights as the blind girl."

Variety, 1.8.36: "Cast, cameraman (John Mescall) and the librettists, along with Director [John M.] Stahl, rate all the bouquets coming their way for the combined good results of their total efforts."

Oakland Tribune [CA], 2.13.36: "Miss Dunne's role of

78   Irene Dunne

twice-victim of the wastrel Tommy is developed with her usual charm and tranquil power. She, too, executes a skilled job in character transition. Her version of valor under fire; sacrifice for love; spirit rising above tribulation leaves nothing to be desired in the essentials of good, sound theater."

Stage, 2.36: "A fair translation of the sensational best seller....Irene Dunne...carries on in her quietly charming way, and almost pulls the film out of limbo."

See also R-3, A-69, B-27, B-116, B-175, B-179, B-201, B-278, B-351, B-393, B-395, B-434, B-440, B-485, B-489

NOTES: Irene Dunne suggested Robert Taylor for the lead in Magnificent Obsession. Taylor had been regarded as a handsome and promising actor, but had had little chance to prove himself at MGM, where he was under contract. Just as Richard Dix had given the unproven Irene a chance in Cimarron, she persuaded Magnificent Obsession director John Stahl to consider Taylor. And, like Irene, the break was just what Taylor's career needed, propelling him to leading roles in important pictures. He remained at MGM for over twenty years.

In his summary of Magnificent Obsession in Magill's Survey of Cinema, DeWitt Bodeen pointed out the popularity of books and films with spiritual tendencies during national periods of stress. The original Lloyd C. Douglas novel was on the fiction bestseller lists for several years during the Depression. Bodeen said its delay in coming to the screen was due to its preachy tone. However, by 1935, audiences were ready for another dose of spiritual uplifting (B-278). Magnificent Obsession opened at Radio City Music Hall in December, 1935. Irene and Taylor reprised their roles on The Lux Radio Theatre (R-7). Magnificent Obsession was remade by Universal in 1954 with Jane Wyman and Rock Hudson, causing the 1935 version to be withheld from television for many years. Ironically, both Irene and Wyman were thirteen years older than their respective leading men.

F-20   Show Boat   (Universal, 1936)   110 minutes

Producer: Carl Laemmle, Jr. Director: James Whale. Assistant director: Joseph A. McDonough. Choreography: LeRoy Prinz. Screenplay: Oscar Hammerstein II. Based on the novel by Edna Ferber and the musical by Oscar Hammerstein II and Jerome Kern. Songs: Jerome Kern and Oscar Hammerstein II. Musical director: Victor Baravelle. Editors: Ted Kent and Bernard Burton. Photography: John Mescall. Art director: Charles D. Hall. Costumes: Doris Zinkeison and Vera West. Sound: Gilbert Kurland. Special effects: John P. Fulton. Technical director: Leighton Brill.

CAST: Irene Dunne (Magnolia Hawks), Allan Jones (Gaylord Ravenal), Charles Winninger (Captain Andy Hawks), Helen Westley (Parthy Hawks), Paul Robeson (Joe), Helen Morgan (Julie), Donald Cook (Steve), Sammy White (Frank), Queenie Smith (Ellie), J. Farrell MacDonald (Windy), Arthur Hohl (Pete), Charles Middleton (Vallon), Hattie McDaniel (Queenie), Francis X. Mahoney (Rubberface), Sunnie O'Dea (Kim, adult), Marilyn Knowlden (Kim, child), Patricia Barry (Kim, toddler), Dorothy Granger, Barbara Pepper, Renee Whitney (Chorus girls), Harry Barris (Jake), Charles Wilson (Jim Green), Clarence Muse (Janitor), Stanley Fields (Jeb), "Tiny" Stanley J. Sandford (Backwoodsman), May Beatty (Landlady), Bob Watson (Lost child), Jane Keckley (Mrs. Ewing), E.E. Clive (Englishman), Helen Jerome Eddy (Reporter), Donald Briggs (Press agent), LeRoy Prinz (Dance director), Eddie Anderson (Young black man), Patti Patterson (Banjo player), Helen Hayward (Mrs. Brecenbridge), Flora Finch (Woman), Theodore Lorch (Simon Legree), Arthur Housman (Drunk), Elspeth Dudgeon (Mother superior), Monte Montague (Old man), Lois Verner (Small girl), Grace Cunard (Mother), Maralyn Harris (Little girl), Jimmy Jackson (Young man), Eddy Chandler, Lee Phelps, Frank Mayo, Ed Peil, Sr., Edmund Cobb, Al Ferguson (Gamblers), Maude Allen (Fat woman), Artye Folz, Barbara Bletcher (Fat girls), Forrest Stanley (Theatre manager), Jack Latham (Juvenile), George H. Reed (Old black man), Georgia O'Dell (School teacher), Selmer Jackson (Hotel clerk), George Hackathorne (YMCA worker), Ernest Hilliard, Jack Mulhall, Brooks Benedict (Race fans).

SYNOPSIS: The Cotton Blossom is a showboat operated by Captain Andy Hawks and his wife Parthy. Their teenage daughter Magnolia dreams of becoming an actress, but Parthy prohibits her. When the showboat docks, Magnolia meets and falls in love with a gambler, Gaylord Ravenal. To keep out of jail, Gaylord hitches a ride on the showboat. After leading lady Julie LaVerne rebuffs an ex-boyfriend, he tells the sheriff that mulatto Julie is married to a white man. Julie and her husband flee, leaving Magnolia and Gaylord to take over the leads. Although Captain Andy hears rumors about Gaylord, Andy is happy the new leads are a success. Magnolia marries Gaylord, despite Parthy's warning that Gaylord killed a man. Marriage does not reform Gaylord; he is gambling when his daughter Kim is born. On a winning streak, Gaylord moves the family to Chicago. When his luck runs bad, he leaves Magnolia and Kim, deciding they would be better off without him. Magnolia gets a job in a nightclub when Julie deliberately gets drunk and breaks her contract to give her old friend a break. Magnolia becomes a success, thanks to her father's coaching. Years pass and Kim follows her mother into show business. Magnolia meets Gaylord at their daughter's Broadway debut. He is now a stage doorman. They reconcile to rejoice in Kim's success.

REVIEWS:
New York Times, 5.15.36: "Miss Dunne is splendid in the Norma Terris role of Magnolia Ravenal, nee Hawks, daughter of Captain Andy of the showboat Cotton Blossom."

Variety, 5.20.36: "Irene Dunne and Allan Jones are superb in the roles originally created by Norma Terriss [sic] and Howard Marsh [on Broadway]....Irene Dunne maintains the illusion of her Magnolia throughout - from her own secluded girlhood; into sudden stardom on the Cotton Blossom; and later, as a more mature artist, carrying the torch for the disappeared Ravenal and rearing her own child in professional prominence....Of the songs, besides the familiars, Irene Dunne registers with a native Negro strut, under cork; a new ditty, 'Gallavantin' Around,' and a reprise of 'After the Ball' which would have pleased the late Charles K. Harris."

Liberty, 6.13.36: "The most gratifying surprise of the picture, though, is its star, Irene Dunne. Catching every shade in a role that spans a lifetime, she imbues the part with her usual warm intelligence. But one is hardly prepared for her gay comedy flare - a flare she has kept, up to now, hidden from the screen."

Stage, 6.36: "...musical sustains the flavor of both the stage production and the original screen production. These...are mighty heights to sustain....Irene Dunne makes a charming and humorous Magnolia..."

Real Screen Fun, 9.36: "Irene Dunne is superb as the leading lady of the troupe and sings like an angel. Her comedy antics are swell, especially the goofy dance."

See also T-17, T-30, D-24, D-25, S-2, B-18, B-26, B-84, B-87, B-89, B-116, B-126, B-131, B-148, B-165, B-172, B-178, B-179, B-193, B-248, B-249, B-252, B-253, B-276, B-277, B-290, B-294, B-393, B-454, B-465, B-468

NOTES: Although Edna Ferber's novel was also filmed in 1929 and 1951, most film historians consider the 1936 version the best. One explanation is that the actors were familiar with the material, as most had played their film roles on stage: Irene Dunne (1929-30 tour), Allan Jones (St. Louis Municipal Opera), Hattie McDaniel (west coast production), and Helen Morgan and Charles Winninger (original Broadway cast). Another reason the 1936 version is preferred is that it sticks closest to the original script of the Broadway musical. A complete discussion of the 1936 version can be found on Criterion's CAV set of three laser discs of the film, or in the book Show Boat: The Story of a Classic American Musical by Miles Kreuger (B-252). Founder and head of the Institute of the American Musical, Kreuger is a Show Boat authority whose vast collection of stills, plus surviving footage of the 1929 film, can be seen on the laser discs.

Show Boat premiered at Radio City Music Hall on May 14, 1936. Scenes involving the docked Cotton Blossom were filmed on a five-acre tract along the Los Angeles River. Although there was some reluctance among the film community over the hiring of James Whale, a British director primarily known for horror films, critics praised Whale's cinematic expertise in handling Show Boat. But despite its popularity, Irene Dunne told film historian John Kobal that she thought Whale was not the right director for the movie, as he knew little about American showboat life. She also criticized the "stupid" ending of the film (B-250).

Irene sang "Can't Help Lovin' Dat Man," "Make Believe," "I Have the Room Above," "Gallavantin' Around," "After the Ball," and "You Are Love." Irene and Allan Jones filmed a scene in a backfiring automobile, in which they sang "Why Do I Love You?" however the scene was cut from the film. The song can be found on Cut! Outtakes from Movies (D-13). Irene, Jones, and Winninger recreated their roles on The Lux Radio Theatre on June 24, 1940 (R-16).

The 1929 Universal film starred Laura LaPlante and Joseph Schildkraut. It was silent, with some talking sequences, and a special prologue performed by members of the Broadway cast. In 1938, MGM bought the rights from Universal and planned to remake the film with Jeanette MacDonald and Nelson Eddy. This version was never produced. A segment of the Jerome Kern biographical film, Till the Clouds Roll By (MGM, 1946), was devoted to Show Boat, serving as a tryout for the remake that followed in 1951. Kathryn Grayson sang Magnolia in Till the Clouds Roll By; Tony Martin was Ravenal. The 1951 version was filmed in color by MGM, with Kathryn Grayson and Howard Keel as Magnolia and Ravenal. For many years, the 1936 version was withheld from circulation because of the remake.

F-21   Theodora Goes Wild   (Columbia, 1936)   94 minutes

    Associate producer: Everett Riskin. Director: Richard Boleslawski. Assistant director: William E. Muel. Screenplay: Sidney Buchman. Based on the story by Mary McCarthy. Musical director: Morris Stoloff. Editor: Otto Meyer. Photography: Joseph Walker. Art director: Stephen Goosson. Costumes: Bernard Newman. Sound: George Cooper.

    CAST: Irene Dunne (Theodora Lynn), Melvyn Douglas (Michael Grant), Thomas Mitchell (Jed Waterbury), Thurston Hall (Arthur Stevenson), Rosalind Keith (Adelaide Perry), Spring Byington (Rebecca Perry), Elizabeth Risdon (Aunt Mary), Margaret McWade (Aunt Elsie), Nana Bryant (Ethel Stevenson), Henry Kolker (Jonathan Grant), Leona Maricle (Agnes Grant), Robert Greig (Uncle John), Frederick Burton (Governor Wyatt), Mary Forbes (Mrs. Wyatt), Grace Hayle (Mrs. Cobb), Sarah Edwards (Mrs. Moffat), Mary MacLaren (Mrs.

Wilson), Wilfred Hari (Toki), Laura Treadwell (Mrs. Grant), Corbet Morris (Artist), Ben F. Hendricks (Taxi driver), Frank Sully (Clarence), James T. Mack (Minister), William Benedict (Henry), Carolyn Lee Bourland (Baby), Paul Barrett (Adelaide's husband), Leora Thatcher (Miss Baldwin), Billy Wayne, Harold Goodwin, Jack Hatfield (Photographers), Harry Harvey, Don Brodie, Eddie Fetherstone, Ed Hart, Lee Phelps, Sherry Hall, Ralph Malone, Beatrice Curtis (Reporters), Maurice Brierre (Waiter), Sven Borg (Bartender), Dennis O'Keefe (Man), Rex Moore (Newsboy), Georgia Cooper, Jane Keckley, Jessie Perry, Noel Bates, Betty Farrington, Stella Adams, Isabelle LaMal, Georgia O'Dell, Dorothy Vernon (Women).

SYNOPSIS: When Jed Waterbury publishes the first installment of a racy novel in his New England newspaper, the townspeople are up in arms. Theodora Lynn, a proper Sunday school teacher and church organist, whose forefathers founded the town, is urged by her two maiden aunts to protest the book's publication. The aunts do not know that the book was written by Theodora under the nom de plume Caroline Adams. Theodora goes to New York to instruct her publisher to keep her identity a secret. She meets artist Michael Grant, who illustrated the cover of her book. She sets out to prove she is as wild as Caroline Adams, but sophisticated Michael quickly sees through her. He is attracted to Theodora's prim ways so he follows her back to Lynnfield, where he convinces the aunts to hire him as a gardener. His overly familiar attitude embarrasses Theodora. He vows to help her flee Lynnfield to live her own life. When the townspeople chastise Theodora's relationship with Michael, an angry Theodora tells them off and admits she loves Michael. Less than thrilled with her announcement, he returns to New York. Theodora follows and learns he is also a virtual prisoner of circumstance, forced to stay in an unhappy marriage because of his father's political ambitions. Theodora vows to free him as he freed her. She moves into Michael's apartment, launches a publicity campaign, and gets caught in a compromising position with her publisher. Michael promises to marry her in two years, when his father's term is over and Michael can divorce his wife. He begs Theodora to leave town before the governor's ball to avoid a scandal. Instead, Theodora shows up at the ball, dancing with the governor and causing chaos. Michael's wife agrees to the divorce after photographers catch Theodora and Michael in an embrace. Despite the scandal, Theodora's aunts stick by her. When she returns to Lynnfield with a baby, everyone assumes it is hers. The commotion allows Adelaide Perry and her husband to sneak home, having kept their marriage and child a secret from Adelaide's mother Rebecca, the town gossip. Michael goes to Lynnfield, but is scared off by the baby. After Theodora hands it over to Rebecca, she and Michael reunite.

REVIEWS:

New York Times, 11.13.36: "Although she goes wild, she also goes silly; and farce does not set too well upon the lovely shoulders of Irene Dunne. The one thing we cannot abide is studied cuteness and that goes for Shirley Temple, Robert Taylor and Miss Dunne - much as we adore them all....[Melvyn] Douglas and Miss Dunne are a splendid comedy team when there's comedy to be played, but neither fits well in the farce sequences."

Variety, 11.18.36: "...it should strengthen the following of Irene Dunne who takes the hurdle into comedy that so many dramatic actresses have made in the last year or two with versatile grace."

Time, 11.23.36: "For cinema patrons who like rollicking farce, Theodora Goes Wild amounts to a feast. It begins rollicking in Reel One, rollicks faster and more furiously from there on. Most rollicking shot: the wife of Theodora's publisher peeking out of her door to see her drunken husband and Theodora rollicking harmlessly on the floor."

Stage, 12.36: "Somewhere in this idea is an excellant farce. The situations are not believable enough. Miss Dunne is called upon to be _too_ kittenish _too_ long. What we mean is, Theodora goes too wild."

The New Statesman and Nation, 2.13.37: "Miss Dunne, who so outsparks this spark, has become quite a comedienne, and gives an imitation of ZaSu Pitts, too. This film has all the makings of a pleasant evening, all you need to bring to it is the memory of a good dinner and the right frame of mind."

Film Fun, 2.37: "And they don't come any wilder than Irene Dunne or better than this rollicking comedy."

See also R-5, R-30, A-11, B-3, B-22, B-47, B-74, B-75, B-84, B-87, B-88, B-140, B-153, B-165, B-166, B-168, B-175, B-177, B-205, B-255, B-258, B-278, B-285, B-290, B-303, B-368, B-391, B-398, B-438

NOTES: Theodora Goes Wild marked a turning point in Irene Dunne's career, proving that her talents went far beyond dramas and musicals. When Irene signed a contract with Columbia in June, 1935, she decided that a comedy would be a delightful change of pace. However, as the shooting date for Theodora Goes Wild approached, she began to worry about taking such an abrupt turn in her career. She and her husband went on a six-week European vacation to avoid making the film, although she claimed the purpose of the trip was to meet with the daughter of Madame Curie before filming a biographical movie on the scientist for Universal. Irene returned to Hollywood, hoping that Theodora had been assigned to another actress. Instead, she was put on suspension until she agreed to do the film. Despite her

84   Irene Dunne

inital skepticism, Irene later cryptically told reporters that she was a lot like the screwball Theodora. In the film, she sang a hymn, "Be Still My Heart," and "Three Blind Mice."

Richard Boleslawski was a former director of the Moscow Art Theatre. Initially, Irene had little faith in his ability to direct an American comedy. Columbia studio head Harry Cohn urged her to give Boleslawski a chance. If he did not work out after a week, Irene could replace him. She was impressed with Boleslawski's direction and he stayed to complete the picture.

The film premiered at Radio City Music Hall on November 12, 1936. Although popular with the public, many critics deemed it too lightweight. Irene received her second Academy Award nomination, but lost to Luise Rainer for The Great Ziegfeld. Irene recreated her role on The Lux Radio Theatre (R-10).

F-22   **High, Wide and Handsome**   (Paramount, 1937)
       110 minutes

   Producer: Arthur Hornblow, Jr. Director: Rouben Mamoulian. Assistant director: Joe Youngerman. Choreography: LeRoy Prinz. Screenplay: Oscar Hammerstein II and George O'Neil. Songs: Jerome Kern and Oscar Hammerstein II. Musical director: Boris Morros. Orchestrator: Russell Bennett. Editor: Archie Marshek. Photography: Victor Milner and Theodor Sparkuhl. Art directors: Hans Dreier and John Goodman. Costumes: Travis Banton. Sets: A.E. Freudeman. Sound: Charles Hisserich and Don Johnson. Special effects: Gordon Jennings. Technical adviser: William Gilmore Beymer.

   CAST: Irene Dunne (Sally Watterson), Randolph Scott (Peter Cortlandt), Dorothy Lamour (Molly Fuller), Raymond Walburn (Doc Watterson), Alan Hale (Walter Brennan), Elizabeth Patterson (Grandma Cortlandt), Charles Bickford (Red Scanlon), William Frawley (Mac), Akim Tamiroff (Joe Varese), Ben Blue (Zeke), Irving Pichel (Stark), Lucien Littlefield (Mr. Lippincott), Helen Lowell (Mrs. Lippincott), Roger Imhof (Pop Bowers), Purnell Pratt (Colonel Blake), Edward Gargan (Foreman), Tommy Bupp (Boy), Russell Hopton (John Thompson), Billy Bletcher (Shorty), Stanley Andrews (Lem Moulton), Frank Sully (Gabby Jonson), Jack Clifford (Walsh Miller), James Burke (Stackpole), Claire MacDowell (Seamstress), Ivan Miller (Marble), Raymond Brown (P.T. Barnum), Constance Bergen (Singer), Paul Kruger (Man), Claire McDowell (Seamstress), Fred Warren (Piano player), Rolfe Sedan (Photographer), Marjorie Cameron (Blonde singer), John T. Murray (Mr. Green), Sherry Hall (Piano player), Edward Keane (Jones), Pat West (Razorback), John

Maurice Sullivan (Old gentleman), Ernest Wood (Hotel clerk), Lew Kelly (Carpenter), Dell Henderson (Bank president), John Marshall (Teller), Philip Morris (Teamster), Harry Semels (Bartender).

SYNOPSIS: Sally Watterson and her father are stranded in a western Pennsylvania town when their medicine show wagon catches fire. Farmer Peter Cortlandt saves Sally and invites the Wattersons to stay with him and his grandmother. In his spare time, Peter drills for oil, forseeing its future in power. Sally falls in love with Peter and the picturesque community. During their wedding reception, Peter's rig hits oil. Preoccupied with the petroleum boom, Peter neglects his marriage. The farmers band together to commercialize the untapped local oil supply. They have trouble shipping their oil to the refineries because the railroad owners, headed by corrupt Walter Brennan, raise their freight rates. Peter organizes a boycott and searches for another way to transport the oil. Sally befriends Molly Fuller, a shanty boat singer, and tries to get her a job with a carnival. Peter and his neighbors build a pipeline to the refinery. In order to get a mandatory piece of land for the pipe, Peter sells the land where he and Sally planned to build their home. When Peter and Sally have a fight, she joins the carnival where her father is working. Brennan tries to sabotage the pipeline. When that does not work, he buys the bank that holds the farmers' mortgages. Molly warns Sally that Brennan is giving Peter a two-day deadline to complete the pipeline, a nearly impossible task. Despite an offer to sing in New York, Sally returns to Peter and inspires him to keep working. She enlists the help of her carnival friends and they finish the pipeline on time.

REVIEWS:
New York Times, 7.22.37: "Miss Dunne's voice is as delightful as she is..."

Variety, 7.28.37: "Miss Dunne is perhaps a shade too mature for the ingenue role she opens with, as the daughter of the medicine-show owner whose wagon burns down, stranding the troupe in a western Pensy burg."

Newsweek, 7.31.37: "Irene Dunne and Randolph Scott are at their best in roles to which they are admirably suited..."

See also R-8, D-21, D-26, S-3, B-4, B-9, B-101, B-126, B-148, B-172, B-178, B-248, B-249, B-276, B-408, B-465

NOTES: Determined to create "a new Show Boat" for Irene Dunne, Jerome Kern and Oscar Hammerstein II wrote an original screen musical about the founding of the Tidewater Oil Company. Irene sang "High, Wide and Handsome," "To Fool a Simple Maiden," "The Folks Who Live on the Hill," "Allegheny Al," and "Can I Forget You?." Gary Cooper was the original choice for the role of Peter Cortlandt. High, Wide and Handsome cost $1.9 million to produce. It opened at New York's Astor Theatre on July 21, 1937. The film originally ran 110 minutes, but Paramount edited the length for its general release in 1937.

Irene told John Kobal that she disliked the film because of her unhappy memories of making it. In addition to being aggravated by long rides back and forth to Chino, California, where some of the picture was shot, Irene's mother died during the filming. The Hollywood premiere took place at the Carthay Circle Theatre. Irene was seated directly in front of Helen Hayes. Irene recalled, "I didn't like myself in that film, and all the time I was conscious of Helen Hayes breathing down my neck" (B-250).

F-23 <u>The Awful Truth</u>   (Columbia, 1937)   90 minutes

    Producer: Leo McCarey. Associate producer: Everett Riskin. Director: Leo McCarey. Assistant director: William Mull. Screenplay: Vina Delmar. Based on the play by Arthur Richman. Songs: Ben Oakland and Milton Drake. Musical director: Morris Stoloff. Editor: Al Clark. Photography: Joseph Walker. Art directors: Stephen Goosson and Lionel Banks. Costumes: Kalloch. Sets: Babs Johnstone.

    CAST: Irene Dunne (Lucy Warriner), Cary Grant (Jerry Warriner), Ralph Bellamy (Daniel Leeson), Alexander D'Arcy (Armand Duvalle), Cecil Cunningham (Aunt Patsy), Molly Lamont (Barbara Vance), Esther Dale (Mrs. Leeson), Joyce Compton (Dixie Belle Lee [Toots Binswanger]), Robert Allen (Frank Randall), Robert Warwick (Mr. Vance), Scott Colton (Mr. Barnsley), Mary Forbes (Mrs. Vance), Claud Allister (Lord Fabian), Zita Moulton (Lady Fabian), Wyn Cahoon (Mrs. Barnsley), Paul Stanton (Judge), Mitchell Harris (Jerry's attorney), Alan Bridge, Edgar Dearing (Motor cops), Leonard Carey (Butler), Miki Morita (Japanese servant), Frank Wilson (Emcee), Vernon Dent (Police sergeant), George C. Pearce (Caretaker), Bobby Watson (Hotel clerk), Byron Foulger (Secretary), Kathryn Curry (Celeste), Edward Peil, Sr. (Bailiff), Bess Flowers (Viola Heath), John Tyrrell (Hank), Edward Mortimer (Lucy's attorney), Asta (Mr. Smith).

SYNOPSIS: Jerry Warriner tells his wife Lucy that he has been in Florida, although he never left New York. Despite his own deceit, he is upset when he returns to an empty apartment. Jerry is suspicious when Lucy comes home with her voice teacher, Armand Duvalle. Both Warriners jump to conclusions over the other's infidelity and get a divorce. They battle in court over the custody of their dog, Mr. Smith, with the judge awarding custody to Lucy. Although Lucy and Jerry go their separate ways, they are still attracted to each other. Lucy's Aunt Patsy urges Lucy to go out while awaiting her final decree. Aunt Patsy introduces her to wealthy Oklahoma rancher Daniel Leeson. Despite his

Irene's slapstick antics in *The Awful Truth* (Columbia, 1937) earned her a third Academy Award nomination. Here, Cary Grant casts doubts about her relationship with Ralph Bellamy. (Ralph Bellamy collection)

lack of sophistication, Lucy accepts his proposal. Dan's mother worries when she hears rumors about Lucy and Armand. Jerry sarcastically defends Lucy, trying to break up the romance. Lucy admits to Patsy that she loves Jerry and therefore must break up with Dan. Before she has the chance, Dan and his mother catch Lucy with Armand and Jerry in her bedroom, ending the engagement. Later, Lucy reads that Jerry is dating socialite Barbara Vance. Lucy decides to get even with her soon-to-be ex-husband. She masquerades as Jerry's crude sister, performing a mock striptease and embarrassing him in front of his future in-laws. Thinking Lucy is drunk, Jerry offers to drive her to Patsy's cabin. Lucy arranges for the car to roll into a ditch so Jerry cannot go back to town. Finding themselves alone, save the caretaker, Jerry and Lucy sleep in adjoining rooms with a door that keeps swinging open. Jerry admits he was wrong and the Warriners reconcile before their divorce decree is final.

REVIEWS:
Variety, 10.20.37: "Interesting, too, is that Irene Dunne, in the comedy lead, was first brought out as a celluloid comedienne by Columbia in 'Theodora Goes Wild.' She tops that performance by almost an Alp in 'Awful Truth'....Miss Dunne goes vocal several times, once impersonating a phony Deep Dixie warbler (Joyce Compton), who works out a burlesque song in a nightclub sequence. Other time is when Miss Dunne duets with [Ralph] Bellamy in a comedy chanting of 'Home on the Range.'"

Arizona Republic [Phoenix], 10.24.37: "Irene Dunne...is the personification of perhaps one of the most complete reversals registered in the cinema world....she introduced in Theodora Goes Wild, a personality vivacious, winsome, delightfully feminine, and at the same time so completely clothed in comedy that she became an overnight hit....In The Awful Truth in which she is scoring a success at the Orpheum, she goes even more carefree, in a rollicking portrayal of young married life."

Time, 11.1.37: "Irene Dunne...put her foot down last year, demanded comedy. Her astonishing hoe-down interlude in Show Boat indicated her aptitude for lighter things. Theodora Goes Wild gave her the first full-length try. The Awful Truth establishes her with her peers, Claudette Colbert and Jean Arthur."

New York Times, 11.5.37: "Miss Dunne and [Cary] Grant as the couple who get undivorced, and Ralph Bellamy as the rich respectable suitor from Oklahoma have fun with their roles, and the pleasure seems to be shared, on the whole, by the...audience."

Stage, 11.37: "Irene Dunne and Cary Grant play opposite, around and against each other endowing a very giddy piece with smooth and varied comic acting."

The New Statesman and Nation, 1.29.38: "The Awful Truth is a new Irene Dunne, but a much feebler vehicle for that delightful comedienne than Theodora Goes Wild....Miss Dunne has some excruciatingly funny moments, notably when pretending to be a very loud and fast chorus-girl at a stiff Four Hundred dinner party; but where Theodora was sophisticated and subtle, The Awful Truth is a naive romp."

See also R-9, R-32, A-12, A-65, B-24, B-31, B-35, B-43, B-84, B-114, B-120, B-140, B-145, B-151, B-160, B-165, B-166, B-175, B-177, B-215, B-235, B-245, B-258, B-261, B-266, B-277, B-290, B-293, B-301, B-303, B-323, B-347, B-382, B-391, B-395, B-417, B-438, B-450, B-450, B-464

NOTES: The Awful Truth combined the expert timing of Irene Dunne and Cary Grant with the experienced comic direction of Leo McCarey. Having worked with "Our Gang," Laurel and Hardy, W.C. Fields, Mae West, and the Marx Brothers, McCarey knew how to handle the slapstick aspects of the script, as well as the verbal quips. Much of the action was improvised on the set. The film had a troubled beginning. It was rushed into production to fulfill Irene's contract. Tay Garnett, who directed Joy of Living, turned down The Awful Truth. The part played by Ralph Bellamy was written for Roland Young. Despite the film's classic status today, Cary Grant was so afraid of making it that he offered to buy his way out of the movie. He also suggested trading roles with Bellamy. The studio refused to listen to him.

The Awful Truth is recognized as one of the best efforts of romantic screwball comedy. In his book on the genre, Wes D. Gehring noted that Ralph Bellamy's attempt to read romantic poetry to Irene Dunne parodied Gary Cooper's poetry recitations to Jean Arthur in Mr. Deeds Goes to Town (B-140). Irene sang a classical selection, "My Dreams Have Gone with the Wind," and "Home on the Range."

Based on the 1922 play of the same name, The Awful Truth had previously been filmed in 1925 with Agnes Ayres and in 1929 with Ina Claire, who had originated the role of Lucy Warriner on stage. It was remade by Warner Bros. in 1953 as Let's Do It Again with Jane Wyman and Ray Milland. Leo McCarey won an Academy Award for Best Director for the 1937 film. Irene Dunne was nominated for Best Actress, but lost to Luise Rainer in The Good Earth. Irene and Grant reprised their roles on The Lux Radio Theatre (R-83).

F-24   Joy of Living   (RKO, 1938)   90 minutes

Producer: Felix Young. Director: Tay Garnett. Assistant director: Kenneth Holmes. Screenplay: Gene Towne, Graham Baker, Allan Scott, Dorothy Fields, and Herbert Fields. Songs: Jerome Kern and Dorothy Fields. Musical director: Frank Tours. Orchestral arrangements: Russell Bennett. Editor: Jack Hively. Photography: Joseph Walker. Art directors: Van Nest Polglase and Carroll Clark. Costumes: Edward Stevenson and Kalloch. Sets: Darrell Silvera. Sound: John E. Tribby. Special effects: Vernon L. Walker.

CAST: Irene Dunne (Margaret "Maggie" Garret), Douglas Fairbanks, Jr. (Dan Brewster), Alice Brady (Minerva Garret), Guy Kibbee (Dennis Garret), Jean Dixon (Harrison), Eric Blore (Potter), Lucille Ball (Salina Pine), Warren Hymer (Mike), Billy Gilbert (Cafe owner), Frank Milan (Bert Pine), Dorothy Steiner (Dotsy Pine), Estelle Steiner (Betsy Pine), Phyllis Kennedy (Marie), Franklin Pangborn (Radio broadcast orchestra leader), James Burke (Mac), John Qualen (Oswego), Spencer Charters (Magistrate), George Chandler (Taxi driver), Grady Sutton (Florist), Charles Lane (Dress extra), Pat Flaherty (Autograph hound), Harry Woods (Cop/autograph hound), Bert Roach (German waiter), Charles Williams (Sideshow barker), Fuzzy Knight (Sideshow piano player), Frank Moran (Cop with gravel voice), Dennis O'Keefe (Man in building lobby), Frank M. Thomas.

SYNOPSIS: Maggie Garret is a successful Broadway and radio star with a parasitic family. Despite their outrageous spending, which is causing Maggie income tax problems, she swears the family will stick by her in time of trouble. Free spirited Boston ship owner Dan Brewster rescues Maggie from a hoard of autograph hunters on her opening night. Maggie misinterprets his actions and has him arrested as a masher. To keep him from going to jail, Maggie agrees to be his probation officer. Dan tells her he believes in doing what makes him happy, ignoring responsibilities. He urges her to do something for herself before her family bankrupts her. Although Maggie claims she dislikes him, she is upset when he plans to sail. She agrees to a date, which includes dancing, drinking, and roller skating, causing her to lose her inhibitions. Drunk, they return to her house. The next morning, Maggie's family concludes that Dan and Maggie have had an affair. Instead of worrying about her, they worry about how the publicity will affect her show. When Dan tells them off, Maggie orders him out. Regretting her decision, she goes to the dock and proposes to him. Although Dan promises to stay in New York, he secretly plans for them to sail to China. After Dan and Maggie elope, they argue about her family and their future. He promises to get an annulment. Maggie soon sees her family's selfishness. She hurries to Dan and a life of doing what she wants.

REVIEWS:
Variety, 3.23.38: "Important to the list [of distinguished writing and composing talent] is Jerome Kern, who composed four songs that have lyrics by Dorothy Fields and excellent presentation by Miss Dunne, who sings

engagingly."

<u>Newsweek</u>, 4.4.38: "...<u>Joy of Living</u> starts off briskly under Tay Garnett's direction but slows down at the halfway mark to puff home in a series of gag situations. But even these interpolated scenes are sustained by [Douglas] Fairbanks' diligence and Irene Dunne's comic ability to drink beer like a high-school freshman, yet hiccup like a lady and do justice to a pleasant Dorothy Fields-Jerome Kern score."

<u>New York Times</u>, 5.6.38: "It is always depressing to watch a couple of characters change into a pair of caricatures. When Miss Dunne, who has a pleasing voice, begins to go 'cluck-cluck-cluck' and when [Douglas] Fairbanks, who was such a debonair Rupert of Hentzau, flaps his arms while the sound track picks up Mr. Disney's D. Duck I surrendered, gritted my teeth and knew that nothing worse could befall....The saving grace is the Jerome Kern score - with 'Just Let Me Look at You,' 'You Couldn't Be Cuter,' 'What's Good About Goodnight' and 'A Heavenly Party' - which Miss Dunne sings most effectively considering the slapstick static she has to contend with."

<u>Stage</u>, 5.38: "Another of those loony shows, with Irene Dunne playing a hard-working, family-ridden prima donna of the stage....Miss Dunne...is delightfully giddy as the heroine."

See also D-22, S-4, B-18, B-24, B-59, B-84, B-105, B-138, B-172, B-176, B-178, B-238, B-249, B-290, B-301, B-327, B-409, B-460, B-462

NOTES: Ann Sothern and John Boles originally were announced as the stars of <u>Joy of Living</u>, but they were replaced by Irene Dunne and Douglas Fairbanks, Jr. The film was originally titled <u>Joy of Loving</u>, until the censors pointed out that it was too risque. Director Tay Garnett was quoted as saying, "They didn't think loving should be joyous, and were afraid that people would think it was a sex picture" (B-176). According to <u>The RKO Story</u>, the film cost over a million dollars to produce (B-238).

One of the most unique aspects of the film was its approach to presenting the songs. Irene rehearsed "Just Let Me Look at You" in a moving limosine. She sang "You Couldn't Be Cuter" as a lullaby for her twin nieces, picking out the tune on a toy piano. "What's Good about Good Night?" was performed on a radio broadcast. A carnival recording booth was the scene for "A Heavenly Party." Jerome Kern was supposed to write a more complete score, but had a heart attack before the production began. <u>Joy of Living</u> marked Irene's last Kern musical.

F-25   <u>Love Affair</u>   (RKO, 1939)   87 minutes

Producer: Leo McCarey. Director: Leo McCarey. Assistant director: James Anderson. Screenplay: Delmer Daves, Donald Ogden Stewart, Mildred Cram, and Leo McCarey. Musical score: Roy-Webb. Songs: B.G. DeSylva, Harold Arlen, and Ted Koehler. Editors: Edward Dmytryk and George Hively. Photography: Rudolph Mate. Art directors: Van Nest Polglase and Al Herman. Costumes: Howard Greer and Edward Stevenson. Sets: Darrell Silvera. Sound: John L. Cass. Montages: Douglas Travers. Special effects: Vernon L. Walker.

CAST: Irene Dunne (Terry McKay), Charles Boyer (Michel Marnet), Maria Ouspenskaya (Grandmother Janou), Lee Bowman (Ken Bradley), Astrid Allwyn (Lois Clarke), Maurice Moscovich (Maurice Cobert), Scotty Beckett (Boy on ship), Bess Flowers, Harold Miller (Couple on deck), Joan Leslie (Autograph seeker), Dell Henderson (Cafe manager), Carol Hughes (Nightclub patron), Ferike Boros (Boarding house keeper), Frank McGlynn, Sr. (Orphanage superintendent ["Picklepuss"]), Oscar O'Shea (Priest), Tom Dugan (Drunk with Christmas tree), Lloyd Ingraham, Leyland Hodgson (Doctors), Phyllis Kennedy (Maid), Gerald Mohr (Extra).

SYNOPSIS: Playboy Michel Marnet is sailing to New York to marry heiress Lois Clarke. On ship he meets Terry McKay, a former singer who is being kept by her wealthy fiance, Ken Bradley. Michel flirts with Terry and proposes a shipboard romance. Despite their mutual attraction, Terry decides that they should not see each other because of their respective fiances. When the boat docks at Madeira, Michel introduces Terry to his grandmother. Terry learns that Michel is a talented artist who has stopped painting. Grandmother encourages Terry to reform Michel. Back on the boat, their feelings come out. They agree to meet in six months atop the Empire State Building if Michel can find a job and give up his playboy lifestyle. Terry moves to Philadelphia and returns to nightclub singing. Michel gets a job painting signs when his art does not sell. En route to their rendevous, Terry is hit by a car. Afraid of burdening Michel with a cripple, she does not get in touch with him. When Terry does not appear at the Empire State Building, Michel thinks she has married Ken. Michel returns to Madeira, but finds his grandmother has died. He continues to paint and tries to return to his playboy ways. Still in a wheelchair, Terry gets a job teaching music in an orphanage. After Michel and Lois run into Terry and Ken, Michel feels melancholy. He visits Terry to ask why she did not keep their date. When Terry realizes Michel has given up his playboy ways to concentrate on his painting, she vows to learn to walk again.

REVIEWS:
Stage, 3.15.39: "Irene Dunne and Charles Boyer are the

principals involved in the plot's rich and variegated emotions, and Director Leo McCarey is the man responsible for shifting, with no detectable trickery, from the brittle comedy of the early sequences to the genuine emotionalism of the later. It is superior entertainment all the way through."

Variety, 3.15.39: "Miss Dunne is excellent in a role that requires both comedy and dramatic ability....Two songs have been inserted. Miss Dunne presents one, 'Sing My Heart,' by Harold Arlen and Ted Koehler, in a night club setting."

New York Times, 3.17.39: "As co-author, director and producer, [Leo McCarey] must be credited primarily for the film's success, but almost as large a measure of acknowledgement belongs to Irene Dunne and Charles Boyer for the facility with which they have matched the changes of their script - playing it lightly now, soberly next, but always credibly, always in character, always with a superb utilization of the material at hand."

See also R-14, R-69, A-15, A-64, A-65, S-5, B-12, B-30, B-81, B-87, B-104, B-151, B-166, B-175, B-213, B-226, B-233, B-238, B-278, B-290, B-293, B-295, B-297, B-309, B-314, B-324, B-328, B-349, B-382, B-407, B-408, B-430

NOTES: Both Irene Dunne and Charles Boyer called Love Affair their favorite film. Much of the script was improvised, with producer/director Leo McCarey taking suggestions from the cast. Although dismissed by some as too sentimental or melodramatic, Love Affair was believable and entertaining, thanks to McCarey's eye for imagery and the performances by Irene and Boyer. In Magill's Survey of Cinema, Blake Lucas mentioned the way the film's songs expressed an aspect of the film's meaning. "Plaisir D'Amour," sung during the visit with Grandmother, hints that there could be tragedy in store for the couple. "Sing My Heart," was performed by Irene in a nightclub scene shortly before her character was paralyzed, dashing the happy ending she sang about. Her pupils sang "Wishing." Lucas wrote, "The song beautifully expresses what the audience wants to believe and what the film wills to be truth, that 'wishing will make it so'" (B-278).

The censors also influenced the ending of Love Affair. Since it was implied that Irene's character had been a kept woman before meeting Boyer, she had to pay for her sin, hence the accident, before finding happiness.

Irene received her fourth Academy Award nomination for Best Actress, but lost to Vivien Leigh for Gone with the Wind. Irene and Boyer reprised their roles on The Lux Radio Theatre (R-25). Love Affair was remade by 20th Century-Fox in 1957 as An Affair to Remember, with Deborah Kerr and Cary Grant. Leo McCarey directed the color remake, which was twenty-eight minutes longer than the original,

94   Irene Dunne

added songs by Harry Warren, and was filmed in CinemaScope. The 1957 version kept <u>Love Affair</u> out of circulation for many years. In 1975, the Los Angeles International Film Exposition (Filmex) paid for a new negative to be struck from the only extant print, which belonged to the Museum of Modern Art, so that <u>Love Affair</u> could be shown at Filmex's tribute to Irene Dunne. Since then, the film has been more widely circulated, even appearing on videocassette.

F-26   <u>Invitation to Happiness</u>   (Paramount, 1939)
       95 minutes

   Producer: Wesley Ruggles. Director: Wesley Ruggles. Screenplay: Claude Binyon and Mark Jerome. Song: Frank Loesser and Frederick Hollander. Editor: Alma Macrorie. Photography: Farciot Edouart and Leo Tover. Art directors: Hans Dreier and Ernst Fegte. Costumes: Edith Head. Sets: A.E. Freudeman. Sound: Earl Hauman and Richard Olson.

   CAST: Irene Dunne (Eleanor Wayne), Fred MacMurray (Albert "King" Cole), Charlie Ruggles (Hank "Pop" Hardy), Billy Cook (Albert Cole, Jr.), William Collier, Sr. (Mr. Wayne), Marion Martin (Lola), Oscar O'Shea (Divorce judge), Burr Caruth (Butler), Eddie Hogan (The champ), Gordon Jones (Dutch Arnold), Allen Wood, Don Laterre (Youths), Mack Gray (Usher), Bob Evans (Galliette), Jack Roper (Scat), Billy Newell (Waiter), Heinie Conklin (Cook), Franklin Parker, Wheaton Chambers, Joseph Franz, Jack Gargan, Jack Knoche, Robert Stevenson, Jerry Fletcher, Harry Hayden (Reporters), Lee Moore (Headwaiter), Doodles Weaver (Band leader), Myra Marsh (Maternity nurse), Virginia Brissac (Eleanor's nurse), William Orr (Bellboy), Bill Knudsen (Attendant), Emerson Treacy (Photographer), Hank Hankison (Fighter), Joe Cunningham (Announcer), Guy Usher (Spectator), Joe Caits (Man in office), Russ Clark, Charles Randolph (Referees).

SYNOPSIS: Hank "Pop" Hardy visits his former oil partner, Mr. Wayne, and asks him to invest in his latest venture, heavyweight fighter Albert "King" Cole. Eleanor Wayne tries to discourage her father from investing, despite King's prospects. King does not want Pop to give up a percentage. He insults Eleanor and storms off. Despite the initial fireworks, Eleanor sees a sensitive side to King and is happy when her father buys half his contract. King confesses that he lives to be champion and cannot imagine what he will do if he ever loses a fight. King and Eleanor elope, despite their class differences. She soon learns that her homelife is not what she imagined, with King always on the road and in training. He is not even present when his son Albert is born. After ten years, Eleanor sees how King's frequent absences hurt Albert. She resents King trying for the championship, despite having earned enough money to support the family. After seeing King with his former girlfriend, Eleanor files for divorce. King gets temporary custody, trying to prove to Albert how much he loves him. King refuses to go to training camp before the championship, enabling him to spend time with Albert, but jeopardizing his championship chances. The sight of his son gives King the strength to get up after repeatedly being knocked down during the match. King loses the fight, but regains the love and respect of Eleanor and Albert. No longer afraid of failure, King can get on with his life and marriage.

REVIEWS:
Variety, 5.10.39: "Miss Dunne switches to a straight dramatic role from her recent cycle of comedies and farces, and does a most capable job in the assignment."

Stage, 5.15.39: "There is the most terrifying and agonizing prize-fight [sic] you ever saw on the screen, and fine, glib dramatic performances by [Fred] MacMurray and Irene Dunne."

New York Times, 6.8.39: "We confess a delighted appreciation of the scenes in which Miss Dunne and William Collier Sr. (as her father) face the advent of the tiny stranger, and that in which she claims her triumph over King Cole's pre-marital blonde..."

Time, 6.19.39: "Invitation to Happiness...is not exactly up Cinemactress Dunne's gay alley, but it is a setup for headstrong Cinemactor MacMurray, a field day for Character Actors William Collier Sr. and Charles Ruggles..."

See also B-58, B-101, B-169

NOTES: Invitation to Happiness reunited Irene Dunne with Wesley Ruggles, the director of Cimarron. The producer/director was the brother of actor Charlie Ruggles, who played Pop Hardy in Invitation to Happiness. It was Irene's first of two screen appearances with Fred MacMurray.

F-27   When Tomorrow Comes   (Universal, 1939)   90 minutes

   Producer: John M. Stahl. Director: John M. Stahl. Assistant director: Joseph A. McDonough. Screenplay: Dwight Taylor. Based on the unpublished novel by James M. Cain. Musical director: Charles Previn. Editor: Milton Carruth. Photography: John J. Mescall. Art directors: Jack Otterson and Martin Orzina. Costumes: Vera West and Howard Greer. Sets: R.A. Gausman. Sound: Bernard B. Brown.

   CAST: Irene Dunne (Helen), Charles Boyer (Philip Andre Chagal), Nydia Westman (Lulu), Onslow Stevens (Holden), Fritz Feld (Nicholas, the butler), Barbara O'Neil (Madeleine Chagal), Nella Walker (Mrs. Dumont), Constance Moore (Bride), Jerry Marlowe (Groom), Doris

Weston, Frances Robinson, Bobbe Trefts, Helen Lynd, Myrtis Crinley, Kitty McHugh, Florence Lake, Dorothy Granger, Mary Treen, Inez Courtney, Helen MacKellar, Helen Brown, Ruth Warren, Dorothy Appleby, Virginia Sale, Mira McKinney, Claire Du Brey, Greta Granstedt, Diana Gibson, Jane Barnes, Sally Payne, Jennifer Gray, Claire Whitney, Mary Field (Waitresses), Harry C. Bradley (Minister), Milton Parsons (Organist), William Davidson (Army captain), Addison Richards (Refugee leader), Tom Dugan (Bum), Greta Meyer (Nurse), Howard Hickman (Wealthy man), Natalie Moorhead, Margaret McWade, Gladys Blake (Women), Frank Darien (Boathouse caretaker), George Humbert (Vendor), Wade Boteler (Policeman), Milburn Stone (Bus boy head), Emmett Vogan (Head waiter), Gaylor Steve Pendleton (Bus boy), Edward Keane Alden, Stephen Chase, Landers Stevens, John Dilson (Men), Vinton Haworth, Gordon Jones, Stanley Taylor (Radio technicians), Eddie Acuff (Bus driver), Edward Earle (Assistant manager), Philip Trent (Service man), James Flavin (Coast Guard man), Otto Hoffman (Farmer), Mickey Kuhn, Tommy Bupp, Ray Nichols, Payne Johnson, Sonny Bupp, Delmar Watson (Boys), Hally Chester (Newsboy), Lilian Elliott (Character woman), James Morton (Chef), Ed Peil, Sr. (Janitor), George Offerman, Jr. (Farmer's son), Dick Winslow (Accordian player).

SYNOPSIS: Helen is a poor waitress with Communist leanings; Philip Andre Chagal is a wealthy French pianist. After meeting Helen at her restaurant, Philip immediatly is attracted to her and follows her to a union rally. Helen speaks at the meeting, urging the waitresses to strike. Philip applauds her speech, but tells her he dislikes unions. Despite their differing backgrounds, they begin dating. While Helen and Philip are out on his boat, a storm comes up, forcing them to take refuge in his Long Island house. The storm reaches hurricane proportions, but Helen insists on going back to town after Philip kisses her. En route to the city, the weather worsens and they spend the night in a deserted church. Although Philip confesses that he loves her, Helen heads back to New York without him when she learns he is married. Philip follows, introducing her to Madeleine, his psychologically unstable wife. Philip begs Helen to continue their relationship, despite his marriage. While Helen is considering the offer, Madeleine confronts Helen about Philip. Although Helen loves him, she steps aside, allowing Philip to return to his wife.

REVIEWS:
Variety, 8.16.39: "Miss Dunne and [Charles] Boyer are ideally teamed to provide a sincere and understanding romance, despite the obstacles presented for a happy conclusion."

New York Times, 8.17.39: "[Charles] Boyer, with the charm that has made him one of our few authentic matinee idols, and Miss Dunne, always a pleasant and sincere performer, are unequal to the task of bringing life and conviction to James Cain's made-to-order script."

See also B-18, B-116, B-150, B-179, B-293, B-370, B-430, B-459, B-463

NOTES: When Tomorrow Comes tried to cash in on the popularity of Love Affair by reuniting the actors in a similar story about star-crossed lovers. Although audiences enjoyed the second film, it never reached the classic status of Love Affair. The working title of When Tomorrow Comes was A Modern Cinderella. Irene Dunne sang "Solidarity Forever," a union anthem using the tune of "The Battle Hymn of the Republic," and Schubert's "Serenade." Time reported that director John Stahl lost nineteen pounds during the filming, as repeated retakes caused him trouble (August 21, 1939). When Tomorrow Comes was remade as Interlude in 1957 and 1968. The 1957 version starred June Allyson and Rossano Brazzi; the 1968 version, made in England, starred Oskar Werner and Barbara Ferris.

F-28 My Favorite Wife   (RKO, 1940)   88 minutes

Producer: Leo McCarey. Director: Garson Kanin. Assistant directors: James H. Anderson and Ruby Rosenberg. Screenplay: Bella and Samuel Spewack, and Leo McCarey. Editor: Robert Wise. Photography: Rudolph Mate. Art directors: Van Nest Polglase and Mark-Lee Kirk. Costumes: Howard Greer. Sets: Darrell Silvera.

CAST: Irene Dunne (Ellen Wagstaff Arden), Cary Grant (Nick Arden), Randolph Scott (Stephen Burkett), Gail Patrick (Bianca), Ann Shoemaker (Ma), Scotty Beckett (Tim Arden), Mary Lou Harrington (Chinch Arden), Donald MacBride (Hotel clerk), Hugh O'Connell (Johnson), Granville Bates (Judge), Pedro de Cordoba (Dr. Kohlmar), Brandon Tynan (Dr. Manning), Leon Belasco (Henri), Harold Gerald (Assistant clerk), Murray Alper (Bartender), Earle Hodgins (Court clerk), Cyril Ring (Contestant), Clive Morgan, Bert Moorhouse (Lawyers), Florence Dudley, Jean Acker (Witnesses), Joe Cabrillas (Phillip), Frank Marlowe (Photographer), Thelma Joel (Miss Rosenthal), Horace MacMahon (Truck driver), Chester Clute (Little man), Eli Schmudkler (Janitor), Franco Corsaro (Waiter), Cy Kendall (Detective), Pat West (Caretaker).

SYNOPSIS: After Ellen Arden has been missing at sea for seven years, her husband Nick has her declared legally dead so that he can marry Bianca. As he heads off on his honeymoon, the shipwrecked Ellen returns, rescued by a boat that went off course. Ellen goes to Nick's hotel and confronts him. He claims he wants to return to Ellen, but needs time to break the news to Bianca. Meanwhile, Ellen

98   Irene Dunne

pretends to be an old friend of the family and moves in with the Ardens. She befriends her children, who are too young to remember her. Nick gets jealous when he learns Ellen was on a deserted island for seven years with Stephen Burkett, a handsome, athletic anthropologist. To quiet Nick, Ellen gets a bald shoe salesman to pose as Stephen, not knowing that Nick has already tracked down the real Burkett. Meanwhile, Nick's strange behavior prompts Bianca to call in a psychiatrist. As Nick tries to explain the truth to Bianca, he is arrested for bigamy. The judge annuls his second marriage, but Nick cannot make up his mind. Stephen invites Ellen to return to the island, but she still loves her husband. Nick takes Ellen and the children to their moutain home to wait until he makes his decision at Christmas. Realizing he still loves Ellen, Nick is reluctant to leave. His mother calls and tells Ellen that she and Nick are legally married since the annulment has been filed and the judge has declared her alive. Ellen strings Nick along, making him sleep in the attic. He admits he wants her, but she insists he wait until Christmas as he originally planned. He returns in a Santa suit and they reconcile.

REVIEWS:
Variety, 5.1.40: "Irene Dunne and Cary Grant appear in the second of their series of wife-and-husband romantic farces, picking up the thread of marital comedy at about the point where they left off in 'The Awful Truth.' With these two stars working again with Leo McCarey, a surefire laughing film is guaranteed....Principals perform with cleverness..."

New York Times, 5.31.40: "[Leo] McCarey is, without compare, a master of the technique of the prolonged and amorous tease; and with an actress such as Miss Dunne through whom to apply it - she with her luxurious and mocking laughter, her roving eyes and come-hither glances - mere man is powerless before it."

Movie-Radio Mirror, 6.1.40: "...My Favorite Wife... [has] an excellent chance of winning anybody's nomination as the most laughingly entertaining film of the current season....Cary Grant and Irene Dunne surpass their last comedy efforts (in The Awful Truth) here..."

See also R-17, R-65, A-70, B-12, B-18, B-31, B-43, B-72, B-140, B-145, B-160, B-165, B-185, B-211, B-214, B-215, B-238, B-245, B-277, B-290, B-315, B-336, B-347, B-391, B-407, B-428, B-457, B-459, B-464

NOTES: The team that created The Awful Truth hoped to rekindle some of the spark with My Favorite Wife. However, director Leo McCarey had to hand over the directing reins to Garson Kanin when McCarey was injured in an automobile accident shortly before the filming began. Critics pointed out the similarities in the films. In

Magill's Survey of Cinema, Judith M. Kass illustrated several comparisons: the other man, the understanding mother, the outrageous behavior Irene Dunne's characters go through to confuse the other women. "Most importantly," Kass wrote, "Both films share the episode of an awkward night, during which Nick devises a number of stratagems to reconcile himself with Ellen, at the end of which the couple is reunited" (B-277).

Irene was paid one hundred thousand dollars for the film, plus a percentage of the profits. The premiere took place in her hometown of Louisville, with Irene and her husband joining McCarey and RKO executives at the special event, which happened to coincide with the Kentucky Derby. The film opened in New York on May 4, 1940 at Radio City Music Hall. Irene and Grant reprised their roles on *The Screen Directors' Playhouse* in 1950 (R-74).

Like the Alfred Lord Tennyson poem "Enoch Arden" on which it was based, *My Favorite Wife* concerned a shipwrecked spouse who returned after being declared legally dead. Ironically, director Leo McCarey originally planned the film, then titled *Woman Overboard*, for Jean Arthur. However, Arthur made a similar film entitled *Too Many Husbands* (Columbia, 1940). In 1963, 20th Century-Fox remade the film as *Move Over, Darling* with Doris Day and James Garner. An uncompleted version, entitled *Something's Got to Give*, was filmed by 20th Century-Fox in 1962 with Marilyn Monroe and Dean Martin. Unreleased, it was Monroe's last screen appearance. Because of the remake, *My Favorite Wife* was withheld from television for many years. In 1989, Turner Entertainment Company colorized *My Favorite Wife*.

F-29   *Land of Liberty*   (MGM, 1941)   137 minutes

> Producer: Motion Picture Producers and Distributors of America. Narration: Jeanie MacPherson and Jesse Lasky, Jr. Editors: Herbert L. Moulton, William H. Pine, and Francis S. Harmon, under the supervision of Cecil B. DeMille. Historical consultant: Professor James T. Shotwell of Columbia University.
>
> CAST: Don Ameche, Edward Arnold, John Barrymore, Lionel Barrymore, Warner Baxter, Wallace Beery, George Brent, Bob Burns, Claudette Colbert, Gary Cooper, Bette Davis, Irene Dunne, Henry Fonda, Fredric March, Joel McCrea, Robert Montgomery, Anna Neagle, George Raft, Randolph Scott, James Stewart, Lewis Stone, Margaret Sullavan, Spencer Tracy, Loretta Young.

SYNOPSIS: The film is a history of the United States, from colonial times to the 1930s, emphasizing the constant urge for freedom. It was updated in 1941 to include references to the war in Europe.

REVIEWS:

100   Irene Dunne

<u>New York Times</u>, 6.17.39: "But for all its gaps, [<u>Land of Liberty</u>] is a fascinating record and tribute to Hollywood as well as to our democracy. For it serves again to remind us of the cinema's skill in evoking the past, of its ability to make a permanent record of the present."

<u>Variety</u>, 6.21.39: "Film is cleverly put together and narrated, and it should be of immense value as an educational subject, either in its entirety or at the rate of one reel per week."

<u>Variety</u>, 1.15.41: "Picture is a grand parade of cinema figures over the last 10 years or so, besides being the most comprehensive single picture document on American history ever put together."

<u>New York Times</u>, 1.30.41: "As a cinematic mosaic, it is impressive - and incidentally it affords one much delight in recalling the films from which its scenes are clipped. But for any one who wasn't already familiar with the epic of America, it wouldn't mean a thing."

NOTES: <u>Land of Liberty</u> was a compilation of scenes from 112 features and shorts, made by many different film companies. It premiered at the New York World's Fair on June 15, 1939, running 137 minutes. Much of the initial criticism was that the film ran too long. Therefore, when <u>Land of Liberty</u> was released by MGM in 1941, it was trimmed to ninety-eight minutes. The distributors' profits from the film were donated to war emergency welfare work. A flier for the film heralded, "139 stars! 200 scenes! 1000 thrills! Cavalcade of screen wonders snatched from the treasures of 51 Hollywood producers. 150 years of breathless American drama...adventure...romance... packed into one mighty show!" Irene Dunne was seen in a clip from <u>Cimarron</u>.

F-30   <u>Penny Serenade</u>   (Columbia, 1941)   125 minutes

Producer: George Stevens. Associate producer: Fred Guiol. Director: George Stevens. Assistant director: Gene Anderson. Screenplay: Morrie Ryskind. Based on the story by Martha Cheavens. Music: W. Franke Harling. Musical director: Morris Stoloff. Editor: Otto Meyer. Photography: Joseph Walker. Art director: Lionel Banks.

CAST: Irene Dunne (Julie Gardiner Adams), Cary Grant (Roger Adams), Beulah Bondi (Miss Oliver), Edgar Buchanan (Applejack Carney), Ann Doran (Dotty), Eva Lee Kuney (Trina, age six), Leonard Willey (Dr. Hartley), Wallis Clark (Judge), Walter Soderling (Billings), Baby Biffle (Trina, age one), Edmund Elton (Minister), Billy Bevan (McDougal), Nee Wong, Jr. (Sung Chong), Michael Morris (Bill collector), Grady Sutton, Stanley Brown (Men), Beryl Vaughn (Flower girl), John Tyrrell (Press operator), Iris Han (O-Hanna-San), Otto Han (Cook Sam), Ben Taggart (Policeman), Frank Moran (Cab driver), Lyton Brent (Reporter), Al Seymour (Bootlegger), Dick Wessel (Joe), Charles Flynn (Bob), Arline Jackson, Mary Bovard, Georgia Hawkins (Girls), Fred "Snowflake" Toones (Train porter), Ed Peil, Sr. (Train conductor), Eddie Laughton (Cab driver), Doris Herbert (Minister's wife), Bess Flowers (Mother), John Ferguson (Father), Lani Lee (Chinese waitress), Rollin Moriyama, Ben Kumagai (Rickshaw boys), Lillian West (Nurse), Henry Dixon (Old printer), Dorothy Adams (Mother), Albert Butterfield (Boy).

SYNOPSIS: As Julie Adams prepares to leave her husband Roger, she plays a series of records on the phonograph which remind her of their life. The story flashes back to the Adams' meeting in a New York record store. Roger, a reporter, buys a stack of records from Julie and soon falls in love with her. When he gets an assignment in Tokyo, they marry. Julie soon learns that Roger is impractical with money, as he splurges on a home in Japan and lavishly spends his inheritance. They are thrilled when Julie learns she is pregnant. Their happiness is short-lived, as Julie has a miscarriage during an earthquake, destroying her chances to bear children. Roger buys a small newspaper outside San Francisco and brings his friend Applejack Carney west to be press manager. Sensing Roger and Julie's longing for a baby, Applejack suggests they try adoption. Despite their shaky financial situation, Julie and Roger adopt baby Trina with the help of kindly Miss Oliver, the head of the adoption agency. Roger is enchanted by his daughter, although he had requested a two-year-old boy. When Roger's newspaper has financial difficulties before the adoption is finalized, they almost lose Trina. However, Roger's heartfelt appeal convinces the judge to let them keep her. When Trina is six, she dies suddenly, leaving her parents angry and grieving. Feeling as if they do not need each other anymore, they decide to separate. They reconsider when Miss Oliver offers them a two-year-old boy, as they had originally requested.

REVIEWS:
<u>Variety</u>, 4.16.41: "Film marks the return of Miss Dunne after an extended vacation, the only effects of which seem to be that she proves again her place among the handful of women screen stars. In the role of a not too prosperous wife of a small-town struggling newspaper publisher, she is gay and earnest, and plays the sentimental passages with restraint. She has had more spectacular roles, but none that required sustaining quite the mood of her latest film."

<u>Newsweek</u>, 4.28.41: "In their fictional past Irene Dunne and Cary Grant have played fast and twice as loose with the tie that binds, specifically in <u>The Awful Truth</u> and <u>My Favorite Wife</u>. Their turnabout in Columbia's <u>Penny</u>

Serenade is something less than fair play. Here the comedy team produces a sentimental film that, sniffle for sniffle, ranks with the best in the tear-jerker class....But whenever sentiment threatens to get out of hand, George Stevens' shrewd direction and the sincerity of the Dunne-Grant performances restore order and credibility."

Time, 5.5.41: "Stars Grant and Dunne successfully weather the serious competition of two pairs of identical twins (who play the Adams' child at different ages, one of each subbing for the other to save shooting time). The awkward, embarrassed ineptitude of their first night of parenthood is one of the most deliciously human, truly comic sequences out of Hollywood in many moons."

New York Times, 5.23.41: "...you can't help but feel that somebody has slipped a fast one over on you....Maybe it is Miss Dunne, who originally succumbs to one of the most severe cases of galloping nostalgia we have ever witnessed on the screen....some very credible acting on the part of [Cary] Grant and Miss Dunne is responsible in the main for the infectious quality of the film."

The New Statesman and Nation, 7.12.41: "*Penny Serenade* is long enough to enjoy, to sleep through, and then enjoy again....Irene Dunne gives a charming, individual performance..."

Screenland, 7.41: "You liked Irene Dunne and Cary Grant in *The Awful Truth* - and now they're together again in this charming picture which is often as funny as that first hit, and also grand and weepy - so bring out the hankies.... Irene Dunne is just right as the wife - she is an irresistible compound of womanly tenderness and understanding, always believable as a small-town matron, never reminding of the Hollywood star."

Silver Screen, 7.41: "Irene Dunne and Cary Grant - the most popular team in Hollywood - play husband and wife in a serious drama for a change....Handkerchiefs will be in order, and, naturally, women will like this better than men."

See also R-34, B-18, B-31, B-43, B-63, B-140, B-145, B-160, B-175, B-177, B-245, B-258, B-266, B-278, B-292, B-347, B-395, B-408, B-451, B-464, B-465, B-468

NOTES: Unlike earlier Irene Dunne-Cary Grant collaborations, *Penny Serenade* was not a comedy. Although the film had some humorous and touching scenes, it was basically a tearjerker. The film used a phonograph as the connecting device, easing into flashbacks as Irene Dunne's Julie played records which triggered her memory. The uncredited singer was Johnny Johnston, who later married Kathryn Grayson. Ironically, Grayson reprised Irene's roles in the remakes of *Show Boat* and *Roberta*.

Penny Serenade was a critical and financial success, earning Grant his first Academy Award nomination. Irene and Grant recreated their roles on The Gulf Screen Guild Theater (R-22). Irene often said Penny Serenade was her favorite film because it reminded her of her own adopted daughter.

F-31   Unfinished Business   (Universal, 1941)   96 minutes

Producer: Gregory La Cava. Director: Gregory La Cava. Screenplay: Eugene Thackrey. Song: Jimmy McHugh and Jack Frost. Musical director: Franz Waxman. Photography: Joseph Valentine. Art director: Jack Otterson. Sound: Bernard B. Brown.

CAST: Irene Dunne (Nancy Andrews), Robert Montgomery (Tom Duncan), Eugene Pallette (Elmer, the butler), Preston Foster (Steve Duncan), June Clyde (Clarisse), Phyllis Barry (Sheila Duncan), Thomas W. Ross (Lawyer), Richard Davies (Jimmy), Esther Dale (Aunt Mathilda), Walter Catlett (Billy Ross), Samuel S. Hinds (Uncle), Dick Foran (Frank), Kathryn Adams (Katy, the bride), Chester Clute, Paul Everton, John Sheehan, Matt McHugh, Larry Kent, Fred Santley, Reed Hadley, Boyd Irwin, Quen Ramsey (Men), Pierre Watkin (Lawyer), Helen Land, Phyllis Kennedy, Margaret Armstrong, Grace Hayle, Dorothy Vaughan, Grace Stafford, Dorothy Granger, Dora Clement, Hillary Brooke, Sheila Darcy, Flo Wix, Virginia Engels, Gwen Seager, Isabelle LaMal, Dorothy Hass, Ruth Dwyer (Women), Paul Fix, Jack Voglin, Eddie Fetherstone (Reporters), Virginia Brissac (Aunt), Josephine Whittell (Wardrobe woman), Mary Gordon (Charwoman), Harry Rosenthal (Pianist), George Davis, Bob Perry (Waiters), Helen Millard (Helen), Fortunio Bonanova (Impresario), Reverend Neal Dodd (Minister), Hope Landin (Groom's mother), Frank Coghlan, Jr. (Page boy), Jacques Vanaire (Head waiter), Yolande Mellot (Manicurist), Frank Shannon (Groom's father), Hugh Beaumont (Groom), Eugene Jackson (Bootblack), Lester Dorr (Yes man), Mary Jo Ellis (Bridesmaid), Amanda McFarland (Baby).

SYNOPSIS: After marrying off the sister she raised, Nancy Andrews leaves her small Ohio town for adventure. En route to New York, she meets wealthy playboy Steve Duncan. Despite his line, she promptly falls in love with him. In New York, Nancy auditions for singing jobs while waiting for Steve to call. Her roommate urges Nancy to forget him. Nancy is hired to answer phones in a nightclub, where she runs into Steve and his fiancee. Not knowing about the past, Steve's brother Tom tries to comfort her. Nancy is distressed when Steve marries. Although she still loves Steve, she marries Tom after a few drinks. Nancy throws herself into the social whirl, but continues to have feelings for Steve. During their first dinner party, Tom's ex-girlfriend and Steve show up. The girlfriend spies Nancy kissing Steve, although their relationship is over. Tom learns that Steve and Nancy met before. Nancy leaves before he can question her. Disgruntled with his life, Tom joins the army. On leave a year later, he sees Nancy singing in the chorus of an opera. He tries to convince her to return to him, but thinks she still loves Steve when she refuses. Steve tries to tell him the truth, but Tom does not believe him. Tom finds Steve at Nancy's apartment and tries to beat him up, facing up to his brother for the first time. Tom and Nancy reconcile when he learns they have a son.

REVIEWS:
Variety, 8.27.41: "Miss Dunne grooves neatly to carry the main role...Miss Dunne sings 'When We Were Young Maggie,' in addition to a brief excerpt from an operatic aria."

New York Times, 9.2.41: "Any picture which brings Irene Dunne and Robert Montgomery to a state of matrimony, with the directorial blessing of Gregory La Cava, must...have a great deal to recommend it....Miss Dunne, even though she must combine the naivete of Cinderella with devastating wit of Dorothy Parker, is charming..."

Newsweek, 9.8.41: "If Universal's Unfinished Business is disappointing, it is chiefly because the critical moviegoer has come to expect considerably better of Gregory La Cava. Even so, the producer-director's handling of a well-chosen cast, the expert directorial touches, and the crisp, amusing dialogue make up for a lot....[Irene Dunne, Robert Montgomery, and Preston Foster] are adept enough in trying roles..."

The Spectator, 10.3.41: "Unfinished Business...is only too anxious to flourish its psychological pretentions. Without them, Robert Montgomery and Irene Dunne might have made a very pleasant little comedy..."

The New Statesman and Nation, 10.4.41: "...despite the artificialities of the plot, it is a film two-thirds agreeable, and Irene Dunne has a native charm that survives all obstacles."

See also B-116, B-179, B-240, B-286, B-316, B-318, B-436

NOTES: Unfinished Business reunited Irene Dunne with Gregory La Cava, who directed Symphony of Six Million. Although their previous collaboration had been a soap opera, Irene had high hopes for the comic possibilities of Unfinished Business, as La Cava had directed Carole Lombard in the screwball classic My Man Godfrey. Unfinished Business never reached the heights of My Man Godfrey, but it proved popular with wartime audiences. According to Lombard biographer Larry Swindell, Unfinished Business originally was to star Lombard and Robert Montgomery, and be produced by a company formed by Lombard,

La Cava, and agent Myron Selznick. Negotiations broke off before the film began (B-431). Irene sang "I Love Thee Now," "Happy Birthday," snatches of an aria, and "When We Were Young Maggie," and performed in the chorus of the opera Martha. She reprised her role on The Lux Radio Theatre (R-21).

F-32 Lady in a Jam   (Universal, 1942)   78 minutes

Producer: Gregory La Cava. Director: Gregory La Cava. Assistant director: Joseph A. McDonough. Screenplay: Eugene Thackrey, Frank Cockrell, and Otho Lovering. Music: Frank Skinner. Musical director: Charles Previn. Editor: Russell Schoengarth. Photography: Hal Mohr. Art directors: Jack Otterson and Martin Obzina. Costumes: Bernard Newman of I. Magnin & Co. Sets: R.A. Gausman. Jewelry: Brock and Company, Los Angeles. Sound: Bernard B. Brown.

CAST: Irene Dunne (Jane Palmer), Patric Knowles (Dr. Enright), Ralph Bellamy (Stanley), Eugene Pallette (Billingsley), Queenie Vassar (Cactus Kate), Jane Garland (Strawberry), Robert Homans (Faro Bill), Samuel S. Hinds (Dr. Brewster), Hobart Cavanaugh (Reporter), Mira McKinney (Lady of the evening), Sarah Padden (Miner's wife), Clara Blandick (Tourist), Sam H. Underwood (Desert rat), Kathleen Howard, Josephine Whittell, Kitty O'Neil, Veda Ann Borg, Claire Whitney, Mona Barrie (Women), Russell Hicks (Carter), Irving Bacon (Motel proprietor), Hardie Albright (Xilton), Charles Lane (Government man), Edward McWade (Ground-Hog), Isabel LaMal (Josephine), Ed Gargan (Deputy), Fuzzy Knight, Eddie Fetherstone (Cab drivers), Robert Emmett Keane (Coupe driver), Charles Cane (Cop), Holmes Herbert, Garry Owen, Reed Hadley, Charles Coleman (Men), Phyllis Kennedy (Drunk tourist), Rex Lease, Syd Saylor, Ruth Warren (Drunks), Eddie Dunn (Bartender), Thomas Kilshaw (Auctioneer), Chief Thundercloud (Himself), Eddy Chandler (Waiter), Lester Dorr (Assistant manager), Al Bridge (Furniture mover), Fred Stanley (Tourist), Dick Alexander (Fighter), Billy Benedict (Barker), Bess Flowers (Nurse), Casey MacGregor (Case keeper), Jack Gardner (Auctioneer's clerk).

SYNOPSIS: Jane Palmer is a spoiled spendthrift who relies on numerology and vibrations to breeze through life. Billingsley, the executor of her grandfather's estate, is worried about her extravagance. He enlists the help of Dr. Enright, who works for a psychiatric foundation supported by the Palmers. Enright agrees to help teach Jane some responsibility. He convinces her to hire him as a chauffeur, claiming he is taking a leave from his practice because of a woman. Meanwhile, Jane is astounded to learn she is bankrupt. Although Billingsley promises to salvage what he can, she accuses him of absconding with her money. After Jane's possessions are auctioned off, Enright convinces her to confront her past in Arizona. Jane tries to persuade her gun-toting grandmother Cactus Kate to give her enough money to prosecute Billingsley. Kate refuses, but points out the Lost Hope mine, where Jane's grandfather excavated the family fortune. Falling in love with Enright, Jane tries to please him by aiming for self-sufficiency and working in the mine. When Jane is ready to give up on Enright and the mine, Kate salts it with gold. Jane is soon back to her wacky ways and Enright is furious. To make him jealous, she flirts with Stanley, her childhood flame. When a government man offers to buy the mine because it contains millions of dollars in quick silver, Enright has had enough. Knowing that money will corrupt Jane, he returns to New York and his practice. The foundation staff notices strange behavior upon his return, with Enright discussing numerology and vibrations. Although engaged to Stanley, Jane follows Enright to New York. She explains that she gave the government money to Kate and confesses that she loves Enright. He screams at the lunacy of love.

REVIEWS:
Variety, 7.1.42: "Miss Dunne handles the lead excellently..."

Newsweek, 7.13.42: "In a uniformly good cast, the mainstay is Irene Dunne, whose Jane Palmer is a charming, inarticulate nitwit who goes bankrupt....Whether she is panning for gold that isn't there, encouraging a lovesick cowboy..., or merely baffling saner folk, the star doesn't miss a flutter-brained inflection of her role."

New York Times, 9.11.42: "Universal wasn't kidding when it tagged Irene Dunne's new picture 'Lady in a Jam.' For never, in our recollection, has the generally delectable Miss Dunne been made to appear to less advantage than she is in this vapid confusion..."

See also B-94, B-116, B-179

NOTES: Irene Dunne and director Gregory La Cava were reteamed in Lady in a Jam. In The RKO Gals, James Robert Parish suggested that La Cava's recurring illnesses during the shooting caused the film to "bomb" (B-343). In any case, the comedy was slight, even for wartime audiences looking for an escape. Lady in a Jam marked the final screen pairing of Irene and Ralph Bellamy.

F-33   A Guy Named Joe   (MGM, 1943)   118 minutes

Producer: Everett Riskin. Director: Victor Fleming. Screenplay: Dalton Trumbo, Frederick Hazlitt Brennan, Chandler Sprague, and David Boehm. Music: Herbert Stothart. Song: Roy Turk and Fred Ahlert. Editor: Frank Sullivan. Photography: George Folsey and Karl

Freund. Art directors: Cedric Gibbons and Lyle Wheeler. Costumes: Irene. Sound: Douglas Shearer. Special effects: Arnold Gillespie, Donald Jahraus, and Warren Newcombe. Technical advisor: Major Edward G. Hillery.

CAST: Spencer Tracy (Pete Sandidge), Irene Dunne (Dorinda Durston), Van Johnson (Ted Randall), Ward Bond (Al Yackey), James Gleason (Colonel "Nails" Kilpatrick), Lionel Barrymore (The General), Barry Nelson (Dick Rumney), Don DeFore (James "Powerhouse" Rourke), Henry O'Neill (Colonel Hendricks), Addison Richards (Major Corbett), Charles Smith (Sanderson), Mary Elliott (Dancehall girl), Earl Schenck (Colonel Schenck), Maurice Murphy (Captain Robertson), Gertrude Hoffmann (Old woman), Mark Daniels (Lieutenant), William Bishop (Ray), Esther Williams (Ellen Bright), Eve Whitney (Powerhouse girl), Kay Williams (Girl at bar), Walter Sande (Mess sergeant), Gibson Gowland (Bartender), John Whitney, Kirk Alyn (Officers in heaven), James Millican (Orderly), Ernest Severn (Davy), Edward Hardwicke (George), Raymond Severn (Cyril), Yvonne Severn (Elizabeth), Christopher Severn (Peter), John Frederick (Lieutenant), Frank Faylen, Phil Van Zandt (Majors), Marshall Reed, Blake Edwards (Fliers), Matt Willis (Lieutenant Hunter), Peter Cookson (Sergeant Hanson), Jacqueline White (Helen), Bill Arthur, John Bogden, Herbert Gunn, Bob Sully, Johnny Dunn, James Martin, Richard Woodruff, Ken Scott, Louis Hart, Fred Beckner (Cadets), Craig Flannagan, Melvin Nix, Earl Kent, Michael Owen (U.S. lieutenants), Joan Thorsen, Leatrice Gilbert, Mary Ganley (Girls in Chinese restaurant), Charles King II (Lieutenant Collins), Eddie Borden (Taxi driver), Arthur Speace (San Francisco airport captain), Alan Wilson (Sergeant in jeep), Leslie Vincent (Sentry), Elizabeth Valentine (Washerwoman's child), Arthur Stenning, George Kirby (Fishermen), Mary McLeod, Aileen Haley (Hostesses), Oliver Cross (American mayor), Wyndham Standing (English colonel), Violet Seton (Bartender's wife), Becky Bohannon (English girl), Harold S. Landon (Cadet), Jean Prescott (Mother), Simon Oliver (Boy), Richard Graham (Crew member), James Warren (Irish guard), George Atkinson (Waiter), Howard Davies (Bartender), Carlie Taylor (English captain), Jack Saunders (American captain), Stanley Orr (English captain), William Bishop (Ray), Allen Wood (Tough corporal), Eddie Coke (Corporal), Carey Harrison (American major in Red Lion Inn), Dora Baker (Scrub woman), Clarence Straight (Flight sergeant), Verno Downing (English liaison officer), William Manning (Co-pilot), Jesse Tai Sing (Headwaitress), Martin Ashe (Sergeant in Chinese restaurant).

SYNOPSIS: Pete Sandidge is an American bomber pilot

stationed in Britain during World War II. His grandstanding maneuvers and disobedience of orders lead to his being transferred to Scotland. Despite Pete's daredevil antics, he worries about his girlfriend Dorinda Durston, a ferry command pilot. He urges her to get a desk job, but she refuses. When the Colonel is offered a position teaching fliers in the United States, he invites Pete to join him. Fearing Pete is going to be killed, Dorinda begs him to take the commission. During his last emergency maneuver in Scotland, Pete crashes his plane into a German aircraft carrier and dies. In heaven, Pete learns he will be sent back to earth to help Air Force cadets. He starts with Ted Randall, a young millionaire who is afraid to fly. Pete instills confidence, both on and off the airfield. Although it takes Pete's coaxing to get Ted to ask canteen worker Ellen Bright to dance, he is soon a lady killer. Meanwhile, Dorinda continues to mourn Pete's death by throwing herself into her work. Pete's former partner Al urges her to get on with her life. She meets Ted and soon falls in love with him, although he reminds her of Pete. When Ted and Dorinda get engaged, Pete is jealous. He encourages Ted to do some daredevil flying, hoping it will get Ted in trouble. Instead of punishment, Ted is given a dangerous assignment. Ordered back to heaven, Pete reconsiders his jealousy and agrees to let Dorinda find happiness with Ted. Meanwhile, Dorinda breaks her engagement, telling Ted she still loves Pete. When she learns of Ted's mission, she takes his place, hoping to get killed in the line of duty so she can join Pete. With Pete's spirtual help, she completes the mission and returns to Ted.

REVIEWS:
New York Times, 12.24.43: "...Miss Dunne is as lovely and fetching as we've seen her - maybe even a little more so."

Variety, 12.29.43: "...Miss Dunne is nifty to look at and turns in a sufficiently restrained but emotionally convincing portrayal."

Time, 1.10.44: "It would succeed more thoroughly if Miss Dunne's grief and her scenes with Van Johnson were not...so smoothly soft peddled. But Miss Dunne's early scenes with the living Pete have unusual friendliness."

See also S-6, B-73, B-83, B-100, B-108, B-135, B-153, B-280, B-290, B-311, B-348, B-465

NOTES: MGM had originally planned to have Dorinda die during the bombing mission and end up in heaven with Pete, leaving Ted to find happiness with Ellen Bright. However, preview audiences found this ending too depressing so it was discarded.

Spencer Tracy took an immediate dislike to Irene Dunne during filming. According to most reports, he considered her too prudish, so he and his drinking buddy Victor

Fleming, the film's director, teased her unmercifully, often reducing her to tears. Conversely, Tracy took young actor Van Johnson under his wing during filming. When Johnson was seriously injured in a car accident, causing a metal plate to be inserted in his forehead, Tracy insisted MGM shut down production. MGM mogul Louis B. Mayer wanted to replace Johnson with another contract player like John Hodiak or Peter Lawford, however Tracy threatened to quit if Johnson were replaced. Mayer agreed to hold off the production until Johnson's recovery if Tracy would treat Irene with respect. Irene began shooting The White Cliffs of Dover during the interim. When Johnson returned to work, Irene acted in the two films concurrently.

Irene Dunne told a different version of the Tracy disagreement to film historian James Harvey. She said that Tracy was her hero and it disturbed him that she would be disillusioned after working with him. Despite the initial sparks, Irene said they worked things out and became friends (B-290).

According to American Magazine, the script for A Guy Named Joe called for Irene to sing "It's Three O'Clock in the Morning," a song she openly disliked. She suggested they revive an old song instead. When the music department gave her a choice between "My Wonderful One" and "I'll Get By," she selected the latter, which became a big hit after the movie (B-21).

A Guy Named Joe earned more than $4 million during its initial release. It ranked in the top ten films of 1943-44. A Guy Named Joe was remade in 1989 as Always, starring Richard Dreyfuss and Holly Hunter.

F-34   The White Cliffs of Dover   (MGM, 1944)
       126 minutes

   Producer: Sidney Franklin. Director: Clarence Brown. Screenplay: Claudine West, Jan Lustig, and George Froeschel. Based on the poem "The White Cliffs" by Alice Duer Miller, with additional poetry by Robert Nathan. Music: Herbert Stothart. Editor: Robert J. Kern. Photography: George Folsey. Art directors: Cedric Gibbons and Randall Duell. Costumes: Irene and Gile Steele. Sets: Edwin B. Willis and Jacques Mersereau. Sound: Douglas Shearer. Makeup: Jack Dawn. Technical adviser: Major Cyril Seys Ramsey-Hill. Special effects: Arnold Gillespie and Warren Newcombe.

   CAST: Irene Dunne (Susan Ashwood), Alan Marshall (Sir John Ashwood), Frank Morgan (Hiram Porter Dunn), Roddy McDowall (John Ashwood II, as a boy), Peter Lawford (John Ashwood II, age 24), Dame May Whitty (Nanny), C. Aubrey Smith (Colonel Forsyth), Gladys Cooper (Lady Jean Ashwood), Van Johnson (Sam Bennett), John

Warburton (Reggie Ashwood), Jill Esmond (Rosamund), Brenda Forbes (Gwennie), Norma Varden (Mrs. Bland), Elizabeth Taylor (Betsy, age 10), June Lockhart (Betsy, age 18), Charles Irwin (Farmer Kenney), Jean Prescott (Mrs. Kenney), Tom Drake (American soldier), Isobel Elsom (Mrs. Bancroft), Edmond Breon (Major Bancroft), Miles Mander (Major Loring), Ann Curzon (Miss Lambert), Steven Muller (Gerhard), Norbert Muller (Dietrich), Molly Lamont (Helen), Lumsden Hare (Vicar), Arthur Shields (Benson), Emily Fitzroy (Spinster in boarding house), Emily Massey (Elegant lady in boarding house), Guy D'Ennery (Curate in boarding house), Lal Chand Mehra (Indian student in boarding house), Clifford Brooke (Indian major in boarding house), Elton Burkett, Eldon Burkett (Twins in boarding house), Doris Lloyd (Plump lady in the boarding house), Matthew Boulton (Immigration officer), Ethel Griffies (Woman on train), Herbert Evans (Footman), Keith Hitchcock (Duke of Waverly), Vera Graaff (Duchess), Anita Bolster (Miller), Ian Wolfe (Skipper), Alec Craig (Billings), Clyde Cook (Jennings), Bunny Gordon (John, age six months), George Kirby (Old man), Wilson Benge (Chauffeur), Harry Allen (English cabby), Nelson Leigh (British naval officer), Mabel Row (Housemaid), James Menzies (Telegraph boy), Kay Deslys (Blonde woman), Leo Mostovoy (Bandmaster), George Davis (Boots), Matthew Boulton (Immigration officer).

SYNOPSIS: Red Cross volunteer Susan Ashwood worries about her soldier son as she waits for the wounded to arrive at a British hospital during World War II. She recalls her life as she waits. American Susan sails for England for a two-week visit in 1914. On her last night, an elderly colonel takes her to a ball where she meets British baronet John Ashwood. John urges Susan to extend her stay. She meets his mother and learns about his family history. Although Susan loves John, she is reluctant to marry him and give up her country. She finally gives in as World War I errupts. While John is serving, Susan gives birth to John Ashwood II. She is thrilled when the Americans join the war, hoping John, Sr. will soon get to see his son. Instead, John is killed in action. Bitter, Susan vows to keep her son out of the army. As years pass, John develops into a caring, noble boy like his father. Susan's father urges her to bring John to the United States, afraid another war will claim him. When her mother-in-law dies, Susan agrees. John feels guilty about leaving the tenants on his manor and deserting his country; he convinces Susan to stay in England. When World War II breaks out, John joins his father's regiment. He is brought in with the wounded at the Red Cross hospital where Susan is working. She is powerless to save him from his fatal injuries. She finds strength in her patriotism, as she sees British and American troops marching together.

REVIEWS:

Filmography   111

<u>Variety</u>, 3.15.44: "Miss Dunne gives an excellent performance..."

<u>New York Times</u>, 5.12.44: "...Metro has followed the outline of the poem, but has put its particular emphasis upon the romantic aspects of the tale. As a consequence, long stretches of the picture are played in blissful solitude by Irene Dunne and Alan Marshall as the American lady and the English man. Miss Dunne gives to her character a nice glow of American charm..."

<u>San Francisco Chronicle</u>, 7.28.44: "This picture is superbly acted. Irene Dunne has been cast in a role which magnificently suits her talent for reserved power."

<u>The Spectator</u>, 8.18.44: "[<u>The White Cliffs of Dover</u>] is excellently acted, particularly by Irene Dunne..."

See also A-70, B-32, B-74, B-100, B-207

NOTES: Filmed at the same time as <u>A Guy Named Joe</u>, <u>The White Cliffs of Dover</u> was directed at promoting British-American relations during World War II. The film opened at Radio City Music Hall on May 10, 1944. Irene Dunne read the poem which inspired the film on a broadcast from Canada (R-35). She and C. Aubrey Smith recreated their film roles on <u>Academy Award</u> (R-41).

F-35   <u>Follow the Boys</u>   (Universal, 1944)   122 minutes

Producer: Charles K. Feldman. Associate producer: Albert J. Rockett. Director: Eddie Sutherland. Assistant director: Howard Christie. Screenplay: Lou Breslow and Gertrude Purcell. Choreographer: George Hale. Songs: Richard A. Whiting, W. Franke Harling, Leo Robin, Isham Jones, Gus Kahn, Jack Yellen, Shelton Brooks, Roy Turk, Fred E. Ahlert, Jule Styne, Sammy Cahn, Larry Marks, Dick Charles, Chopin, Earl Robinson, and Lewis Allan. Musical director: Leigh Harline. Editor: Fred R. Feitshans, Jr. Photography: David Abel. Special effects: John Fulton.

CAST: George Raft (Tony West), Vera Zorina (Gloria Vance), Charles Grapewin (Nick West), Grace MacDonald (Kitty West), Charles Butterworth (Louie Fairweather), George Macready (Walter Bruce), Elizabeth Patterson (Annie), Theodor von Eltz (William Barrett), Regis Toomey (Dr. Jim Henderson), Ramsey Ames (Laura), Spooks (Junior), Mack Gray (Lt. Reynolds), Molly Lamont (Miss Hartford, the secretary), John Meredith (Blind soldier), John Estes, Ralph Gardner (Patients), Doris Lloyd (Nurse), Charles D. Brown (Col. Starrett), Nelson Leigh (Bull Fiddler), Lane Chandler (Ship's officer), Cyril Ring (Laughton, <u>Life</u> photographer), Emmett Vogan (Harkness, <u>Life</u> reporter), Addison

Irene Dunne

Richards (MacDermott, *Life* editor), Frank LaRue (Mailman), Tony Marsh (First officer), Stanley Andrews (Australian officer), Leslie Denison (Reporter), Leyland Hodgson (Australian reporter), Bill Healy (Ship's officer), Frank Jenks (Chick Doyle), Ralph Dunn (Loomis), Billy Benedict (Joe, a soldier), Grandon Rhodes (George Grayson), Howard Hickman (Dr. Wood), Edwin Stanley (Taylor, film director), Roy Darmour (Eddie, assistant director), Carl Vernell (Terry Dennis, dance director), Tony Hughes (Man), Wallis Clark (Victory Committeeman), Richard Crane (Marine officer), Frank Wilcox (Captain Williams, Army doctor), Jimmy Carpenter, Bernard Thomas (Soldiers), Carey Harrison (Colonel), George Riley (Jimmy), Steve Brodie (Australian pilot), Jack Wegman (Mayor), Billy Wayne (Columnist), Clyde Cook, Bobby Barber (Stooges), Dick Nelson (Sergeant), John Whitney, Walter Tetley, Joel Allen, Carlyle Blackwell, Michael Kirk, Mel Schubert, Stephen Wayne, Charles King (Soldiers), Anthony Warde (Captain), William Forrest (Colonel), Tom Hanlon (Announcer), Don McGill, Franklin Parker (Men in office), Dennis Moore (H.V.C. officer), Odessa Lauren, Nancy Brinckman (Telephone operators), Martin Ashe (Man in office), Duke York (M.P.), Lennie Smith, Bob Ashley (Jitterbugs), Jackie Lou Harding, Genevieve Bell (People in montage), Edwin Stanley (Room clerk), Don Kramer, Allan Cooke, Luis Torres Nicholai, John Duane, Ed Browne, Clair Freeman, Bill Meader, Eddie Kover (Dancers), Lee Bennett (Acrobat), Daisy (Fifi), John Cason (Soldier of radio), George Eldredge (Submarine officer), Marie Osborne (Nurse), Nicodemus Stewart (Lt. Reynolds), George "Shorty" Chirello (Welles's assistant), Janice Gay, Jane Smith, Marjorie Fectean, Doris Brenn, Rosemary Battle, Lolita Leighter, Mary Rowland, Eleanor Counts, Linda Brent (Magic maids), Bill Wolf (Zoot suiter), Jeanette MacDonald, Orson Welles's Mercury Wonder Show, Marlene Dietrich, Dinah Shore, Donald O'Connor, Peggy Ryan, W.C. Fields, the Andrews Sisters, Arthur Rubinstein, Carmen Amaya and Her Company, Sophie Tucker, Delta Rhythm Boys, Leonard Gautier's Bricklayers, Agustin Castellon Sabicas, Ted Lewis and His Band, Freddie Slack and His Orchestra, Charlie Spivak and His Orchestra, Louis Jordan and His Orchestra, Louise Beavers, Clarence Muse, Maxie Rosenbloom, Maria Montez, Susanna Foster, Louise Allbritton, Robert Paige, Alan Curtis, Lon Chaney, Jr., Gloria Jean, Andy Devine, Turhan Bey, Evelyn Ankers, Noah Beery, Jr., Gale Sondergaard, Peter Coe, Nigel Bruce, Thomas Gomez, Lois Collier, Samuel S. Hinds, Randolph Scott, Martha O'Driscoll, Elyse Knox, Philo McCullough (Guest stars), Joan Bennett, Hedy Lamarr, Martha Scott, Irene Dunne (Stars in film clips).

SYNOPSIS: Hoofer Tony West is so busy with his career and

war efforts, organizing the Hollywood Victory Committee, that he neglects his wife Gloria Vance. She leaves him and has a baby. Tony learns he has become a father just before his ship sinks. Tony's work with the Hollywood Victory Committee, a wartime group of radio and film actors, gave the film the opportunity to showcase many stars.

REVIEWS:
<u>Variety</u>, 3.29.44: "Prime trouble with <u>Follow the Boys</u> is its over-generosity. The two hours and two minutes running time show that a good thing can be overdone. However, by and large, this salute to show business, with its galaxy of names, even though many are walk-throughs, makes '<u>Boys</u>' a cinch for biz boxoffice."

<u>New York Times</u>, 4.26.44: "Perhaps there are plenty of people who can take entertainment this way - with performers just standing before microphones and tossing it out loud and long. But it makes for cheap screen entertainment - and hardly a tribute to the players it presents."

NOTES: Released on May 5, 1944, <u>Follow the Boys</u> was Universal's answer to the all-star wartime musicals produced to boost morale. The film included clips of Irene Dunne, Joan Bennett, Hedy Lamarr, and Martha Scott doing U.S.O. appearances. Producer Charles K. Feldman was Irene's agent.

F-36 <u>Together Again</u>   (Columbia, 1944)   93 minutes

Producer: Virginia Van Upp. Director: Charles Vidor. Assistant director: Milton Feldman. Screenplay: Virginia Van Upp, F. Hugh Herbert, Stanley Russell, and Herbert Biberman. Music: Werner R. Heymann. Musical director: Morris W. Stoloff. Editor: Otto Meyer. Photography: Joseph Walker. Art directors: Stephen Goosson and Van Nest Polglase. Costumes: Jean Louis. Sets: Fay Babcock.

CAST: Irene Dunne (Anne Crandall), Charles Boyer (George Corday), Charles Coburn (Jonathan Crandall, Sr.), Mona Freeman (Diana Crandall), Jerome Courtland (Gilbert Parker), Elizabeth Patterson (Jessie), Charles Dingle (Morton Buchanan), Walter Baldwin (Witherspoon), Fern Emmett (Lillian), Frank Puglia (Leonardo), Janis Carter (Miss Thorn), Adele Jergens (Gilda LaVerne), Edwin Mills (Potter Kid), Virginia Sale (Secretary), Jessie Arnold, Isabel Withers, Virginia Brissac (Women), Sam Flint, Ferris Taylor, Fred Howard, Charles Marsh (Men), Carole Mathews, Shelley Winters, Adelle Roberts, Ann Loos (Girls), Carl "Alfalfa" Switzer (Elevator boy), Jimmy Lloyd (Master of ceremonies), Rafael Storm (Artist), Nina Mae McKinney (Maid), Ralph Dunn, James Flavin (Policemen), Constance Purdy, Jody Gilbert (Fat women), Wally Rose (News cameraman), Charles Arnt (Clerk), Paul Burns, Milton Kibbee (Workmen), Nora

Cecil (Woman at recital), Dudley Dickerson (Porter), Hobart Cavanaugh (Perc Mather), Jimmy Carpenter, Billy Lord, Bobby Alden (Newsboys), Billy Newell (Cab driver).

SYNOPSIS: Anne Crandall has been the mayor of a small Vermont town since her husband's death five years ago. She holds the position more out of family honor than for her own political aspirations. Newspaper editor Mort Buchanan runs against Anne, vowing to get rid of the Crandall rule. Her father-in-law Jonathan worries about Anne devoting her life to politics and her neurotic step-daughter Diana. Jonathan urges Anne to remarry and find her own life. When lightning hits a statue of Anne's dead husband, Jonathan takes it as a sign to find her a new mate. He sends her to New York to find a sculptor to commission a new statue, hoping she will fall in love. Anne meets artist George Corday. She is offended when he mistakes her for one of his models and orders her to take off her clothes, though she agrees to have dinner with him. Through a misunderstanding, Anne is arrested during a nightclub raid. She leaves New York hurriedly, embarrassed by the publicity and George's attentions. Despite Anne's insistance that George will not fit in Brookhaven, he follows her back to Vermont. Anne and George fall in love. She turns down his proposal because she feels a duty to the town. Diana soon develops a crush on George and mistakenly thinks he is proposing to her. Anne flirts with Diana's boyfriend to make Diana jealous. In order to get the lovers with their proper mates, Jonathan tells Mort about Anne's arrest. When a scandal errupts, Diana insists George marry Anne. Brookhaven rallies around Anne, believing no Crandall would cause a scandal. George tries to get her to withdraw from the election, but she refuses. Anne regrets her decision when he leaves town. Jonathan and Anne take it as a sign that she should resign her post when lightning knocks the head off the new statue, not knowing George loosened it. Free of her responsibilities, Anne returns to George in New York.

REVIEWS:
Variety, 11.8.44: "Miss Dunne and [Charles] Boyer competently team in the top spots - she as the pursued and he as the pursuer in the love match."

New York Morning Telegraph, 11.24.44: "Both principals [Irene Dunne and Charles Boyer] play their parts to the hilt..."

New York Times, 11.24.44: "In bringing Irene Dunne and Charles Boyer together again yesterday..., Columbia Pictures has fashioned a buoyant, featherweight entertainment that is eminently suited to its principals' talents....Miss Dunne and Mr. Boyer are...altogether diverting, and so is 'Together Again.'"

New York World-Telegram, 11.24.44: "The [Irene]

Dunne-[Charles] Boyer combination is a guarantee of deft handling of any such light humors as the picture offers."

See also R-42, R-67, B-74, B-97, B-112, B-177, B-250, B-258, B-391, B-416, B-430

NOTES: The title was an allusion to the re-teaming of Irene Dunne and Charles Boyer. The working title was <u>A Woman's Privilege</u>. Irene sang "Adios Muchachos." She and Boyer reprised their film roles on <u>The Screen Guild Players</u> (R-76).

F-37 <u>Over 21</u>   (Columbia, 1945)   102 minutes

    Producer: Sidney Buchman. Director: Charles Vidor. Assistant director: Ray Nazarro. Screenplay: Sidney Buchman. Based on the play by Ruth Gordon. Music: Marlin Skiles. Musical director: Morris W. Stoloff. Editor: Otto Meyer. Photography: Rudolph Mate. Art directors: Stephen Goosson and Rudolph Sternad. Sets: Louis Diage. Sound: Howard Fogetti.

    CAST: Irene Dunne (Paula Wharton), Alexander Knox (Max Wharton), Charles Coburn (Robert Gow), Jeff Donnell (Jan Lupton), Loren Tindall (Roy Lupton), Lee Patrick (Mrs. Foley), Phil Brown (Frank MacDougal), Cora Witherspoon (Mrs. Gates), Charles Evans (Colonel Foley), Pierre Watkin (Joel I. Nixon), Anne Loos (Mrs. Dumbrowski), Nanette Parks (Mrs. Clark), Adelle Roberts (Mrs. Collins), Jean Stevens (Mrs. Greenberg), Billy Lechner (Little boy), Robert Williams (Taxi driver), Abigail Adams, Francine Ames, Pat Jackson, Marilyn Johnson, Carole Mathews, Jo Gilbert (Officer candidates' wives), Charles Marsh (Howell), Dan Stowell (Male secretary), Robert Emmett Keane (Kennedy), Forbes Murray (Meredith), Cosmo Sardo (Barber), Alfred Allegro, Lillian Bronson (Secretaries), George Carleton (Hinkle), Doug Henderson, Michael Owen, George Peters, John James, Bob Merredith, William Hudson (Officer candidates), James Flavin (Captain), Rube Schaefer (Athletic instructor), George Bruggeman, Chuck Hamilton, LeRoy Taylor (Lieutenants), Gladys Blake (Girl), Wallace Pindell (Publicity man).

SYNOPSIS: Max Wharton is the managing editor of the <u>Bulletin</u>, a liberal New York newspaper. His wife Paula is a novelist and screenwriter. Max resigns from the newspaper and enlists in the army so that he can observe and comment on the post-war world from a soldier's viewpoint. The Whartons move to Florida, where Max struggles through officer candidate school and Paula gets used to crowded war conditions and rationing. Robert Gow, the <u>Bulletin's</u> publisher, wants Max back as editor and threatens to sell the paper if he does not return. Paula tries to prevent Robert from telling Max that the newspaper is failing

116 Irene Dunne

without him. She is afraid that the news will force Max to choose between his loyalty to the paper and his country, and that he will blame Robert if he fails his officer's exam. She writes a series of editorials under Max's name, incorporating his ideas about a post-war world of international cooperation. She keeps the editorials a secret from Max, wanting him to devote his complete attention to his studies. When Max is asked to speak at the graduation ceremonies, Paula realizes he knows about her writing. Max receives his commission and convinces Robert to hire Paula to replace him for the duration of the war.

REVIEWS:
Variety, 7.25.45: "As with the others, the character [of Paula] is slightly superficial, but in Miss Dunne's hands comes out as a choice job of miming."

New York Times, 8.17.45: "...to say that the sleek Miss Dunne plays it with [creator Ruth] Gordon's fluttery finesse - or even in a passing imitation - would be granting a little too much. She tries hard, that's plain - and she manages some amusing confusions at times. And, once in a while, she exhibits some fetching contrivances of her own. But the strong urge to ape Miss Gordon, not only in manner but in voice (although it may have been strictly unconscious), becomes monotonous and distracting after a time."

Time, 8.27.45: "...[Over 21] was supposed to have echoed, faintly at least, the fuming sincerity of PM's Ralph Ingersoll and the virtually unduplicable wit of Dorothy Parker. [Ruth] Gordon [who originated the role on Broadway] was well qualified to reverberate the Parker echoes. Miss Dunne, despite her own kinds of charm and humor, is not."

Theatre Arts, 10.45: "...Irene Dunne and Alexander Knox as the leading actors have put flesh and blood into [playwright Ruth] Gordon's more or less paste and paper characters....Irene Dunne, who can time a line so precisely that no seconds are wasted, and who wields a sizable vocabulary in the inflection of her voice, plays the spirited and resourceful wife with a generous undertone of warmth and understanding..."

See also B-139, B-177

NOTES: Ruth Gordon wrote and starred in the Broadway production of Over 21, which ran for 221 performances in 1944. The character of Paula was loosely based on writer Dorothy Parker. Many reviews pointed out the dissimilarity between Gordon and Irene Dunne, implying that Irene was miscast. Irene and Alexander Knox recreated their roles on The Lady Esther Screen Guild Theater (R-40).

F-38 Anna and the King of Siam (20th Century-Fox,

Filmography   117

1946)   128 minutes

Producer: Louis D. Lighton. Director: John Cromwell. Assistant director: Saul Wertzel. Screenplay: Talbot Jennings and Sally Benson. Based on the biography by Margaret Landon and books by Anna H. Leonowens. Music: Bernard Herman. Editor: Harmon Jones. Photography: Arthur Miller. Art directors: Lyle Wheeler and William Darling. Costumes: Bonnie Cashin. Sets: Thomas Little and Frank E. Hughes. Sound: Bernard Fredericks and Roger Heman. Makeup: Ben Nye. Special camera effects: Fred Sersen.

CAST: Irene Dunne (Anna Owens), Rex Harrison (King Mongkut), Linda Darnell (Tuptim), Lee J. Cobb (Kralahome), Gale Sondergaard (Lady Thiang), Mikhail Rasumny (Alak), Dennis Hoey (Sir Edward), Tito Renaldo (Prince, adult), William Edmunds (Moonshee), Richard Lyon (Louis Owens), John Abbott (Phya Phrom), Leonard Strong (Interpreter), Mickey Roth (Prince, child), Connie Leon (Beebe), Diana Van Den Ecker (Princess Fa-Ying), Si-lan Chen (Dancer), Marjorie Eaton (Miss MacFarlane), Helena Grant (Mrs. Cortwright), Stanley Mann (Mr. Cortwright), Addison Richards (Captain Orton), Neyle Morrow (Phra Palat), Yvonne Rob (Lady Sno Kim), Julian Rivero (Government clerk), Lorette Lucz, Chabing, Marianne Quon, Lillian Molieri, Buff Cobb, Sydney Logan (Wives of king), Oie chan (Old woman), Ted Hecht, Ben Weldon (Judges), Aram Katcher, Rico DeMontes (Guards), Pedro Regas (Guide), Hazel Shon (Slave), Chet Voravan (Siamese guard), Dorothy Chung, Jean Wong (Amazon guards).

SYNOPSIS: British widow Anna Owens goes to Siam in 1862 to teach the wives and children of King Mongkut. Anna is upset to learn that women have no rights in Siam and she sets out to change it. She is distressed when the king reneges on his promise to give her a house, forcing Anna and her son Louis to live in the harem. The king is enchanted by Anna and western ways, yet clings to barbaric traditions like groveling. Anna proves a fitting intellectual match, challenging his ideas. She preys on his conscience by teaching her pupils English proverbs, causing the king to build her a proper house. When she threatens to leave Siam, the prime minister convinces her to stay and advise the king about saving his country. She helps the king entertain European dignitaries and prove he is not a barbarian. Siam welcomes consulates from Europe and the United States. Anna grows to like and respect the king, but is repulsed when he executes a runaway wife without a trial. Anna plans to leave Siam, but the king's first wife begs her to stay and teach the heir to the throne, the only hope for the country. After Louis is killed in a riding accident, the king gets Anna out of her mourning by sending her back to work. As years go by, she takes a special interest in the first prince. On his deathbed, the king thanks Anna for helping his children and always being honest with him. The prince becomes king when his father dies. His first edict is abolishing the act of groveling that Anna so resented. She smiles with pride at the progress she helped initiate.

REVIEWS:
Variety, 6.5.46: "Irene Dunne does a superb enactment of Anna, the woman who influenced Siamese history by being teacher and confidante to a kingly barbarian."

New York Times, 6.21.46: "...Miss Dunne makes a regular bandbox heroine. She carries her bonneted head high, demonstrates wit with pretty modesty and eventually drops a tender, touching tear. Her lady is on a level with some that Greer Garson has played."

Newsweek, 6.24.44: "Anna Leonowens (Anna Owens for screen purposes) is impersonated by Irene Dunne with charm, good sense, and a nice appreciation of Occidental independence in an Oriental oligrachy....Miss Dunne's Anna is a plucky rebel in an Asiatic nest of extremely simple folk."

The Spectator, 8.16.46: "There is no sense of enchantment about Anna and the King of Siam. This is a charade more lavish than anything the wealthiest Edwardian country house could have provided. Everyone dresses up and plays around with [the] story....Rex Harrison and Irene Dunne go through their dressing-up and their lines with suitable skill."

The New Statesman and Nation, 8.17.46: "...the film is enormously long and spoilt [sic] by the usual miscastings and jumbled accents. It took me more than half an hour to get used to an Englishwoman talking American (Irene Dunne) and a Siamese King replying in pidgin English (Rex Harrison). An odd, clumsy, entertaining film."

See also R-66, D-11, B-164, B-175, B-263, B-266, B-277, B-305, B-310, B-442

NOTES: 20th Century-Fox purchased the screen rights to Margaret Landon's book from galley proofs in 1944. It took eighty-eight days to film the epic. Irene Dunne sang "There's No Place Like Home." Anna and the King of Siam premiered at Radio City Music Hall on June 20, 1946. In Hollywood, co-stars Irene Dunne and Rex Harrison put their foot and hand prints in the cement in front of Grauman's Chinese Theatre on July 8, 1946 to promote the film.

Time reported that Anna and the King of Siam was one of the first postwar films to use lavish pre-war style props. The movie's press agent valued the set, which spread over five acres of lot, at three hundred thousand dollars, the King's crowns at eighty-four thousand dollars, and the costumes at twenty-three thousand dollars ("The New Pictures." Time. June 24, 1946. p. 98.). The film won

Oscars for Cinematography and Art Direction and Interior Decoration, in addition to three other Academy Award nominations.

Linda Darnell, who played the king's runaway wife Tuptim, had a deadly fear of fires. The film called for her to be burned at the stake after the king thought she was unfaithful. Ironically, Darnell died in a fire in 1965.

Irene and Rex Harrison recreated their roles on The Lux Radio Theatre (R-44). Anna and the King of Siam was musicalized by Richard Rodgers and Oscar Hammerstein II in 1951. The Broadway production of The King and I starred Gertrude Lawrence and Yul Brynner. The musical was filmed by 20th Century-Fox in 1956 with Brynner and Deborah Kerr. Brynner continued touring in productions of the musical until his death in 1985. Additionally, he starred with Samantha Eggar in a non-musical TV series called Anna and the King for three months in 1972. Because of its many incarnations, Anna and the King of Siam was withheld from television until 1969. Some critics have noted that Irene would have been a prime candidate for the film The King and I if she had been younger. Marni Nixon dubbed most of Kerr's vocals in the movie. During the 1950s, Irene occasionally sang selections from the musical on television variety shows.

F-39 Life with Father (Warner Bros., 1947)
      118 minutes color

  Producer: Robert Bucker. Director: Michael Curtiz. Assistant director: Robert Vreeland. Dialogue director: Herschel Daugherty. Screenplay: Donald Ogden Stewart. Based on the play by Howard Lindsay and Russel Crouse, and the books by Clarence Day, Jr. Music: Max Steiner. Musical director: Leo F. Forbstein. Orchestral arrangements: Murray Cutter. Editor: George Amy. Photography: Peverell Marley and William V. Skall. Technicolor directors: Natalie Kalmus and Monroe W. Burbank. Art director: Robert Haas. Costumes: Milo Anderson. Sets: James Hopkins. Sound: C.A. Riggs. Technical advisor: Mrs. Clarence Day, Jr. Makeup: Perc Westmore. Montages: James Leicester. Special effects: William McGann and Ray Foster.

  CAST: William Powell (Clarence Day), Irene Dunne (Vinnie Day), Elizabeth Taylor (Mary Skinner), Edmund Gwenn (Rev. Dr. Lloyd), ZaSu Pitts (Cora Cartwright), Jimmy Lydon (Clarence Day, Jr.), Emma Dunn (Margaret), Moroni Olsen (Dr. Humphries), Elizabeth Risdon (Mrs. Whitehead), Derek Scott (Harlan Day), Johnny Calkins (Whitney Day), Martin Milner (John Day), Heather Wilde (Annie), Monte Blue (Policeman), Nancy Duff (Delia), Mary Field (Nora), Queenie Leonard (Maggie), Clara Blandick (Miss Wiggins), Frank Elliott (Dr. Somers),

Clara Reid (Scrub woman), Philo McCulough (Milkman), Lois Bridge (Corsetierre), George Meader (Salesman), Douglas Kennedy (Mr. Morley), Phil Van Zandt (Clerk), Russell Arms (Stock quotation operator), Faith Kruger (Hilda), Jean Del Val (Francois), Michael and Ralph Mineo (Twins), Creighton Hale (Father of twins), Jean Andren (Mother of twins), Elaine Lange (Ellen), Jack Martin (Chef), Arlene Dahl (Girl in Delmonico's), Gertrude Valerie, David Cavendish, Henry Sylvester, Hallene Hill, Laura Treadwell (Churchgoers), John Beck (Perkins, the clerk), James Metcalf (Customer), Joe Bernard (Cashier), Lucille Shamberger (Nurse maid).

SYNOPSIS: The Days are a Victorian New York family headed by an irascible patriarch, Clarence. He complains about finances, religion, and politics, frightening the Days' servants. Annoyed with his wife Vinnie's penchant for buying useless knickknacks, he agrees to open charge accounts to improve her bookkeeping. Clarence is furious when he is forced to entertain cousin Cora and her young friend Mary Skinner, who soon takes an interest in Clarence, Jr. The elder Day is even more upset when an innocent question from Mary reveals that he was never baptized. The family gangs up on Clarence, trying to convince him that he is headed for hell without baptism. Vinnie takes to her bed, upset by her husband's stubbornness. To earn money for a new suit to impress Mary, Clarence, Jr. sells tonic. Believing Vinnie's illness is real, he gives her some tonic and nearly poisons her. Vinnie uses her illness to maneuver Clarence to church. Worrying his wife is dying, he agrees to be baptized. Vinnie recovers and charges an ugly china dog. She arranges Clarence's baptism, although he tries to break his promise. When Vinnie agrees to exchange the dog, the family heads off for Clarence's baptism.

REVIEWS:
Good Housekeeping, 7.47: "It's always fun to talk about pictures we can recommend wholeheartedly. Life with Father is one....William Powell is the tyrannical father, Irene Dunne the mother."

Hollywood Reporter, 8.15.47: "Irene Dunne is Vinnie and a happier choice for the assignment would be difficult to imagine. Miss Dunne, stunning in the period costumes, etches a rich, warm portrait of an American mother whose grace and charm are born of forbearance and tolerance."

New York Times, 8.16.47: "It is almost unpardonable not to have mentioned Irene Dunne before this because she interprets Vinnie Day with charm, wit and an exactness that perfectly complement [William] Powell's Father. The way she finally cajoles her rebellious husband into making the journey up to Audubon Park to submit to the baptismal rites which his parents had somehow overlooked is handled by Miss Dunne with great charm and feminine wile."

Newsweek, 8.18.47: "Miss Dunne is nearly perfect in her role, playing the meek, yet adamant, Vinnie with a toned-down version of her own particular brand of comedy, and getting her effects by suggestion more often than by outright action."

Variety, 8.20.47: "Miss Dunne and [William] Powell have captured to a considerable extent the play's charm....Miss Dunne compares very favorably with the Dorothy Stickney original [stage] role, exacting the comedy from the part without overplaying it."

Chicago Tribune, 8.22.47: "Irene Dunne's Mrs. Day is gently willful and charming to see in the demure furbelows of the '80s....[The film] is completely entertaining, and I can't imagine any person to whom it would not be entirely satisfactory fare."

Time, 8.25.47: "...Irene Dunne seems to understand Mother. Father was put on film when the play was already an enormous success. It is filmed like a success; it has the glitter, the good humor and the rather beefy adroitness of a success. The chances are a hundred to one that it will be a success."

Theatre Arts, 10.47: "...no effort has been spared to reproduce the proven delights of the original [Broadway production]....They have cast it with care and drawn splendid portrayls from the players, all the way from William Powell and Irene Dunne as Father Day and Vinnie his wife down to Derek Scott, the scowling charmer who portrays the littlest Day."

See also D-14, B-18, B-38, B-92, B-129, B-134, B-180, B-278, B-290, B-313, B-362, B-424, B-470

NOTES: The stage version of Life with Father ran 3,224 performances, holding the record for the longest non-musical run on Broadway. The play was almost sidetracked. Clarence Day, Jr. was on his deathbed when he wrote the books God and My Father, Life with Father, and Life with Mother, which became the basis for the play and film. Day was ready to sell the rights to his books to Paramount, but changed his mind when he learned they planned to use them as vehicles for W.C. Fields. Playwrights Russel Crouse and Howard Lindsay stepped in and turned the books into a stage comedy. After numerous stars turned down the Broadway roles, Lindsay and his wife Dorothy Stickney became Clarence and Vinnie Day. After a five-year run, the show closed and Lindsay and Crouse wrote a sequel entitled Life with Mother, which ran for 265 performances with Lindsay and Stickney reprising their roles.

Lillian Gish appeared in the Chicago production of Life with Father. She told her friend Mary Pickford that the role would be a perfect vehicle for her screen comeback.

However, Pickford procrastinated about obtaining the film rights, and Warner Bros. acquired the play. Pickford made several tests for the role of Vinnie, but the studio worried about her box office popularity after a thirteen-year absence from the screen. In the end, director Michael Curtiz vetoed her. He preferred Irene Dunne, who repeatedly refused the role, insisting Vinnie was unsympathetic. At the last minute, Irene gave in and accepted the part. Casting Clarence was much easier. Initially, William Powell had tried to convince MGM to purchase the film rights to Life with Father, but they were outbid by Warner Bros. Lindsay disqualified himself after testing for the role, leaving Warner Bros. to borrow Powell's services from MGM and cast him as Clarence.

Before filming began, the cast was taken to Perc Westmore's salon to have their hair dyed red on a Sunday morning. When it was time to rinse the dye, the beauticians discovered that the water had been turned off for the entire block because they were repairing the street. Because dyes were so strong then, leaving them on could have caused the cast to lose their hair. Luckily, someone suggested diluting the dye with cold cream. Further troubles ensued when it came time for Warner Bros. to give its stars equal billing. To satisfy fans of William Powell and Irene Dunne, as well as their agents, the studio had flashing lights alternate each name in the opening credits. Print advertising also alternated, top billing Irene one day and Powell the next.

Shooting began in August, 1946. Lindsay and Crouse, as well as Clarence Day, Jr.'s widow, were on the set most of the time and were given veto power on all aspects of the film. According to David Chierichetti, Mrs. Day approved of Irene's characterization and lent Irene some jewelry that belonged to the real Vinnie (B-278). Irene sang "Sweet Marie."

Life with Father had its world premiere on August 14, 1947 in Skowhegan, Maine, where the play had its initial performance eight years before. Warner Bros. rereleased the film in 1948. Although there was no remake to hold back a television sale, as with many of Irene's films, Life with Father was withheld from television for many years. Chierichetti explained that when the studio first sold a package of films to television, Life with Father could not be included because Warner Bros. had agreed not to distribute the film to any media after 1954. In 1970, the studio, authors, and producer reached a new agreement that provided a network television sale (B-278). Leon Ames and Lurene Tuttle portrayed Clarence and Vinnie in a TV version, which ran on CBS from 1953-55. Life with Father was Irene's only full-length color film. Despite its popularity, Irene continued to call Vinnie the only character she disliked.

F-40   I Remember Mama   (RKO, 1948)   134 minutes

Executive producers: George Stevens and Dore Schary. Producer: Harriet Parsons. Director: George Stevens. Assistant director: John H. Morse. Screenplay: DeWitt Bodeen. Based on the novel <u>Mama's Bank Account</u> by Kathryn Forbes and the play <u>I Remember Mama</u> by John Van Druten. Music: Roy Webb. Musical director: Constantin Bakaleinikoff. Editors: Robert Swink and Tholen Gladden. Photography: Nicholas Musuraca. Art directors: Albert S. D'Agostino and Carroll Clark. Costumes: Edward Stevenson and Gile Steele. Sets: Darrell Silvera and Emile Kuri. Sound: Richard Van Hessen and Terry Kellum. Makeup: Gordon Bau. Hairstyles: Hazel Rogers. Special effects: Russell A. Cully and Kenneth Peach.

CAST: Irene Dunne (Mama), Barbara Bel Geddes (Katrin), Oscar Homolka (Uncle Chris), Philip Dorn (Papa), Sir Cedric Hardwicke (Mr. Hyde), Edgar Bergen (Peter Thorkelson), Rudy Vallee (Dr. Johnson), Barbara O'Neil (Jessie Brown), Florence Bates (Florence Dana Moorehead), Peggy McIntyre (Christine), June Hedin (Dagmar), Steve Brown (Nels), Ellen Corby (Aunt Trina), Hope Landin (Aunt Jenny), Edith Evanson (Aunt Sigrid), Tommy Ivo (Cousin Arne), Lela Bliss, Constance Purdy (Nurses), Stanley Andrews (Minister), Franklyn Farnum (Man), Cleo Ridgley (Schoolteacher), George Atkinson (Postman), Howard Keiser (Bellboy), Ruth Tobey, Alice Kerbert, Peggy McKim, Peggy Kerbert (Girls).

SYNOPSIS: Writer Katrin Hanson types a story about her Norwegian immigrant family, headed by her wise and generous mother. As Katrin reads, a series of flashbacks recalls her youth in 1910 San Francisco and how it influenced her writing. The family is introduced to the classics through their border, Mr. Hyde, who reads aloud to them every night. When he flees without paying his rent, he leaves his books behind, with Mama assuring the family that he gave them something far more valuable than money. Katrin remembers a right of passage after her eighth grade graduation. When Katrin learns Mama sold her heirloom broach to buy Katrin a coveted dresser set, Katrin exchanges the gift and returns Mama's broach. Feeling her daughter is an adult, Mama gives her the broach and her first cup of coffee. Katrin recalls boisterous Uncle Chris, the family patriarch who scares everyone but Mama. On his deathbed, the family learns Chris had a soft side. Instead of squandering his money on liquor and women, as they suspected, Chris paid for operations to help lame people walk. Katrin remembers how her mother influenced her writing. After receiving many rejection notices, Katrin is ready to give up her career. Mama takes her stories to novelist Florence Dana Moorehead, trading recipes for a critique of her daughter's talent. Moorehead says Katrin is gifted, but encourages her to write what she knows. Moorehead passes along her agent's address. Katrin sells a story about Mama for five hundred dollars and insists it go into the family bank account. Mama confesses that she made up the bank account to give the children security, but they no longer need to worry. Katrin reads her story to the family.

REVIEWS:
Variety, 3.10.48: "Irene Dunne, who played a New York mom in Warners's 'Life with Father,' is the central pillar of this production. In holding down the most demanding role of her career, she earns new honors as an actress of outstanding versatility. Her Norwegian dialect sounds queer for the first couple of minutes but soon establishes itself solidly as a natural part of her lingo. In general, her role is marked by a great strength and sympathy that makes her symbolize all mothers. That won't hurt the [box office] either."

New York Times, 3.12.48: "As Mama, the wheel-horse of the family, Irene Dunne does a beautiful job, in a blonde, braided wig and in dresses which actually appear to be worn. Handling with equal facility an accent and a troubled look, Miss Dunne has the strength and vitality, yet the softness, that the role requires."

Newsweek, 3.29.48: "Irene Dunne, wearing a blond wig and conjuring up an acceptable accent, does a fine job as Mama..."

Time, 4.5.48: "The casting is wise and the acting is almost entirely satisfying. Miss Dunne, who has been prone to hurt her serious roles with snobbish or ironic undertones, takes her tongue out of her cheek and gives a performance that is warm, disciplined and unaffected."

Life, 4.12.48: "Director [George] Stevens has astutely guided his cast into some of the most convincing performances on record. Most notable: Irene Dunne, with a charming Norwegian accent, as Mama..."

The Spectator, 7.23.48: "On Mama rests the whole burden of living, and Miss Irene Dunne, patient and resourceful without being pi [sic], is admirable in the part."

The New Statesman and Nation, 7.24.48: "Mama is a charmer; with Miss Irene Dunne playing the part, and subduing her fun artfully, she could hardly fail to be....I Remember Mama is little more than a series of sketches strung together, too sweet at times, too intentionally endearing in its fun, but possessed of a decided charm."

See also R-59, R-65, A-27, A-31, A-32, A-70, B-18, B-85, B-120, B-166, B-187, B-202, B-213, B-218, B-238, B-278, B-290, B-312, B-321, B-345, B-347, B-371, B-372, B-373, B-374, B-375, B-382, B-421, B-468, B-490

Filmography   125

NOTES: Producer Harriet Parsons, daughter of columnist Louella Parsons, was enchanted by Kathryn Forbes's tales of her Norwegian family in Mama's Bank Account. When Parsons learned that her studio, RKO, had purchased the rights to the book, she asked to produce the film. During preproduction, Richard Rodgers and Oscar Hammerstein II acquired the rights from RKO. They hired John Van Druten to write and direct a stage production based on the book. I Remember Mama marked the first play produced by composers Rodgers and Hammerstein. It was a critical and financial success, opening on October 19, 1944 and running for 714 performances. Mady Christians starred as Mama; Marlon Brando made his Broadway debut as son Nels. RKO re-acquired the film rights. Despite the attention of other producers, the studio returned the property to Parsons.

The role of Mama was originally offered to Greta Garbo, who turned it down. Irene Dunne was reluctant to take the part, since it might typecast her in character roles. However, she agreed to make the film, providing RKO hire one of five directors of her choosing. They agreed on George Stevens, who had directed Irene in Penny Serenade. The film was partially shot on location in San Francisco. Irene sang a Norwegian lullaby.

I Remember Mama premiered at Radio City Music Hall in March, 1948. According to The RKO Story, it failed to turn a profit because of an excessive negative cost of over $3 million, despite critical and popular acclaim (B-238). The film received five Academy Award nominations, including Irene's fifth Best Actress nod. She lost to Jane Wyman for Johnny Belinda. In April, 1948, Louella Parsons awarded the film Cosmopolitan's Citation for the best picture of the month and Irene Dunne Cosmopolitan's Citation for best feminine starring performance. I Remember Mama came in third in Film Daily's twenty-seventh annual "Best Picture" poll, placing behind Gentleman's Agreement and Johnny Belinda. Irene, Barbara Bel Geddes, and Oscar Homolka recreated their roles on The Lux Radio Theatre (R-54).

A TV version, entitled Mama, ran from 1949-56 on CBS. Ironically, Mama was played by Peggy Wood, who Irene replaced in a tour of The Clinging Vine in 1924. Richard Rodgers and Martin Charnin wrote a musical version of I Remember Mama in 1979. The Broadway show, which was Rodgers's last, starred Liv Ullman.

F-41 Never a Dull Moment   (RKO, 1950)   89 minutes

Producer: Harriet Parsons. Director: George Marshall. Screenplay: Lou Breslow and Doris Anderson. Based on the novel Who Could Ask for Anything More by Kay Swift. Songs: Kay Swift. Music: Frederick Hollander. Musical director: C. Bakaleinikoff. Editor: Robert Swink. Photography: Joseph Walker. Art directors: Albert S. D'Agostino and Walter E. Keller. Costumes: Travis Banton. Sets: Darrell Silvera and Jack Mills. Sound: Phil Brigandi and Clem Portman. Makeup: Mel Berns. Hair: Larry Germain.

CAST: Irene Dunne (Kay Kingsley), Fred MacMurray (Chris Hayward), William Demarest (Mears), Andy Devine (Orvie), Gigi Perreau (Tina Hayward), Natalie Wood (Nan Hayward), Philip Ober (Jed), Jack Kirkwood (Papa Dude), Ann Doran (Jean Morrow), Margaret Gibson (Pokey), Lela Bliss (Mama Dude), Irving Bacon (Tunk Johnson), Victoria Horne, Connie Van, Virginia Mullen, Edna Holland (Women), Gene Evan, Olin Howlin, Paul Newman (Hunters), Ann O'Neal (Julia Craddock), Chester Jim Hawkins (Chalmers), Alan Dinehart III (Sonny Boy), Jo Ann Marlowe (Sister), Jacqueline De Witt (Myra Van Elson), Bob Thom, Carl Sklover, Art Dupuis (Vendors).

SYNOPSIS: Kay Kingsley is a Manhattan songwriter who meets widowed rancher Chris Hayward at a rodeo benefit. His ranch hand Orvie intercedes, dragging Chris to Kay's apartment for a date. After a whirlwind courtship, they fall in love and marry. Chris takes his bride to his Wyoming ranch, where she has trouble winning over his daughters and adjusting to rural living. She befriends Chris's former girlfriend, who teaches Kay how to be a ranch wife. Kay's former partner Jed tries to convince her to collaborate on a new show. She considers the offer so that she can buy a bigger ranch with its own water supply so the Haywards do not have to depend on their stingy neighbor, Mr. Mears. However, Kay decides Chris needs her too much to spare her even a few weeks, so she turns down Jed's offer. Running short on water, Kay convinces Mears to expand their rights. However the celebration is short-lived when she accidently shoots his prize bull. Furious, Mears cuts off their water supply completely. Kay and Chris have an argument and Kay returns to New York. Chris goes back on the rodeo circuit to make enough money to buy another ranch; she tries to write Jed's show. Both find they cannot work without the other. Orvie reunites the family and they head back to the ranch.

REVIEWS:
Variety, 11.1.50: "Comedy is broad as played by Irene Dunne, Fred MacMurray and others, and the star names will give it some marquee help....Three songs are spotted in the footage, all written by Kay Swift, who authored the novel on which the Lou Breslow-Doris Anderson script was based. Numbers are 'Once You Find Your Guy,' 'The Man with the Big Felt Hat,' and 'Sagebrush Lullaby,' all sung by Miss Dunne with just moderately successful vocals."

New York Times, 11.22.50: "Pretending to tell the story of a lady song writer who marries a rodeo hand and goes to live with him on his ranch in Wyoming, with supposedly comical results, its sole achievement as entertainment is the presentation of Irene Dunne in a series of rustic encounters that are about as funny as stepping on a nail."

<u>Library Journal</u>, 12.1.50: "This amiable lighthearted comedy does not always live up to its title for there are occasional dull moments and forced incidents....Irene Dunne is the Park Avenue heroine of the story and most of the laughs derive from her attempt to adapt herself to the way of life on a Western cattle ranch. She is at home in the New York episodes, but never seems completely assimilated by her Western world..."

<u>Newsweek</u>, 12.4.50: "The best that can be said for this somewhat undernourished farce is that [Irene] Dunne,... tackles her indoctrination as a 'fair hand' about the place with commendable stamina....Between pratfalls Miss Dunne takes advantage of a pleasant number called 'The Man with the Big Felt Hat' to demonstrate she can still sing when she gets a chance."

<u>The Christian Century</u>, 1.24.51: "Film depends on obvious slapstick for most of its fun, is often labored but provides good escapist entertainment."

See also B-238

NOTES: <u>Never a Dull Moment</u> reunited Irene Dunne with her <u>Invitation to Happiness</u> co-star, Fred MacMurray. She sang "Once You Find Your Guy," "Ti-Yi-Yippee-Yippee-Yay," "Sagebrush Lullaby," and "The Man with a Big Felt Hat." <u>Never a Dull Moment</u> was called <u>Come Share My Love</u> before its release. The film was based on Kay Swift's 1943 autobiographical novel <u>Who Could Ask for Anything More</u>. Swift also wrote the film's songs.

F-42 <u>The Mudlark</u>   (20th Century-Fox, 1950)   99 minutes

> Producer: Nunnally Johnson. Director: Jean Negulesco. Screenplay: Nunnally Johnson. Based on the novel by Theodore Bonnett. Music: William Alwyn. Editor: Thelma Myers. Photography: Georges Perinal. Art director: C.P. Norman. Sound: Buster Ambler. Special effects: W. Percy Day. Dialogue coach: George More O'Ferrall.
>
> CAST: Irene Dunne (Queen Victoria), Alec Guinness (Prime Minister Benjamin Disraeli), Andrew Ray (Wheeler the mudlark), Beatrice Campbell (Lady Emily Prior), Finlay Currie (John Brown), Anthony Steel (Lieutenant Charles McHatten), Raymond Lovell (Sergeant Footman Naseby), Marjorie Fielding (Lady Margaret Prior), Constance Smith (Kate Noonan), Ronan O'Casey (Slattery), Edward Rigby (Watchman), Robin Stevens (Herbert), William Strange (Sparrow), Kynaston Reeves (General Sir Henry Ponsonby), Wilfred Hyde-White (Tucker), Ernest Clark (Hammond), Eric Messiter (Ash, lieutenant of police), Pamela Arliss

Fans disliked Irene Dunne hiding beneath makeup and padding to portray Queen Victoria in *The Mudlark* (20th Century-Fox, 1950). (Doug McClelland collection)

(Princess Christian), Ian Selby (Prince Christian), Maurice Warren (Christian), Michael Brooke (Albert), Jane Short (Victoria), Howard Douglas (Broom), Richmond Nairne (Didbit), George Dillon (Jailer), Leonard Sharp (Ben Fox), Vi Kaley (Mrs. Feeney), Freddie Watts (Iron George), Y. Yanai (Al Hook), Paul Garrard (Petey), Leonard Morris (Hooker Morgan), Marjorie Gresley (Meg Bownes), Bob Head (Dandy Fitch), Vi Stevens (Mrs. Dawkins), Alan Gordon (Disraeli's valet), Grace Denbeigh Russell (Queen's maid), Patricia Hitchcock.

SYNOPSIS: Wheeler is a poor, illiterate, nine-year-old orphan, who finds a medallion picturing Queen Victoria. When Wheeler hears the queen is the mother of England, his curiosity peaks. He decides to go to Windsor Castle to meet the queen, despite the fact that she is in seclusion, still mourning the death of Prince Albert after fifteen years. Wheeler sneaks through the gate and falls down a coal chute, landing in the castle. Meanwhile, Prime Minister Disraeli urges the queen to get on with her life so that they may work on England's reform program, which includes assistance and education for the poor. Wheeler hides in the castle, in hopes of meeting the queen. He falls asleep behind a curtain in the dining room and the queen hears his snoring. He is jailed by the guards, who fear he is part of a plot to assassinate the queen. After the experience, the queen decides to remain in seclusion, despite Disraeli's protests. She insists Disraeli not discuss the matter in Parliament. An Irish representative asks Disraeli to deny any Irish conspiracy involving Wheeler during the Parliament session. Despite the queen's orders, Disraeli uses the occasion to express need for reform in England and for the queen to return to public life. Disraeli arranges for Wheeler to be cared for and educated. Wheeler returns to the castle and charms the queen. To Disraeli's delight, she changes her mind about returning to public life.

REVIEWS:
Variety, 11.8.50: "The Queen's eventual meeting with the young mudlark is an emotional triumph for both Miss Dunne and Andrew Ray, and is a certain tear-jerker for the femme customers....Intricate makeup for Miss Dunne brought about an astounding likeness to Victoria. Despite its obvious restrictions on facial expressions, she brought to life the lonely Mother of England who shunned the outer world and canonized her Prince."

Saturday Review of Literature, 12.23.50: "...Irene Dunne's natural exuberance has been effectively cloaked by the clothes and mask of Queen Victoria, the charm of her speaking voice converted into the hoarse, measured tones of an old woman. Hers is less a performance than an impersonation, a diligent but unpersuasive reading of an impossible role."

New York Times, 12.25.50: "Alongside of [Alec Guinness's performance], the performance of Irene Dunne in the Victoria role is labored and superficial. Unfortunately, through no fault of hers, she is not possessed of the nature of the talent to do this job. And although she is made up stoutly to look like the overstuffed queen, she conveys very little illusion or real emotion, which is sadly missed."

Library Journal, 1.1.51: "Within the framework of a disciplined queen, Irene Dunne is authentically impressive."

Time, 1.1.51: "At the head of an otherwise all-British cast, Actress [Irene] Dunne shares honors with her make-up [sic] man for a competent, unspectacular performance."

New Yorker, 1.6.51: "The makeup man has converted [Irene] Dunne into a reasonable likeness of the Queen, but the actress conveys none of the stubborn vitality that made Victoria such a handful."

See also B-8, B-29, B-34, B-227, B-276, B-289, B-290, B-304, B-404, B-442, B-468, B-469, B-481

NOTES: In March, 1950, British Actors Equity protested the choice of Irene Dunne to portray Queen Victoria, arguing that the role should be essayed by an English actress. By the time the film began shooting in England that summer, the furor had disappeared. On October 30, 1950, The Mudlark was chosen as a Command Performance for the royal family, causing another outcry in the British press. According to Newsweek, the American press reported that the film helped cement relations between the United States and England. However, Newsweek quoted several London sources, which labeled The Mudlark "dull" and called Irene Dunne's performance "the most unmoved Victoria we have had so far" ("Royal Trouble." November 13, 1950.). Despite the acting challenge it provided Irene, most of her fans disliked her hiding behind makeup and padding. She later admitted that the film was a mistake. Irene and Sir Cedric Hardwicke performed The Mudlark on The Lux Radio Theatre (R-77).

F-43 It Grows on Trees   (Universal, 1952)   84 minutes

Producer: Leonard Goldstein. Director: Arthur Lubin. Assistant director: John Sherwood. Screenplay: Leonard Praskins and Barney Slater. Music: Frank Skinner. Editor: Milton Carruth. Photography: Maury Gertsman. Art directors: Bernard Herzbrun and Alexander Golitzen. Costumes: Bill Thomas. Sets: Russell A. Gausman and Julia Heron. Sound: Leslie I. Carey and Richard DeWeese. Makeup: Bud Westmore. Hairstyles: Joan St. Oegger.

CAST: Irene Dunne (Polly Baxter), Dean Jagger (Phil Baxter), Joan Evans (Diane Baxter), Richard Crenna (Ralph Bowen), Edith Meiser (Mrs. Pryor), Sandy

Descher (Midge Baxter), Dee Pollock (Flip Baxter), Les Tremayne (Finlay Murchison), Malcolm Lee Beggs (Henry Carrollman), Forrest Lewis (Dr. Harold Burrows), Frank Ferguson (John Letherby), Bob Sweeney (McGuire), Emile Avery (TV man), John Damler (Cleanshave), Clark Howat (Mustache), Elmer Peterson (Commentator), Dee J. Thompson (Miss Reid), Thurston Hall (Sleamish), Cliff Clark (Sergeant), Madge Blake (Woman), Hal K. Dawson (Tutt), Jimmy Dodd (Treeburger proprietor), Anthony Radecki, Perc Launders, Charles Gibb, Charles McAvoy (Policemen), Mary Benoit, Vera Burnett (Assistants), William O'Leary (Gonnigle), Bob Carney (Bus driver), Burman Bodel (Badge vendor), Ralph Montgomery (Umbrella vendor), Jack Reynolds (Reporter), Bob Edgecomb (Interviewer), Jeanne Blackford (Lady), Frank Howard, Robert Strong (Ad lib cameramen), Walter Clinton (Delivery man), Chuck Courtney (Paper man).

SYNOPSIS: The Baxters are a loving, middle-class family, plagued by financial woes. Polly and Phil are startled when a five-dollar bill floats through the window, temporarily taking care of their problems. More money turns up unexpectedly and Polly insists that it is coming from a higher power who knows they need it. Phil refuses to believe her whimsical notions and prohibits her from spending any of the mysterious cash. Polly discovers that the five- and ten-dollar bills are growing on some new trees in their backyard, but keeps it a secret. After Polly receives a light-hearted response from the Treasury Department about the authenticity of the cash, she goes on a spending spree and pays off the mortgage. Phil returns from a business trip with tales of being in jail for passing counterfeit money. Like leaves, the bills crumble after a few days. Polly is horrified, but does not tell anyone. Daughter Diane's fiance Ralph ends up in jail when he refuses to tell the bank who paid off a mortgage with the disintegrating cash. Polly tells Phil about the trees, but he does not believe her. A reporter picks up on the story, turning the Baxters' home into a tourist attraction. Government representatives ask Polly to make a statement, claiming the whole thing was a joke. Polly, still believing that the world needs more wonder, insists the money tree is real. A government botanist verifies her claim and insists she turn over the trees for the sake of the economy. Polly is reimbursed for the money she spent. However, the government men quickly take back their checks when a frost kills the trees. Undaunted, Polly opens a basket of treasures she bought at a blind auction. She discovers a lamp and rubs it optimistically, never losing her wonder as smoke begins to pour out.

REVIEWS:
Variety, 11.5.52: "Miss Dunne and [Dean] Jagger are a slick pairing and capably sell the whimsy and the folksy flavor that predominates the presentation."

132   Irene Dunne

New York Times, 11.29.52: "...Miss Dunne's arch refinement throughout underlines the basic coyness of a joke that makes its point and dingdongs itself to death."

See also B-116, B-179, B-289

NOTES: *It Grows on Trees* was Irene Dunne's final film. She was later quoted as saying that it might have been more successful with the light touch of a leading man like Cary Grant or with a big name director. She said she took the role because of the fantasy involved, but the finished film came out too realistically.

FILM SHORTS:
FS-1   *The Stolen Jools* (AKA *The Slippery Pearls*)
       (1932)   2 reels

       CAST: Buster Keaton, Joe E. Brown, Norma Shearer, Barbara Stanwyck, Frank Fay, Stan Laurel, Oliver Hardy, Edward G. Robinson, Irene Dunne, Maurice Chevalier, Mitzi Green, Wallace Beery, Our Gang, Joan Crawford, William Haines, Winnie Lightner, Fifi D'Orsay, Warner Baxter, Bert Wheeler, Robert Woolsey, Richard Dix, Gary Cooper, Eugene Pallette, Douglas Fairbanks, Jr., Loretta Young, Richard Barthelmess, Charles Butterworth, Ben Lyons, Bebe Daniels, Jack Oakie, Polly Moran, Jack Hill, Hedda Hopper, Eddie Kane, Dorothy Lee, El Brendel, Charlie Murray, Victor McLaglen, Claudia Dell, Edmund Lowe, Lowell Sherman, George Sidney, Fay Wray, Stuart Erwin, George "Gabby" Hayes, Skeets Gallagher, J. Farrell MacDonald, Buddy Rogers, George E. Stone, Wynne Gibson, Little Billy.

SYNOPSIS: After a celebrity-studded party, Norma Shearer discovers that her pearl necklace is missing. Thieves Edward G. Robinson and George E. Stone confess they wanted to steal it, but someone beat them to it. Detective Eddie Kane questions the all-star cast in a series of corny vignettes. Mitzi Green confesses that she saw Robinson and Stone hiding the necklace so she took it.

NOTES: The short was produced for the Masquers Club by National Variety Artists and Chesterfield cigarettes. Irene Dunne was questioned by Eddie Kane in a hotel lobby.

FS-2   *Show Business at War*   (20th Century-Fox, 1943)

       CAST: Louis Armstrong and his Band, Ethel Barrymore, Jack Benny, Linda Darnell, Marlene Dietrich, Irene Dunne, Kay Francis, Rita Hayworth, Hedy Lamarr, George Murphy, Lily Pons, Ginger Rogers, Anne Shirley, Frank Sinatra, Lana Turner, Orson Welles, Darryl F. Zanuck.

NOTE: Filmed by 20th Century-Fox for the "March of Time" series, *Show Business at War* showed film stars doing their bit during World War II.

FS-3 **Irene Dunne American Red Cross Fund Appeal**   (1949)
      2 minutes

NOTES: Irene Dunne was the campaign vice chairman for the 1949 American Red Cross Fund appeal. The short ran in thirteen thousand theatres around the country.

FS-4 **You Can Change the World**   (Cascade Pictures, 1949)
      30 minutes

    Producer: William Perlberg. Director: Leo McCarey. Assistant director: Alvin Ganzer. Screenplay: Richard Breen and Eugene Ling. Based on the books **You Can Change the World** and **Three Minutes a Day** by Father James Keller. Song: Johnny Burke and Jimmy Van Heusen. Editor: Paul Weatherwax. Art director: William E. Flannery.

    CAST: Irene Dunne, William Holden, Loretta Young, Bob Hope, Jack Benny, Eddie "Rochester" Anderson, Paul Douglas, Ann Blyth, Bing Crosby, Johnny Burke, Jimmy Van Heusen, Father James Keller.

SYNOPSIS: Jack Benny invites a group of his celebrity friends over to meet Father James Keller and discuss making a film for the Christophers. The stars talk about how each individual can play a part in changing the world for the better.

See also B-33, B-50, B-51, B-354

NOTES: This short was produced by the Christophers, a non-sectarian, anti-totalitarian, anti-Communist group, founded in 1945 by Father James Keller, a Maryknoll priest. In 1949, Keller announced that the Christophers would produce thirty non-profit films, which would "help throw out evil from American life." The project was budgeted at a million dollars, averaging thirty thousand dollars per film. The stars and director donated their talents to help the cause. **You Can Change the World** was filmed at the Hal Roach studio on November 30, 1949. Two hundred prints of the short were offered, without charge, to any interested groups throughout the country. At the time of the shooting, plans for the other twenty-nine shorts were pending, while the Christophers waited for donations. By the mid 1950s, sixteen films had been produced. **You Can Change the World** was released for television in 1952. Bing Crosby introduced the song "Early American" in the film.

FS-5 **A Story of Two Men**   (c. 1956)   30 minutes

    CAST: Irene Dunne, Ross Elliott, Aline Towne.

NOTES: This short, produced by the Christophers,

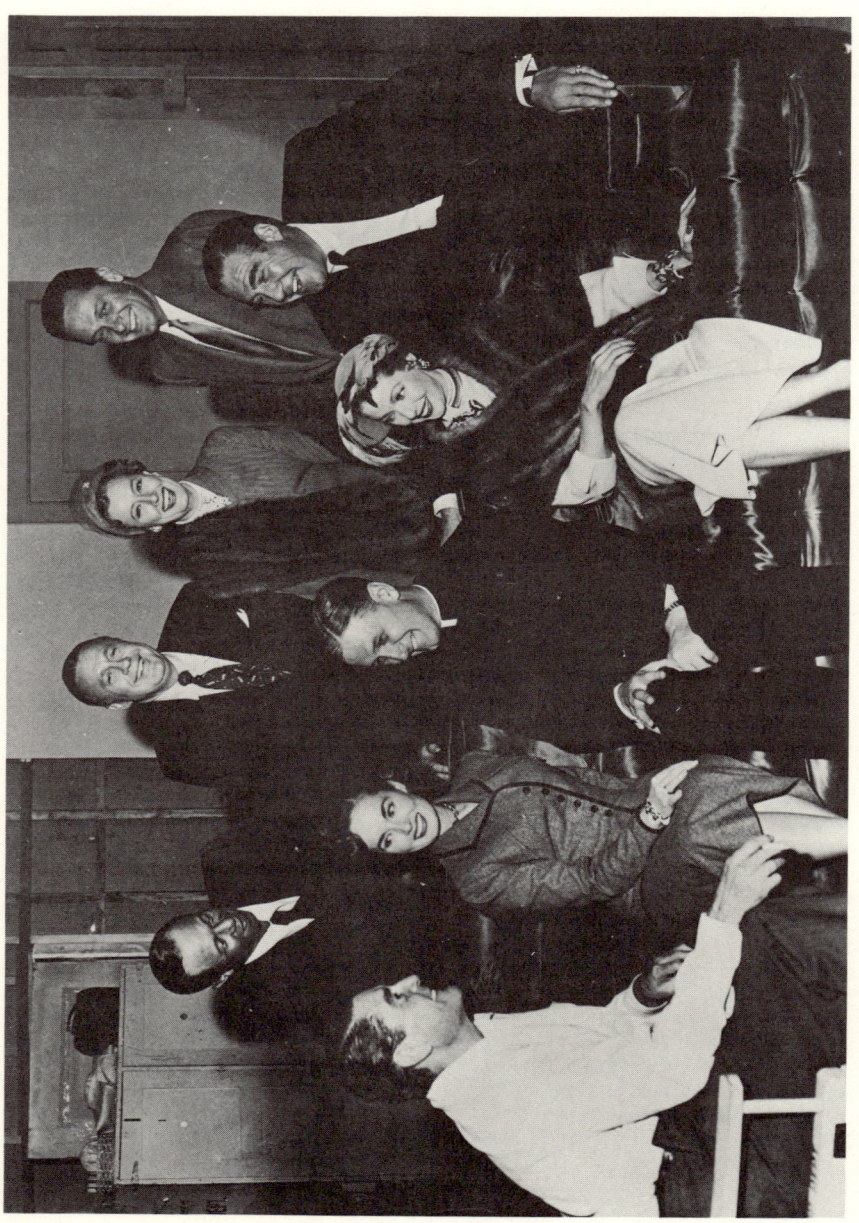

The cast of *You Can Change the World* (Cascade Pictures, 1949). *Back row:* Eddie "Rochester" Anderson, Jack Benny, Irene Dunne, William Holden. *Front row:* Director Leo McCarey, Ann Blyth, Father James Keller, Loretta Young, Paul Douglas. (The Christophers)

dramatized the life of Mentor Graham, Abraham Lincoln's first teacher. Irene Dunne introduced the story.

Radio

This chapter is a chronological listing of Irene Dunne's national radio appearances. Each entry is preceded by the letter "R." A typical entry includes the name of the series, episode title, date of broadcast, network, cast, and a brief description. Selected reviews are also provided.

A key to abreviations follows:
AFRS	Armed Forces Radio Service
ant	anthology
Mut	Mutual broadcasting network
NN	Non-Network (did not appear on ABC, CBS, NBC, or Mut)
ser	series
sp	special

R-1   Hollywood Hotel   1.25.35   CBS
Variety program with master of ceremonies Dick Powell, performances by Frances Langford, the Ted Fio Rito Orchestra, Jane Williams, Muzzy Marcellino, and Joy Hodges, and celebrity interviews by columnist Louella Parsons. Irene Dunne and Fred Astaire performed scenes from Roberta.

R-2   The Lux Radio Theatre   ant   "Secrets"   3.24.35   NBC
Irene Dunne appeared in this sixty-minute broadcast.

See also B-206

R-3   Hollywood Hotel   10.11.35   CBS
Variety program with master of ceremonies Dick Powell, interviews by Louella Parsons, and musical selections by Frances Langford, the Raymond Paige Orchestra, Anne Jamison, and Igor Gorin. Irene Dunne, Robert Taylor, and Sara Haden performed scenes from Magnificent Obsession.

138   Irene Dunne

R-4   **The Lux Radio Theatre**   ant   "Bitter Sweet"
      5.11.36   CBS
      Irene Dunne starred in this sixty-minute adaptation of
      Noel Coward's operetta, which was filmed in 1933 with
      Anna Neagle and Fernand Gravet, and in 1940 with
      Jeanette MacDonald and Nelson Eddy.

R-5   **Hollywood Hotel**   11.20.36   CBS
      Dick Powell was master of ceremonies for this variety
      program, which featured interviews by Louella Parsons,
      and musical selections by Frances Langford and the
      Raymond Paige Orchestra. Irene Dunne and Melvyn
      Douglas performed scenes from **Theodora Goes Wild**.

R-6   **Elza Schallert**   1936
      Irene Dunne was interviewed by Elza Schallert.

R-7   **The Lux Radio Theatre**   ant   "Magnificent
      Obsession"   4.26.37   CBS
      Irene Dunne and Robert Taylor recreated their screen
      roles in this sixty-minute adaptation.

R-8   **Hollywood Hotel**   8.6.37   CBS
      Variety program with Jerry Cooper, Louella Parsons,
      Frances Langford, and the Raymond Paige Orchestra.
      Irene Dunne and Randolph Scott performed scenes from
      High, Wide and Handsome.

REVIEW:
Variety, 8.11.37: "**Hollywood Hotel** program was given a
much needed assist Friday evening with a resume of **High,
Wide and Handsome**, co-starring Irene Dunne and Randolph
Scott, providing 25 minutes of entertaining dialog [sic]
plus [a] couple of vocals by Miss Dunne. Songs were 'High,
Wide and Handsome' at beginning of script and 'People Who
Live on the Hill,' [sic] further down. Miss Dunne was in
usual good singing voice and reception was clear."

R-9   **Hollywood Hotel**   10.15.37   CBS
      Variety program with master of ceremonies Ken Murray,
      interviews by Louella Parsons, and songs by Frances
      Langford and the Raymond Paige Orchestra. Irene
      Dunne, Cary Grant, and Ralph Bellamy performed scenes
      from **The Awful Truth**.

R-10 **The Lux Radio Theatre**   ant   "Theodora Goes Wild"
      6.13.38   CBS
      Irene Dunne recreated her film role in this
      sixty-minute adaptation. Cary Grant played the part
      essayed by Melvyn Douglas on screen.

R-11 **The Gulf Screen Guild Show**   ant   "Alone in Paris"
      4.30.39   CBS
      Irene Dunne, Cary Grant, Walter Connolly, and Herman
      Bing appeared in this thirty-minute broadcast.

Irene Dunne posed with an NBC microphone to promote her appearance on *The Lux Radio Theatre* in 1935. (Author's collection)

140   Irene Dunne

R-12   **The Lux Radio Theatre**   ant   "The Sisters"
       10.9.39   CBS
       Irene Dunne and David Niven starred in this
       sixty-minute story about three sisters' marital
       problems. Movie-Radio Guide columnist Evans Plummer
       reported that Irene forgot to bring her pocketbook to
       the broadcast and had to borrow a quarter from mikeman
       Mel Ruick to pay the parking attendant ("Hollywood
       Showdown." October 21, 1940.). The 1938 film version
       starred Bette Davis and Errol Flynn.

R-13   **The Silver Theatre**   ant   "Romeo and Juliet"
       1.7.40   CBS
       Cary Grant starred in this thirty-minute adaptation of
       Shakespeare's tragedy. Reports conflict about his
       leading lady: Irene Dunne or Margot Stevenson. The
       play was filmed in 1936 with Norma Shearer and Leslie
       Howard.

R-14   **The Lux Radio Theatre**   ant   "Love Affair"   4.1.40
       CBS
       Irene Dunne and William Powell played the roles
       performed by Irene and Charles Boyer on screen in this
       sixty-minute adaptation.

R-15   **Hawaii Calls**   5.18.40   Mut
       Irene Dunne was interviewed while on vacation in
       Hawaii.

R-16   **The Lux Radio Theatre**   ant   "Show Boat"   6.24.40
       CBS
       Irene Dunne, Charles Winninger, and Allan Jones
       recreated their screen roles in this sixty-minute
       adaptation of the film. With Verna Felton, Hal K.
       Dawson, Ynez Seabury, Gloria Holden, Kristam Poppin,
       Earle Ross, Edward Marr, Barbara Jean Wong, Arthur Q.
       Bryan, James Eagles, Sarah Selby, musical director
       Louis Silvers.

See also D-25

R-17   **The Gulf Screen Guild Theater**   ant   "My Favorite
       Wife"   3.23.41   CBS
       Irene Dunne recreated her screen role in this
       half-hour adaptation. Robert Montgomery played the
       part originated by Cary Grant.

See also B-446

R-18   **Friendship Bridge**   5.20.41   NN
       Program of the British-American Ambulance Corps
       featuring Irene Dunne, George Murphy, and a group of
       British evacuees who spoke to their parents in
       England during the broadcast.

See also B-124

R-19   Your Happy Birthday   5.23.41   NBC
        Irene Dunne was a guest on this quiz show, which
        featured "Birthday Man" Edmund "Tiny" Ruffner, singer
        Helen O'Connell, and the Jimmy Dorsey Orchestra.

R-20   United Service Organization Benefit   6.29.41   CBS
        Broadcast from the Hollywood Bowl, this program was
        part of a $10 million drive to provide entertainment
        and religious facilities for enlisted men. Irene
        Dunne and Cary Grant appeared in a skit together.

See also P-14, B-125, B-453

R-21   The Lux Radio Theatre   ant   "Unfinished Business"
        10.6.41   CBS
        Irene Dunne recreated her screen role in this
        sixty-minute adaptation. Don Ameche played the
        character originated by Robert Montgomery.

R-22   The Gulf Screen Guild Theater   ant   "Penny
        Serenade"   11.16.41   CBS
        Irene Dunne and Cary Grant recreated their film roles
        in this half-hour adaptation.

R-23   The Cavalcade of America   ant   "Cimarron"
        12.1.41   NBC
        Irene Dunne recreated her film role in this
        thirty-minute adaptation.

R-24   Red Cross Show   c. 5.42   NBC
        Irene Dunne, Bob Hope, Deanna Durbin, and Marlene
        Dietrich were among the stars who appeared in this
        benefit for the Red Cross.

See also B-449

R-25   The Lux Radio Theatre   ant   "Love Affair"   7.6.42
        CBS
        Irene Dunne and Charles Boyer recreated their film
        roles in this sixty-minute adaptation.

R-26   Stagedoor Canteen   9.3.42   CBS
        Irene Dunne, Orson Welles, Martha Scott, James Melton,
        and Lou Holtz were the guests on this World War II
        variety program, hosted by Bert Lytell. Irene sang "I
        Left My Heart at the Stage Door Canteen" with Melton
        and the serviceman audience, and gave a pitch for war
        bond purchases. Although audiences were led to
        believe it was coming direct from the canteen, the
        show was really broadcast from the CBS studios.

REVIEW:
Variety, 9.9.42: "Windup of the show was throat-catching,
as the servicemen studio audience joined [James] Melton and
Miss Dunne in singing 'Left My Heart at the Stage Door
Canteen' theme tune."

142   Irene Dunne

R-27   **The Lux Radio Theatre**   ant   "To Mary, With Love"
11.16.42   CBS
Irene Dunne, Ray Milland, and Otto Kruger starred in this sixty-minute broadcast about a shaky marriage. The 1936 film starred Myrna Loy and Warner Baxter.

R-28   **The Charlie McCarthy Show**   4.25.43   NBC
Edgar Bergen and Charlie McCarthy welcomed guest Irene Dunne to their variety hour.

R-29   **The Lady Esther Screen Guild Theater**   ant
11.29.43   CBS
Irene Dunne starred in this thirty-minute broadcast. Title unavailable.

R-30   **Front Line Theatre** #88   ant   "Theodora Goes Wild"
11.29.43   AFRS
Irene Dunne reprised her film role. Cary Grant and Hanley Stafford played the characters originated by Melvyn Douglas and Thomas Mitchell.

R-31   **Everything for the Boys**   ant   "Lady of the House"
1.25.44   NBC
Ronald Colman was the star of this half-hour anthology, which aimed to provide servicemen with dramatic entertainment. Irene Dunne appeared in a twenty-minute adaptation of "Lady of the House." The remaining ten minutes consisted of shortwave interviews with servicemen stationed around the world.

R-32   **The Goodyear Program**   ant   "The Awful Truth"
2.6.44   CBS
Irene Dunne recreated her film role in this thirty-minute version. Walter Pidgeon played the Cary Grant part.

R-33   **Information Please** #28   4.29.44   AFRS
Irene Dunne and Deems Taylor were guests on the quiz program, which was moderated by Clifton Faddiman.

R-34   **The Lux Radio Theatre**   ant   "Penny Serenade"
5.8.44   CBS
Irene Dunne and Edgar Buchanan reprised their film roles in this sixty-minute adaptation. Joseph Cotten played the character essayed by Cary Grant on screen.

R-35   **Canada War Bonds Show**   1944
Irene Dunne recited Alice Duer Miller's "The White Cliffs" in this broadcast from Ontario. The poem served as the basis for Irene's film *The White Cliffs of Dover*.

R-36   **Command Performance** #152   3.10.45   AFRS
Stars donated their services for this war-time variety program, written by Glenn Wheaton of the War Department. With Irene Dunne, the Hoosier Hot Shots,

Radio 143

        Connie Haines, Johnny Mercer, Jerome Kern, Jimmy
        McHugh, Jimmy Van Heusen, and Johnny Burke.

R-37   America's Town Meeting of the Air   3.45   ABC
       George Denny moderated this sixty-minute forum, with
       guests Eddie Cantor, Irene Dunne, and Dr. Smith.

R-38   The Cavalcade of America   ant   "Doctora in Mexico"
       4.16.45   NBC
       Irene Dunne starred in this half-hour drama about the
       real adventures of Dr. Katherine Dale.

R-39   America's Town Meeting of the Air   9.45
       Irene Dunne was a guest in the audience, introduced
       during this sixty-minute forum.

R-40   The Lady Esther Screen Guild Theater   ant   "Over
       21"   2.18.46   CBS
       Irene Dunne and Alexander Knox recreated their film
       roles in this half-hour adaptation.

R-41   Academy Award   ant   "White Cliffs of Dover"
       9.18.46   CBS
       Irene Dunne and C. Aubrey Smith recreated their
       film roles in this half-hour adaptation.

R-42   The Lux Radio Theatre   ant   "Together Again"
       12.9.46   CBS
       Irene Dunne reprised her film role in this
       sixty-minute adaptation. Walter Pidgeon played the
       Charles Boyer character.

R-43   The Charlie McCarthy Show   12.22.46   NBC
       Edgar Bergen and Charlie McCarthy welcomed guest Irene
       Dunne to their variety hour.

R-44   The Lux Radio Theatre   ant   "Anna and the King of
       Siam"   1.20.47   CBS
       Irene Dunne and Rex Harrison reprised their film roles
       in this sixty-minute adaptation.

See also D-11

R-45   The Family Theatre   ant   "J. Smith and Wife"
       2.27.47   Mut
       Irene Dunne, Bing Crosby, and Dana Andrews appeared in
       this thirty-minute drama. Produced by Father Patrick
       Peyton, the series presented a variety of genres, from
       melodramas to westerns to science fiction, with all
       the stories stressing the value of family love and
       prayer. Irene was a regular guest and occasionally
       hosted the program.

REVIEW:
Variety, 3.5.47: "The story of the married couple (who
die in a boat sinking) outside the gates of the Elysian

144   Irene Dunne

Fields was full of tenderness and beauty, keyed to the thematic purpose of the 'Family' series."

R-46   The World's Greatest Mother   sp   5.11.47   Mut
Thirty-minute broadcast honoring the Virgin Mary, with Irene Dunne, Loretta Young, Ethel Barrymore, Ruth Hussey, Rosalind Russell, Charles Boyer, George Murphy, Pat O'Brien, Margaret O'Brien, Don Ameche, Bing Crosby, and Meredith Willson's orchestra. The program, broadcast on Mother's Day, included dramatic skits, narratives, monologues, bible readings, prayer, and music.

REVIEW:
Variety, 5.14.47: "It was on a much higher spiritual plane than one would have expected from the title or the cast (composed of glamour names from the film world). If radio represented the true religious spirit on any occasion, it was here....One well-known voice after another picked up the skein, with no fanfare, no false trumpeting, not even a mention of their name for any publicity purpose. There were no false notes."

See also B-5

R-47   Hollywood Fights Back   10.26.47   ABC
Screen stars banded together to speak out in favor of the First Amendment after the House Un-American Activities Committee (HUAC) began its investigation into alleged Communist activity in Hollywood. Organized by John Huston, the broadcast featured Judy Garland, Irene Dunne, Claudette Colbert, Myrna Loy, Senator Elbert D. Thomas (D-Utah), Senator Harley M. Kilgore (D-West Virginia), Senator Glen H. Taylor (D-Idaho), Senator Claude Pepper (D-Florida), producers Walter Wanger and William Wyler, New York lawyer Arthur Garfield, poet Archibald MacLeish, ASCAP president Deems Taylor, and Dr. Harlow Shapley, director of the Harvard Observatory. The Committee for the First Amendment, described by the New York Times as "a non-political organization campaigning only for honesty, fairness and the accepted rights of any American citizen," sent about thirty representatives to Washington to counteract the negative publicity about Hollywood and to convince HUAC to stop its investigation.

See also B-173

R-48   The Family Theatre   ant   "Our Lady's Juggler"
12.25.47   Mut
Irene Dunne hosted this thirty-minute broadcast, which was an adaptation of an Anatole France story. The program starred John Nesbit and John Charles Thomas.

R-49   The Camel Screen Guild Players   ant   "Brief

Encounter" 1.26.48 CBS
Irene Dunne, Herbert Marshall, and Tom Conway appeared in this thirty-minute drama about two married people who are drawn into a romance after meeting at a train station. The story was adapted from Noel Coward's one-act play Still Life. A British film version was released in 1945 with Celia Johnson and Trevor Howard.

R-50   The Louella Parsons Show   3.7.48   ABC
Irene Dunne was interviewed by the columnist.

R-51   The Cavalcade of America   ant   "Queen of Heartbreak Trail"   5.17.48   NBC
Irene Dunne starred in a half-hour story about Alaska.

R-52   The Theatre Guild on the Air   ant   "Reflected Glory"   5.30.48   ABC
Irene Dunne, Roger Pryor, and Audrey Christie starred in a story by George Kelly.

R-53   Cal York's   6.48
Irene Dunne was a guest while in New York.

R-54   The Lux Radio Theatre   ant   "I Remember Mama"   8.30.48   CBS, AFRS
Irene Dunne, Barbara Bel Geddes, and Oscar Homolka reprised their film roles in this sixty-minute adaptation.

R-55   Hallmark Playhouse   ant   "Cimarron"   9.9.48   CBS
Irene Dunne recreated her film role in this thirty-minute adaptation. James Hilton was the host-narrator.

R-56   The Family Theatre   ant   10.48   Mut
Irene Dunne hosted a broadcast.

R-57   The Cavalcade of America   ant   "Bryant's Station"   10.25.48   NBC
Irene Dunne appeared in this thirty-minute drama.

R-58   Dewey-Warren Bandwagon Show   11.1.48   CBS, NBC
Irene Dunne made a speech, sang, and appeared in a playlet about an ex-convict who died while voting in this hour-long political program. The all-star cast included Robert Montgomery, Lionel Barrymore, Jeanette MacDonald, Frank Morgan, Leo Carrillo, Bud Abbott and Lou Costello, Ray Milland, ZaSu Pitts, Fred Waring, Tex McCrary, Jinx Falkenburg, Victor Moore, James Melton, Harold Peary, Robert Ripley, Arthur Lake, George Murphy, and Gov. Earl Warren. At the end of the program, Republican Presidential candidate Thomas E. Dewey gave a five-minute speech.

REVIEW:
Variety, 11.3.48: "Several dramatic skits with Ray

146 Irene Dunne

Milland, Irene Dunne, Tex McCrary, Jinx Falkenburg and ZaSu Pitts were okay for the occasion, despite apparent weaknesses."

See also B-194

R-59   The Louella Parsons Show   1.2.49   ABC
Irene Dunne was interviewed and sang a lullaby from I Remember Mama.

R-60   We, the People   1.18.49   CBS
Irene Dunne gave "We the People" speech about American intolerence as she was honored by the National Conference of Christians and Jews. With Bill Veeck, Bill Leonard, and Elizabeth C. Bagg.

R-61   The Theatre Guild on the Air   ant   "The Late Christopher Bean"   1.30.49   ABC
Irene Dunne and Thomas Mitchell appeared in the drama by Sidney Howard. Lawrence Langner was host.

R-62   The Screen Directors' Playhouse   ant   "Magnificent Obsession"   2.13.49   NBC
Irene Dunne recreated her film role in this thirty-minute adaptation. Director John Stahl introduced the broadcast and, after the story, discussed making the film with Irene.

R-63   The Cavalcade of America   ant   "Citizen Mama"   4.4.49   NBC
Irene Dunne starred in this half-hour drama.

R-64   The Triumphant Hour   sp   "A Special Rosary"   4.17.49   Mut
Irene Dunne, Ethel Barrymore, Dan Daily, Bing Crosby, Fibber McGee and Molly, Jimmy Durante, Rosalind Russell, Dennis Day, Anne Jamison, Rita Johnson, Christopher Lynch, Dorothy Mayner, J. Carroll Naish, Robert Ryan, Lizebeth Scott, Dean Stockwell, Loretta Young, Pedro de Cordoba, and Father Patrick Peyton participated in this Easter program, which originated from both New York and Hollywood.

REVIEW:
Variety, 4.20.49: "Seldom has any religious program marshaled such an array of Hollywood talent as did this full hour, with some 19 film and radio names spotted through the varied scenes of the Resurrection, the Ascension and Coronation of Mary....With no advance announcement as to the identities of the stars, the naming of those in the cast at the close provided a surprise twist for those dialers who might not have recognized the players' voices."

R-65   Community Bond Drive Show   sp   5.16.49
all networks
Among the stars launching the Treasury Department's

Opportunity Bond drive were Jack Benny, Bob Hope, Bing
Crosby, Rochester, Al Jolson, Lionel Barrymore, Jo
Stafford, Irene Dunne, Edward Arnold, Edward G.
Robinson, Roy Rogers, Betty Garrett, Esther Williams,
Gene Kelly, Frank Sinatra, Jules Munshin, Fred Waring
and Glee Club, Red Skelton, and Alan Ladd. The show
mixed dramatic skits with comedy and music, urging
listeners to buy bonds. President Harry Truman and
Treasury Secretary Snyder closed the program with
brief messages. The stars were brought on the show by
Cornwell Jackson, radio consultant to the Treasury
Department and the husband of Gail Patrick, Irene
Dunne's co-star in My Favorite Wife.

REVIEW:
Variety, 5.18.49: "Hour-long stanza kicking off the new
savings bond drive presented some of radio's top performers
in a fast-moving, well-paced variety show, but missed the
dramatic impact that gets people to dig into their pockets.
Typical of the muff was the use of Irene Dunne acting the
role of the mother in I Remember Mama, Edward G. Robinson,
playing his usual tough, and Edward Arnold, as a banker, all
selling the advantages of bonds. If the stars spoke as
themselves, rather than as characters, it would have been a
more compelling argument."

See also B-419

R-66   The Lux Radio Theatre   ant   "Anna and the King of
       Siam"   5.30.49   CBS
       Irene Dunne recreated her film role in this
       sixty-minute adaptation. James Mason played the part
       created by Rex Harrison.

R-67   The Camel Screen Guild Guild Players   ant
       "Together Again"   6.16.49   NBC
       Irene Dunne recreated her film role in this half-hour
       adaptation. Walter Pidgeon essayed the Charles Boyer
       part.

R-68   Fibber McGee and Molly   sp   9.13.49   NBC
       Hour-long program honoring the fifteenth anniversary
       of Fibber McGee and Molly's radio program on NBC,
       featuring many guest stars, including Irene Dunne, Bob
       Hope, Dennis Day, Phil Harris, Alice Faye, Dinah
       Shore, Perry Como, Robert Young, William Bendix, and
       Harold Peary as the Great Gildersleeve.

REVIEW:
Phoenix Republic, 9.20.49: "Miss Irene Dunne of the
movies bobbed up just long enough to deliver a rather
strange compliment. She said - and I quote - 'Fibber and
Molly have never abused the good American air in our homes.'
I don't know what that means exactly but I guess I endorse
it."

148   Irene Dunne

See also B-377

R-69   <u>The Prudential Family Hour of Stars</u>   ant   "Love Affair"   10.2.49   CBS
Irene Dunne recreated her film role in this half-hour adaptation by Jean Holloway. Co-stars were Paul Frees, Parley Baer, Bea Benaderet, Gerald Mohr, and Rolfe Sedan. This was the first show of the <u>Prudential Family Hour of Stars's</u> 1949 season. Although Irene was heralded as one of six rotating stars, she disappeared after her second broadcast.

REVIEW:
<u>Variety</u>, 10.5.49: "Production was slick and Miss Dunne's acting surefire."

See also B-204, B-324

R-70   <u>The Lux Radio Theatre</u>   ant   "Mr. Blandings Builds His Dream House"   10.10.49   CBS
Sixty-minute adaptation of the comedy about a city couple attempting to build a home in the country. Cary Grant recreated his film role, while Irene Dunne played the character originated by Myrna Loy.

R-71   <u>Hallmark Playhouse</u>   ant   "Bride of Fortune"   11.10.49   CBS
Irene Dunne starred in this thirty-minute broadcast, which was hosted by James Hilton.

R-72   <u>Prudential Family Hour of Stars</u>   ant   "The Barretts of Wimpole Street"   11.27.49   CBS
Irene Dunne played Elizabeth Barrett in this thirty-minute drama about her romance with fellow poet Robert Browning. The 1934 film starred Norma Shearer and Fredric March.

R-73   <u>Hallmark Playhouse</u>   ant   "The Story of Florence Nightingale"   10.5.50   CBS
Irene Dunne starred in this thirty-minute drama about the famous nurse. James Hilton was host.

R-74   <u>The Screen Directors' Playhouse</u>   ant   "My Favorite Wife"   12.17.50   NBC
Irene Dunne and Cary Grant reprised their film roles in this sixty-minute broadcast. With Frank Nelson.

R-75   <u>Hallmark Playhouse</u>   ant   "Joy Street"   4.12.51   CBS
Irene Dunne starred in this thirty-minute broadcast.

R-76   <u>The Screen Guild Players</u>   ant   "Together Again"   5.3.51   ABC
Irene Dunne and Charles Boyer recreated their film roles in this one-hour comedy.

R-77 **The Lux Radio Theatre** ant   "The Mudlark"
      8.27.51   CBS
      Irene Dunne reprised her screen role in this
      sixty-minute drama, which featured Sir Cedric
      Hardwicke in the part created by Alec Guiness.

R-78 **Bright Star** ser 1952 NBC
      Irene Dunne and Fred MacMurray starred in this
      fifteen-minute comedy/drama series. The thirty-two
      episodes centered around a small town newspaper.
      Irene played Susan, the owner/editor of the
      financially troubled Hillsdale Morning Star.
      MacMurray portrayed George, the paper's star reporter.
      The cynic-idealist theme was prevalent, as George
      handled the day-to-day operations of running the paper
      and Susan indulged in philanthropy. Harry Von Zell
      was the announcer.

See also B-269

R-79 **Hallmark Playhouse** ant   "January Thaw"   1.11.53
      CBS
      Irene Dunne starred in this thirty-minute broadcast.

R-80 **The Cavalcade of America** ant   "The Short Straw"
      2.3.53   CBS
      Irene Dunne starred in this half-hour drama.

R-81 **The Lux Radio Theatre** ant   "June Bride"
      12.28.53   CBS, AFRS
      Irene Dunne and Fred MacMurray starred in this
      sixty-minute comedy about magazine writers inspired by
      their article on June brides. Some sources credit
      Joan Fontaine rather than Irene Dunne. The 1948 film
      version starred Bette Davis and Robert Montgomery.

R-82 **Heart Fund of 1954** #3 1954 NN
      Irene Dunne, Eddy Arnold, and the Pickens Sisters
      appeared in this fifteen-minute program soliciting
      donations for the Heart Fund.

R-83 **The Lux Radio Theatre** ant   "The Awful Truth"
      1.18.55   NBC, AFRS
      Irene Dunne and Cary Grant recreated their film roles
      in this sixty-minute adaptation.

DATE AND TITLE UNKNOWN:
R-84 ? 1935
      Irene Dunne sang "Here Am I" from Sweet Adeline, as
      heard on Hollywood on the Air Presents "The
      Feminine Touch" (D-18).

R-85 ? 1935
      Irene Dunne, Fred Astaire, and Ginger Rogers promoted
      Roberta. Irene sang "Smoke Gets in Your Eyes" and

"Lovely to Look At." Broadcast was released as <u>Hollywood on the Air</u> (D-17).

Television

This chapter is a complete chronological listing of Irene Dunne's national television appearances. Theatrical motion pictures shown on TV, telethons, or repeats are not included. Each entry is preceded by the letter "T." A typical entry includes the name of the series, the episode title, the date of broadcast, the network, and a brief synopsis of the type of series and Miss Dunne's role. Selected reviews are also provided. This chapter also features a guide to the twenty-six episodes of <u>Schlitz Playhouse of Stars</u>, which were hosted by Miss Dunne. The episodes are labled with the prefix "SP."

A key to abreviations follows:
```
ant       anthology
com       comedy
gm        game
NN        Non-Network (did not appear on ABC, CBS, or
             NBC)
rel       religious
ser       series
sp        special
var       variety
```

T-1   <u>Schlitz Playhouse of Stars</u>   ant ser
      5.30.52-11.21.52   (26 episodes)   CBS   30 minutes

   Producer: Edward Lewis. Directors: Robert Aldrich, William Asher, John Brahm, Phil Brown, Robert Florey, Richard Haydn, Leigh Jason, Roy Kellino, Herbert Kline, Lew Landers, Edward Mann, Arthur Pierson. Writers: Katharine Albert, Theodore Apstein, Oliver Crawford, Robert Riley Crutcher, Luther Davis, Robert Dennis, Richard DeRoy, Dale Eunson, Adrian Gendot, Zachary Gold, L. Gorog, Jack Guss, Aben Kandel, Herbert Kline, Al Laszlo, Val Lindberg, Dennis Locke, Vincent McConnor, Leonard Praskine, Dean Riesner, Arthur Ross, Barney Slater, L.C. Stoumen, Therese

Vernon.

Schlitz Playhouse of Stars premiered on October 5, 1951 as an hour-long anthology. Beginning May 30, 1952, the program was shortened to a half hour and Irene Dunne became the hostess. Her job was to establish the mood of the episode in a short prologue. She also appeared in an epilogue to tie up the proceedings. Irene left the show after twenty-six weeks in November, 1952. Critics often said hosting the show was a waste of her talents. Several reports claimed Irene left because too many of her fans protested about her appearance on a program sponsored by a brewery. After Irene's departure, the series used the guest stars in the prologue. Joan Bennett was originally asked to host the series. Only the episodes hosted by Irene Dunne are listed below.

FIRST SEASON   5.30.52-9.26.52
SP-1   "A Quarter for Your Trouble"   5.30.52
        Richard Haydn starred in this story about tracking down a murderer.

REVIEWS:
<u>Daily Variety</u>, 6.2.52: "Miss Dunne, looking much younger than her years, swept on the stage to set the scene and intro the characters. She partook of a few dialog [sic] exchanges and came on at the finish to invite the viewers back next week."

<u>Variety</u>, 6.4.52: "For the initial program, a detective drama..., Miss Dunne 'set the mood' via a quickie portrayal of a gum-chewing clerk in a department store information bureau. Within the 90-second to two-minute span, it is Miss Dunne's duty to put the audience in condition, in what amounts to one of TV's most extravagant and pretentious marquee come-ons."

SP-2   "Souvenir from Singapore"   6.6.52
        Dan Duryea starred as an Irish renegade who broke up a gang of rubber hijackers.

REVIEW:
<u>Daily Variety</u>, 6.9.52: "Irene Dunne's opening bit, to set the mood, is sprightly with an edging of humor....the camera follows her from her entrance through the door across the stage in hurrying stride and then to the business of acting out an atmospheric scene."

SP-3   "Dress in the Window"   6.13.52
        Teresa Wright portrayed a newspaper reporter who rescued a gangster's girlfriend from an apartment surrounded by police.

REVIEW:

Daily Variety, 6.16.52: "Irene Dunne's intro is pleasantly done."

SP-4   "Say Hello to Pamela"   6.20.52
        Leif Erickson played a salesman who innocently fell into a trap with a cheating wife. He visited the woman, played by Barbara Britton, on the advice of a fellow peddler, not knowing she was married or that her jealous husband had a gun.

REVIEW:
Daily Variety, 6.23.52: "Irene Dunne took her usual long walk in the prologue to set the mood, but gave the heavy dramatics a humorous flavoring. It didn't seem to fit."

SP-5   "The Von Linden File"   6.27.52
        Steve Brodie played an insurance agent who assigned his secretary, Joan Leslie, to trap a suspected jewel thief.

REVIEW:
Daily Variety, 6.30.52: "Irene Dunne's long walk to intro is becoming somewhat tiresome, and her 'cute' dialogue to set the scene doesn't seem to serve any particular purpose, other than giving a name to the series."

SP-6   "The House of Death" (AKA "Death House")
        7.4.52
        Boris Karloff starred in a story about a British girl who was receiving anonymous death threats after moving to New York.

REVIEW:
Daily Variety, 7.7.52: "There's more eerie suspense during Irene Dunne's walking marathon introduction than is generated by Vincent McConnor's slow-moving teleplay....Chief fault continues to be the Dunne intros which promise more than *Playhouse* delivers."

SP-7   "A Southern Lady"   7.11.52
        Jane Wyatt played a woman who allegedly had not left her room since the death of her twin brother nineteen years ago. When her greedy family arrived to con her out of her fortune, they discovered the charwoman was neither wealthy, nor a recluse.

REVIEW:
Daily Variety, 7.14.52: "Even the overlong Irene Dunne intro, supposedly limning the poignancy of loneliness in a big city, fails to arouse any interest in or sympathy for the characters."

154   Irene Dunne

SP-8   "Early Space Conquerors"   7.18.52
        Bobby Driscoll starred in a fantasy about
        space.

REVIEW:
Daily Variety, 7.22.52: "Irene Dunne hoves into
view for an invitation to come back next Friday. She
does, however, drop a clue when after her opening
stroll through the doors and down hallways ('I'm on my
way') she prologues, 'this is all about the remarkable
toys they sell for children these days.'"

SP-9   "A Man's World"   7.25.52
        With Pat O'Brien. Synopsis unavailable.

SP-10   "Crossroads"   8.1.52
        In a tale set during the early days of the
        French republic, Sir Cedric Hardwicke plotted
        to replace the leader with his own candidate,
        hoping to eventually come to power himself.

REVIEW:
Daily Variety, 8.4.52: "Irene Dunne's prolog [sic]
this time is a takeoff on a Scandanavian woman
applying for citizenship."

SP-11   "So Help Me"   8.8.52
        Jean Wallace portrayed a Broadway chorus girl
        who married a jealous millionaire, played by
        Walter Coy.

REVIEW:
Daily Variety, 8.11.52: "...Irene Dunne prologing
and epiloging, though it's her series, seems a waste
of time both for the star and the viewer, but it's all
done in good style and for less discriminating
audiences it's a passable half-hour sitback."

SP-12   "Double Exposure"   8.15.52
        John Beal and Amanda Blake played a husband and
        wife who both thought the other wanted to
        murder him.

REVIEW:
Daily Variety, 8.18.52: "It might have been better
for Irene Dunne to have explained the dark doings in
an epilog [sic] rather than her opening clue that
'somebody is always trying to kill someone else.'"

SP-13   "Mr. and Mrs. Trubble"   8.22.52
        Virginia Field and Willard Parker starred in a
        mystery involving stolen jewels.

REVIEW:
Daily Variety, 8.25.52: "Irene Dunne tips the clue
in the prolog [sic] when, as a gabby manicurist, she

points up la femme's intuitive detectiving."

SP-14 "Port of Call" 8.29.52
Victor McLaglen and Gertrude Michael acted in a story about a hunt for a stolen jewel, set in Mexico.

SP-15 "Homecoming" 9.5.52
Leif Erickson played a former college athlete who tried to get by on his past achievements. Helen Westcott was the wife who made him grow up.

REVIEW:
Daily Variety, 9.9.52: "Irene Dunne has cut down on her long walks in the prolog [sic]..."

SP-16 "The Marriage of Lit-Lit" 9.12.52
Rita Moreno and Don DeFore starred in the story about a marriage of convenience. Moreno played an Indian maiden whose father swapped her for provisions; DeFore was the store manager who wanted a woman to look after his children.

REVIEW:
Daily Variety, 9.16.52: "In these brewed brevities Irene Dunne has been both functional and decorative. She not only sets the scene but gives a clue to which turn the plot will take. Here she is of little help on the latter count, merely intoning 'this is a Jack London story about marriage.'"

SP-17 "I Want to Be a Star" 9.19.52
Elinor Donahue played a starstruck teenage girl who spent the afternoon at a drugstore, hoping to be discovered like Lana Turner. James Dunn starred as her father, who was discovered by a talent scout when he came to retrieve her.

REVIEW:
Daily Variety, 9.22.52: "Irene Dunne's intro, in which she is seen playing football, using a dummy infant as the ball, makes as much sense as the rest of the film."

SP-18 "The Trial" 9.26.52
Lon Chaney, Jr. starred in this tale of greed set in the Alaskan gold fields.

REVIEW:
Daily Variety, 9.29.52: "New lead-ins with Irene Dunne now keep her immobile to set the scene. It allows more time for the dramatics and Schlitz commercials, which are never resented."

SECOND SEASON   10.3.52-11.21.52

156   Irene Dunne

SP-19   "Come What May"   10.3.52
        Wallace Ford portrayed a suspicious father who
        tried to trap his daughter's boyfriends.

REVIEW:
Daily Variety, 10.7.52: "Only improvement is in
Irene Dunne's intro, who now simply tells a bit about
the star and the story."

SP-20   "Trouble on Pier Twelve"   10.10.52
        Akim Tamiroff played a murderous sea captain
        who hired a private eye, portrayed by John
        Howard, to give him an alibi. When the private
        eye realized the death was not a case of self
        defense, the captain tried to kill him. The
        detective was saved by his wife, played by
        Rochelle Hudson.

SP-21   "This Plane for Hire"   10.17.52
        Lloyd Bridges starred as a flier who was forced
        at gun point to pilot a Mexican gangster out of
        the country.

REVIEW:
Daily Variety, 10.20.52: "...Irene Dunne's prolog
[sic] was meaningless."

SP-22   "Drawing Room A"   10.24.52
        Joan Camden played a girl with amnesia who
        wandered into the drawing room of an army
        psychiatrist, portrayed by William Bishop. In
        a turn of events, it developed that the
        psychiatrist was really the one with amnesia
        and the girl was his wife, attempting to shock
        him back to reality.

SP-23   "Enchanted Evening"   10.31.52
        Eddie Albert and his real-life wife Margo
        played a couple who were planning to take his
        boss to the theatre. Trouble errupted when one
        of their children hid the tickets.

SP-24   "Tango"   11.7.52
        Cesar Romero and Ann Savage starred as a washed
        up dance team in a Panama club. The wife
        became suspicious of her husband when a wealthy
        admirer was murdered and the husband flashed a
        large bankroll.

SP-25   "The House of Pride"   11.14.52
        Robert Hutton played a Hawaiian patriarch who
        ordered a man and his mother off the island
        because they knew too much about his family.

REVIEW:
Daily Variety, 11.17.52: "As the third [Jack]

London fable in this series, which has one more week to go before the 'new winter' collection of plays takes over and immobilizes Irene Dunne, it has passable quality and is an improvement over the others filmed in Mexico City."

SP-26 "The Pussyfootin' Rocks"   11.21.52
Joan Blondell and Buddy Ebsen starred as Calamity Jane and a man who smuggled aliens in this western parody.

See also B-110, B-198, B-232

GUEST APPEARANCES BY IRENE DUNNE:
T-2 What's My Line?   gm   2.1.53   CBS   30 minutes

Irene Dunne was the mystery guest on this game show hosted by John Daly. Panelists included Arlene Francis, Dorothy Kilgallen, and Bennett Cerf.

T-3 Colgate Comedy Hour   var   11.15.53   NBC
60 minutes

Martha Raye hosted this variety program, with guests Irene Dunne, Rocky Graziano, and Cesar Romero. Irene sang "Smoke Gets in Your Eyes" and participated in a comedy sketch.

REVIEW:
Variety, 11.18.53: "Other guest was Irene Dunne, who opened with 'Smoke Gets in Your Eyes,' the Jerome Kern number which she essayed in Roberta in 1935. Miss Dunne contributed to a comedy sequence also toward the end of the show."

T-4 The Jack Benny Show   com   "The Irene Dunne Show"
12.6.53   CBS   30 minutes

Producer: Ralph Levy. Associate producer: Hilliard Marks. Director: Ralph Levy. Writers: Sam Perrin, George Balzer, Milt Josefsberg, and John Tackaberry. Musical director: Mahlon Merrick. Editor: Stanley Frazen. Photography: Phil Tannura.

Irene Dunne, Gregory Ratoff, Vincent Price, and Rex Evans guested on the first filmed episode of Jack Benny's comedy program (prior broadcasts were performed live). The plot involved Benny trying to replace Price as Irene's leading man, despite Ratoff's protest. A Variety critic noted that the same story line was used in a previous episode of The Jack Benny Show with Claudette Colbert and Robert Montgomery.

REVIEWS:
Daily Variety, 12.7.53: "Only the skeleton plot [of a previously used story] was retained, but with Irene Dunne,

Gregory Ratoff, Vincent Price and a butler named Rex Evans as co-protagonists it bagged more laughs than the limit allows....with Benny and his polished helpers, it was a classical gem of atomic humor."

Variety, 12.9.53: "Miss Dunne was capitally correct and, to borrow from Louella [Parsons], 'never looked lovlier.'...Luckily...this one was on film. It'll be around many times again, the standby for any emergency or just plain reprising because it's just plain so howling good."

See also T-29, B-110, B-242

T-5   Academy Awards   3.25.54   NBC

The twenty-sixth annual Academy Awards was a bi-coastal event, with hosts Donald O'Connor at Hollywood's RKO Pantages Theatre and Fredric March at New York's NBC Century Theatre. Irene Dunne presented the Best Director Oscar to Fred Zinnemann for From Here to Eternity.

REVIEW:
Variety, 3.31.54: "Fluffs were few and hardly noticeable despite the complexities of the format, varied origination points, split-screen trickery and extensive use of film clips. It was unusually deft organization, skillfully prepared and executed."

T-6   Easter Parade of Stars   sp   4.6.54   CBS
      30 minutes

      Producer: Martin Manulls. Director: Byron Paul.

      CAST: Irene Dunne, Phyllis Kirk, Nancy Olson, Ann Rutherford, Buff Cobb, Roxanne, Robin Chandler, Denis Lors, Eva Gabor, Evelyn Ay, Rex Marshall, others.

Auto-Lite spark plugs sponsored this program, which originated from New York. Segments included the Easter Parade of Stars Auto Show at the Waldorf-Astoria Hotel and a dinner for the Army Emergency Relief Fund. Irene Dunne was Mistress of Ceremonies.

REVIEW:
Variety, 4.14.54: "Irene Dunne made a charming conferencier, although the job had her a bit confused at times. After all, the load of names of sales officials, company presidents, the various cars, etc., would make for a trying session for quite a few people."

T-7   Ford Television Theatre   ant   "Sister Veronica"
      4.15.54   NBC   30 minutes

      Producer: Michael Kraike. Director: Ted Post.
      Teleplay: Erna Lazarus. Based on characters created by Vivian Cosby. Editor: Henry Batista.

Photography: Burnett Guffey.

CAST: Irene Dunne (Sister Veronica), John Hudson (Scott Averill, Jr.), Taylor Holmes (Gerald Fitzgerald), Morris Ankrum (Dr. Clark), Herbert Hayes (Scott Averill, Sr.), Frances Robinson (Sister Barbara), Stephanie Griffin (Claire), Alan Dexter, Laurie Mitchell.

SYNOPSIS: Sister Veronica is the head of a hospital who risks being removed by the bishop when she interferes in the marriage of a young couple. When the pregnant wife arrives at the hospital with a fractured skull sustained in a fall, her wealthy father-in-law demands that she be treated in his home to avoid publicity. Sister Veronica disagrees and reunites the young couple.

REVIEW:
Daily Variety, 4.19.54: "...Miss Dunne gives a sterling performance with all the sympathetic charm of her calling. She is taken through a series of changing emotions, becoming dramatic and capricious by turns."

NOTES: This was Irene Dunne's dramatic TV debut. Taylor Holmes was the father of Phillips Holmes, who co-starred with Irene in The Secret of Madame Blanche.

T-8   Ford Television Theatre   ant   "A Touch of Spring"
      2.3.55   NBC   30 minutes

Producer: Irving Starr. Director: James Neilson. Teleplay: Margaret Fitts. Based on a story by Robert Bassing. Editor: Richard Fantl. Photography: Charles Lawton, Jr. Art director: Ross Bellah.

CAST: Irene Dunne, Kathryn Grant, Frank Wilcox, and Gene Barry.

SYNOPSIS: Temporarily stricken with spring fever, a married woman (Dunne) lets a lonely young man (Barry) pick her up for an innocent afternoon flirtation. When she tells her husband (Wilcox), he invites the young man to his house while he is gone, letting the wife make her own decision about what she wants to do. The wife reveals her marriage to the young man and remains faithful.

REVIEW:
Daily Variety, 2.8.55: "Miss Dunne turns in an effortlessly effective portrayal, neatly underplayed, of the briefly smitten wife."

NOTES: Kathryn Grant married Bing Crosby in 1957. According to Dr. Joseph Link, Grant and Irene Dunne used to go on religious retreats together (B-475).

T-9   Academy Award Nominations Special   sp   2.12.55

160   Irene Dunne

NBC   90 minutes

Producer: Alan Handley. Director: Alan Handley.
Writer: Richard Breen.

Irene Dunne, Jack Webb, Louella Parsons, Donna Reed, and Humphrey Bogart emceed the special, which announced the Oscar nominations for 1954-55. The live show emanated from NBC's Burbank studio, Ciro's, Romanoff's, and the Coconut Grove, where the expected nominees were supposed to congregate. However, few of the candidates were on hand for the special. According to author James Robert Parish, Irene refused to wear glasses and squinted to read the nominations. It was the first and last time the Oscar nominations were announced in a primetime program.

REVIEWS:
Daily Variety, 2.14.55: "Louella Parsons was placed in the embarrassing position of screwing up her face and squinting to read the monitored cards, putting the burden on Irene Dunne, who shared the name-calling."

Variety, 2.16.55: "Of the other 'assistants' to [Jack] Webb, Irene Dunne and Greer Garson were properly gracious in making with the introductions."

T-10 Dateline Disneyland   ant   7.17.55   ABC
      90 minutes

Producer: Sherman Marks. Musical director: Walter Schumann.

Live episode of the anthology series celebrating the opening day of the Anaheim theme park, hosted by Art Linkletter, Ronald Reagan, Bob Cummings, and George Murphy. Irene Dunne christened the Mark Twain, the park's 105-foot sternwheeler. Among the fifteen thousand guests invited by Walt Disney were Fess Parker, Buddy Ebsen, Alan Young, Danny Thomas, and the Mouseketeers.

REVIEWS:
Daily Variety, 7.18.55: "Many picture and TV stars were shown on the rides and Irene Dunne christened the river boat."

Variety, 7.20.55: "Perhaps ABC-TV played it smart in corralling a major chunk of Hollywood talent and celebs for on-camera participation (Irene Dunne, who christened the Mark Twain river boat as one of the visual facets of Frontierland)..."

T-11 The Loretta Young Show   ant   "Slander"   10.30.55
      NBC   30 minutes

Producer: Bert Granet. Director: Richard Morris.
Writer: Richard Morris. Musical director: Harry

Lubin. Photography: Norbert Brodline.

CAST: Irene Dunne, Laraine Day, Ken Tobey, Corey Allen, Betty Caulfield, Irene Tedrow, Adrienne Marden.

Irene Dunne hosted this episode of the anthology series, which concerned the effects of vicious small town gossip on an aristocrat's wife.

T-12   The Loretta Young Show   ant   "Tropical Secretary"
       11.6.55   NBC   30 minutes

Producer: Bert Granet. Director: Harry Keller. Teleplay: William Bruckner. Based on a story by Elizabeth S. Holding. Music: Harry Lubin. Photography: Norbert Brodine.

Irene Dunne substituted for an ailing Loretta Young as hostess of this anthology. This episode starred Phyllis Kirk, Rod Cameron, Dabbs Greer, Walter Coy, and John Harmon.

REVIEW:
Daily Variety, 11.8.55: "Irene Dunne pinch-hits for Miss Young in the narration."

T-13   Benefit Show for Retarded Children   sp   11.12.55
       CBS   30 minutes

Jack Benny hosted this special, which launched National Retarded Children's Week (November 12-28). Guests included Irene Dunne, Art Linkletter, Bob Crosby, Cathy Crosby, the Modernaires, Marge and Gower Champion, Liberace, George Liberace, Oreste Kirkip, and Don Wilson.

REVIEW:
Variety, 11.16.55: "Irene Dunne and Art Linkletter made effective pitches for the retarded kids..."

T-14   The Christophers   rel   "The Fun of Teaching"
       c. 1955   NN

Irene Dunne, Jerry Jerome, and Dean Jagger were the guests on this episode of the religious series. Irene presented the seven points on the challenge and fun of teaching.

T-15   Ford Television Theater   ant   "On the Beach"
       4.12.56   NBC   30 minutes

Producer: Irving Starr. Director: James Neilson. Teleplay: N.B. Stone, Jr. and Joan Bourland. Editor: Robert L. Swanson. Photography: Gert Andersen. Art director: Walter Holscher.

CAST: Irene Dunne, Richard Denning, Jo Ann Lilliquist, David Kasday, Lucien Littlefield, Elizabeth Patterson, Gordon Howard.

162   Irene Dunne

SYNOPSIS: A widow (Dunne) meets a beachcomber (Denning) while vacationing in a New England fishing village with her daughter. The widow learns that the beachcomber is a former executive who has been deathly afraid of trains since his wife was killed in a train wreck. In the end, the widow reforms him and gets rid of his train phobia, with implications that they will marry.

REVIEW:
Daily Variety, 4.17.56: "Miss Dunne looks properly attractive and inspiring, but does little beyond this."

T-16   Ford Television Theater   ant   "Sheila"   5.24.56
       NBC   30 minutes

   Producer: Irving Starr. Director: James Neilson. Teleplay: Mary C. McCall, Jr. Based on a story by Manya Starr and Carol Gluck. Editor: Robert L. Swanson. Photography: Gert Andersen. Art director: Cary Odell.

   CAST: Irene Dunne, Elinor Donahue, Stephanie Griffin, Philip Ober, Peter Miller, Howard Wright.

SYNOPSIS: The headmistress of an exclusive girls school (Dunne) thinks her daughter (Donahue) has been dating the handyman's nephew (Miller). In time, the headmistress learns that it is really a poor little rich girl (Griffin) who is dating the boy. The headmistress re-establishes her relationship with her daughter and marries the rich girl's widowed father (Ober).

REVIEW:
Daily Variety, 5.28.56: "In the field of noble suffering on the screen, Irene Dunne has few equals, and this...story gives her talents full rein....Miss Dunne registers the required emotions with the skill of long practice."

See also B-491

NOTE: NBC reran "Sheila" as an episode of Festival of Stars on September 8, 1956.

T-17   The Perry Como Show   var   9.15.56   NBC
       60 minutes

   Producer: Robert S. Finkel. Director: Gray Lockwood. Writers: Goodman Ace, Jay Burton, Mort Green, and George Foster.

   CAST: Perry Como, Irene Dunne, Sal Mineo, Patience and Prudence, Robert W. Sarnoff, Ray Charles Singers, Frank Gallop, Mitchell Ayres Orchestra.

REVIEWS:
Daily Variety, 9.17.56: "It was a 10-strike to shove

off with such a name and talent as Irene Dunne, all grace and poise with a singing voice of such fine timbre that those home lookers who don't recall her operettas must have been pleasantly surprised....For Miss Dunne was routined a hit revue of her own, topped off with songs from Show Boat, which she did as a film. Most of the songs she sang while seated on a couch in a flouncy gown, which easterners saw in color but out west in black-and-white."

Variety, 9.19.56: "The only nostalgia they settled for was to guest-star Irene Dunne to recreate some of the top tunes from Show Boat which she understudied back in '28 [sic]. Miss Dunne's gown was fetching in compatible tint, but the NBC big and expensive push rated a better display than this....even with Miss Dunne encountering surprisingly little difficulty hurdling those Jerome Kern octaves, the show unfortunately was devoid of any spark."

NOTES: According to Perry Como's secretary, Vera Hamilton, Irene Dunne appeared on Como's variety series on September 28, 1957. Hamilton claimed Irene sang selections from Show Boat and joined Como, puppets Kukla and Ollie, and twelve United Nations children in singing "Getting to Know You." TV Guide and trade reviews stick by the September 15, 1956 date and description.

T-18   Ike Day Surprise Birthday Party   sp   10.13.56
        CBS   30 minutes

        Producer: David Lowe.   Director: David Lowe.

In honor of President Dwight Eisenhower's birthday, an alleged surprise party was telecast, with segments originating from the White House, Washington's Hotel Statler, Hollywood, and New York. Performers, including Kathryn Grayson, Howard Keel, Eddie Fisher, Nat King Cole, the Voices of Victory, and the Fred Waring Orchestra, sang the President's favorite tunes. Helen Hayes cut the birthday cake. Irene Dunne and James Stewart hosted the program. Irene and Charles H. Percy, president of Bell and Howell, were credited with organizing the Ike Day festivities.

REVIEW:
Variety, 10.17.56: "End result was to supply a fairly entertaining show with lotsa [sic] top name stars, along with a sugar-coated political message that could hardly have failed to register. With the genuine admiration expressed by the stars for Ike, along with his modest and gracious acceptance of the situation, this show was easily a bigger vote-getter than a half-dozen speeches."

T-19   Academy Awards   4.6.59   NBC

Bob Hope, David Niven, Tony Randall, Mort Sahl, Laurence Olivier, and Jerry Lewis hosted the thirty-first Oscar ceremonies from the RKO Pantages Theatre in Hollywood. Irene Dunne and John Wayne presented the Best Actor award to David Niven for Separate Tables.

REVIEWS:
Daily Variety, 4.7.59: "It was a super spec in the Hollywood tradition of colossals, brilliantly staged but marred by a muddled finish that left the show groping for something to fill at least 15 minutes short of the scheduled two hours."

Variety, 4.8.59: "This newest outing was the most uneventful in memory, probably striking a new nadir in the use of the talent - plus said talent's indifference....all in all, the show had mammoth dimensions cast-wise, and little sparkle."

T-20   The June Allyson Show   ant   "The Opening Door"
       10.5.59   CBS   30 minutes

   Producer: Alvin Cooperman. Director: Jack Smight. Teleplay: Henry Greenberg and David Horne. Editor: Chandler House. Photography: George Diskan.

   CAST: Irene Dunne, Harry Townes, Virginia Christine, Melinda Plowman, Douglass Dumbrille, Claudia Bryar, Scott Davey.

SYNOPSIS: When a brain-damaged child (Davey) gets out of control, his mother (Christine) takes him to Dr. Gina Kersten (Dunne), who specializes in such cases. Although Dr. Kersten usually admits only promising youngsters, she agrees to accept the child on a trial basis. The child's father (Townes) insists that his son belongs in an institution. After Dr. Kersten gives him therapy and affection, the child is able to go back to school for further treatment.

REVIEW:
Daily Variety, 10.7.59: "Time was when Miss Dunne was insurance against mediocrity, but not even her charm and acting finesse could overcome this pallid story....For Miss Dunne, one of our finest, it was a valiant effort to make something out of what wasn't there."

NOTE: Dr. Gina Kersten, whom Irene Dunne portrayed in this anthology episode, was a real-life physician who treated mentally retarded children.

T-21   The Big Party   var   11.5.59   CBS   90 minutes

Irene Dunne hosted this episode of the pseudo-variety show, the premise of which was to recreate a Hollywood soiree, with celebrities dropping by to entertain. Irene's melange of guests included composer Jule Styne, stripper/author Gypsy Rose Lee, singer Pearl Bailey, comedian Jack Carter, singer/comedienne Dorothy Loudon, singer Cesare Siepi, comedienne Ruth Gilbert, and tumbler Les Charlivels. Irene sang "Shall We Dance," dueted with Carter on "I Still Get Jealous," and joined the crowd to warble "Together." The script was written by Goodman Ace and Abe Burrows. Historically, the most interesting segment of the faux party was Gypsy Rose Lee singing "Let Me Entertain You" and "Everything's Coming Up Roses," which were written by Jule Styne for the musical Gypsy, based on her autobiography.

REVIEWS:
Daily Variety, 11.9.59: "Miss Dunne was a gracious hostess and joined the fun by singing, dancing and keeping the party gay."

Variety, 11.11.59: "Irene Dunne is an attractive and charming hostess but even she couldn't lift CBS-TV's Big Party out of the routine vaudeo groove....Miss Dunne got her singing and terping licks in too with a workover of 'Shall We Dance.'"

T-22   The Christophers   rel   c. 1959   NN

Irene Dunne guested on this religious series, which highlighted ways and means of promoting respect for the law. She was joined by Supreme Court Justice Tom Clark, Federal Court Judge Irving R. Kaufman, Fordham University Dean Joseph W. McGovern, and Ross Malone, president of the American Bar Association.

T-23   Eleanor Roosevelt's Diamond Jubilee Plus One
       sp   10.7.60   NBC   60 minutes

       Producer: Michael Abbott. Director: Dick Schneider.
       Writer: Reginald Rose.

This special saluted the former First Lady and solicited funds for the Eleanor Roosevelt Cancer Foundation. Guests included Mrs. Roosevelt, Bob Hope, Jack Benny, Carol Channing, George Burns, Nat King Cole, Paul Newman, Joanne Woodward, Jimmy Durante, Mahalia Jackson, Irene Dunne, Mary Martin, the kids from The Sound of Music, Simone Signoret, Lucille Ball, Gen. Omar Bradley, John F. Kennedy (then a Senator), Richard Nixon (then Vice President), and Dr. Tom Dooley. Irene performed a five-minute "commercial" for the Roosevelt Cancer Foundation.

REVIEW:
Variety, 10.12.60: "...the biggest star, backstage or onstage, was writer Reginald Rose. He penned 'commercials' for Dr. Tom Dooley, Simone Signoret, Lucille Ball, Paul Newman and Joanne Woodward and Irene Dunne that were great."

T-24   Frontier Circus   ant   "Dr. Sam"   10.26.61   CBS
       60 minutes

Ellen Corby, Irene Dunne, and Chill Wills starred in an episode of *Frontier Circus* in 1961. (Author's collection)

Irene Dunne played Dr. Sam, a pioneer who brought women's rights to the old west. With Chill Wills, John Derek, Ellen Corby, and Richard Jaeckel.

T-25   G.E. Theatre   ant   "Go Fight City Hall"   1.28.62
       CBS   30 minutes

Irene Dunne played a widow who became politically active. Despite rumors, Irene denied that the episode would lead to a series about a lady politician. Allyn Joslyn co-starred.

See also B-198

T-26   Saints and Sinners   ant   "Source of Information"
       10.15.62   NBC   60 minutes

   Teleplay: Joseph Stefano.

   CAST: Irene Dunne (Anita Farrell), Dennis Morgan (Chad Hamilton), Scott Marlowe (Frederick Brennen), Nick Adams (Nick), John Larkin (Grainger), Richard Erdman (Klugie), Hayden Rorke.

SYNOPSIS: Promoter Frederick Brennen submits a play to actress Anita Farrell and persuades her to finance the production. Although Nick is the author, Frederick pretends that he wrote the play.

T-27   Hollywood without Makeup   sp   c. 1965   60 minutes

Ken Murray hosted this selection of his home movies of celebrities. Irene Dunne looked chic in a hat and suit at a party given by Cary Grant in Malibu.

T-28   Academy Awards   4.10.67   ABC

   Producers: Joseph Pasternak and Richard Dunlap. Director: Richard Dunlap. Writers: Hal Kanter, L.A.L. Diamond, and Mort Lachman. Musical director: John Green.

Bob Hope hosted the thirty-ninth annual Academy Awards from the Santa Monica Civic Auditorium. Irene Dunne presented the Jean Hersholt Humanitarian Award to George Bagnall, president of the Motion Picture Relief Fund.

REVIEW:
Variety, 4.12.67: "Irene Dunne, looking great, presented the Jean Hersholt Award to Motion Picture Relief Fund president George Bagnall..."

T-29   Jack Benny's Twentieth Anniversary Special   sp
       11.16.70   NBC   60 minutes

Frank Sinatra, Bob Hope, Dinah Shore, Mary Livingstone, Dennis Day, Rochester, and Don Wilson joined the comedian to celebrate his twentieth year in television. According to Benny producer Irving Fein, clips from The Jack Benny Show were the highlight of the program. They included a snippet from Irene Dunne's 1953 appearance (T-4).

REVIEW:
Variety, 11.18.70: "In the finale quarter hour, [Benny]...segued into some silent film clips of past greats he'd had on his shows in the past 20 years. Nostalgia is not his bag, as Benny pointed out, but the tightly-edited montage hit the memory right when now-gone performers like Fred Allen, Gary Cooper, Marilyn Monroe, Nat Cole, Ronald Colman, and Humphrey Bogart flashed by."

See also B-110

T-30 Kennedy Center Honors   sp   12.27.85   CBS
      120 minutes

>Producers: Nick Vanoff and George Stevens, Jr. Director: Don Mischer. Writers: George Stevens, Jr., Sara Lukinson, Bob Shrum, and L.T. Iglehart, Jr. Special musical material: Ray Charles. Musical director: Nick Perito.

>CAST: Walter Cronkite, Don Ameche, Mikhail Baryshnikov, Carol Burnett, Chevy Chase, Gloria and Rodolfo Dinzel, Kirk Douglas, Robert Goulet, Rex Harrison, Louis Jourdan, Michele Lee, Merce Cunningham Dance Co. members, Sherrill Milnes, Anthony Newley, New York City Opera, Liz Robertson, Maureen Stapleton, James Stewart, Frederica von Stade, Washington Opera Chorus, 82nd Airborne Chorus, Soldiers Chorus of the U.S. Army Field Band, U.S. Navy Band Sea Chanters, U.S. Marine Corps Basic School Choir, Fife and Drum Corps.

Irene Dunne, Bob Hope, Beverly Sills, Merce Cunningham, Alan Jay Lerner, and Frederick Loewe were honored for their contributions to the arts. Irene was unable to attend the ceremony, but was saluted with a film tribute narrated by James Stewart. He noted that Irene was the only actress ever nominated for three Academy Awards in three different genres. Frederica von Stade sang "Smoke Gets in Your Eyes" from Roberta and "You Are Love" from Show Boat in her honor.

REVIEW:
Variety, 1.1.86: "...[Irene] Dunne [was] unable to make the broadcast as she had been felled with illness at the last minute. The 'Honors' format is to run a retrospective of each honoree as part of each guest's segment, usually composed of film footage. There is also an on-stage performance of some sort to round out the segment....Dunne [was saluted] by a performance of songs she had introduced, performed by opera star Frederica von Stade."

See also A-68, B-47, B-48, B-53, B-132, B-136, B-137, B-158, B-159, B-466, B-468, B-478, B-480

Discography

     This chapter is divided into three sections: 78s, LPs, and compact discs (CDs). Recordings made in the 78 speed are listed chronologically by the date of recording; they include song title, musical from which it came, matrix number, date and city of recording, labels on which the song was released, and record numbers. The LP and CD sections are listed alphabetically by album title. They include movie soundtracks, radio broadcasts, and compilations which feature the songs originally released on 78s. Listings include label, record or CD number, songs sung by Irene Dunne, and the musical from which the song was taken.

<u>78s</u>:
D-1   "When I Grow Too Old to Dream" from <u>The Milk Maid</u>
     With Nat Shilkret Orchestra
     # B-17247-2   recorded 4.4.35, New York
     Brunswick 7420, Brunswick 02048, Columbia DB-1805, Epic SN-6059

D-2   "Lovely to Look At" from <u>Roberta</u>
     With Nat Shilkret Orchestra
     # B-17248-2   recorded 4.4.35, New York
     Brunswick 7420, Brunswick 02048, Columbia DB-1805, Epic SN-6059

NOTES: Irene Dunne's recording of "Lovely to Look At" made <u>Billboard</u>'s popular sales chart, hitting #20 the week of June 8, 1935. According to <u>Variety's</u> June music survey, it was the fifth best-selling Brunswick record in Los Angeles for the month.

D-3   "I've Told Ev'ry Little Star" from <u>Music in the Air</u>
     With Victor Young Orchestra
     # DLA 2552-A   recorded 7.16.41, Los Angeles
     Decca 18201, Decca 40016, Brunswick 03340

D-4   "Smoke Gets in Your Eyes" from <u>Roberta</u>
     With Victor Young Orchestra

172   Irene Dunne

      # DLA 2553-A   recorded 7.16.41, Los Angeles
      Decca 18201, Decca 40016, Brunswick 03340

D-5   "All The Things You Are" from <u>Very Warm for May</u>
      With Victor Young Orchestra
      # DLA 2554-A   recorded 7.16.41, Los Angeles
      rejected

D-6   "Why Was I Born?" from <u>Sweet Adeline</u>
      With Victor Young Orchestra
      # DLA 2605   recorded 7.31.41, Los Angeles
      Decca 18202, Decca 40017

D-7   "Babes in the Wood" from <u>Very Good Eddie</u>
      With Victor Young Orchestra
      # DLA 2626   recorded 8.4.41, Los Angeles
      Decca 18203, Decca 40018

D-8   "They Didn't Believe Me" from <u>The Girl from Utah</u>
      With Victor Young Orchestra
      # DLA 2679   recorded 8.24.41
      Decca 18203, Decca 40018

D-9   "All The Things You Are" from <u>Very Warm for May</u>
      With Victor Young Orchestra
      # DLA 2680   recorded 8.24.41, Los Angeles
      Decca 18202, Decca 40017

D-10   <u>Irene Dunne in Songs by Jerome Kern</u>   Decca 484
      78 album with Victor Young Orchestra, recorded in 1941

      "Smoke Gets in Your Eyes" (<u>Roberta</u>)/"I've Told Ev'ry
        Little Star" (<u>Music in the Air</u>)   Decca 40016
      "All the Things You Are" (<u>Very Warm for May</u>)/"Why
        Was I Born?" (<u>Sweet Adeline</u>)   Decca 40017
      "Babes in the Wood" (<u>Very Good Eddie</u>)/"They Didn't
        Believe Me" (<u>The Girl from Utah</u>)   Decca 40018

NOTES: Album featured the six songs Irene Dunne recorded in 1941. See D-3, D-4, D-6, D-7, D-8, and D-9 for recording information.

<u>LPs</u>:
D-11   <u>Anna and the King of Siam</u>   Sandpiper LP-3
      <u>Lux Radio Theatre</u> broadcast from January 20, 1947,
      starring Irene Dunne and Rex Harrison.

See also R-44

D-12   <u>Christmas Stories from Guideposts</u>   Guideposts
      Irene Dunne and Dick Van Dyke read stories from the
      religious magazine.

D-13   <u>Cut! Out Takes from Hollywood's Greatest Musicals,
      Volume 3</u>   OTF-3

Collection of songs cut from musicals, taken from studio recordings.

> "Why Do I Love You?" (<u>Show Boat</u>) - Irene Dunne, Allan Jones

D-14 <u>Fifty Years of Film</u>   Warner Bros.   3XX2737
Three-record set celebrating the studio's fiftieth anniversary in 1973, featuring scenes from Warner Bros. films.

> Scene from <u>Life with Father</u> - William Powell, Irene Dunne, Johnny Calkins, Derek Scott

NOTE: Set included an illustrated booklet with photographs of the scenes on the record. Irene Dunne and William Powell were shown leading their children down the street, en route to Powell's baptism.

D-15 <u>A Guide to "Dimension: An Exhibition of Sculpture for the Sighted and Blind"</u>   Capitol SPRO-4924/4925
Irene Dunne narrated this oral guide to the exhibition "Dimension," which was sponsored by the California Arts Commission. The album was recorded at the 16-2/3 speed so that it could be played on talking book machines, which the Federal Government made available to anyone who was legally blind.

See also B-11, B-13, B-14, B-77

D-16 <u>Here Come the Girls</u>   Epic 1114 (10" LP) and Epic 3188 (12" LP)
Collection of songs by leading actresses.

> "Lovely to Look At" (<u>Roberta</u>) - Irene Dunne

D-17 <u>Hollywood on the Air</u>   Star-Tone ST-204
1935 radio production promoting <u>Roberta</u>, with Irene Dunne, Ginger Rogers, Fred Astaire. Flip side is <u>Top Hat</u> radio broadcast.

> "Smoke Gets in Your Eyes" - Irene Dunne
> "Lovely to Look At" - Irene Dunne, Fred Astaire

See also R-85

D-18 <u>Hollywood on the Air Presents "The Feminine Touch"</u>
Star-Tone ST-205
Actresses perform songs and scenes from vintage radio broadcasts.

> "Here Am I" (<u>Sweet Adeline</u>, 1935 radio broadcast) - Irene Dunne

See also R-84

174   Irene Dunne

D-19 **Hollywood Sings: Volume 1 (The Girls)**   Ace of
      Hearts AH-67; Coral CP-96
      British compilation of songs by female film stars.

      "Smoke Gets in Your Eyes" (*Roberta*) - Irene Dunne

D-20 **Hollywood Story**   Festival 214
      French collection of film songs.

      "Here Am I" (*Sweet Adeline*) - Irene Dunne

D-21 **Jerome Kern in Hollywood: 1934-1938**   JJA 19747
      Excerpts from original soundtracks composed by Jerome
      Kern, including *Sweet Adeline*, *Roberta*, *High,
      Wide and Handsome*, and *Joy of Living*.

      Sweet Adeline
      "Here Am I" - Irene Dunne
      "We Were So Young" - Irene Dunne
      "Why Was I Born?" - Irene Dunne
      "Lonely Feet" - Irene Dunne
      "'Twas Not So Long Ago" - Joseph Cawthorn, Irene
         Dunne, Phil Regan, Hugh Herbert, Nydia Westman
      "Lonely Feet" - Irene Dunne, Chorus
      "We Were So Young" - Irene Dunne, Phil Regan, Chorus
      "Don't Ever Leave Me" - Irene Dunne

      Roberta
      "Russian Folk Song" - Irene Dunne
      "Yesterdays" - Irene Dunne
      "Smoke Gets in Your Eyes" - Irene Dunne
      "Lovely to Look At" - Irene Dunne

      High, Wide and Handsome
      "High, Wide and Handsome" - Irene Dunne
      "The Folks Who Live on the Hill" - Irene Dunne
      "Allegheny Al" - Irene Dunne, Dorothy Lamour
      "Can I Forget You?" - Irene Dunne

      Joy of Living
      "Main Title"/"What's Good About Good Night?" - Irene
         Dunne, Chorus
      "You Couldn't Be Cuter" - Irene Dunne
      "Just Let Me Look at You" - Irene Dunne
      "What's Good about Good Night?" - Irene Dunne
      "A Heavenly Party" - Irene Dunne, Douglas Fairbanks,
         Jr.

D-22 **Jerome Kern In Hollywood, Volume 2**   JJA 19784
      More songs by composer Jerome Kern.

      "Why Was I Born?" (*Sweet Adeline*) - Irene Dunne
      "Smoke Gets in Your Eyes" (*Roberta*) - Irene Dunne
      "I've Told Ev'ry Little Star" (*Music in the Air*) -
         Irene Dunne
      "Babes in the Wood" (*Very Good Eddie*) - Irene Dunne

"All the Things You Are" (<u>Very Warm for May</u>) - Irene Dunne
"Lovely to Look At" (<u>Roberta</u>) - Irene Dunne
"They Didn't Believe Me" (<u>The Girl from Utah</u>) - Irene Dunne

NOTES: "Lovely to Look At" was taken from the film soundtrack; other songs were from Irene Dunne's Decca 78s.

See also D-3, D-4, D-6, D-7, D-8, D-9

D-23 <u>Roberta</u>   Classic International Filmusicals
CIF 3011; Sandy Hook SH 2061
Soundtrack from 1935 film with Irene Dunne, Ginger Rogers, and Fred Astaire.

"Russian Song" - Irene Dunne and Balalaika Orchestra
"Yesterdays" - Irene Dunne
"Smoke Gets in Your Eyes" - Irene Dunne and Balalaika Orchestra
"Lovely to Look At" - Irene Dunne, Chorus

NOTE: The <u>Roberta</u> soundtrack was also released in cassette form by Sandy Hook (SH 2061).

D-24 <u>Show Boat</u>   Xeno 251; Vertinge 2004
Soundtrack from 1936 film with Irene Dunne, Allan Jones, Helen Morgan, Paul Robeson, Hattie McDaniel, Queenie Smith, Sammy White. Orchestra: Robert Russell Bennett. Conductor: Victor Baravelle.

"Make Believe" - Irene Dunne, Allan Jones
"Can't Help Lovin' Dat Man" - Helen Morgan, Hattie McDaniel, Irene Dunne, Paul Robeson
"I Have the Room Above" - Allan Jones, Irene Dunne
"Gallavantin' Around" - Irene Dunne, Chorus
"You Are Love" - Irene Dunne, Allan Jones
"Can't Help Lovin' Dat Man" - Irene Dunne
"After the Ball" - Irene Dunne, Chorus
"You Are Love" (reprise) - Irene Dunne, Allan Jones

D-25 <u>Show Boat</u>   Sunbeam P-501
<u>Lux Radio Theatre</u> broadcast from June 24, 1940, with Irene Dunne, Allan Jones, and Charles Winninger; conductor: Louis Silvers.

"Make Believe" - Irene Dunne, Allan Jones
"You Are Love" - Irene Dunne, Allan Jones
"Why Do I Love You?" - Irene Dunne, Allan Jones
"Can't Help Lovin' Dat Man" - Irene Dunne

See also R-16

D-26 <u>Sweet Adeline/High, Wide and Handsome</u>   Titania 506
Soundtracks from the 1935 film with Irene Dunne, Phil Regan, Joseph Cawthorn, and chorus, and the 1937 film

176   Irene Dunne

with Irene Dunne, Dorothy Lamour, William Frawley, and chorus.

Sweet Adeline
"Here Am I" - Irene Dunne
"We Were So Young" - Irene Dunne
"Why Was I Born?" - Irene Dunne
"Lonely Feet" - Irene Dunne
"'Twas Not So Long Ago" - Joseph Cawthorn, Irene
    Dunne, Phil Regan, Hugh Herbert, Nydia Westman
"Lonely Feet" - Irene Dunne, Chorus
"We Were So Young" - Irene Dunne, Phil Regan, Chorus
"Don't Ever Leave Me" - Irene Dunne

High, Wide and Handsome
"High, Wide and Handsome" - Irene Dunne
"The Folks Who Live on the Hill" - Irene Dunne
"Allegheny Al" - Irene Dunne, Dorothy Lamour
"Can I Forget You?" - Irene Dunne

D-27   Those Legendary Leading Ladies of Stage, Screen & Radio, Vol. 2   Harmony KH-32423
Collection featuring Broadway, film, and radio stars.

"Lovely to Look At" (Roberta) - Irene Dunne

D-28   Those Wonderful Girls of Stage, Screen & Radio
Epic SN-6059; Epic BSN-159
Compilation album of songs by Broadway, film, and radio personalities.

"Lovely to Look At" (Roberta) - Irene Dunne

COMPACT DISKS:
D-29   Love Is the Sweetest Thing - "Great Love Songs of the 30s"   The Compact Selection TQ 153
British compact disc released in 1987, including songs by Ruth Etting, Bing Crosby, and Ginger Rogers.

"Lovely to Look At" (Roberta) - Irene Dunne

D-30   Makin' Whoopee - Favorites of Stage and Screen
Conifer TQ 132
British compact disc with songs by film and stage personalities.

"Lovely to Look At" (Roberta) - Irene Dunne

D-31   Puttin' on the Ritz   SVL 188
British compact disc of songs from the stage and screen.

"Lovely to Look At" (Roberta) - Irene Dunne

NOTE: The collection was also available in cassette format

(CSVL 188).

D-32 <u>Those Sensational Swinging Sirens of the Silver Screen</u>
Collection of songs performed by the leading ladies of film, including Joan Crawford, Lena Horne, Rita Hayworth, and Alice Faye.

"Lovely to Look At" (<u>Roberta</u>) - Irene Dunne

Awards and Honors

The following is a list of awards, nominations, honors, and degrees received by Irene Dunne. Since it is impossible to catalogue all honors, keys to the city, etc., the list is meant to be a representative sampling.

A-1   Scholarship for a musical course at the Oliver Willard Pierce Academy of Fine Arts, Indianapolis, IN. Awarded by the Madison, IN Current Events Club, c. 1910s.

A-2   Scholarship to the Chicago Musical College, 1918-19 school year.

A-3   Gold medal for vocal excellence at the Chicago Musical College annual contest, 1919.

A-4   Senior diploma in voice from the Chicago Musical College, June 19, 1919.

A-5   Scholarship for further study at the Chicago Musical College, 1919-20 school year.

A-6   Academy Award nomination for Best Actress, 1930-31, for Cimarron; lost to Marie Dressler for Min and Bill. The ceremony was held at the Sala D'Oro of the Biltmore Hotel in Los Angeles on November 10, 1931.

A-7   One of fifty actresses chosen to participate in a popularity poll, which named Ronald Colman as their favorite actor, 1934.

A-8   Irene's recording of "Lovely to Look At" ranked #20 in Billboard's popular sales chart during the week of June 8, 1935.

A-9   Irene's recording of "Lovely to Look At" named fifth best seller by Brunswick in Variety's June record

180   Irene Dunne

list, 1935.

A-10 Named a runner-up in a "most popular film star" poll conducted by the trade journal <u>Boxoffice</u>, January, 1937.

A-11 Academy Award nomination for Best Actress, 1936, for <u>Theodora Goes Wild</u>; lost to Luise Rainer for <u>The Great Ziegfeld</u>. Irene Dunne attended the ceremony, which was held at the Biltmore Bowl of the Biltmore Hotel in Los Angeles, on March 4, 1937.

A-12 Academy Award nomination for Best Actress, 1937, for <u>The Awful Truth</u>; lost to Luise Rainer for <u>The Good Earth</u>. The ceremony was held at the Biltmore Bowl of the Biltmore Hotel in Los Angeles, on March 10, 1938. Irene Dunne was in New York at the time.

A-13 Selected as the most accomplished female speaker in a survey conducted by the American Society for the Hard of Hearing, August, 1938.

A-14 Named one of the ten most glamorous women in Hollywood by actor George Brent.

A-15 Academy Award nomination for Best Actress, 1939, for <u>Love Affair</u>; lost to Vivien Leigh for <u>Gone with the Wind</u>. The ceremony was held at the Coconut Grove at the Ambassador Hotel in Los Angeles on February 29, 1940. Irene Dunne did not attend.

A-16 Unanimously named the favorite film star of explorers residing in the South Pole in a poll conducted by Schenectady shortwave radio station WGEO, July, 1940.

A-17 Member of the Beverly Hills United Service Organization (U.S.O.).

A-18 Placed first in Elsa Maxwell's list of "The 10 Great Ladies in the Contemporary World," 1941.

A-19 Received a certificate from the U.S. Treasury Department for National War Savings Program for her efforts selling war bonds, September 9, 1942.

A-20 Granted honorary membership in the music fraternity Sigma Alpha Iota.

A-21 Awarded Honorary Doctor of Music degree from the Chicago Musical College, June 14, 1945.

A-22 Named tenth runner-up in "America's favorite film star" poll conducted by <u>Boxoffice</u>, November, 1945.

A-23 Put foot and hand prints in cement at Grauman's

Irene Dunne and Rex Harrison put their foot and hand prints in the cement in front of Grauman's Chinese Theatre to promote *Anna and the King of Siam,* July 8, 1946. (Wisconsin Center for Film and Theater Research)

Chinese Theatre, July 8, 1946.

A-24   Received the Distinguished Service Award from the American Cancer Society, 1947.

A-25   Named runner-up in "All-American Popularity" poll conducted by <u>Boxoffice</u>, November, 1947.

A-26   Named Honorary National Commander of the Field Army by the American Cancer Society, March 31, 1948.

A-27   Awarded <u>Cosmopolitan's</u> Citation for "Best Performance of the Month" for <u>I Remember Mama</u> by Louella Parsons, April, 1948.

A-28   Named a member of the delegation from California at the Republican National Convention in Philadelphia, June 21-25, 1948; seconded nomination of Earl Warren for Vice President.

A-29   Honored by the National Conference of Christians and Jews for her contribution to the anti-prejudice movement, February 4, 1949.

A-30   Headed women's committee of the American Heart Association's 1949 drive, which lasted from February 7 to February 28, 1949.

A-31   Awarded a diamond heirloom crown by the Society of Norwegian Playwrights for her performance in <u>I Remember Mama</u>, February 12, 1949.

A-32   Academy Award nomination for Best Actress for <u>I Remember Mama</u>, 1948; lost to Jane Wyman for <u>Johnny Belinda</u>. Ceremony was held at the Academy Theatre on March 24, 1949.

A-33   Received the American Heart Association's first annual gold award for distinguished service and leadership in the 1949 national campaign, June 4, 1949.

A-34   Awarded Honorary Doctor of Laws degree from Mount Saint Mary's College, June 5, 1949.

A-35   Awarded Laetare Medal from the University of Notre Dame, June 29, 1949. The medal was given to an outstanding member of the Roman Catholic laity.

A-36   Named Vice Chairman of the American Red Cross Fund Appeal, 1949.

A-37   Received the American Cancer Society Award for Distinguished Service, 1949.

A-38   Awarded a citation from the Mission Helpers of Alabama from the Benefactors of the Diocese of Mobile,

Awards and Honors   183

1949.

A-39   Received the Certificate of Honor from the American
       National Red Cross for distinguished achievement
       during the 1949 Red Cross fund drive.

A-40   Elected president of the Saint John's Hospital
       Foundation, 1951.

A-41   Appointed to serve on the Defense Advisory Committee,
       which was set up to advise the Defense Department on
       policies concerning women in the armed forces, August,
       1951.

A-42   Ranked as one of fifteen favorite American actresses
       in a poll conducted by RKO in eleven European
       countries, 1951.

A-43   Awarded the Lateran Cross by the Lateran Basilica
       Chapter of Canons for her "exemplary life and service
       to the Roman Catholic Church," September, 1951.

A-44   Received Award of Merit from the Sister Elizabeth
       Kenny Foundation, June 1, 1953. Irene was recognized
       for her outstanding community service on behalf of
       polio stricken children during the 1953 campaign.

A-45   Received a citation for distinguished service from the
       Community Chests of America.

A-46   Received the Pro Deo Et Juventute Award from the
       National Council of Catholic Youth, 1957.

A-47   Appointed an alternate delegate to the United Nations
       Twelth General Assembly, August, 1957.

A-48   Received honorary Doctor of Laws from the University
       of Notre Dame, 1958.

A-49   Received honorary degree from Loyola University of Los
       Angeles, 1958.

A-50   Named Indiana Woman of the Year by the Indianapolis
       alumnae chapter of Theta Sigma Phi (now Women in
       Communications), 1958.

A-51   Addressed fund campaign rally at a meeting of the Los
       Angeles chapter of the American Red Cross at the
       Biltmore Bowl, March 10, 1960.

A-52   Honorary Chairman of the Century Ball, a charity
       fundraiser for Saint John's Hospital.

A-53   Named to the Mayor's Community Advisory Committee for
       the City of Los Angeles.

184   Irene Dunne

A-54 Awarded a star on the Hollywood Walk of Fame for her film contributions, located at 6440 Hollywood Boulevard.

A-55 Named Chairman of the Saint John's Hospital Foundation, 1963; resigned June 28, 1966, but continued to work with the developmental council.

A-56 First woman elected to the board of directors, Technicolor, Inc., 1965.

A-57 First woman to receive the Bellarmine College Medal, 1965. Irene was cited for her contribution to "American society in the entertainment arts and in a variety of civic and philanthropic activities."

A-58 One of four recipients honored at Delta Kappa Alpha awards banquet, January 15, 1967. Other honorees were Frank Capra, Jack Oakie, and William Wyler.

A-59 Recipient of the Golden Eve Award from the Mannequins of the Assistance League of Southern California, May 17, 1967. Irene was recognized for repeatedly being nominated as one of Southern California's best dressed women.

A-60 Appointed member of the California Arts Commission, 1967; served three years.

A-61 Named one of Colorado's Women of Achievement, June 15, 1968.

A-62 Honored with a film retrospective, sponsored by the Los Angeles County Museum and the California Palace of the Legion of Honor, November, 1970. Tribute included a screening of <u>Roberta</u> and a question-and-answer period.

A-63 Acted as master of ceremonies of the Chaminade Mothers Club fashion show "Flight into Fashion," which was sponsored by Delta Airlines, December 5, 1970.

A-64 Honored at the Los Angeles International Film Exposition (Filmex) on March 23, 1975. The five-hour program included clips from fifteen films and two TV shows, as well as a screening of <u>Love Affair</u>, and a twenty-five-minute question-and-answer period. The program was coordinated by David Chierichetti and moderated by Roddy McDowall.

A-65 Honored by the American Film Institute on August 25, 1979. Tribute included a screening of <u>Love Affair</u>, clips from <u>The Awful Truth</u>, and a question-and-answer session.

A-66 Saint John's Hospital and Health Center dedicated a

life-size bust of Irene Dunne on May 7, 1985, to honor her fundraising contributions.

A-67 Honored by the National Art Association at a dinner at the Beverly Wilshire Hotel's Grand Ballroom, May 18, 1985. The tribute included film clips and musical selections sung by John Raitt.

A-68 One of six recipients of the Kennedy Center Honors, December, 1985. Other honorees were Beverly Sills, Merce Cunningham, Bob Hope, Frederick Lowe, and Alan Jay Lerner. Irene was present at the dinner at the State Department on December 7, but was unable to attend the gala tribute on December 8.

A-69 Honored with "The Best of Irene Dunne," a two-day film festival presented by the Los Angeles County Museum of Art, December 5 and 6, 1986. <u>Back Street</u> and <u>Magnificent Obsession</u> were screened on December 5; <u>Roberta</u> and <u>Sweet Adeline</u> were shown on December 6.

A-70 Posthumous birthday film festival on TNT, December 20, 1990. The cable network aired <u>The Secret of Madame Blanche</u>, <u>Roberta</u>, the colorized <u>My Favorite Wife</u>, <u>I Remember Mama</u>, <u>The White Cliffs of Dover</u>, and <u>Sweet Adeline</u> to honor Irene Dunne.

Song Sheets

   The following song sheets feature photographs of Irene Dunne.

S-1   <u>Roberta</u>   (1935)
   "(When Your Heart's on Fire) Smoke Gets in Your Eyes"
   "Let's Begin"
   "Yesterdays"
   "I'll Be Hard to Handle"
   "Lovely to Look At"
   "I Won't Dance"

Fred Astaire and Ginger Rogers danced in the upper left while a closeup of Irene Dunne graced the lower right corner of this green and gray song sheet.

S-2   <u>Show Boat</u>   (1936)
   "Make Believe"
   "Can't Help Lovin' Dat Man"
   "Ol' Man River"
   "Why Do I Love You?"
   "Bill"
   "You Are Love"
   "I Have the Room Above"
   "I Still Suits Me"

At left, Irene Dunne towered over a sketch of a showboat, while headshots of co-stars Charles Winninger, Helen Morgan, Paul Robeson, and Allan Jones lined the right.

S-3   <u>High, Wide and Handsome</u>   (1937)
   "Can I Forget You"
   "Allegheny Al"
   "The Things I Want"
   "High, Wide and Handsome"
   "The Folks Who Live on the Hill"
   "Will You Marry Me Tomorrow, Maria"

Surrounded by a circle of lace, Irene Dunne and Randolph

Scott were pictured sitting on the grass in this blue and gray song sheet.

S-4   Joy of Living   (1938)
        "A Heavenly Party"
        "Just Let Me Look at You"
        "What's Good about Good-Night?"
        "You Couldn't Be Cuter"

A glamorous, circular closeup of Irene Dunne in purplish tones towered over a green rainbow of stars.

S-5   Love Affair   (1939)
        "Sing My Heart"
        "Wishing (Will Make It So)"

Charles Boyer and Irene Dunne faced each other in profile at the bottom of the pink and blue tinted song sheet.

S-6   A Guy Named Joe   (1943)
        "I'll Get By (As Long as I Have You)"

Irene Dunne and Spencer Tracy looked toward the sky in black and white as a dark blue plane shadowed above them in the gray-blue background.

S-7   Stingaree   (1934)
        "Tonight Is Mine"

Black and white headshots of Irene Dunne and Richard Dix hovered above the film title and a bright red heart.

Annotated Bibliography

This bibliography is intended to be a representative sampling of the different types of sources which wrote about Irene Dunne and her work. It features reviews and articles from newspapers, books, news magazines, fan magazines, trade papers, and tabloids. It is interesting to note the type of publicity Miss Dunne received throughout her career, always reinforcing her image as a lady. Gossip items concerned innocuous topics like gardening or hairstyles. Somewhat racy magazines, like <u>Film Fun</u>, which featured corny jokes and scantily-clad women, ran innocent film stills of Miss Dunne. <u>Silver Screen</u>'s Elizabeth Wilson best summed up the reporters' feelings about the actress: "Terrible copy - but awfully charming."

B-1 "According to Schedule." <u>Film Fun</u>. April, 1934. p. 60.
Irene Dunne was set to star in <u>Transient Love</u> with Ralph Bellamy. The film was released as <u>This Man Is Mine</u> in 1934.

B-2 "According to Schedule." <u>Film Fun</u>. March, 1935. p. 62.
Report that the filming of <u>Roberta</u> was "progressing nicely" at RKO, with Irene Dunne, Fred Astaire, and Ginger Rogers in the leads. Director William Seiter hoped to make the film surpass the hit stage version.

B-3 "According to Schedule." <u>Film Fun</u>. January, 1937. p. 62.
After Irene Dunne finished shooting <u>Theodora Goes Wild</u>, she was supposed to film <u>Madame Curie</u> for Universal. John Boles was tentatively cast as Pierre Curie, the scientist's husband and co-discoverer of radium. The picture was canceled. <u>Madame Curie</u> was filmed by MGM in 1943 with Greer Garson and Walter Pidgeon.

B-4 "According to Schedule." <u>Film Fun</u>. February, 1937. p. 61.

Irene Dunne and Randolph Scott, teamed in *High, Wide and Handsome*, were called "the newest and most impressive" of the new screen romance teams.

B-5 "Actress, Charity Backer Irene Dunne Dead at 88." *Catholic Telegraph*. September 14, 1990. p. 15-A.
Obituary focusing on Irene Dunne's involvement with the Catholic church. In addition to mentioning the Laetare Medal that she was awarded, the article talked about her work with the Family Rosary Crusade. Founded by Holy Cross Father Patrick Peyton, the crusade promoted family prayer through the media. Father Peyton first met Irene on August 5, 1945 at Good Shepard Church in Beverly Hills. He had invited a group of stars to perform on his radio series, *The Family Theatre*. Father Peyton recalled that Irene misunderstood him at first, thinking he wanted her to portray the Blessed Virgin. She protested, insisting she "wouldn't be worthy of it." When Father Peyton explained that he wanted her simply to guest on the show, Irene agreed and appeared many times. She also became a benefactor to the organization. Father Peyton said, "She was a dignified woman with the air of a queen."

B-6 "Actress Irene Dunne, 88, starred in Movie Classics." *Chicago Tribune*. September 5, 1990.
Irene Dunne's career was recalled in this obituary. Her daughter Mary Frances Griffin Gage said Irene had been bedridden for the last month of her life. Irene's business manager, John Larkin, added that she had been suffering from an irregular heartbeat for a year. Article acknowledged the discrepancy in Irene's birthdate in many sources, but listed her age as eighty-eight instead of ninety-one.

B-7 "Actress Wins New Laurels." *Los Angeles Times*. August 10, 1932.
Irene Dunne's work in *Back Street* was praised.

B-8 "An American Queen: Extra Chins Help Irene Dunne Portray Victoria." *Life*. September 11, 1950.
Irene Dunne was pictured in the four stages of putting on her makeup for *The Mudlark*. The process, which included applying a cosmetic latex chinpiece, took ninety minutes. Although article claimed Irene cheerfully submitted to the makeup application, she complained, "I have to cut a strawberry in four pieces to get it down."

B-9 "Americana Set to Music is Paramount's *High, Wide and Handsome*." *Life*. September 27, 1937.
Reviews from around the country were quoted in this two-page pictorial spread, advertising *High, Wide and Handsome*. Irene Dunne was seen in four stills. The final panel said, "Till *Life* is wired for sound, can make its pictures move, we cannot do justice to a picture as colorful, as spectacular, as thrilling as Paramount's *High, Wide and Handsome*."

B-10   "Anti Bias Award for Irene Dunne." <u>New York Times</u>.
       February 5, 1949.
The National Conference of Christians and Jews gave Irene
Dunne a citation for her contribution to the anti-prejudice
movement. Bernard M. Baruch praised her "strength of
character and mind and her nobility of spirit." The
citation commended Irene for her "exemplification of
religious principles which have helped her as an artist and
which she has helped to spread through the medium of stage
and screen." In accepting the award, Irene said, "Trying to
build the brotherhood of man without the Fatherhood of God
is like having the spokes of a wheel without the hub."

B-11   Ardmore, Jane. "Irene Dunne: She'll Always Be
       Hollywood's Perfect Lady." <u>Photoplay</u>. December,
       1975.
Biographical sketch of Irene Dunne, accompanied by three
photographs, including one from the 1970s. Irene recalled
her acting technique of becoming the character. "But," she
said, "When the day's work was over, I left 'her' and 'him'
and went home to my own very wonderful life." Irene
confessed that her mother probably wanted to be an actress
"way way down deep in her heart." Adelaide Dunn had
graduated from the Cincinnati Conservatory of Music. Since
the death of Irene's husband Francis ("Frank") Griffin in
1965, she had been handling his business affairs. She
called her brother Charles "my mainstay," as he gave up his
position after Frank's death to help Irene. In addition to
her fundraising work with Saint John's Hospital, Irene
served on the California Arts Commission for three years.
The commission's goal was to bring culture to the small
communities of the state. One of the projects sponsored
during Irene's term was a sculpture show for the blind.

B-12   Arnold, Gary. "Stars! Celebration! AFI's 10th
       Anniversary Toast." <u>Washington Post</u>. November 6,
       1977.
The American Film Institute (AFI) planned a twelve-day
celebration for their tenth anniversary. Beginning November
6, 1977, the festivities included premieres, retrospectives,
and seminars, as well as a stellar fundraising gala, which
was televised by CBS. Special events were held at the
Eisenhower Theatre in Washington, D.C.. Irene Dunne
introduced <u>Love Affair</u>, and clips from <u>Roberta</u> and <u>My Favorite Wife</u>. Following the screening, Irene answered
questions. Tickets cost five dollars for members of AFI and
seven dollars for nonmembers.

B-13   "Art Perception through the Sense of Touch." <u>San Francisco Chronicle-Examiner</u>. January 4, 1970.
Irene Dunne, blind pianist George Shearing, and Nancy Reagan
(then First Lady of California) planned to attend the
opening ceremonies for "Dimension" at San Francisco's M.H.
de Young Memorial Museum on January 12, 1970. Presented by
the California Arts Commission, of which Irene was a member,
"Dimension" was billed as an exhibition of sculpture for the

sighted and the blind. The purpose of the show was to make art more accessible to the blind and to give the sighted a new perspective. The thirty pieces of sculpture were selected because of their varied textures. The exhibit included a Braille map to lead visitors through the gallery, Braille inscriptions along a rail surrounding the gallery, and a study area with talking books and Braille material on art and art history. Valued at more than half a million dollars and spanning 3,100-year period, the works were borrowed from California museums and galleries. Although there was a permanent gallery for the blind in North California, "Dimension" marked the first touring exhibit aimed at bringing art to the handicapped. Los Angeles, Sacramento, San Diego, Fresno, and Long Beach were among the cities which hosted the exhibit.

B-14   "Art with a New 'Dimension.'" Oakland Tribune. January 13, 1970.
Irene Dunne was pictured, guiding the fingers of a blind student over sculptures of St. Peter and St. Anthony, at the opening of "Dimension." The exhibit, put together by the California Arts Commission (CAC), allowed visitors to touch the sculptures. Among the celebrities attending the opening of the exhibit at San Francisco's M.H. de Young Memorial Museum were CAC member Irene Dunne, Nancy Reagan (wife of California governor Ronald Reagan), Mayor Joseph Alioto, and John W. Grossman, chairman of the CAC.

B-15   "At Debutantes' Party." New York Herald Tribune. November 27, 1953.
Photograph of Irene Dunne and her daughter Mary Frances Griffin at the Gotham Debutante Ball. The ball, a benefit for the New York Foundling Hospital, was held at the Plaza Hotel. Mary Frances was then a student at Manhattanville College. She was adopted through the New York Foundling Hospital.

B-16   Austin, Jay. "It Was Rumored..." American Movie Classics Magazine. March, 1989. p. 11.
Irene Dunne was urged to come out of retirement to play the role of Aunt Alicia in the film Gigi. Irene declined, preferring to stay in retirement. The role also was offered to Yvonne Printemps and Ina Claire, before Isabel Jeans was cast.

B-17   Badder, David and Baker, Bob. "Irene Dunne. Film Dope. No. 13, January, 1978. pp. 35-37.
Brief career study of Irene Dunne, including a list of her film and television appearances. A career essay urged film-goers to re-examine Irene's performances to better understand her versatility. Article included several photographs from her films.

B-18   Barris, Alex. Hollywood's Other Women. A.S. Barnes and Co., Inc. Cranbury, New Jersey. 1975. pp. 13, 18, 23, 39, 53, 66, 82, 89, 104, 191.

Irene Dunne's starring roles were contrasted with those of the second female leads in this book about supporting actresses. Irene was mentioned in sections on Gail Patrick (her co-star in <u>My Favorite Wife</u>), Barbara O'Neil (<u>When Tomorrow Comes</u>), Frances Dee (<u>The Silver Cord</u>), Beulah Bondi (<u>Penny Serenade</u>), Jean Dixon and Lucille Ball (<u>Joy of Living</u>), and Helen Westley (<u>Show Boat</u>). Irene also was painted as a charming matriarch in <u>Life with Father</u> and <u>I Remember Mama</u>.

B-19   Bart, Peter. "Elections Arouse Hollywood Stars." <u>New York Times</u>. October 13, 1964.
Bart claimed that the 1964 Presidential election was the first time a majority of entertainment figures openly supported candidates. In addition to offering monetary support, the stars appeared in television spots, spoke at rallies and luncheons, and even toured in satirical revues. Irene Dunne was one of the stars who signed an ad in one of the trade papers supporting Republican candidate Barry Goldwater. Later, Irene claimed she was a Nixon Republican, rather than a Goldwater Republican, saying she disliked extremism.

B-20   _____. "Liberals Vs. Their Movies." <u>New York Times</u>. August 29, 1965.
Bart discussed the political activism of current film stars, noting that the studios discouraged any activity that might be deemed controversial during the 1930s and '40s. Although the article focused on supporters of liberal causes, Irene Dunne was listed among the "small coterie of old-time stars who had long decorated conservative banquets" at a fundraiser for Republican candidate Barry Goldwater during the 1964 Presidential campaign.

B-21   Beatty, Jerome. "Lady Irene." <u>American Magazine</u>. November, 1944. pp. 28-29, 117-19.
Interview with Irene Dunne, recalling her career, her war work, and details of her personal life. She claimed she had few friends in the film business, aside from Loretta Young. Irene preferred to keep her life away from the studio private. Because she and her husband kept such a low profile, Irene said, "When we go out the photographers don't pay any attention to me. They concentrate on Doctor." Although Beatty erroneously claimed that Irene recorded songs from <u>Show Boat</u> during her tour of the musical, he included some other interesting trivia about Irene's performances. He recalled spilling ink on Irene's tablecloth during his first meeting with the actress. His jitters disappeared when Irene insisted milk would take out the stain, remaining a perfect lady throughout the interview.

B-22   "The Beauty from Within..." <u>Stage</u>. February, 1937.
Irene Dunne was pictured in an ad for Elizabeth Arden makeup. The ad claimed, "From the humor of <u>Theodora Goes</u>

Wild to the exacting dramatic moods of Madame Curie, her next picture, Miss Dunne moves with grace and distinction, the quality of her own beauty made real by Screen-Stage Make-up [sic] by Elizabeth Arden."

B-23   "The Bended Knee." Time. April 4, 1949. p. 40.
Irene Dunne was pictured clutching a bouquet of flowers, accompanying the announcement that the University of Notre Dame had awarded her the Laetare Medal. The medal, given to an outstanding member of the Roman Catholic laity, was awarded only three months after Irene was honored by the National Conference of Christians and Jews. The conference named Irene as "the person who has done most in 1948 to promote better understanding among people of all faiths."

B-24   Best, Katharine. "Dead Ringers." Stage.
       August, 1938. pp. 26-27.
Discussion of Hollywood's trend toward copying a successful film's format, like the whimsical family in You Can't Take It with You. Best complained about the use of gag situations, violent offstage noises, symbolism, and comedy built on incongruity. She found The Awful Truth embodied all the qualities she disliked. Irene Dunne was pictured in stills from The Awful Truth and Joy of Living.

B-25   Biery, Ruth. "Irene's Secret Marriage."
       Photoplay. April, 1931. pp. 35, 135.
Irene Dunne debated about keeping her marriage to Dr. Francis Griffin a secret when she entered films because she thought it might be detrimental to her career. After Cimarron was released, reporters clamored to interview her. Irene was relieved when Photoplay uncovered the truth about her marital status. She openly discussed her relationship with Frank, who had watched her test for Cimarron and advised her on every move. She recalled that Frank had been opposed to her career at the beginning of their marriage, but now encouraged her to act. Irene said that the long distance marriage cost the Griffins a fortune in telephone bills, averaging seven hundred dollars a month.

B-26   Bird, Adelia. "And the Bride Wore..." Modern
       Screen. July, 1936. pp. 64-66, 80-81.
Screen wedding gowns were discussed, including the one worn by Irene Dunne in Show Boat.

B-27   _____. "What They Like to Wear." Modern
       Screen. March, 1936. pp. 56-57, 86-88.
Irene Dunne and director John Stahl were pictured selecting costumes for Magnificent Obsession from Hattie Carnegie's salon.

B-28   Birmingham, Stephen. "What Have They Done to Irene
       Dunne." McCall's. August, 1964. pp. 100, 131-32.
Interview with Irene Dunne in her Los Angeles home. Since her United Nations appointment, many people thought Irene had retired from show business. She insisted she was not

retired, although she had turned down many scripts. She
confessed that she had read many plays, looking for a role
that "said something." Birmingham described Irene as aloof,
quoting her friend Mildred Knopf, who said, "You never get
really close to Irene. There's always something withheld."
Movie colleagues recalled her ambition. Irene said she
built a private life, focusing on community service and her
family, knowing that acting was not everything there was.
Her hobbies included spending time with her husband, walking
with their black French poodle Sanka, reading aloud to each
other, and visiting her grandchildren. Because Irene
disliked shopping, designers submitted sketches to her, from
which she selected three or four dresses a year. She
credited her youthful looks to getting plenty of rest and
fresh air. She admitted that she enjoyed watching her
movies on television and tried to view them objectively.
Irene stressed the importance of faith, in religion and the
faith of possibilities.

B-29   Blum, Daniel and Kobal, John. <u>A New Pictorial
        History of the Talkies</u>. G.P. Putnam's Sons. New
        York. 1973. pp. 20, 34, 45, 48, 68, 76, 85, 95,
        127, 135, 152, 158, 173, 174, 183, 206.
Chronological arrangement of stills, presenting a history of
sound films. Irene Dunne was seen in a 1930 portrait, as
well as in scenes ranging from <u>Cimarron</u> to <u>The Mudlark</u>.

B-30   Boyer, Charles. "Irene." <u>Photoplay</u>. October,
        1939.
The star of <u>Love Affair</u> discussed his leading lady, Irene
Dunne.

B-31   Brady, Gloria. "A Salute to Cary Grant." <u>American
        Movie Classics Magazine</u>. January, 1989. pp. 4-5.
Overview of the actor's career as American Movie Classics
cable station aired a film tribute. Irene Dunne was
mentioned as his co-star in <u>The Awful Truth</u> and <u>My
Favorite Wife</u>, and pictured in a scene from <u>Penny
Serenade</u>.

B-32   Brady, Thomas F. "Hollywood Collides with the Wage
        Ceiling." <u>New York Times</u>. November 8, 1942.
Myrna Loy retired from the screen after marrying John Hertz,
Jr. in May, 1942. Loy's departure from MGM forced the
studio to find a replacement to star opposite William Powell
in the <u>Thin Man</u> series. MGM signed Irene Dunne to a
contract, which also provided that she would star in <u>The
White Cliffs of Dover</u> and <u>Gaslight</u>. Loy settled her
dispute with the studio and returned to make two more <u>Thin
Man</u> movies. <u>Gaslight</u> was filmed by MGM in 1944 with
Ingrid Bergman, Charles Boyer, and Joseph Cotten. Irene
starred in <u>The White Cliffs of Dover</u> for MGM in 1944.

B-33   _____. "Stars Help Make Religious Picture." <u>New
        York Times</u>. December 1, 1949.
Irene Dunne was one of the stars of <u>You Can Change the</u>

World, a thirty-minute short produced by the Christophers. Although founded by a priest, the Christophers claimed to be a non-sectarian group who wanted citizens to put their moral concepts to work in society. Other stars who donated their services to make the short included Jack Benny, Loretta Young, and Bob Hope.

B-34 "British Score U.S. Stars." *New York Times*. March 19, 1950.

The House of Commons planned to address the issue of granting labor permits to American artists and senior technicians, following a brouhaha about *The Mudlark*. British Actors Equity protested the choice of Irene Dunne to play Queen Victoria in the film. Despite the protest, *The Mudlark* was shot at a studio in Shepperton, with Irene as the monarch.

B-35 Brockman, Alfred. *The Movie Book: The 1930s*. Crescent Books. New York. 1987. pp. 22, 74, 76, 81, 102, 110, 111, 112, 113, 145, 166, 167, 175, 186, 203, 245, 268, 278, 290, 310, 313, 428, 451, 453, 454, 458.

Pictorial history of 1930s films, with stills of Irene Dunne in most of her first twenty-seven features. Inexplicably, *Thirteen Women*, *The Secret of Madame Blanche*, *If I Were Free*, *This Man Is Mine*, and *The Awful Truth* were not included.

B-36 Burden, Janet. "Parted but Happily Married." *Motion Picture*. July, 1932. pp. 26-27, 75, 77.

Despite the fact that Irene Dunne worked in Hollywood and her husband Dr. Francis ("Frank") Griffin worked in New York, they maintained a solid marriage. Although the Griffins had seen each other only seven times over the last twenty months, Burden reported that they were the happiest screen couple she knew. Irene said she tried to maintain Frank's professional dignity by keeping him out of her interviews as much as possible. In addition to frequent telephone conversations, the couple spent Irene's film hiatuses together. When Irene visited New York, the Griffins lived in the apartment they first rented as newlyweds. Frank spent the rest of the year in bachelor quarters at his club. She estimated their phone bills ran $350 per month. Irene was quoted as saying, "It's a temporary situation that has become permanent, and it's impossible - for any length of time ahead." She continued, "But for just today - well, we manage. And we keep hoping that something will happen so we can be together." Despite Burden's dour predictions that the marriage would end in divorce like previous Hollywood happy couples', the Griffins were together until Frank's death in 1965. Article included a full-page portrait of Irene, as well as a photo of the Griffins.

B-37 "Bust Is Dunne and Dedicated." *Los Angeles Herald Examiner*. May 8, 1985.

Irene Dunne and her grandson Mark Shinnick were pictured at the dedication at Saint John's Hospital and Health Center, where a life-size bronze bust of Irene by sculptor Artis Lane was unveiled.

B-38   Cades, Hazel Rawson. "Life with Bangs." _Woman's Home Companion_. September, 1947. pp. 7-8.

Irene Dunne and Elizabeth Taylor, stars of _Life with Father_, modeled hairstyles with bangs. Cades confessed that Irene's movie bangs were hair pieces, designed to save the actress time in the makeup department each morning. When not in use, the bangs were attached to a wig block with Irene's name on it, which was made in proportion to her head. Cades recalled an amusing incident involving a wig block mixup. The _Life with Father_ rehearsals were halted one morning so that Irene could try on a new set of bangs. Cades wrote, "The hairdresser checked the fit and Irene was about to put the bangs back when she noticed the sign. The bangs had been delivered on the wrong head. The block read: Eddie Cantor." Cades could not imagine the curly, feminine bangs on the comedian and concluded, "Now that's something I should like to see."

B-39   Calhoun, Dorothy. "Off with the New Clothes, and On with the Old!" _Motion Picture_. June, 1933. pp. 54-55, 92-93.

The popularity of period films and costumes were discussed in this article, which included Irene Dunne in a costume from _The Secret of Madame Blanche_.

B-40   "California Callers." _Washington Post_. December 1, 1954.

Perle Mesta gave a small party for Irene Dunne while she was in Washington with a group of friends from California. The columnist reported that Irene wore a dark red decollete gown "that fitted her superb figure like the paper on the wall." He continued, "She's the most different person in the acting business this columnist has ever met. Instead of talking about herself,...she shows such an interest in you and your surroundings that you forget to ask her what's cooking in Hollywood."

B-41   "Cardinal Hosts Evening for Bob, Dolores Hope." _Los Angeles Times_. December 5, 1980.

Pictorial showing guests at a benefit for Catholic charities hosted by Cardinal Timothy Manning. Bob and Dolores Hope were honored in an evening of memories at the benefit, which was held at the Beverly Wilshire Hotel on December 3, 1980. Irene Dunne was pictured with Daniel Donohue.

B-42   Carpozi, Jr., George. _The Great Ladies of Hollywood_. Manor Books, Inc. New York. 1978.

B-43   _Cary Grant: In the Spotlight_. Galley Press. New York. 1980. pp. 40, 44, 46-47, 49, 134-35, 138, 140-41.

Pictorial overview of Cary Grant's life and career. Irene Dunne was mentioned in conjunction with The Awful Truth, My Favorite Wife, and Penny Serenade. Book included a full-page publicity photograph from The Awful Truth and half-page stills from The Awful Truth and Penny Serenade.

B-44   "Cast Changes." Variety. May 29, 1929.
Irene Dunne replaced Norma Terris in the touring company of Show Boat, then playing in Boston.

B-45   Cerf, Phyllis. "Irene Dunne's First Job." Good Housekeeping. February, 1958. p. 116.
Irene Dunne reminisced about her earliest days in New York when she tried to give producer Florenz Ziegfeld a letter praising her talents from his father, the founder of Irene's alma mater, the Chicago Musical College. Irene recalled how she turned down Ziegfeld's offer of a chorus position, however he hired her later for the lead in Show Boat. Irene, then an alternate representative to the United Nations, praised her new career. She was quoted as saying, "No play or motion picture I was ever in had as much drama. I am a fortunate woman to be allowed to play this new role of trying to promote better understanding among people."

B-46   Champlin, Charles. "Dunne: Recalling a Hollywood Rarity." Los Angeles Times. September 7, 1990.
Arts editor Champlin reminisced about Irene Dunne's stellar performances following her September 4 death. Champlin praised Irene's happy marriage and her charitable efforts. However, he said her one vanity was her sensitivity about her age. He recalled that a woman wrote to him after his 1985 article "Irene Dunne: Always a Lady of the House" appeared (B-47). The woman claimed her mother was born in the same Indiana hospital as Irene - in 1896. Other sources insist Irene was born in Louisville, so the woman's claim does not seem valid. In any case, Champlin concluded, "It is ungallant to raise this matter at all...and my own view is that a woman is as young as she says she is." He continued, "By any reckoning, 86, 89, 92 or 94 years, Irene Dunne had had a long and splendid life, and brought an uncommon dignity to an industry where it is never in long supply."

B-47   _____. "Irene Dunne: Always a Lady of the House." Los Angeles Times. December 5, 1985.
Interview with Irene Dunne concerning the Kennedy Center Honors. She discussed her love of comedy, which she considered easier than drama, but not as rewarding. After the death of her husband in 1965, Irene set up an office in her home to take care of the Griffin business interests, which included a part ownership of the Beverly Wilshire Hotel. Although she was still active in a few charities, including Saint John's Hospital, Irene said she seldom attended public events. Despite her stereotype as a lady, Irene said friends found she more closely resembled the

madcap Theodora in <u>Theodora Goes Wild</u>.

B-48 _____. "Irene Dunne Receives Kennedy Center Award." <u>Asbury Park Press</u> [New Jersey]. December 15, 1985.
Reprint of "Irene Dunne: Always a Lady of the House," including a photograph of Irene Dunne from the 1970s.

B-49 Chierichetti, David. "Irene Dunne Today." <u>Film Fan Monthly</u>. February, 1971.
Detailed account of Irene Dunne's career by film historian Chierichetti, who coordinated the 1975 Filmex tribute to the actress.

B-50 "Christophers Plan Films in War on Evil Influences." <u>Hollywood Reporter</u>. September 19, 1949.
Director Leo McCarey suggested a thirty-film series to counteract the evil influences in government, labor management, education, and the media. The series was produced by the Christophers, a non-sectarian group founded by Father James Keller. McCarey volunteered to direct the first short. Other celebrities who offered their services gratis were Irene Dunne, Loretta Young, Jack Benny, Spencer Tracy, and Jimmy Durante. The shorts were based on Keller's books <u>You Can Change the World</u> and <u>Three Minutes a Day</u>.

B-51 "Christophers to Put $1 Million in Movies to 'Throw Out Evil.'" <u>Valley Times</u> [North Hollywood]. September 19, 1949.
Father James Keller, founder of the Christophers, announced that the group would produce thirty half-hour shorts to promote morality. Among the stars who volunteered their services were Irene Dunne, Spencer Tracy, Rosalind Russell, Jimmy Durante, and Jeanne Crain.

B-52 Christy, George. "The Great Life." <u>The Hollywood Reporter</u>. May 8, 1985. p. 15.
A bronze bust of Irene Dunne was unveiled at Saint John's Hospital and Health Center in Santa Monica. The festivities included a Mass and luncheon honoring Irene, whom the Sisters of Charity called "The First Lady of Saint John's." The bust, by Artis Lane, is located in the hospital's fountain court.

B-53 _____. "The Great Life." <u>The Hollywood Reporter</u>. December 12, 1985. p. 22.
Account of the two-day festivities surrounding the Kennedy Center Honors, which included dinner at the State Department, a luncheon at Washington's Ritz Carlton, a reception at the White House, and a star-studded gala at Kennedy Center. Although Irene Dunne was in Georgetown Hospital during the gala, she was able to attend the State Department dinner. James Stewart called Irene "an American thoroughbred" in his tribute at the gala. At a dance following the White House reception, Roddy McDowall confessed that he had an ongoing "fantasy love match" with

200   Irene Dunne

Irene since he first saw her on film. A photograph of the six honorees, taken before the State Department dinner, was included.

B-54   Churchill, Douglas W. "Discord in Hollywood." New York Times. October 26, 1941.
Deanna Durbin's dispute with Universal Studios was discussed. Irene Dunne was mentioned as one of the stars with whom Universal had a contract. Churchill claimed that Durbin's revolt would have been disasterous for the studio, had they not recently signed such "money-makers" as Irene, Charles Boyer, Margaret Sullavan, and Bud Abbott and Lou Costello.

B-55   _____. "Hollywood Letter." New York Times. November 3, 1935.
Discussion of the talent trading that was going on between the studios, with film companies loaning out their stars to appear in movies made by their rivals. Among the trades mentioned was a deal that never materialized. RKO star Ann Harding wanted to make The Indestructable Mrs. Talbot, but Paramount owned the rights. RKO traded the services of Harding and Irene Dunne, who were scheduled to appear in The Old Maid, in exchange for the rights to The Indestructable Mrs. Talbot. The Indestructable Mrs. Talbot became The Lady Consents, released by RKO in 1936. The Old Maid was filmed in 1939 by Warner Bros. with Bette Davis and Miriam Hopkins.

B-56   _____. "Hollywood Scorns the Alter Ego." New York Times. June 6, 1937.
Twenty-two actors who doubled for the stars were getting a chance to work together in the film Once a Hero. Churchill profiled some of the doubles, including Mary Miner, who was Irene Dunne's stand-in during her RKO years.

B-57   _____. "Hollywood's War Boom." New York Times. March 16, 1941.
Although Ginger Rogers and Irene Dunne had been announced as candidates for the lead in RKO's Sister Carrie, the film was abandoned. Paramount finally brought Theodore Dreiser's controversial novel to the screen in 1952 as Carrie, starring Jennifer Jones.

B-58   _____. "Latest Scarlett Letter." New York Times. December 18, 1938.
Fresh from a trip abroad, Wesley Ruggles planned to make Invitation to Happiness appealing to American, as well as European, audiences. He predicted that the film would be successful, noting that Irene Dunne was a "great favorite" abroad and that American prizefights were also popular.

B-59   _____. "Methods in Madness." Stage. March, 1938. pp. 29-30.
Profile of screenwriters Gene Towne and Graham Baker, who authored the script for Joy of Living. The screenwriters,

known for their wacky antics, often appeared on the set to instruct Irene Dunne and Douglas Fairbanks, Jr. how to play a scene. The story included two stills of Irene and Fairbanks from the film, plus photos of Towne and Baker showing how the scenes should be played.

B-60 _____. "The New Production Set-up at Fox." New York Times. November 24, 1940.
Agent Charles Feldman and his clients Irene Dunne, Charles Boyer, Ronald Colman, Lewis Milestone, and Anatole Litvak, formed Group Productions, in association with 20th Century-Fox. The company planned to make films at the Fox studios with Fox money. The major participants would be paid on a profit-sharing basis. Churchill summed up Group Productions' affiliation with Fox, stating that it would "strengthen the star roster and...enable the studio to trade in talent more advantageously."

B-61 _____. "Nobody Loves the Film City." New York Times. November 4, 1934.
Irene Dunne's contract insisted that her name must be "mentioned first and in larger type than any other member of the cast." Such was the case in Roberta, which also starred Fred Astaire and Ginger Rogers. It was announced that RKO planned to use only "Smoke Gets in Your Eyes" from the Broadway score and have Jerome Kern write new songs for the film. Instead, only two songs were added to the original score: "Lovely to Look At" and "I Won't Dance."

B-62 "Clark Gable No. 1 in New Film Poll." New York Times. January 4, 1937.
Clark Gable was named the most popular film star in a poll conducted by Boxoffice, a trade journal. Irene Dunne was one of the runners-up. Independent theatre owners, newspaper columnists, and civic groups were among those polled.

B-63 "Clear the Way for Comedy." Movie-Radio Guide. March 15, 1941.
Penny Serenade was named "co-picture of the week," with Footsteps in the Dark. Both films were given a one-page pictorial review. It was noted that the prop men had some difficulty locating musical jugs and counterfeit bootleg liquor labels for a scene early in Penny Serenade. They were finally found in the garage of one of the prop men.

B-64 Clifford, Charles V. St. Louis' Fabulous Municipal Theatre. Charles V. Clifford. St. Louis. 1969. pp. 71-72.
Irene Dunne's summer season with the St. Louis Municipal Opera was discussed in this history of the theatre. Clifford said that rain interrupted the end of the second act of Victor Herbert's Eileen, the show in which Irene made her Municipal Opera debut. Despite strong winds, which blew over some scenery, the cast finished the performance. Some of Irene's former classmates recalled that she had not

202   Irene Dunne

participated in school plays and had little interest in dramatics while attending St. Louis's Loretto Academy.

B-65   "Clinging Vine Opens." Billboard. December 23, 1922.
Producer Henry W. Savage planned a special performance of the musical for the critics and an invited audience on December 24, 1922 at the Knickerbocker Theatre. The musical's official opening was December 25. The Clinging Vine marked Irene Dunne's Broadway debut.

B-66   "Clip of Diamonds, Sapphires." Indianapolis Star. October 27, 1940.
Several movie stars' wardrobes were described, including Irene Dunne, who was seen at Ciro's in a white and navy print crepe dinner dress.

B-67   "Clipped from Interviews." Film Fun. May, 1937. p. 58.
Stars were quoted (or misquoted) in these snippets from interviews from other publications. Irene Dunne said, "It's a good idea to get a slant on your own stature every now and then!"

B-68   "Coffin Nailers Busy Boxing Axis Rulers." New York Times. September 9, 1942.
Irene Dunne sold war bonds and urged patrons to nail the coffins of Hitler, Horohito, and Mussolini, which were set up in Times Square for the rally. Irene was on tour as part of the movie industry's billion-dollar war bond sales campaign.

B-69   Cole, Hubert. "Is She Too Versatile?" Picturegoer and Film Weekly. November 4, 1939.
British reporter Cole posed the question about Irene Dunne's versatility, stating, "The point is that Miss Dunne seems to be able to do so many things - and to do them all remarkably well." He summed up her career as "effortless," recounting her successes in drama, comedy, and musicals, which seemed to occur with equal ease.

B-70   Condon, Frank. "She Made a Hole in One." Saturday Evening Post. June 11, 1932. pp. 91-92.
Irene Dunne's early career was recalled in this profile. Condon said Irene enjoyed golf, but was evasive about her scores. She confessed that she once broke one hundred at the Oyster Harbor course at Cape Cod and got a hole in one at the Pebble Beach course in Carmel, California. Despite Irene's elaborate tale of how she scored the hole in one, Condon was dubious. Among the trivia he reported was that Irene liked to eat hard-boiled eggs dipped in vinegar, was depressed by good-looking men, and won first prize at a dahlia show. She did not drink, and smoked only when in mixed company "who might point her out as an oddity if she didn't."

B-71   Considine, Shaun. <u>Bette and Joan: The Divine</u>
        <u>Feud</u>. E.P. Dutton. New York. 1989. pp. 110,
        113, 145, 204.
Irene Dunne was mentioned in a list of the ten most
glamorous women in Hollywood, as named by actor George Brent
in the 1930s. Bette Davis, then dating Brent, was annoyed
that she was omitted from the list. Irene was a guest at a
dinner given by Joan Crawford to honor Noel Coward in the
1940s.

B-72   Coons, Robbin. "Irene Dunne Gets Dunked Before
        Lens." <u>Richmond News Leader</u> [Virginia].
        February 23, 1940.
The press was invited to the filming of a scene from <u>My</u>
<u>Favorite Wife</u>, in which Irene Dunne fell in a swimming pool
fully clothed. Because of numerous retakes on a previous
scene, the "Dunking of Dunne," as Coons dubbed it, was
delayed until the next day. Coons recalled other scenes, in
which usually lady-like film celebrities engaged in raucous
behavior. Coons concluded, "There is something extremely
humanizing about such scenes. Irene Dunne knows it. The
Dunking of Dunne wouldn't be in there if Irene didn't like
it."

B-73   "Costume and Make-up [sic]." <u>What's Happening in</u>
        <u>Hollywood</u>. April 5, 1943.
With the government restricting fabric for film costumes
during World War II, designer Edith Head discussed her
economizing measures. Irene Dunne's costumes for <u>A Guy</u>
<u>Named Joe</u> were among those affected.

B-74   Creelman, Eileen. "Irene Dunne Talks of '<u>Together</u>
        <u>Again</u>,' Columbia Comedy which Opens Thursday."
        <u>New York Sun</u>. November 21, 1944.
Interview with Irene Dunne about <u>Together Again</u>. She
compared the film to <u>Theodora Goes Wild</u>, saying both
comedies took place in small towns. Because Irene was in
New York when retakes were shot, she was not in the final
scene of the film. She said, "...they have two streaks of
lightning, a male lightning and a female lightning...for the
final love scene. I don't understand it; but everyone says
it's wonderful and very funny." She contrasted <u>Together</u>
<u>Again</u> director Charles Vidor with Sidney Franklin, director
of <u>The White Cliffs of Dover</u>. Irene said Vidor liked a
spontaneous quality in his films, while Franklin researched
every detail.

B-75   Crewe, Regina. "Irene Dunne to Go to Europe as Two
        Movies Await Her." <u>New York American</u>. June 5,
        1936.
As Irene Dunne prepared for a European holiday, she
discussed her past and future films, which included
<u>Theodora Goes Wild</u>. Crewe mentioned that Irene had turned
down roles in <u>Valiant Is the Name for Carrie</u> [sic] and
<u>The Old Maid</u>. Irene actually turned down <u>Sister Carrie</u>.
<u>Valiant Is the Word for Carrie</u> was a 1936 film with

204   Irene Dunne

Gladys George. Ironically, George was nominated for an Academy Award for the film at the same time Irene was nominated for Theodora Goes Wild.

B-76   Croce, Arlene. The Fred Astaire and Ginger Rogers Book. Outerbridge and Lazard, Inc. New York. 1972. pp. 44-53.
Chapter on Roberta included credits, synopsis, production notes, and descriptions of musical numbers. In addition to stills from the film, a photo of the song sheet was provided.

B-77   Cross, Miriam Dungan. "'Dimension' Brings Art to the Blind." Oakland Tribune. January 11, 1970.
"Dimension" was the first touring art exhibit for the blind, as well as the first major exhibition for the California Arts Commission (CAC), of which Irene Dunne was a member. Established by the State Legislature in 1964, the CAC fostered growth of the arts in California communities. California galleries loaned their works and assisted the CAC in compiling an elaborate catalogue with pictures and essays on the thierty sculptures. Irene Dunne narrated a talking book about the exhibit, which toured California for eleven months. Art crtic Cross detailed some of the works involved and suggested that a second show for the blind feature contemporary works by California sculptors or works that involved some sound.

B-78   Cruickshank, _____. "Irene Gets the Plum." Silver Screen. October, 1933.

B-79   Cumulated Dramatic Index, 1909-1949. G.K. Hall and Co. Boston. 1965.
Extensive list of articles, photographs, and reviews from a variety of periodicals, including news, movie, and fashion magazines. While much more comprehensive in length than other film star bibliographies, the Cumulated Dramatic Index generally provided only source, date, and page number.

B-80   Cuskelly, Richard. "A Five-hour Irene Dunne Film Festival." Los Angeles Herald-Examiner. March 23, 1975.
Irene Dunne was interviewed in conjunction with the retrospective of her career at the Los Angeles International Film Exposition (Filmex). She admitted that she felt a twinge of regret over her self-imposed retirement while watching Katharine Hepburn and Laurence Olivier in the telefilm Love Among the Ruins. She said, "For an instant I felt the old acting itch. That show was done so beautifully, in such good taste. Sir Larry was the one actor I yearned to work with and never did." Irene confided that she and Olivier were scheduled to do a film together in the 1930s for RKO, but it was canceled after the costume fittings. Irene recalled that she and Claudette Colbert were among the first actresses to free-lance. Although RKO

was her home base during the 1930s, her contract allowed her to make one film a year for Columbia and Universal as well. Irene said she retired in 1952, despite numerous offers, because she did not want to become a character actress. She felt sorry for current actors who had no studio to protect them. Although she claimed that the recent press had treated her fairly, she recalled the studio clearing up rumors about her father living in poverty during the height of her career, while, in fact, he had died when she was a child.

B-81 _____. "Irene Dunne Retrospective." Los Angeles Herald-Examiner. March 24, 1975.
Chronicle of the Los Angeles Film Exposition (Filmex) tribute to Irene Dunne, which was held at the Plitt Theatre on March 23, 1975. The tribute included clips from Irene's film and TV appearances, as well as a complete screening of Love Affair. During a question-and-answer session hosted by Roddy McDowall, Irene revealed that she did not like her real name. "I would have preferred to be called Irene Barkley - the Barkley I was going to steal from my favorite uncle," she said. "Instead I just added an 'E' to my real name, Dunn."

B-82 Daily Variety. September 11, 1990. p. 2.
Loretta Young was the only celebrity in attendance at Irene Dunne's funeral. Irene's business manager, John Larkin, said she did not want the event turned into a circus, therefore only thirty people were invited. Even former President Ronald Reagan was refused when he called to request an invitation.

B-83 Davidson, Bill. Spencer Tracy: Tragic Idol. E.P. Dutton. New York. 1987. pp. 3, 92.
Van Johnson recalled how Spencer Tracy saved Johnson's career by insisting that Johnson could not be replaced after he was injured during the filming of A Guy Named Joe. Author Davidson said A Guy Named Joe "also was a film in which, semi-drunk, [Tracy] needled Irene Dunne to such an extent (about her clothes, her hairdo, her bustline, her slightly longish nose) that she threatened to walk out of the picutre until [MGM mogul] Louis B. Mayer himself had to intercede to restore peace."

B-84 Devine, John F. "Irene Goes Wild." Modern Movies. April, 1937. pp. 34-35, 73-75.
Fans of Irene Dunne were used to surprises from their favorite star. After her meteoric rise in Cimarron, she was typecast as a dramatic actress. When she was given a chance to sing in Stingaree, it triggered her musical cycle. According to Devine, Irene decided to try her hand at comedy after the reaction to her blackface dance in Show Boat. Theodora Goes Wild and The Awful Truth brought her rave reviews. One trade paper was quoted as calling her work in The Awful Truth "the most captivating portrait in her film album," and describing Irene as "one of the

Melvyn Douglas recalled director Richard Boleslawski's unusual method of getting a surprised look from Irene Dunne in *Theodora Goes Wild* (Columbia, 1936). The film marked Irene's first comedy. (Doug McClelland collection)

screen's foremost commediennes." Devine claimed that Irene appreciated her comic roles, as they gave her fans the chance to see that she was not the "cold, stand-offish, always dignified lady" she played on screen. Article included stills from her upcoming film, Joy of Living.

B-85   "Do You Remember Mama?" Life. August 9, 1948. p. 101.
Irene Dunne was pictured in her costume from I Remember Mama in this ad for U.S. Savings Bonds. The ad tied in to the film, stating, "I Remember Mama proves...that, with a reserve fund in the present, you face the future with a confidence and faith that helps you get results."

B-86   Donnelly, Antoinette. "Attitudes Play Role in Remaining Active." New York Daily News. August 6, 1960.
Discussion of aging, citing Irene Dunne as an outstanding example of the older woman who stayed young. Article included a photograph of Irene.

B-87   Dooley, Roger. From Scarface to Scarlet. Harcourt Brace Jovanovich, Publishers. New York. 1979. pp. 38, 41, 42, 45, 114, 120, 132, 135, 237, 254, 267, 268, 269, 304, 342, 414, 426, 470, 471, 539, 544, 548, 549, 558, 567, 611, 612, 618.
Chronicle of 1930s films, broken down by genre. Dooley described Irene Dunne's performance in Theodora Goes Wild, stating, "[Her] slow, insinuating laugh reminded some reviewers of Lynn Fontanne's." Photographs from Symphony of Six Million, Show Boat, and Love Affair were included.

B-88   Douglas, Melvyn and Arthur, Tom. The Autobiography of Melvyn Douglas. University Press of America, Inc. Lanham, Maryland. 1986. p. 110.
Irene Dunne's co-star in Theodora Goes Wild recalled director Richard Boleslawski's unusual method for eliciting a look of surprise from Irene for an important scene. Douglas wrote, "The director warned the cast and crews, then crept up behind her and fired a blank cartridge from a hand gun held just below her buttocks." He continued, "If you look at the film,...you will be rewarded with one of the most breathless, bewildered on-camera entrances ever recorded."

B-89   Druxman, Michael B. Make It Again, Sam. A.S. Barnes and Co., Inc. Cranbury, New Jersey. 1975. pp. 185-91.
A chapter was devoted to Show Boat in this book on movie remakes. Druxman discussed the Edna Ferber novel and the three films based on it, claiming the 1929 version stuck closest to the book. Chapter included stills from all three films, two of which featured Irene Dunne.

B-90   Dunne, Irene. "Dignified." American Magazine.

August, 1942. pp. 84-85.
Irene Dunne explained why she disliked hearing herself described as "dignified." She recalled her first musical audition for a scholarship at the Chicago Musical College with renowned opera coach Edouardo Sacerdote. He relaxed the nervous Irene with a wink, giving her the confidence to sing and win the scholarship. She concluded, "But how different my story would have been if the man at the piano had been dignified instead of kind. Which is why, when I am called 'dignified,' I feel like saying to the accuser, 'When you say that, smile!'"

B-91 _____. "Do You Have a Problem?" <u>Silver Screen</u>. September, 1947 through May, 1952.
Irene Dunne dispensed advice in this monthly column.

B-92 _____. "Everybody's Etiquette." <u>Philadelphia Bulletin</u>. September 18, 1949.
The actress was a guest contributor in the weekly column devoted to giving "the right answers." Irene answered a question about what to do when someone makes a racial or ethnic slur during a social gathering. As the winner of an award from the National Conference of Christians and Jews, Irene said, "I try to deflect the aim of the slurs by pointing out the unreliabilty of generalities. If even this be termed rudeness - well, frankly, I call it being rude with reason." She was pictured with playwrights Howard Lindsay and Russel Crouse, who wrote <u>Life with Father</u>.

B-93 _____. "Freedom Is Responsibility." <u>Vital Speeches</u>. February 15, 1959. pp. 283-84.
Former United Nations delegate Irene Dunne delivered this speech at the Conference on Family Security, sponsored by the Insurance Company of North America, at Disneyland on January 9, 1959. Irene stressed the need for responsibilities in a free world. She said U.S. citizens must be capable of thinking rationally and making moral decisions. While she admitted this was sometimes difficult, she said it was easier than having someone else do the thinking and acting, as in Communist countries. Irene tied together her speech with a personal anecdote involving insurance. She said that her father's foresight to invest in insurance paid for her education and musical training. Irene concluded, "We Americans should put a little more living into our lives. That is the main challenge of ours."

B-94 _____. "How I Stay Normal in Hollywood." <u>Movie-Radio Mirror</u>. April 25, 1942. pp. 2-3.
Irene Dunne promoted her latest film, the madcap <u>Lady in a Jam</u>, with a look at how she "stayed normal" off screen. Irene said she never wanted to do outrageous things like the characters she played, despite the public perception that actors were unusual and eccentric. She wrote, "I confess to liking a well-ordered existence." Article included eight stills from the film, as well as a shot of Irene wallowing in black mud on location in Arizona to get a feel for her

Bibliography   209

role. Irene was also pictured on the cover.

B-95   _____. "Report on Economic Conditions in
        Non-self-governing Territories." <u>U.S. Department of
        State Bulletin</u>. December 2, 1957. p. 895.
United Nations Representative Irene Dunne gave the report to
the U.N. General Assembly on October 21, 1957.

B-96   _____. "Wish You Were Here." <u>Guideposts</u>.
        December, 1951. pp. 1-2, 23-24.
Irene Dunne discussed her religious philosophy, which
included the belief that the best way to keep one's religion
was to share it with others. She compared spreading her
religion to sharing details of a vacation. Although
vacations and religion both entailed making sacrifices, the
benefits each gave were more than worth it. Born a
Catholic, Irene said she took her faith for granted when she
was young. She recalled making the sign of a cross before
the opening of an early musical, an automatic response. She
credited her mother's steady faith with giving her strength.
Irene said she took her mother's presence for granted and
was shattered when Adelaide died. "How alone I would have
been at that time if she had not pointed the way to another
Comforter who would never leave me!" Irene said. Article
included a photograph of Irene and her husband kneeling at
the Holy Door of St. Paul's Basilica during their Holy
Pilgrimage to Rome in 1950.

B-97   "Dunne - in the Romantic Mood." <u>Motion Picture</u>.
        February, 1945. p. 58.
Irene Dunne modeled three costumes from <u>Together Again</u>.

B-98   "Dunne to Sing." <u>Movie-Radio Guide</u>. August 16,
        1941.
Irene Dunne was invited to sing with the Philadelphia
Symphony, an honor extended to only one star a year.

B-99   Durling, E.V. "On the Side." <u>New York Journal-
        American</u>. October 21, 1941.
Columnist Durling praised Irene Dunne's acting by calling
her "the Kentucky [Eleanora] Duse." Durling claimed he knew
Irene's pet name for her husband, but promised not to
disclose it.

B-100   Eames, John Douglas. <u>The MGM Story</u>. Crown
        Publishers, Inc. New York. 1975. pp. 74, 77, 97,
        128, 184, 198, 199, 210, 296.
Brief synopis, credits, and critique from MGM features made
between 1924 and 1974. Irene Dunne was mentioned in entries
for <u>The Great Lover</u>, <u>The Secret of Madame Blanche</u>, <u>A
Guy Named Joe</u>, and <u>The White Cliffs of Dover</u>.
Photographs included a full-page still of Irene and Alan
Marshall from <u>The White Cliffs of Dover</u>.

B-101   _____. <u>The Paramount Story</u>. Crown Publishers,
        Inc. New York. 1985. pp. 128, 137.

In another studio history, Eames presented credits, critique and summaries of Paramount films released between 1916 and 1984. Irene Dunne was listed in entries about *High, Wide and Handsome* and *Invitation to Happiness*. She also was seen in a still from the former.

B-102 "Event of the Week." *Movie-Radio Guide*.
August 24, 1940.
Nearly five thousand dollars was raised for the British War Relief Association of Southern California through a celebrity-studded performance of Noel Coward's play cycle *Tonight at 8:30* at the El Capitan Theatre. The August 5 premiere featured Constance Bennett and Douglas Fairbanks, Jr. in *We Were Dancing*, Binnie Barnes and Reginald Gardiner in *Red Peppers*, and Basil Rathbone and Gladys Cooper in *The Astonished Heart*. Irene Dunne was one of the celebrities in attendance on opening night. She was accompanied by producer Homer Curran. During the next two weeks, six other Coward plays were performed by volunteers from the screen community.

B-103 "Event of the Week." *Movie-Radio Guide*.
October 19, 1940. p. 6.
Irene Dunne was one of the celebrities who attended a Chinese Garden Festival at Pickfair on October 6, 1940. The event, which cost three dollars a head, benefited China's first orthopedic hospital and the Chinese war orphans. Rosalind Russell was committee chairman and Dr. T.K. Chang, Chinese consul at Los Angeles, served as honorary chairman. Other guests included Mary Martin, Dorothy Lamour, Anna May Wong, and Cesar Romero. The celebrity-signed guest book was sent to Madame Chiang Kai-Shek.

B-104 Everson, William K. *Love in the Film*. Citadel
Press. Secaucus, New Jersey. 1979. pp. 151-54.
Discussion of *Love Affair*, including credits, synopsis, and stills from the film. Everson praised director Leo McCarey's ability to build the film's structure like a comedy, yet evoke drama and pathos. Everson said, "Irene Dunne's underplayed farewell to Maria Ouspenskaya is a suddenly tender and poignant moment, as it would be in life, but as such moments all too rarely are in film."

B-105 Fairbanks, Jr., Douglas. *The Salad Days*.
Doubleday. New York. 1988. p. 277.
Fairbanks recalled his work with Irene Dunne in *Joy of Living*, calling her "one of the finest of screen actresses." He said, "Everyone adored Irene. She had an impeccable offstage reputation - as the virtuous wife of a doctor....She was fun to work with, yet wonderfully concentrated."

B-106 Faith, Willaim Robert. *Bob Hope*. G.P. Putnam's
Sons. New York. 1982. pp. 319, 360.
Irene Dunne was one of the many celebrated guests at Bob Hope's daughter's wedding on January 11, 1969 at North

Hollywood's St. Charles Borromeo Church. Irene also
attended a memorial for Jack Benny.

B-107   "Fashion of the Week." Movie-Radio Guide.
        September 28, 1940.
Irene Dunne and her husband were pictured at the opening of
the Ice Follies at the Pan-Pacific Auditorium.

B-108   "Fashion-Wise." What's Happening in Hollywood.
        November 13, 1943.
Current costume trends were discussed, including the fact
that Irene Dunne would be wearing mostly uniforms in A Guy
Named Joe.

B-109   Father Ted, S.S.P. Stars in My Heaven. St. Paul
        Monastery Press. Canfield, Ohio. 1948. pp. 32-39.
Catholic celebrities, including Loretta Young, Pat O'Brien,
Bing Crosby, and Joan Leslie, discussed their faith in this
booklet distributed by the Apostolate of the Press. A
chapter was devoted to Irene Dunne. Don Ameche was quoted
as saying that Irene's name was "synonymous with everything
that Catholicism stands for - a woman who has faith and
tolerance, pity and piety - everything." In order to
balance her career, family, home, and religion, Irene
avoided nightclubs and publicity stunts. She discussed her
life and career, insisting her routine was similar to that
of other women. Despite her many radio appearances, she
claimed she disliked the medium. She was always afraid of
disappointing the listeners. Irene said she preferred
singing to acting, however she admired people who could
express themselves on paper, a talent she wished she
possessed. Sense of humor was important to Irene; she
enjoyed playing pranks, as well as being the recipient. She
attended Mass daily and found it easy to rear her daughter
under the guidance of the church. When asked about
ambitions, she said she would like to sing opera, but did
not think she was good enough. Irene predicted that if she
entered a new career, it would be in politics, rather than
music. A self-confessed conservative, Irene concluded, "I
was, and I hope to continue to be what I am - myself."

B-110   Fein, Irving A. Jack Benny. G.P. Putnam's Sons.
        New York. 1976. pp. 16, 152, 153, 181, 260.
Irene Dunne was mentioned as one of the celebrities
attending Benny's funeral on December 29, 1974. She was
also on the dais at a 1957 Friars Club tribute, which raised
money for the Heart Fund. Although Fein, who was executive
producer of The Jack Benny Show, claimed Irene made her
television debut on the series, she had already hosted
twenty-six episodes of Schlitz Playhouse of Stars, and
appeared on What's My Line? and The Colgate Comedy Hour
before guesting on Benny's series.

B-111   Fernbach, Lyn. "22 Nations Raise $31,439,752 for
        U.N. Refugee Relief Fund." New York Herald
        Tribune. October 5, 1957.

212   Irene Dunne

Irene Dunne announced the United States' pledge to help refugees in Europe and the Middle East. It was Irene's first presentation before the United Nations General Assembly. Article included a photograph of Irene speaking at the General Assmebly on October 4.

B-112   Field, Alice Evans. "Costume Design." <u>Hollywood, U.S.A.: From Script to Screen</u>. New York. Vantage. 1952. pp. 114-21.
This book on costume design mentioned the pyschological importance of Irene Dunne's wardrobe in <u>Together Again</u>.

B-113   <u>Film Fun</u>. July, 1934. p. 15
Irene Dunne and Ralph Bellamy both reached for a book in a still from <u>This Man Is Mine</u>.

B-114   <u>Film Fun</u>. December, 1937. p. 73.
A tuxedoed Cary Grant straddled a motorcycle, flanked by Irene Dunne and Marguerite Churchill in this still from <u>The Awful Truth</u>.

B-115   "First Prize for 'Flour' Arrangement." <u>New York Daily News</u>. September 24, 1958.
Photograph of Irene Dunne presenting a twenty-five thousand dollar check to the winner of the Pillsbury's Best Tenth Grand National Bake-Off at New York's Waldorf-Astoria.

B-116   Fitzgerald, Michael G. <u>Universal Pictures</u>. Arlington House. New Rochelle. 1977. pp. 34, 143, 175, 176, 199, 228, 587.
Brief synopsis, credits, and critique of Universal films made between 1930 and 1976. Irene Dunne was mentioned in listings for <u>Back Street</u>, <u>Magnificent Obsession</u>, <u>Show Boat</u>, <u>When Tomorrow Comes</u>, <u>Unfinished Business</u>, <u>Lady in a Jam</u>, and <u>It Grows on Trees</u>. She was also seen in stills from the first four films.

B-117   "Five-time Academy Award Nominee Dunne Dead at 88." <u>Sacramento Union</u>. September 5, 1990.
Brief obituary, with Irene Dunne's business manager, John Larkin, claiming she was eighty-eight at the time of her death. Larkin said Irene had been in failing health for a year and "her heart gave out."

B-118   Flagg, James Montgomery. "Irene Dunne Has Charm and Beauty, Flagg Finds." <u>Richmond News Leader</u> [Virginia]. October 9, 1941.
Account of Flagg's visit to Irene Dunne's home, where he found her "a little too ideal to be true." Article included a sketch of Irene by Flagg.

B-119   Fletcher, Adele Whitely. "The True and Tender Story of Irene Dunne's Daughter." <u>Photoplay</u>. June, 1938.
Tale of how Irene Dunne and her husband Francis Griffin adopted their daughter Mary Frances.

B-120   Flint, Peter B. "Irene Dunne, a Versatile Actress of
        the 1930's and 40's, Dies at 91." New York Times.
        September 6, 1990.
Stills from I Remember Mama and The Awful Truth
accompanied this obituary. Irene Dunne's career was
chronicled. Although Flint was one of the few writers to
recognize Irene's correct birthdate, he said she played the
title role in the Chicago company of Irene, when, in fact,
she was in the chorus.

B-121   "Flu Epidemic Hits Movieland." Movie-Radio Guide.
        December 21, 1940. p. 6.
Several film studios had moved shooting outside the
soundstages to combat a contagious strain of flu that had
been hitting the stars. Irene Dunne was one of several
actors who were taken ill at work and had to be sent home
for medical attention the previous week. The epidemic
allegedly traveled to the United States from Hawaii.

B-122   Fontaine, Joan. No Bed of Roses. William Morrow
        and Company, Inc. New York. 1978. pp. 204-5.
Fontaine recalled a State Department-sponsored film junket
in South America during the spring of 1951. Celebrities in
attendance included Irene Dunne, Fred MacMurray, Robert
Cummings, and Patricia Neal. Fontaine remembered an
incident during Rio de Janeiro's Carnival. "At the hotel
one morning during the three-day celebration, I came out of
my suite just as Irene Dunne stepped out of her neighboring
one," Fontaine said. "'How did you sleep last night, Joan?'
inquired beautiful Irene. 'How could I sleep with all those
thousands on the beach chanting under my window 'Joanna
Fontana, Joanna Fontana!'" Fontaine replied wearily. "'Not
at all.' Irene smiled. 'I heard them too. They were
calling out 'Irenee Doonee, Irenee Doonee!'"

B-123   Foose, Thomas T. "B'way 'Boat' on Tour." Variety.
        September 24, 1990.
In a letter to the editor, Brooklyn resident Foose praised
Variety's obituary (B-232) of Irene Dunne and offered one
correction. He objected to the 1929 Show Boat company
being labeled the "Chicago company," as it played Chicago
only sixteen of the seventy-two weeks it toured. He noted
that most of the cast, excluding Irene, were from the
Broadway production.

B-124   "For Britain." New York Post. May 21, 1941.
Photograph of Irene Dunne, George Murphy, and a group of
young British evacuees, who appeared on Friendship Bridge,
the radio program of the British-American Ambulance Drivers.

B-125   "For Entertainment's Sake." Movie-Radio Guide.
        August 9, 1941. pp. 6-7.
Stars from movies, vaudeville, and radio raised over
twenty-three thousand dollars for the U.S.O. during a
three-hour performance at the Hollywood Bowl on June 29,
1941. Broadcast over CBS, the show was part of a $10

million drive to provide entertainment and religious facilities for the armed services. The most dramatic moment in the broadcast was when Edward G. Robinson announced he would donate his salary for his next film, estimated at one hundred thousand dollars, to the cause. Irene Dunne performed a skit with Cary Grant.

B-126 Fordin, Hugh. <u>Getting to Know Him: A Biography of Oscar Hammerstein II</u>. Random House. New York. 1977. pp. 139, 146, 148.

Fordin claimed Irene Dunne was "everyone's first choice" for the role of Magnolia in the 1936 film version of <u>Show Boat</u>. However, he incorrectly stated that she was discovered by a film scout while the touring production of the musical was in Los Angeles. In fact, Irene was discovered in Baltimore. Fordin also discussed <u>High, Wide and Handsome</u>, a film he considered ahead of its time.

B-127 "Foundation Circle Dedication." <u>Los Angeles Times</u>. May 8, 1985.

Irene Dunne was pictured with sculptor Artis Lane and Sister Marie Madeleine at the dedication of Foundation Circle at Saint John's Hospital and Health Center. Foundation Circle honored Irene for her fundraising efforts with a life-size bronze bust.

B-128 Franchey, John R. "Mitchell Manor's Master." <u>New York Times</u>. November 23, 1941.

Interview with character actor Thomas Mitchell, who was getting ready to juggle two film roles, in <u>Song of the Islands</u>, with Betty Grable, and <u>Tales of Manhattan</u>. In the latter, Franchey reported, Mitchell "will be married to Irene Dunne, who will be having an affair with Charles Boyer." Irene was not in the finished film, which was released by 20th Century-Fox in 1942. Rita Hayworth starred in the vignette with Boyer and Mitchell.

B-129 Francisco, Charles. <u>Gentleman: The William Powell Story</u>. St. Martin's Press. New York. 1985. pp. 218-20.

After seeing <u>Life with Father</u> on Broadway, William Powell decided he was perfect for the role of Clarence Day in the film version. He tried to convince MGM mogul Louis B. Mayer to purchase the screen rights to the play, but Mayer refused. When Warner Bros. bought the film rights in 1947, the studio borrowed Powell from MGM for the role. Although Powell was best known for his portrayals in light, sophisticated comedy, he was able to draw laughs from the characterization rather than the usual witty dialogue. Irene Dunne played Powell's screen wife. The film grossed over $6 million during its initial run. Irene and Powell were pictured in a still from the film.

B-130 French, W.F. "Her Love Story." <u>Motion Picture</u>. January, 1935.

B-131   Freulich, Roman and Abramson, Joan. *Forty Years in Hollywood*. Castle Books. New York. 1971. pp. 33, 35.
Memoir by photographer Freulich included two full-page stills from *Show Boat* with Irene Dunne, Sammy White, and Allan Jones.

B-132   Fristoe, Roger. "Irene Dunne." *Louisville Courier-Journal*. December 15, 1985.
Overview of Irene Dunne's career in conjunction with the Kennedy Center Honors. Irene traveled to Washington for the ceremony with her granddaughter Ann Shinnick. Irene attended a dinner in the Benjamin Franklin Dining Room at the State Department where the honorees received the gold medallions on rainbow ribbons that signify the award. However, she had to miss the White House reception and the Kennedy Center gala the following evening because of a back ailment. A *Washington Post* article mentioned that many of the honorees had social ties to the Ronald Reagan White House. Bonita Granville Wrather, a friend of Irene and a member of the Kennedy Center Board, was quoted as saying, "[Irene] is a neighbor of mine and a social friend, and she was already on the artists' comittee list....I think she's long overdue." Fristoe also focused on Irene's Louisville background.

B-133   Funke, Lewis. "Understudy Gets Role, New Star Is Born." *New York Times Magazine*. February 23, 1947. pp. 20, 67-69.,
The myth that all understudies become overnight stars was dispelled. Funke pointed out that acting as an understudy was valuable training, even if it did not lead to fame. He quoted an understudy, who said, "...if you have an opportunity to keep your talent alive by doing something like this, it's better than staying home with your nose in the air, letting your talent die." Famous understudies of the past were pictured, including Irene Dunne, who stepped in for Peggy Wood in *The Clinging Vine*.

B-134   "Furor with Father." *Newsweek*. September 15, 1947.
The religious ribbing in *Life with Father* was not taken lightly by some Protestant groups. The Protestant Motion Picture Council criticized the film's "grave distortions of religious life" and "the use of so serious a matter as baptism as a major comic them." But not all religious groups agreed. The Legion of Decency gave the film a rating of "unobjectional for adults" and both *The Churchman*, an Episcopal periodical, and *The Commonweal*, a Catholic magazine, ran full-page ads for *Life with Father* at the height of the dispute.

B-135   "A Gal Named Dunne." *Lion's Roar*. January, 1944.
Biographical sketch of Irene Dunne, then appearing in *A Guy Named Joe*, in MGM's in-house promotional magazine.

B-136   Gamarekian, Barbara. "Six Receive Kennedy Center
        Honors." <u>New York Times</u>. December 9, 1985.
The recipients of the eighth annual Kennedy Center Honors
gathered in Washington, D.C. for the two-day festivities.
Following a dinner in the Benjamin Franklin Dining Room at
the State Department, gold medallions on rainbow-colored
ribbons were presented to the honorees while James Stewart
read citations. The recipients were Irene Dunne, Merce
Cunningham, Frederick Loewe, Alan Jay Lerner, Beverly Sills,
and Bob Hope. Despite back problems and a "fragile"
appearance, Irene arrived late at the dinner and posed for
photographers, saying, "...as soon as the lights come on, I
seem to manage." On doctor's orders, Irene was unable to
attend the White House reception and the Kennedy Center
gala, but she sent word via James Stewart that the show
should go on. The tribute aired on CBS on December 27,
1985.

B-137   Garcia, Guy D. "People." <u>Time</u>. December 23,
        1985. p. 61.
Report on the eighth annual Kennedy Center Honors, of which
Irene Dunne was one of the recipients. Garcia said that
Irene was unable to attend the gala because back-pain
medication made her ill. She sent word from the hospital
that "the show must go on." Article included a photograph
of the six honorees.

B-138   Garnett, Tay and Balling, Fredda Dudley. <u>Light
        Your Torches and Pull Up Your Tights</u>. Arlington
        House. New Rochelle. 1973.
Director Garnett confessed that he turned down the script
for <u>The Awful Truth</u>, which won director Leo McCarey the
Academy Award. Garnett also recalled that the Hays office,
which censored films, insisted that the title <u>Joy of
Loving</u> be changed to <u>Joy of Living</u>. Garnett explained
their theory, "Loving was conjugality, involving a possible
nod from the stork. All strictly business, and joy be
damned."

B-139   Gassner, John and Nichols, Dudley. <u>Best Film Plays
        - 1945</u>. Crown Publishers. New York. 1946.
        pp. 521-88.
The screenplay for <u>Over 21</u> was considered among the year's
best by editors Gassner and Nichols. Others included
<u>Double Indemnity</u>, <u>The Lost Weekend</u>, and <u>Spellbound</u>.
The script for <u>Over 21</u> was reproduced here, along with
four stills of Irene Dunne from the film. The <u>Best Film
Plays</u> series was reprinted in 1977 by Garland Publishing,
Inc.

B-140   Gehring, Wes D. <u>Screwball Comedy: A Genre of
        Madcap Romance</u>. Greenwood Press. New York. 1986.
        pp. 4, 11, 42-44, 47, 48, 49-50, 55-57, 60, 63-64,
        81, 83, 121-22, 127-34, 142, 159, 165.
Discussion of the screwball comedy genre, including comments
about Irene Dunne's performances in <u>My Favorite Wife</u>,

Theodora Goes Wild, and _The Awful Truth_. Gehring noted recurring themes and symbols in the genre. He said romantic screwball comedies like _My Favorite Wife_ and _The Awful Truth_ had characters repairing their relationships during a sojourn in the country. _Theodora Goes Wild_ also allowed the protagonists to build their relationship while picking berries and fishing in the woods. However, while the country served as a point of sanity, the city was where the screwball antics occurred. Gehring also pointed out the dominance of women in screwball comedy, often reducing men to puppets, as in the final scenes of all three of Irene's screwball films. He added that Irene's leading ladies often feigned eccentricity in order to win their males. Gehring devoted sections of the book to actors and directors, including Leo McCarey, who frequently worked in the genre. He suggested that Katharine Hepburn borrowed her comic high-pitched, self-conscious laugh from Irene, who had used a similar laugh in _Theodora Goes Wild_ and _The Awful Truth_. Gehring compared the screen's two best screwball heroines: Irene Dunne and Carole Lombard. He said Lombard's comedy was based on character, as she was an expert at essaying dizzy roles. Irene's comedy was based on situation. He continued, "Lombard was a free-spirited eccentric whose private life was frequently public. Dunne was forever the lady on screen and off (excepting, of course, those moments of screwball comedy truth when she went 'wild.')" Gehring noted, "Much of the humor in a Dunne screwball comedy is based in the contrast between her proper persona and the slightly unhinged person she decides to let out." Although Irene's characters were often wealthy, he said that they were easy for audiences to identify with. Gehring pointed out the use of music in many of Irene's comedies. Irene was pictured on the set of _The Awful Truth_ with Leo McCarey and Alex D'Arcy, and at the premiere of _Penny Serenade_.

B-141 "Genevieve Tobin Out." _Variety_. March 10, 1926.
Irene Dunne replaced Genevieve Tobin in the Broadway cast of _Sweetheart Time_ on March 8, 1926. The reason for Tobin's departure was not revealed. Although the headline correctly annouced Genevieve Tobin, the body of the article mistakenly called her Vivian. The Tobins were sisters.

B-142 Gill, Ted. "Irene Dunne Works Over Those Tears." _Baltimore Sun_. May 2, 1943.
Irene Dunne discussed crying before the camera. She explained her technique. "Whenever I have to weep for the cameras, I prefer to cry real tears..., provided I have enough time to recover my emotions before I have to make the 'take,'" she said. "But if I have to do another and greatly different scene immediatly afterward...it frequently is easier on my emotions just to put glycerin or some other tear substitute in my eyes." Because she recalled sad situations from her real life to produce the tears, Irene had trouble finding new things to cry over for her many weepy scenes.

B-143 Gloria. "Style Notes from the Gay Musical, Roberta." Screen Book. March, 1935. pp. 48-49.
Irene Dunne and Ginger Rogers each modeled two costumes from Roberta. The film's 150 costumes, which were designed by Bernard Newman, cost fifty thousand dollars. Irene wore fifteen outfits in the film.

B-144 "Glowing Pride." Los Angeles Examiner. November 28, 1953.
Irene Dunne and her daughter Mary Frances Griffin were pictured at the Gotham Debutante Ball, where Mary Frances made her debut. The event was held at New York's Plaza Hotel and benefited the New York Foundling Hospital, from which Mary Frances was adopted.

B-145 Godfrey, Lionel. Cary Grant - The Light Touch. St. Martin's Press. New York. 1981. pp. 86, 100, 104, 154.
Discussion of Irene Dunne's work with Cary Grant in The Awful Truth, My Favorite Wife, and Penny Serenade. Godfrey pointed out that Irene was "a superb screen comedienne, curiously neglected by historians of the cinema."

B-146 "Good Night, Irene Dunne; Hollywood Loses an Airy and Elegant Gal from Film's Golden Age." People. September 17, 1990. p. 119.
A half-page portrait of Irene Dunne from the late 1930s graced this brief chronicle of her career, following her September 4 death. Errors included her age (eighty-five instead of ninety-one) and crediting her as the star of Irene rather than as a member of the chorus. The article claimed Irene did not drink and refused to wear slacks. Columnist Earl Wilson was quoted as saying, "It's very hard to write a good story about Irene because she was too much of a lady to be good copy."

B-147 Grant, Hank. "Rambling Reporter." Hollywood Reporter. December 20, 1977.
Irene Dunne was being nagged to come out of retirement to star in the Story of a House miniseries. The plot concerned a house and its occupants on San Francisco's Nob Hill from Gold Rush days to the present. The miniseries was being developed by Ross Hunter Productions for NBC and a theatrical release was planned for overseas.

B-148 Green, Stanley. Encyclopadeia of the Musical Film. Oxford University Press. New York. 1981. pp. 78, 90, 127-28, 177, 239-40, 256-57.
Brief biography and musical film credits of Irene Dunne. Credits and synopses were given for High, Wide and Handsome, Roberta, and Show Boat. Irene was also mentioned in discussions of the songs "Lovely to Look At," "The Folks Who Live on the Hill," and "Can I Forget You?"

B-149   Green, Stanley and Goldblat, Burt. *Starring Fred Astaire*. Dodd, Mead & Company. New York. 1973. pp. 82-95

A chapter on *Roberta* included many stills from the film, as well as photos of the poster and sheet music. Green discussed the history of the musical and provided detailed credits and synopsis.

B-150   Greer, Howard. "I've Dressed Them All." *Modern Screen*. February, 1934. pp. 44-46, 90-91.

Irene Dunne was pictured being fitted for a Howard Greer costume for an unnamed film. Greer was not given credit for any of Irene's 1934 films so the outfit may not have appeared on screen. He did work on *Love Affair* in 1939.

B-151   Griffith, Richard. *The Talkies*. Dover Publications, Inc. New York. 1971. pp. xvii, 68, 225, 250-52, 312, 321-22, 325.

Reprints of articles and illustrations from *Photoplay*. Irene Dunne was pictured in a scene from *Love Affair* and an ad for *Back Street*. A July, 1938 article entitled "Fashions in Passions" was an open letter to actresses involved in screwball comedy. Reporter Ruth Waterbury complained that she had used the actresses as role models, however their recent forays into slapstick were ruining her romances. Irene Dunne was chided for her raucous performance in *The Awful Truth*. Waterbury said, "...don't you understand that if the rest of us went around invading houses like that our boyfriend would not only think it wasn't funny but have us run out of town for displaying such awful manners?"

B-152   Guttman, Monika. "TVQs." *New York Daily News*. November 29, 1987.

Television question-and-answer column. One viewer wrote to ask if Irene Dunne was the same actress who played Granny on *The Beverly Hillbillies*. Guttman explained that they were confusing Irene Dunne with Irene Ryan.

B-153   Haber, Joyce. "The Sweet Smell of Irene Dunne." *Los Angeles Times*. March 16, 1975.

Irene Dunne discussed her career and the changes in the movie industry. After a screening of *Theodora Goes Wild*, she was asked if she would play a nude scene. Irene answered, "Well, I would never do that because I'm so susceptible to colds I'd catch pneumonia." She recalled that Cary Grant not only admired her comic timing, but called her "the sweetest-smelling actress" he ever knew. Irene said she had no interest in seeing "dirty movies." She professed, "I think you have a choice. I could use all the four-letter words if I wanted to. But you listen to all the Jane Fondas and I don't know why they have to come on so strong." Irene's life and career were reviewed. She "loathed" studying Russian ballet as an aspiring singer. She explained that her husband was beginning to have eye trouble when he moved to California, therefore, "...I

don't think he or I deny great sacrifice." Publicist Emily
Torchia recalled Irene's relationship with macho Spencer
Tracy and director Victor Fleming on the set of A Guy Named
Joe. "It didn't take a week before both of them were
bringing tea for Irene and waiting on her," Torchia said.
"She's a perfect example of the soft-spoken woman who turns
men on more than sexpots."

B-154   Hall, Joe B. "Additions and Corrections." Films in
        Review. January, 1970. pp. 59-60.
Letter to the editor from a longtime Irene Dunne fan,
concerning errors in a career article in the December, 1969
issue of Films in Review (B-276). Among the mistakes Hall
pointed out were that Irene played in the chorus of the
Chicago company of Irene rather than the lead, Irene and
her husband were married on July 16, 1928 rather than June
16, and that The Clinging Vine opened in 1922, not 1923.
Hall also corrected the spelling of many actors listed in
the filmography, as well as the dates of release.

B-155   Hamilton, Sara. "This Is Really Irene Dunne."
        Photoplay. April, 1936.
Interview with the actress, who claimed her private life was
very quiet. Hamilton concluded, "I can guarantee no juicy
bits of intimate gossip. For I know of none. Unless,
perhaps she lies awake nights heartsick about the kitchen
sink in her new home. She's afraid it's too near the door.
Or would you call that juicy? No? No, I thought not."

B-156   Harmetz, Aljean. "Irene Dunne - A Famous Actress Who
        Didn't Look Back." Los Angeles Times.
        November 29, 1970.
Interview with Irene Dunne following the Los Angeles County
Museum of Art retrospective of her films. Although Irene
ended her film career nearly twenty years earlier, two
thousand people were turned away from a screening of
Roberta during the retrospective. Irene discussed her
late husband, for whom she had had a Mass the day prior to
the interview. She said, "It was so joyous I still can't
believe it. For the first time [since his death five years
ago] there was no sorrow, no pain." Since her husband's
death, Irene had taken over his position as president of
some corporations which owned shopping centers in Nevada and
real estate in Beverly Hills. She moved the office to her
home so she could spend her mornings on corporate business.
Governor Ronald Reagan appointed Irene to the California
Arts Commission; she was also active with several charities,
including fund-raising for Saint John's Hospital. Although
she disliked the violence and nudity in recent films, she
was opposed to censorship. Irene praised Katharine
Hepburn's acting, saying that the enrichment of knowledge
and education were necessary to be a good actress. Although
Irene's film contracts had allowed her to start work at
10:00 and leave by 6:00, she was quoted as saying that she
did not have time to enjoy her success. When she was ten
years old, Irene's father advised her to "make up your mind

what you want and go after it. But be prepared to pay well for it." Irene enjoyed her career, but regretted the time she missed with her mother and daughter.

B-157   Harpers Bazaar. May, 1939. p. 81.
Irene Dunne struck a pensive pose in the ruins of the old slave hospital on the golf links at Sea Island, Georgia. She modeled a purple and white checked dress with bright green halter bands and belt.

B-158   Harris, Radie. "Broadway Ballyhoo." Hollywood
        Reporter. December 2, 1985.
Longtime friend Bill Frye planned to escort Irene Dunne to the Kennedy Center Honors. Columnist Harris predicted that Irene would receive "the most thunderous ovation among all the distinguished guests, especially after the clips from some of her most memorable pictures remind everybody what a superb actress she was, before her voluntary retirement."

B-159   _____. "Broadway Ballyhoo." Hollywood
        Reporter. December 12, 1985.
Harris reported on the festivities surrounding the Kennedy Center Honors, whose recipients included Irene Dunne, Bob Hope, Beverly Sills, Merce Cunningham, Frederick Loewe, and Alan Jay Lerner. Harris said, "The only disappointment of the evening was the absence of Irene Dunne, who was taken ill the previous evening at Vice President [George] Bush's dinner. She is now recovering at Georgetown Hospital and her lifelong companion, Bill Frye, assures me that she is recovering rapidly and should be back in Holmby Hills on Saturday."

B-160   Harris, Warren G. Cary Grant: A Touch of
        Elegance. Doubleday. New York. 1987. pp. 81,
        99-100, 107-8.
Irene Dunne was mentioned in conjunction with her work with Cary Grant in The Awful Truth, My Favorite Wife, and Penny Serenade. Grant was dissatisfied with the script for The Awful Truth. Director Leo McCarey was quoted as saying, "I remember he argued, 'Any man married to a lovely lady like Irene Dunne could not be unfaithful to her - it's totally unbelievable.'" Author Harris praised the chemistry between Irene and Grant. "Cary Grant's rapid-fire delivery and his ability to throw away lines, which sometimes made it sound as though he were talking to himself, made him the perfect foil for Irene Dunne's calm, relaxed style." Because Irene was then best known for her roles in romantic melodramas, Harris continued, "The director capitalized on the incongruity of involving such an obviously genteel lady in screwball happenings."

B-161   _____. Gable & Lombard. Simon and Schuster.
        New York. 1974. pp. 18, 66, 92, 144, 168-69.
Irene Dunne was a guest at the White Mayfair Ball on January 25, 1936, the party at which Carole Lombard and Clark Gable began their romance. Irene was also present for the inital

The 1985 Kennedy Center Honors recipients posed wearing their rainbow ribbon awards. The occasion marked Irene Dunne's last public appearance. *Back row:* Merce Cunningham, Beverly Sills, Bob Hope. *Front row:* Alan Jay Lerner, Irene Dunne, Frederick Loewe. (Photo by Jack Buxbaum)

meeting of the Hollywood Victory Committee on December 22, 1941. Set up to enlist the movie industry's help in securing talent to entertain the troops, the committee formed a fifteen-member sub-committee to choose talent for bond rallies, hospital tours, and camp shows. Headed by Gable, the fourteen stars included Irene Dunne, Myrna Loy, Claudette Colbert, Charles Boyer, Bob Hope, John Garfield, Rosalind Russell, Tyrone Power, Bette Davis, Gary Cooper, Ginger Rogers, Ronald Colman, Jack Benny, and Cary Grant. Carole Lombard was one of the first actresses to volunteer her services; she was killed in a plane crash while returning from a bond-selling trip. In January, 1944, Irene christened the U.S.S. Carole Lombard, a Liberty ship named after the actress. Harris noted that Irene had no close ties to Lombard, but, at the time, was making a film at MGM, which helped stage the event. A photograph of Irene launching the ship was included.

B-162   Harrison, Helen. "Screen Style Secrets!" Screenland. April, 1935. pp. 32-33, 75-76.
Bernard Newman discussed some of his costume designs for Roberta. Irene Dunne and Ginger Rogers each modeled two outfits.

B-163   Harrison, Paul. "Irene Dunne Takes a Ride - on a Bus." New York Journal-American. July 17, 1941.
After frequently overhearing her name mentioned as the tour buses passed her Holmby Hills home, Irene Dunne decided to take the tour. Although she was accompanied by three press agents, a secretary, reporter Paul Harrison, the owner of the tour company, and a photographer from one of the movie magazines, Irene almost went unrecognized by the other passengers. When the driver, Glen Smith, realized Irene was on board, he deleted passages from his usual speech and overly praised Irene when the bus passed her home. When the bus stopped at the beach, Irene revealed her identity to the other passengers and signed autographs. Smith became more at ease.

B-164   Harrison, Rex. Rex. William Morrow & Company, Inc. New York. 1975. p. 90.
In his autobiography, Harrison recalled filming Anna and the King of Siam with Irene Dunne. Although Harrison had problems getting along with director John Cromwell, he said Irene had a better working relationship with the director. Harrison wrote, "She was an excellent actress, much more used to the Hollywood scene than I was. She too went her own way, and tactfully used the director, as I later learned to do myself, to her own advantage; she listened to what he had to give, and discarded it or used it, as she wished."

B-165   Hartl, John. "Belle of the Screwball." Chicago Tribune. September 25, 1990.
Hartl complained that Irene Dunne's death was given short shrift, compared to other stars of her era. He said she helped define the term "screwball comedy" with her

224   Irene Dunne

performance in <u>Theodora Goes Wild</u>. He discussed the numerous remakes that Irene's films spawned, noting that both versions should be watched together to compare performances. He contrasted her <u>Show Boat</u> "breezy folksiness" with Kathryn Grayson's "wooden" role. Hartl added that, in <u>The Awful Truth</u> and <u>My Favorite Wife</u>, "the dialogue doesn't need to be witty for her to get her laughs."

B-166   Harvey, James. <u>Romantic Comedy in Hollywood from Lubitsch to Sturges</u>. Alfred A. Knopf. New York. 1987. pp. x, 104, 177, 206, 218, 221-48, 259, 261-63, 266, 269-70, 272 290-91, 298-99, 305, 307, 312, 351, 419-21, 424, 426, 427, 433, 439, 500, 502, 570, 679-92.

Irene Dunne's work in the genre was explored in a chapter; an interview, conducted in September, 1978, which ran in the January/February, 1980 issue of <u>Film Comment</u>, was reprinted in the appendix. <u>Theodora Goes Wild</u> (which Harvey compared to <u>Nothing Sacred</u>) and <u>The Awful Truth</u> were discussed in detail. Harvey concluded, "Of the great women stars who dominated the movie comedies of the thirties (and forties)...Irene Dunne is probably the greatest, the loveliest and funniest and most skilled, the most complex and affecting. She is one of those transcendent comic players who reminds us that there is a comic equivalent...to the tragic experience of being deeply moved." He said that she reminded him of Greta Garbo, conveying a mystery in her playfulness. Irene also was mentioned in chapters on Cary Grant, Jean Arthur, directors Leo McCarey, George Stevens, Preston Sturges, Ernst Lubitsch, and Howard Hawks. Harvey commented on techniques employed by McCarey in <u>The Awful Truth</u> and <u>Love Affair</u>, and compared the handling of romantic comedy elements in Irene's films to those of other stars. Harvey praised Irene's work in <u>I Remember Mama</u>, claiming that she did not seem to act. "It's an utterly plain and undecorated performance: everything, including the Scandinavian accent, done from the inside out," he wrote. Irene was pictured in stills from <u>Back Street</u>, <u>Theodora Goes Wild</u>, <u>The Awful Truth</u>, <u>Love Affair</u>, and <u>I Remember Mama</u>, as well as a photo showing her leaning against a slant-board on the <u>Awful Truth</u> set. Harvey also noted that, when he was a child in parochial school, Irene's name was always the first mentioned when anyone listed Hollywood's "good Catholics."

B-167   Haver, Ronald. <u>David O. Selznick's Hollywood</u>. Alfred A. Knopf, Inc. New York. 1980. pp. 71, 73, 75.

Irene Dunne was pictured three times in this book on the mogul, who was head of production at RKO from 1931 to 1933. Irene was seen on the cover of a vintage issue of <u>Photoplay</u>, in a <u>Cimarron</u> display at Grand Central Station, and in a composite ad art still from <u>Symphony of Six Million</u>.

B-168 "Hay! Hay Makers!" *Film Fun*. May, 1937. pp. 18-19.
Film stills shot outdoors accompanied corny jokes in this two-page spread. Irene Dunne, in plaid shirt and straw hat, fed berries to Melvyn Douglas in a scene from *Theodora Goes Wild*.

B-169 Haynes, Marjorie. "Lest We Forget America." *Movie Mirror*. June, 1939.
While hearing the song "Beautiful Ohio" on the set of *Invitation to Happiness*, Irene Dunne recalled her youth in Madison, Indiana on the banks of the Ohio River. Her nostalgia for her hometown led her to write a letter to First Lady Eleanor Roosevelt, urging Americans to visit their own hometowns. Irene's "Home Town Drive" was intended to promote new understanding among American people and re-establish a unified nation.

B-170 "Heart Association Drive Will Be Aided by Actress." *New York Times*. January 17, 1949.
Announcement that Irene Dunne would head the women's committee in the American Heart Association's $5 million drive. The campaign was scheduled from February 7 to February 28, 1949.

B-171 "Hello There, Miss Dunne." *Photoplay*. November, 1941.
When Irene Dunne heard that the driver of a Hollywood sight-seeing bus was dispensing scandalous tidbits about the stars, she disguised herself and joined the tour. She gloated when the driver praised her as he passed her home, but was dismayed when she learned it was only because he recognized her. As the driver bid her goodbye, he was quoted as saying, "You should _really_ hear what I say on your block sometimes."

B-172 Hemming, Roy. *The Melody Lingers On*. Newmarket Press. New York. 1986. pp. 91, 93, 99-101, 103-4, 113, 115-16, 237, 292.
Chronicle of composers and their movie musicals. Irene Dunne was mentioned frequently in the chapter on Jerome Kern in conjunction with *Sweet Adeline*, *Roberta*, *Show Boat*, *High, Wide and Handsome*, and *Joy of Living*. Hemming cited *Roberta* as one of the few film musicals which was better than its Broadway predecessor. He praised the cast. "First, there's Irene Dunne singing 'Yesterdays' as elegantly and touchingly as anyone has ever sung it, and then, a bit later, making 'Smoke Gets in Your Eyes' one of the great, unforgettably poignant moments in any '30s musical." *Joy of Living* was to have had additional songs, but Jerome Kern had a heart attack prior to the production. Hemming concluded, "[Irene Dunne] came to epitomize in both voice and manner the type of lyrical loveliness and elegance, even classiness, for which Kern is best known. Yet, like Kern himself, she also had a delightfully impish sense of down-to-earth fun that made her stand out from

226   Irene Dunne

other '30s sopranos and which lent itself perfectly to Kern's own efforts to deflate the artiness that sometimes crept into his work." Irene was pictured in stills from Sweet Adeline, Show Boat, and Joy of Living.

B-173 Henreid, Paul with Fast, Julius. Ladies Man. St. Martin's Press. New York. 1984. pp. 180-84.
Actor Henreid recalled his involvement with the House Un-American Activities Committee (HUAC). A subcommittee of HUAC began investigating the film industry in 1947. The committee insisted that Hollywood was making pro-Communist films. The studios were quick to argue, but, fearing the repercussions, agreed that anyone called before the committee should go to Washington to answer its charges. Among those asked to appear were right wing activists Gary Cooper, Irene Dunne, and John Wayne. This caused great confusion, with the public jumping to the conclusion that anyone who appeared before the committee was a Communist, Henreid said. When the Hollywood Ten, a group of writers and directors who refused to cooperate with HUAC, were jailed, writer/director John Huston took action. He formed a committee to counteract HUAC and fight for the First Amendment. Irene Dunne was one of many stars who appeared in Huston's radio broadcast, with the theme that no one should be robbed of his Constitutional rights.

B-174 "Here and There." New York Daily News. September 21, 1979. p. 9.
Irene Dunne was pictured walking with Mrs. William Randolph Hearst, Jr. Column reported that Irene had lunched with Mr. and Mrs. Hearst and designer Arnold Scassi at Quo Vadis on September 20. Irene said she had been traveling around the world and was heading back to Los Angeles to take care of her grandchildren.

B-175 Herschhorn, Joel. Rating the Movie Stars. Beekman House. New York. 1983. pp. 125-26.
Brief biography of Irene Dunne, accompanied by ratings for her films. Overall, she earned a 3.15, with 4 stars being the maximum. Cimarron, Symphony of Six Million, Back Street, Magnificent Obsession, Theodora Goes Wild, The Awful Truth, Love Affair, Penny Serenade, and Anna and the King of Siam each received four stars. Herschhorn concluded, "Irene Dunne's talent never leaped off the screen and grabbed the viewer by the shoulders. Hers was a quiet professionalism that seems more remarkable in retrospect than during her career."

B-176 Higham, Charles. Lucy: The Life of Lucille Ball. St. Martin's Press. New York. 1986. pp. 46-47.
According to Higham, Lucille Ball was irritable throughout the shooting of Joy of Living with Irene Dunne. Ball wanted RKO to loan her services to Universal so that she could appear in Letter of Introduction, but the studio refused. She was also upset when her friend Ann Sothern withdrew from Joy of Living and was replaced by Irene.

Because the actresses played sisters, they had many scenes together and, Higham reported, "The tension was considerable between them."

B-177   Hirschhorn, Clive. <u>The Columbia Story</u>. Crown Publishers, Inc. New York. 1990. pp. 12, 69, 71, 81, 91, 95, 104, 130, 135, 276.
Brief credits, synopsis, critique, and photographs from Columbia films from 1922 through 1988. Irene Dunne was mentioned in entries on <u>Theodora Goes Wild</u>, <u>The Awful Truth</u>, <u>Holiday</u>, <u>His Girl Friday</u>, <u>Penny Serenade</u>, <u>Together Again</u>, <u>Over 21</u>, and <u>Bob and Carol and Ted and Alice</u>. The last was a comment that the marital topics covered in the 1969 film were a far cry from those of screen teams Irene Dunne and Cary Grant, and Myrna Loy and William Powell.

B-178   _____. <u>The Hollywood Musical</u>. Crown Publishers, Inc. New York. 1981. pp. 59, 99, 120, 132, 148.
Hirschhorn critiqued musicals made between 1928 and 1980, with each entry including brief credits, synopsis, and a photograph from the film. Irene Dunne was mentioned in listings for <u>Leathernecking</u>, <u>Sweet Adeline</u>, <u>Show Boat</u>, <u>High, Wide and Handsome</u>, and <u>Joy of Living</u>.

B-179   _____. <u>The Universal Story</u>. Crown Publishers, Inc. New York. 1983. pp. 74, 88, 93, 97, 111, 127, 133, 207, 222, 240, 265, 359.
In another studio history, Hirschhorn presented synopsis, credits, critique, and photographs from Universal films made between 1913 and 1982. Irene Dunne was listed in <u>Back Street</u>, <u>Magnificent Obsession</u>, <u>Show Boat</u>, <u>When Tomorrow Comes</u>, <u>Unfinished Business</u>, <u>Lady in a Jam</u>, and <u>It Grows on Trees</u>.

B-180   _____. <u>The Warner Bros. Story</u>. Crown Publishers, Inc. New York. 1979. pp. 151, 266.
Irene Dunne was pictured in <u>Sweet Adeline</u> and <u>Life with Father</u>, accompanied by brief summaries and critiques of the films. Book covered features made between 1925 and 1978.

B-181   Holland, Jack. "Glamour Does a Pratt Fall." <u>Motion Picture</u>. June, 1941. pp. 24-25, 80-81.
Irene Dunne was among the actresses mentioned who gave up their glamorous images to play comic roles.

B-182   _____. "The Lady Speaks Her Mind." <u>Silver Screen</u>. May, 1946.

B-183   "Hollywood Canteen." <u>Movie-Radio Guide</u>. October 31, 1942.
After visiting the Stage Door Canteen in New York, Bette Davis was inspired to create a similar "home-away-from-home" for servicemen in California. Studio artists and carpenters refurbished and decorated the Old Barn, a former nightclub. Film stars volunteered their services, washing dishes,

228   Irene Dunne

busing tables, and dancing with soldiers. Irene Dunne was pictured giving autographs at the canteen.

B-184 "Hollywood Earfuls." <u>Silver Screen</u>. October, 1941. p. 7.

Long interested in horticulture, Irene Dunne began to suspect that the information she gleaned from books was not entirely correct. After telling gardener Alberti to plant at the wrong time of year, the ever-respectful Alberti advised her, "Miss Dunne, please, when you are out in society, don't talk about flowers."

B-185 "Hollywood Earfuls." <u>Silver Screen</u>. November, 1941. pp. 6, 8.

Irene Dunne was one of the celebrity chess players who frequented the Brown Derby. Restaurant manager Bob Cobb, whose wife Gail Patrick appeared with Irene in <u>My Favorite Wife</u>, had installed several chess boards and a system for keeping track of moves so an unfinished game could be completed during another visit. Irene often played with her husband, as well as directors Lloyd Bacon and John Stahl. In an unrelated item, Irene recalled that the best piece of advice she ever received, came from a lawyer, who told her to be herself.

B-186 "Hollywood Hints...Spring Suits." <u>Screen Romances</u>. April, 1934. pp. 72-73.

Irene Dunne modeled a hat from <u>Transient Love</u>, which was released as <u>This Man Is Mine</u>.

B-187 "Hollywood Loses Pioneer with Death of Miss Dunne." <u>Fayetteville Observer Times</u> [North Carolina]. September 6, 1990.

Irene Dunne would be placed in a crypt beside her husband, following a funeral Mass at Calvary Cemetary's Mausoleum Chapel. She was survived by her daughter Mary Frances, two grandchildren, and a niece. Irene's career was recalled in the obituary. It claimed <u>I Remember Mama</u> was Irene's favorite role. Ginger Rogers described her <u>Roberta</u> co-star as "a fine and loving lady," but one who was difficult to get to know well. Virginia Zamboni, director of community affairs at Saint John's Hospital and Health Center, praised Irene's fundraising efforts. Zamboni was quoted as saying, "She got the actors on <u>How the West Was Won</u> to sign a paper and every time it was shown we got residuals. We still do." Zamboni estimated that the film raised $7-8 million for the hospital. The article included a photograph of Irene from the 1940s and a filmography.

B-188 "Hollywood Via Showboat." <u>Baltimore Morning Sun</u>. May 18, 1930.

Profile of Irene Dunne, who went to Hollywood shortly after closing in the Baltimore production of <u>Show Boat</u>. Among the RKO films in which Irene was scheduled to appear were <u>Present Arms</u> (which became <u>Leathernecking</u>), <u>Babes in Toyland</u> (which was made by MGM in 1934 without Irene) and *Heart of the Rockies*. A portrait of Irene accompanied the article.

B-189 "Hollywood Women at War." *Movie-Radio Guide*. May, 1943.
Film and radio stars' wartime activities were listed beside a photo of each woman. Irene Dunne was a member of the Beverly Hills U.S.O.

B-190 "Hollywood's War Effort." *Hollywood*. January, 1943. pp. 22-23.
Irene Dunne was seen dancing with a young corporal in this pictorial about the Hollywood Canteen.

B-191 "Hollywood's Winter Hat Parade." *Movie-Radio Mirror*. October 11, 1941.
Irene Dunne was pictured at Ciro's, modeling a new chapeau.

B-192 "Honored." *Newsweek*. July 11, 1949.
Irene Dunne was pictured, receiving the the Laetare Medal at the University of Notre Dame on June 29, 1949. She was quoted as saying she would rather win the medal than an Oscar because "God does not read an actress's press clippings."

B-193 Hopper, Hedda. "June Preisser Develops as a Female Mickey Rooney." *San Francisco Chronicle*. May 8, 1940.
Hopper recalled her trip to London with Irene Dunne for the British premiere of *Show Boat*. Both ladies were on the Queen Mary, which docked the night of the film premiere. Because her trunks arrived too late, Irene appeared at the premiere in her traveling clothes. However, Hopper recalled, "...when she went to supper at the Savoy Hotel afterwards, they wouldn't let her in - because she was wearing a hat."

B-194 Houseman, John. *Entertainers and the Entertained*. Simon and Schuster. New York. 1986. pp. 252-53.
Actor Houseman critiqued the three political parties' radio broadcasts during the 1944 Presidential election. The Republicans hosted the *Dewey Bandwagon*, heralded as "an hour of entertainment and good fellowship." Although Houseman praised the talents involved in the program, he called the proceedings "hollow as a drum." He wrote, "The depths of bathos were plumbed when Miss Irene Dunne, Mr. Ray Milland and Believe-It-or-Not Ripley presented a brief dramatic sketch concerning Dan Kelso, an ex-convict who died a-voting."

B-195 "How Hollywood Stands on Prohibition." *Motion Picture*. October, 1932.
Film stars were quoted on the topic, including Irene Dunne, who said, "I am in favor of light wines and beer but, in fairness, before anyone decides it for the people of the United States, they should have the chance to vote on the

whole question."

B-196 "How Would You Like a Dish of Jambalaya?" *Motion Picture*. January, 1932. pp. 78-80, 98.
Cooking with the stars. Irene Dunne was shown preparing fruit salad and gave her recipe.

B-197 Hoyt, Caroline S. "Irene Dunne's True Life Story." *Modern Screen*. December, 1938 and January, 1939.
Two-part biography of Irene Dunne, which included family photographs and film stills. Hoyt painted a picture of a happy, carefree childhood. She said that Irene's parents influenced her career, as Irene inherited her father's sense of humor and her mother's musical talents. Hoyt added that their happy marriage made an impression on their daughter. Although Irene was courted steadily by a series of beaus during a social season in Memphis, she waited until she was established in her career and met Frank Griffin before marrying. Hoyt recounted the story of Irene's stage background, repeating the myth that Irene played the lead in the touring company of *Irene*. Hoyt also claimed that Irene played several performances in the Broadway company.

B-198 Humphrey, Hal. "Irene Dunne Offers Some Reflections on Movie Star Glamour." *Los Angeles Mirror*. January 27, 1962.
Irene Dunne insisted that her appearance on *G.E. Theatre* was not a pilot for a television series, although executives wanted it to be one. She said, "When I was at the Revue Studios filming this show, I felt so sorry for all those people who were there doing series and knowing they were unable to do their best. It just can't be done every week, can it?" Irene was quoted as saying that it was difficult for a TV star to remain glamorous with the tight shooting schedules and having to do commercials. She recalled that many of her fans were upset when she was hosting *Schlitz Playhouse of Stars*, simply because she was associated with beer, although she did not do the commercials.

B-199 Hyams, Joe. "Irene Dunne's Husband: 'Be a Trailer.'" *New York Herald Tribune*. March 20, 1958.
Fifth in a series about the husbands of famous women, this article focused on Dr. Francis ("Frank") Griffin, who was married to Irene Dunne. Frank discussed his own business interests, which included being a partner in the Griffin Equipment Company, distributors of diesel power engines for heavy construction, and the Griffin Wellpoint Company, manufacturers of soil dewatering equipment. Frank described his relationship with Irene. "I'm behind her all the time in everything she does," he said. "She co-operates with me as well and we both work together." Frank recalled giving up his career as a dentist to join his wife in Hollywood. He began handling her business affairs, then retired to put them in more experienced hands. Frank credited their successful marriage to being together. Both arranged

their schedules so that they could accompany each other on business trips. He said that both partners must work toward a common goal.

B-200 "I and Q." *Stage*. July, 1938. pp. 36-37, 50.
Irene Dunne was one of fifteen stars pictured in a quiz, in which readers were asked to match an early career photo with a current shot. Irene was seen in stills from *Leathernecking* (#11) and *Joy of Living* (#20).

B-201 "I.Q." *Stage*. February, 1936. pp. 48-49, 76.
Irene Dunne was one of the stars pictured in a twenty-panel quiz about stars who suffered on the stage and screen. Irene was shown in a still from *Magnificent Obsession*.

B-202 "*I Remember Mama*." *Look*. April 27, 1948.
Pictorial review of the film, including five stills of Irene Dunne. Critic said Irene "gave her best performance" and praised producer/director George Stevens's work. However, he wrote, "[Stevens] might have made it shorter - two hours and 14 minutes is a lot of charm."

B-203 "Ike Names La Dunne UN Envoy." *New York Daily Mirror*. August 10, 1957.
President Dwight Eisenhower nominated ten delegates to represent the United States at the United Nations General Assembly during the 1957 session, including Irene Dunne. A photograph of Irene accompanied the announcement.

B-204 "In Hollywood." *Variety*. September 28, 1949.
Irene Dunne, Ronald Colman, Loretta Young, Dana Andrews, Kirk Douglas, and Jane Wyman were announced as the rotating stars of the *Prudential Family Hour of Stars*.

B-205 "In Re Comedy and Color." *New York Times*. November 15, 1936.
Director Richard Boleslawski discussed his views on comedy and the filming of *Theodora Goes Wild*. He said the highest grade of comedy was that which grew out of the situation, like in *Theodora Goes Wild*. The film's humor arose from the action and plot, rather than the dialogue. Article described Irene Dunne, stating that she "had been all but lost to her own generation in a welter of graying periwigs, [she] goes modern and whimsical for a change."

B-206 "Interrupting a Vacation." *New York Times*. March 24, 1935.
Irene Dunne interrupted her vacation to appear in "Secrets" on *Lux Radio Theatre*. She compared radio to screen work. While she disliked the precision involved in radio, she admired the spontaneity. Radio demanded perfect intonation and timing, as mistakes could not be redone as in films. Irene compared the fan mail that radio and movies generated. "Picture fans write to tell what they thought of the dress with the striped sleeves; radio listeners write for the titles of songs and the names of composers," she said.

232   Irene Dunne

Irene was pictured to promote her appearance in "Secrets."

B-207   "Irene." Current Biography. H.W. Wilson Company.
         New York. 1946. pp. 276-77.
Profile of Irene Gibbons, who had been the chief designer at
MGM since 1942. Irene Dunne's costumes for The White
Cliffs of Dover were mentioned.

B-208   "Irene Dunne." Celebrity Register. Simon and
         Schuster. New York. 1973. p. 149.
A brief review of the actress' life and career, including
her work for the Republican party, Technicolor, Inc., and
the United Nations. Eleanor Roosevelt was quoted as saying,
"Irene Dunne has a warm heart, but she doesn't know a thing
about work laws." The year of Irene's birth was incorrectly
given as 1904. The article included a recent portrait of
the actress.

B-209   "Irene Dunne." Vogue. December 15, 1933. p. 70.
Portrait of the actress in a Henri Bendel bonnet of black
satin.

B-210   "Irene Dunne Adopts Baby." New York Times.
         March 17, 1938.
Irene Dunne and her husband Dr. Francis Griffin adopted a
four-year-old daughter, whom they named Mary Frances. The
child had been living with them for a year. The adoption
order was signed in Surrogate's Court on March 15, 1938.
The adoption papers were witnessed by Sister Dominia Maria,
a registered nurse and mother of the New York Foundling
Home, where Mary Frances had formerly been known as Anna
Mary Bush. Despite the New York Times's "facts," other
sources claim Mary Frances was eleven months old when she
came to live with the Griffins in December, 1936, making her
two at the time of the adoption.

B-211   "Irene Dunne and Cary Grant...Movie Marriage Is
         Amusing." Movie-Radio Guide. April 13, 1940.
The stars were pictured in a full-page portrait from My
Favorite Wife.

B-212   "Irene Dunne Appointed to Defense Committee."
         Washington Post. September 1, 1951.
Irene Dunne was appointed to serve on the forty-nine-member
Defense Advisory Committee on Women in the Services, a group
composed of women leaders in many fields. The committee was
set up to advise the Defense Department on policies
concerning women in the armed forces.

B-213   "Irene Dunne at Filmex Tribute Rates 'Affair,'
         'Mama' Her Best." Daily Variety. March 25,
         1975.
After viewing a clip from Cimarron at the Los Angeles
International Film Exposition (Filmex), Irene Dunne called
her favorite film "awfully hammy." She switched allegiance
to I Remember Mama and Love Affair. The tribute,

which included clips from fifteen movies and two television shows, as well as a viewing of the only extant print of Love Affair, was coordinated by David Chierichetti and moderated by Roddy McDowall. Following the clips, Irene participated in a twenty-five-minute question-and-answer session. McDowall described her as "totally a creature of illusion - she was never an exhibitionist, she was always discreet, and when cornered, she was charmingly vague."

B-214 "Irene Dunne Comes Home for Premiere - and Derby." Louisville Courier-Journal. May 5, 1940.
Pictorial showing Irene Dunne returning to her birthplace for the premeiere of My Favorite Wife and the Kentucky Derby. During the three-day festivities, Irene was given a key to the city.

B-215 "Irene Dunne Dies; Versatile Actress Had 5 Oscar Noms." Hollywood Reporter. September 5, 1990.
Obituary of the actress, which mistakenly said she was eighty-eight when she died. Irene Dunne's career was given a short review, with writer praising "her fine sense of timing [which] made her perfect for screwball comedies like The Awful Truth and My Favorite Wife."

B-216 "Irene Dunne Finds Career in U.N. 'Highlight of My Life.'" New York Herald Tribune. October 16, 1957.
Irene Dunne discussed her career as an alternate representative to the United Nations General Assembly. She was surprised that delegates from other countries were familiar with her films. Although Irene was assigned to the U.N. Trusteeship Committee, she said she would have preferred working with the Social and Humanitarian Committee, since it was a field in which she had more background. Irene considered it "a great honor and a privilege" to serve with the United States delegation.

B-217 "Irene Dunne Gets An LL.D." New York Times. June 6, 1949.
Mount Saint Mary's College for Women awarded Irene Dunne with an honorary degree of Doctor of Laws, "in recognition of her courageous fidelity to Catholic principles in public and private life and for her work in cancer research organizations."

B-218 "Irene Dunne Gets Norway Gift." New York Times. February 13, 1949.
The Society of Norwegian Playwrights presented Irene Dunne with a diamond heirloom crown for her performance in I Remember Mama. Finn Boe, drama critic of the Oslo Aftenposten, made the presentation, thanking Irene for her "contribution to a better understanding of the Norwegian character."

B-219 "Irene Dunne Gets Notre Dame Honor." New York Times. March 28, 1949.

The University of Notre Dame awarded Irene Dunne the Laetare Medal, the highest honor that can go to an American Catholic layman. The Rev. John J. Cavanaugh, president of Notre Dame, said Irene was "an example of talented Christian womanhood in a profession and community unfortunately publicized for the briefness of marriages and careers." Cavanaugh praised Irene's choice of wholesome films, her long marriage, and the respect and popularity she won through her career. The medal derived its name from Laetare Sunday, the fourth Sunday in Lent and the day on which it was awarded.

B-220 "Irene Dunne Gives Fountain Fund Boost." Madison Courier [Indiana]. May 21, 1976.
The former Madison, Indiana resident donated one thousand dollars to the Broadway Fountain Fund, to restore a landmark in her hometown. Irene Dunne asked the chairman to keep her posted on the progress and wrote, "I hope too I may one day see the fountain again."

B-221 "Irene Dunne Here from Hollywood." New York Times. November 15, 1932.
Irene Dunne was in New York to visit her husband, who was convalescing following an emergency appendectomy at St. Vincent's Hospital.

B-222 "Irene Dunne Honored." New York Times. December 20, 1948.
The National Conference of Christians and Jews named Irene Dunne as the person "who has done most in 1948 to promote better understanding among peoples of all faiths." Irene's charitable and religious work was mentioned, including her involvement with the National Heart Committee, the American Cancer Society, and the establishment of a Los Angeles school for minority children. The award was presented on February 4, 1949 at the Waldorf-Astoria.

B-223 "Irene Dunne Honored." New York Times. September 28, 1951.
Irene Dunne was awarded the Lateran Cross by the Lateran Basilica Chapter of Canons. Cardinal Spellman of New York planned to present the medal and parchment certificate to Irene for her "examplary life and service to the Roman Catholic Church."

B-224 "Irene Dunne Invited to Serve on U.N." Washington Post. July 17, 1957.
The Washington Post was waiting for Irene Dunne to accept an invitation to serve as an alternate delegate for the September General Assembly of the United Nations. The official announcement of the appointment had not been given by the White House, however the Post had confirmed that a letter asking Irene to serve had been sent.

B-225 "Irene Dunne, Leading Star of '30s and '40s, Dies at 88." Los Angeles Times. September 5, 1990.

Like many of the actress' obituaries, this article claimed that Irene Dunne was eight-eight when she died and that she starred in the road company of Irene. However, unlike many others, this article gave a comprehensive overview of Irene's career, including her Broadway work, her pioneer efforts as a free-lance film star, and her charitable and political involvements.

B-226 "Irene Dunne Makes Uneasy Appearance." Variety. April 2, 1975. pp. 2, 94.
Account of the Los Angeles International Film Exposition (Filmex) which honored Irene Dunne with a retrospective of her films. The tribute, moderated by Roddy McDowall, included clips from fifteen films and two televison shows, as well as a showing of the only extant 35m print of Love Affair. McDowall commented on Irene's "inner substance and strength." He was quoted as saying, "She always brought stamina to her roles, even the ones that didn't have it." After the film clips, Irene participated in a twenty-five-minute discussion of her films. David Chierichetti coordinated the event.

B-227 "Irene Dunne Meets King." New York Times. June 20, 1950.
While in England to film The Mudlark, Irene Dunne met King George and Queen Elizabeth on June 18. She and her husband later had tea with the Marquess and Marchioness of Cansbrooke in London. Meeting with real-life royalty helped promote the film, which was about Queen Victoria.

B-228 "Irene Dunne Receives Notre Dame's Medal." New York Times. June 30, 1949.
The University of Notre Dame awarded its Laetare Medal to Irene Dunne as "an apostle of sanity." Irene attended the ceremonies in South Bend, Indiana with her husband Francis Griffin and their daughter Mary Frances. A citation accompanying the medal praised the Griffins as an ideal Christian home, stating, "You brought to the cinema wholesome and inspiring drama, stories of encouragement and hope that wrinkled with healing laughter the taut features of a war-racked world."

B-229 "Irene Dunne Signed by Warners." New York Herald Tribune. August 21, 1934.
Sweet Adeline was announced as Irene Dunne's first starring vehicle under her new Warner Bros. contract. Mervyn Le Roy was scheduled to direct.

B-230 "Irene Dunne to Receive Degree." New York Herald Tribune. May 31, 1949.
Mount Saint Mary's College planned to award Irene Dunne with an honorary degree of Doctor of Laws on June 4, 1949. The degree was bestowed "in recognition of her courageous fidelity to Catholic principles in public and private life."

B-231 "Irene Dunne, Top Actress, Singer of '30s-'40s, Dies

at 88." <u>Fayetteville Observer Times</u> [North
Carolina]. September 5, 1990.
Irene Dunne's career was reviewed in this obituary.
Although the article mentioned that sources disagreed about
Irene's birthdate, it mistakenly said she was eighty-eight,
rather than ninety-one, at the time of her death. Despite
the fact that she excelled at comedy, Irene preferred
dramatic roles. She was quoted as saying, "Comedy was easy
for me but it wasn't rewarding in the same way."

B-232 "Irene Dunne, Top-rank Film Star of the '30s and
'40s, Dead at 88." <u>Variety</u>. September 10, 1990.
Detailed obituary of the actress, who died in her home on
September 4, 1990 of heart failure. Several of the common
myths about Irene were repeated: that she was born in 1901
and that she starred in the 1920 tour of <u>Irene</u>. Article
mentioned that she appeared on television in <u>Ford Theatre</u>
and <u>Schlitz Playhouse of Stars</u> after her film retirement,
but failed to point out that she hosted the latter.
Interestingly, a reader objected to the obituary labeling
the <u>Show Boat</u> tour the "Chicago company," but failed to
find any of the other errors (B-123).

B-233 "Irene Dunne, 1898-1990." <u>Entertainment Weekly</u>.
September 21, 1990. p. 70.
Obituary of the actress, who died September 4, 1990.
Article noted that Irene Dunne's career was neglected,
blaming her "quiet, gracious living" for keeping her out of
the public eye. "Her decorous offscreen conduct, happy
marriage, and aversion to publicity left her mostly absent
from tabloids both before and after her retirement from
movies in 1952," reporter said. Turner Network Television
(TNT) planned a birthday salute on December 20, 1990, with
the airing of some of her films. However, <u>Love Affair</u> was
not among them, as TNT will not regain video or broadcast
rights until 1993.

B-234 "Irene Dunne's Design for Living." <u>Screenland</u>.
September, 1941. pp. 56-57, 82-83.
A Dallas teacher asked Irene Dunne for decorating
suggestions in this movie magazine contest. Irene stressed
the importance of working women being able to separate their
business lives from their personal lives. She dispensed
advice about redoing one room at a time, sticking to a
budget, and choosing pieces that pleased her, rather than
what was popular. It was important to be patient while
choosing furniture. Irene said, "If you buy a chair simply
because you need a chair, you will usually find that the
chair lacks all the personality in your home." She
suggested that Saturday night parties or Sunday brunches
were the easiest ways for working women to entertain.
Twelve photos of Irene and her daughter, at home and in her
dressing room, accompanied the article.

B-235 "It's a Fact." <u>Film Fun</u>. July, 1934. p. 52.
Irene Dunne was compiling a library of her films. She was

quoted as saying, "It will not only be interesting to me but to my friends and descendants to view these pictures many years hence." Irene later acquired videotapes of her films. Back Street co-star William Bakewell told the author that Irene loaned him her videos of Back Street and The Awful Truth.

B-236   Jablonski, Edward. Gershwin. Doubleday.
        New York. 1987. p. 331.
In order to convince Gertrude Lawrence to sign a contract to appear in the Broadway musical Lady in the Dark in 1940, playwright Moss Hart threatened to hire Irene Dunne instead. After three months of procrastinating, Lawrence signed. Lady in the Dark opened January 23, 1941 and played for 467 performances. It was filmed in 1944 with Ginger Rogers.

B-237   Jason, Johnny. "Movieland's New Rule: No More
        Ladies!" Hollywood: Then & Now. December, 1990.
        pp. 18-20.
Jason bemoaned the fact that Irene Dunne's death rated little more than one page in People, while Julia Roberts had become the "Queen of Hollywood" overnight, after her role as a hooker in Pretty Woman. He compared current stars to those in the 1940s, concluding that there were no more ladies left on screen. He hoped the pendulum would swing the other way and actresses would return to more genteel roles.

B-238   Jewell, Richard B. and Harbin, Vernon. The RKO
        Story. Arlington House. New York. 1982. pp. 30,
        33, 35, 42, 48, 51, 56, 62, 67, 69, 72, 73, 76, 83,
        120, 129, 148, 227, 250.
Studio history of films made between 1929 and 1960. Each entry gave a brief synopsis, credits, critique, and a photograph from the film. Irene Dunne was mentioned regarding Leathernecking, Cimarron, Bachelor Apartment, Consolation Marriage, Symphony of Six Million, Thirteen Women, No Other Woman, The Silver Cord, Ann Vickers, If I Were Free, This Man Is Mine, Stingaree, The Age of Innocence, Roberta, Joy of Living, Love Affair, My Favorite Wife, I Remember Mama, and Never a Dull Moment.

B-239   "Johnson, Irene Dunne Honored." New York Times.
        June 15, 1945.
The Chicago Musical College awarded Honorary Doctor of Music degrees to Irene Dunne and Edward Johnson, general manager of the Metropolitan Opera Association, on June 14, 1945.

B-240   Johnson, Erskine. "Hollywood Newsreel."
        Hollywood. October, 1941. p. 6.
Irene Dunne watched as Robert Montgomery and Preston Foster argued over her affections in a still from Unfinished Business.

B-241   _____. "Hollywood Newsreel." Hollywood.

238   Irene Dunne

January, 1943. p. 12.
Irene Dunne planned to decorate her playroom with the many keys to the city she had received.

B-242   Josefsberg, Milt. The Jack Benny Show. Arlington
        House. New Rochelle. 1977. pp. 142, 143, 480.
Josefsberg, a writer for Benny's radio and television series, recalled several jokes used in the episode featuring Irene Dunne, which aired on December 6, 1953 (T-4).

B-243   "Jottings from Movietown." Movie-Radio Guide.
        November 21, 1942.
Irene Dunne was announced as Myrna Loy's replacement in the Thin Man series. Columnist wrote, "We can't think of anyone who could do a better job."

B-244   Journee, Maclyn. "Historic Madison Gives World
        Celebrities of Modern Screen." Madison Herald
        [Indiana]. October 21, 1931.
Account of Irene Dunne's early career, focusing on her childhood in Madison, Indiana. Article detailed how Irene won the title role in the road company of Irene. Since Irene was in the chorus of the musical, "facts" of her association with the company should be taken lightly.

B-245   Kanin, Garson. "High Comedy: Irene Dunne and Cary
        Grant." Together Again! Doubleday and Company,
        Inc. Garden City, New York. 1981. pp. 142-49.
Irene Dunne and Cary Grant's work in The Awful Truth, My Favorite Wife, and Penny Serenade was described in a chapter devoted to their screen pairing. Kanin reminisced about directing them in My Favorite Wife. He praised their chemistry, comparing it to a lifetime partnership. Cary Grant was quoted as saying, "Acting with Irene is very like a long, continuing, never-ending flirtation. She's constantly surprising, and that makes every hour of every day working with her...a joy." In turn, Irene praised Grant's generosity on screen. She said, "I know that he's not going to make one false step, and if I do, he'll be there to steady me." Kanin mentioned a story idea he brought to Grant and Irene for a further screen pairing. Despite the fact that both actors liked it, Kanin was drafted before the project got off the ground. Although the chapter was entitled "High Comedy," the majority of the photographs were from the serio-comic Penny Serenade.

B-246   Keenan, _____. Chicago Herald. October 20,
        1929.
Caricature of the Chicago Show Boat cast, including Irene Dunne, Sammy White, Charles Winninger, Howard Marsh, and Eva Puck.

B-247   Knowles, Eleanor. The Films of Jeanette MacDonald
        and Nelson Eddy. A.S. Barnes and Co., Inc.
        Cranbury, New Jersey. 1975. pp. 20, 28, 138, 355.
During the fall of 1920, Jeanette MacDonald appeared in

the musical <u>Irene</u> with Irene Dunne in Chicago. MacDonald played Eleanor Worth, while Irene allegedly essayed the title role. Other sources insist that Irene was in the chorus. In 1933, it was rumored that MacDonald and Lawrence Tibbett would star in a film version of <u>The Merry Widow</u> with Irene in a featured role. The film was made with MacDonald and Maurice Chevalier in 1934. Irene was pictured with MacDonald and her husband Gene Raymond in 1938.

B-248   Kobal, John. <u>Gotta Sing, Gotta Dance</u>. Hamlyn. London. 1971. pp. 158, 162, 177, 178.

Rouben Mamoulian, director of <u>High, Wide and Handsome</u>, recalled his involvement with the film in this book on movie musicals. Mamoulian said he wanted to work with Irene Dunne and Gary Cooper, the original choice for the leading male role, therefore Mamoulian went against his better judgement and accepted the film. He said, "It was a very tough picture to make, half dream, half reality. Some things in it are good, but I don't feel that I succeeded. I don't think it is an organic whole." Irene Dunne was pictured in stills from <u>High, Wide and Handsome</u> and <u>Show Boat</u>.

B-249   _____. "Irene Dunne." <u>Focus on Film</u>. #28, 1977. pp. 17-21.

Irene Dunne discussed her film career, concentrating on the musicals, which Kobal had dealt with in his book, <u>Gotta Sing, Gotta Dance</u> (B-248). Irene disliked <u>High, Wide and Handsome</u> because it was a difficult picture physically, with much of the shooting taking place on location in Chino, California. She also associated it with the death of her mother, which occurred while Irene was filming. Irene had recently viewed the movie on television and reconsidered. She discussed her association with Jerome Kern, who wrote the scores for <u>Show Boat</u>, <u>High, Wide and Handsome</u>, <u>Joy of Living</u>, and <u>Roberta</u>. Kern wrote "Lovely to Look At" especially for Irene to sing in the latter film. She recalled, "To show how your mind can play tricks, I got so nervous over the song because I knew I'd have to be lovely to look at walking down that staircase singing the song. I got no sleep the night before." The cameraman refused to shoot the scene until Irene went home for a couple of days to rest. Irene said that James Whale was not the right director for <u>Show Boat</u>, insisting that the film was never as good as the stage play. She claimed that Whale was more interested in atmosphere and lighting, than in the actors' characterizations. Although Irene felt that <u>Roberta</u> had a silly plot, she said that it held up best of her musical films due to its entertainment value. The only clause Irene had in her contract gave her the choice of director. She said, "I always felt that if the director was good then everything else would fall into proper place." Although she admitted that composers Frederick Loewe and Alan Jay Lerner had offered her a project, possibly implying a role in <u>Gigi</u>, Irene stayed in retirement. Kobal concluded, "...her opinions about the merit of her films seem to be governed more by what was happening in her life at the time than by any aesthetic considerations - thus some of her best films are not her favourites and she still pretends to be displeased at ever having played the 'other woman' in Back Street." The article included ten stills from her film and TV appearances.

B-250 _____. People Will Talk. Alfred A. Knopf. New York. 1985. pp. 303, 317-23, 387, 440, 465, 708.
Extensive 1972 interview with Irene Dunne, focusing on her career in musical films and the directors with which she worked. Chapter included a 1938 portrait of Irene by photographer Ernest Bachrach. An edited version of the interview originally appeared in Focus on Film (B-249). Irene was also mentioned in interviews with Joel McCrea, Loretta Young, Jean Louis, and Ingrid Bergman. McCrea recalled enlisting her help in making a decision to leave RKO. Despite his kind words, his description of Irene was none too flattering. Explaining that their relationship was strictly platonic, he said, "She wasn't a sexy girl, you know. Not in the slightest." Designer Jean Louis credited Irene with helping him stay in America and obtaining his first film. Hattie Carnegie was ready to let him return to Europe, until Irene saw his designs and ordered three dresses. His first film was Together Again. Bergman was unaware that she almost lost the role in The Bells of St. Mary's to Irene, because David Selznick, who owned Bergman's contract, wanted more money.

B-251 Kotsilibas-Davis, James and Loy, Myrna. Myrna Loy: Being and Becoming. Alfred A. Knopf. New York. 1987. pp. 29, 75, 185, 191.
In her autobiography, Loy discussed her work with Irene Dunne in Thirteen Women. Loy played a murderous Javanese-Indian half-caste who killed the schoolmates who had patronized her. Irene was one of the few to escape, causing Loy to comment, "I regretted it every time she got the parts I wanted." When Loy married and moved to New York, the Thin Man series, in which she starred with William Powell, was put on hold. Irene was mentioned as a possible replacement, but fans of the series caused such an uproar that the idea was abandoned and Loy returned to the role of Nora Charles. Loy also recalled that she and Irene were the only actresses invited to social events in Los Angeles for many years, concluding that they were perceived as "'ladies' - whatever that is."

B-252 Kreuger, Miles. Show Boat: The Story of a Classic American Musical. Oxford University Press. New York. 1977. pp. ix, 71, 74, 111-53.
Detailed history of Show Boat and its many stage and film incarnations. Kreuger's in-depth study included rare photographs of scenes cut from the film and several appendixes, which compared the different productions. Kreuger claimed the 1936 film version with Irene Dunne was most faithful to the stage production. He said, "As

Magnolia, Irene Dunne found one of the great roles of her career. Her gradual development from youthful innocence, through the emotional maturing forced upon her by Ravenal's irresponsibility, to dignified middle age is shaded skillfully and with great tenderness." He continued, "The range of her vocals too, from a raucous coon song to the most sedate love ballads, affirms her position as one of the pre-eminent stars of musical film."

B-253   Kriegsman, Alan M. "A Double Vision." Washington
        Post. February 3, 1973. pp. E-1, E-9.
Kriegsman called the Washington, D.C. TV premiere of Show Boat a "must-see." He labeled the 1936 film "unquestionably the best" version, praising James Whale's direction and singling out the performances of Helen Morgan and Paul Robeson. Kriegsman added, "But nothing in the film is more impressive than the sheer visual eloquence of such scenes as the New Year's Eve gala in Chicago, as rich and moving a piece of moviemaking as the age produced."

B-254   Lamour, Dorothy, as told to Dick McInnes. My Side
        of the Road. Prentice-Hall, Inc. Englewood
        Cliffs, New Jersey. 1980. pp. 59, 82, 86, 119, 121.
In her autobiography, Lamour recalled participating in "Stars Over America," a nation-wide War Bond tour. Among the celebrities who joined her were Irene Dunne, James Cagney, Bette Davis, Joan Crawford, and Alice Faye. Lamour also worked with Irene Dunne in the film High, Wide and Handsome.

B-255   Lamparski, Richard. Whatever Became Of...?. Crown
        Publishers, Inc. New York. 1967. pp. 170-71.
Review of Irene Dunne's life and career, including photographs from 1936 and 1966. Mistakes included the statement that Leathernecking and Present Arms were two different films and that Theodora Goes Wild gave Irene her first Academy Award nomination.

B-256   _____. Whatever Became Of...?, Eighth Series.
        Crown Publishers, Inc. New York. 1982. pp. 94-95.
Updated biography of Irene Dunne, with mistakes from the previous volume corrected. Lamparski mentioned that Irene donated the altar of St. Teresa in the Church of the Blessed Sacrament in Hollywood. Article included 1940s and 1980s photographs of Irene.

B-257   _____. Whatever Became Of...?, Giant 2nd Annual.
        Bantam Books, Inc. New York. 1977. pp. 29-35, 168,
        172.
Biographical essay on Irene Dunne, including six photographs dating from the 1934 to 1977. Irene was pictured on the cover of Modern Screen and in an ad for Royal Crown Cola. Lamparski noted that her friends included Mrs. Justin Dart (former screen actress Jane Bryan) and the wife of the owner of the Los Angeles Times.

242   Irene Dunne

B-258   Larkin, Rochelle. <u>Hail, Columbia</u>. Arlington
        House. New Rochelle. 1975. pp. 94, 96-99, 110,
        113, 335, 336.
Irene Dunne's Columbia films were discussed in this history of the studio, which included stills from <u>Theodora Goes Wild</u>, <u>The Awful Truth</u>, <u>Together Again</u>, and <u>Penny Serenade</u>.

B-259   Lease, Rex and Harlan, Kenneth. <u>What Actors Eat - When They Eat</u>. Lymanhouse Publisher. Los Angeles. 1939. p. 78.
Irene Dunne shared her recipe for "Chicken and Ham Casserole," saying it was the first time she had given the secret to anyone outside her family. She recalled watching her grandmother prepare the dish when she was a child.

B-260   Lee, Sonia. "Discovering the Glamour in Irene
        Dunne." <u>Motion Picture</u>. March, 1937.

B-261   Leff, Leonard J. and Simmons, Jerold L. <u>The Dame in the Kimono</u>. Grove Weidenfeld. New York. 1990. pp. 24, 62, 63.
In a chapter entitled "You Can Be Had," Leff and Simmons explained how producers could get around the censors in the 1930s and '40s by stocking the credits with well-respected actors and directors. Irene Dunne and director John Cromwell served this purpose for the controversial <u>Ann Vickers</u>. Leff and Simmons recalled that chief censor Joseph Breen often reached terms of agreement with the producers of sophisticated films. They mentioned several instances in <u>The Awful Truth</u> where somewhat racy behavior got past the censors: Irene Dunne goosing a pompous old woman, Cary Grant offering a double entendre about coal mines, and Joyce Compton bearing her garter and underwear during her song. The end of the film was also questionable with the censors, with Irene sending Grant a telepathic message as she snuggled beneath the covers. A close-up of a cuckoo clock alluded to what happened next, with the clock striking midnight, and male and female figurines appearing from two houses to mark the striking hour. However, when the chime struck, the male followed the female back to her house instead of his. Leff and Simmons surmised, "In a cheaper picture, Breen would have bounced the dialogue, the stage business, and the racy close."

B-262   "Let's Talk It Out!" <u>Movie Mirror</u>. March, 1940.
        p. 58.
Irene Dunne served as "guest conductor" of <u>Movie Mirror's</u> youth forum, leading the magazine's regular body of advisers in answering questions sent in by young readers. The advisers concluded, "The Forum had all heard that Irene Dunne was known as Hollywood's Perfect Lady and...they found out you can be a perfect lady and a perfectly friendly, warm personality, too."

B-263   Levant, Oscar. <u>The Unimportance of Being Oscar</u>.

G.P. Putnam's Sons. New York. 1968. p. 132.
Levant recalled Irene Dunne's diplomacy skills were put to use long before her United Nations appointment. When both were under contract to RKO in the early 1930s, they were called upon to entertain for visiting exhibitors who toured the studio. Levant praised Irene's comedic skills and her work in Anna and the King of Siam.

B-264   Levin, Martin, editor. Hollywood and the Great Fan
        Magazines. Castle Books. New York. 1970.
        pp. 146-47, 215-16.
Reprints of articles from film magazines from the 1930s. "My Husband Is My Best Friend," a Modern Screen story about Irene Dunne by Adele Whitely Fletcher, was included. Irene was quoted as saying that she thought it was more fun to be married for a number of years than to be honeymooners. She explained that married couples understand how their partners think and react. Irene concluded, "...everything that happens to you, even a trifling event, is enriched by some similar thing you've already shared." Irene showed Fletcher the plans for the house she and her husband Frank Griffin were building in Holmby Hills. Fletcher stressed that the plans were labeled "Home of Doctor and Mrs. Francis Griffin," indicating that Irene preferred her role as wife to that of movie star. When asked about the long separations that the Griffins had to endure while Irene was in Hollywood filming and Frank was in New York with his dental practice, Irene was philosophical. She said, "Perhaps if we'd been together all the time during the last four years we wouldn't be such good friends. Perhaps together all the time we'd have come to take each other for granted; and find less zest in each other's company." Fletcher concluded, "It isn't...so much the number of hours two people spend together as what they do with those hours. For with the years, [Irene's] marriage to Frank Griffin has grown into that which can only exist in marriage and is at the same time the ultimate of marriage, namely the greatest friendship in the world." A photograph of Irene and Frank, and two stills from Roberta, accompanied the article.

B-265   Levine, Joni. "Spotlight on Beverly Hills."
        Spotlight Chicago. April 24, 1990.
Irene Dunne, who studied at the Chicago Musical College, had a new great-granddaughter, who was born in Chicago.

B-266   Libby, Bill. They Didn't Win the Oscars.
        Arlington House Publishers. Westport. 1980. pp. 7,
        74, 111, 114, 115, 193, 216.
Five-time Academy Award nominee Irene Dunne was pictured in stills from The Awful Truth, Anna and the King of Siam, and Penny Serenade. A brief biographical sketch summed up the Academy's possible reason for not giving her the Oscar. Libby said, "She was sly. She made it look easy. So it was easy to pass her over." Libby also mentioned that Warner Bros. mogul Jack Warner wanted Irene for the lead in Now, Voyager, but Bette Davis fought to win it.

B-267   Lieber, E. "Just a Nice Person, Eh?" *Photoplay*.
        August, 1952.

B-268   "Little Prima Donna with Small Role." *New York Telegram*. March 29, 1923.
Account of Irene Dunne thanking playwright Zelda Sears for making the role of Tessie in *The Clinging Vine* so brief. Irene's four-minute role allowed her to continue to study music, Italian, and dancing during her off-stage hours.

B-269   *Los Angeles Examiner*. August 14, 1951.
After co-starring in two films, Irene Dunne and Fred MacMurray planned to team up again, this time on radio, with a half-hour comedy series entitled *Bright Star*. Sponsored by the Frederic W. Ziv Company, the series would be transcribed, rather than broadcast live, and syndicated throughout the country. Irene and MacMurray's contracts indicated they would each net a minimum of three hundred thousand dollars over the next few years. The series was syndicated in 1952, but ran only fifteen minutes.

B-270   *Los Angeles Times*. November 9, 1932.
Irene Dunne had to cancel her plans to spend Christmas with her husband Frank Griffin when she was ordered to Hollywood by MGM to begin work on *The Lady*. Irene and Frank had planned trips to Havana and Florida for the holidays. *The Lady* was released as *The Secret of Madame Blanche* and co-starred Phillips Holmes.

B-271   *Los Angeles Times*. February 17, 1934.
Irene Dunne's work on *Stingaree* was postponed when she developed a skin infection on her face caused by sunburn and makeup. Irene got the burn while shooting the film on location on the RKO studio ranch for three days. Irene went to work with the infection, but was sent home because the irritation was visible in the previous day's shots.

B-272   "Love Isn't New but These Love Teams Are." *Motion Picture*. July, 1933. p. 49.
Three movie couples were shown embracing, including Irene Dunne and Joel McCrea, stars of *The Silver Cord*.

B-273   Ludlam, H.F. "Dunne 'Nucleus.'" *Silver Screen*.
        July, 1935.

B-274   Mack, Gloria. "Handfuls of Beauty." *Movie Mirror*.
        April, 1940. p. 102
Irene Dunne offered advice for caring for hands and nails. She was quoted as saying, "Hands are a reflection of character. Keep them true to your own individuality." She suggested women who play piano, golf or type should keep nails short. She also praised her longtime habit of pushing back the cuticle after washing her hands.

B-275   Macpherson, Don. *Leading Ladies*. St. Martin's
        Press. New York. 1986.

B-276   Madden, James. C. "Irene Dunne Projected Gentility
        and Failed to Get an Academy Award." *Films in
        Review*. December, 1969. pp. 605-20.
Detailed overview of Irene Dunne's film career. Madden
observed, "...Miss Dunne's screen personality was so
captivating she scarcely needed to act to be believed - be
she portraying a Russian princess (*Roberta*), a Southern
belle (*Show Boat*), or Queen Victoria (*The Mudlark*). She
may not have needed the acting arts to win audiences, but
she nevertheless was the mistress of most of them - and used
them." Madden claimed 1936 was "the year of the great
divide," both professionally and personally. With *High,
Wide and Handsome* as her last full-fledged screen musical,
Irene focused her attention on comedy. It also marked
changes in her personal life, with the death of her mother,
her husband moving to California, and the adoption of Mary
Frances. The article included a filmography and eighteen
photographs.

B-277   Magill, Frank N., editor. *Magill's Survey of
        Cinema, first series*. Salem Press. Englewood
        Cliffs, New Jersey. 1980.
Collected essays on classic movies, written by a series of
film historians. Articles not only discussed the plot of
the movies, but often gave background information about the
shooting and critical analysis. Irene Dunne was mentioned
in pieces on her films *Anna and the King of Siam*, *The
Awful Truth*, *Cimarron*, *My Favorite Wife*, and *Show
Boat*.

B-278   _____. *Magill's Survey of Cinema, second series*.
        Salem Press. Englewood Cliffs, New Jersey. 1981.
Second set of critical/historical essays on classic films.
Among the Irene Dunne movies profiled were *I Remember
Mama*, *Life with Father*, *Love Affair*, *Magnificent
Obsession*, *Penny Serenade*, *Roberta*, and *Theodora Goes
Wild*.

B-279   *Magnificent Costumes*. Sotheby Parke Bernet. Los
        Angeles. 1971.
This auction catalogue from Max Berman & Sons, Inc. listed
uniforms, as well as film and theatre costumes. Two of
Irene Dunne's *Cimarron* outfits were offered. The auction
took place in June, 1971.

B-280   Mahar, Ted. "'Just Folks' People Film; Kubrick
        Features Coldness." *Oregonian* [Portland].
        February 22, 1976.
Discussion of the treatment of religion in *A Guy Named Joe*
and *2001: A Space Odessey*. Mahar compared *Joe's*
spirits to the Greek gods. He said, "...the afterlife is
simply this life with a few limited preternatural powers.
Just like the Greek gods, who carried on petty jealousies
against mortal men and each other." Although Mahar
described *2001's* deities as "emotionally aloof," he
admitted they were more logical than *Joe's* spirits.

Mahar described Irene Dunne's character in <u>A Guy Named Joe</u> as "a very Katharine Hepburnish ferry plane pilot with a very Hepburnish love-antagonism relationship brewing with [Spencer] Tracy."

B-281 "Mammy's Day by Courtesy of the Cradle." <u>Movie Life</u>. May, 1938.
Two-page pictorial spread about the Cradle, an Evanston, Illinois adoption home. Irene Dunne was pictured, along with other actors whose children were adopted with the help of the Cradle. The caption read, "Irene Dunne's little girl will be called Mary Frances Griffin," implying she was not yet adopted at presstime. According to most sources, Mary Frances was adopted from the New York Foundling Home.

B-282 Manners, Dorothy. "You're Twice as Pretty as You Think You Are!" <u>Motion Picture</u>. July, 1932. pp. 32, 53, 86.
RKO's fashion consultant, Mrs. Brock Pemberton, offered advice for improving the appearance and commented on stars who changed their look for the better. Among the actresses she discussed were Irene Dunne, Constance Bennett, and Ann Harding. Pemberton criticized Irene's matronly appearance. In addition to suggesting a brightly colored wardrobe, Pemberton erased years by styling Irene's hair in a wavy bob. Pemberton advised, "If you are the Irene Dunne type, here is just one last word of warning: preserve your real youth - don't waste it on dark, matronly garments and firm, set marcel waves." Irene was shown in before and after photos.

B-283 Marilyn. "Clothes Gossip from Hollywood." <u>Motion Picture</u>. March, 1933. pp. 44-47, 84.
Irene Dunne modeled a costume from <u>The Lady</u>, which was released as <u>The Secret of Madame Blanche</u>.

B-284 Markfield, Wallace. "'Play It Again, Sam' - and Again." <u>Saturday Evening Post</u>. April 22, 1967. pp. 72-76, 78-79.
Paean to the late show, in which Markfield insisted that the old films shown on television were much more memorable than the TV series. After recalling favorites of all genres, he concluded, "Irene Dunne may have been only the most brilliant comedienne of them all."

B-285 Martin, Sally. "Fashions." <u>Movie Classic</u>. December, 1936. pp. 42-43.
Irene Dunne modeled two costumes from <u>Theodora Goes Wild</u>.

B-286 Marvin, Courtenay. "That 'Finishing' Business." <u>Screenland</u>. July, 1941. pp. 56-57, 80-82.
Irene Dunne, Carole Lombard, and Claudette Colbert were mentioned as three actresses who possessed beauty, charm, and a good figure in this article on grooming. Irene gave her tips in several photos taken on the set of <u>Unfinished Business</u>. She advised taking time to keep up on current

events to improve conversation and taking advantage of spare moments, such as her signing autographs between takes. Irene also was seen in two stills from the film.

B-287 Maxwell, E. "A Very Special Woman." *Photoplay*.
       January, 1948.

B-288 Maxwell, V. "Don't Live with Your Mother-in-Law."
       Photoplay. September, 1933.

B-289 McClelland, Doug. *Hollywood Talks Turkey*. Faber
       and Faber. Boston. 1990.
Actors, directors, and screenwriters spoke out about films they considered flops. Screenwriter Albert Hackett recalled being embarrassed when he met Irene Dunne after *The Secret of Madame Blanche*, a film he deemed "awful." However, he was amused when Irene presented him with a check from the Christophers for the screenplay for *Father of the Bride*. As she greeted Hackett, she told him, "I have a friend who thinks the best picture you ever wrote was *The Secret of Madame Blanche*!" Irene was quoted about her work in *The Mudlark* and *It Grows on Trees*. After commenting on the elaborate makeup involved in portraying Queen Victoria, Irene confessed that, while the film did not do her career any good, she enjoyed making it. She concluded, "Maybe if I'd done it earlier in my career when my image wasn't so fixed, it would have been better received." Irene's comments about *It Grows on Trees* were even more succinct. "Maybe if we'd had a bigger director and a 'name' leading man, it might have been successful. But we didn't and it wasn't. My movie career was over."

B-290 McCourt, James and Harvey, James. "Irene Dunne:
       The Awesome Truth." *Film Comment*.
       January/February, 1980. pp. 26-32.
Irene Dunne's screen persona was described by McCourt in an article accompanying Harvey's interview with the actress. Irene reflected on the shyness of some actors, which led them to bury themselves in character parts. She recalled her own character role in *The Mudlark*, "Nobody liked it, but I loved playing it." When Harvey told her he was writing a book on romantic films of the 1930s and 1940s, Irene confessed that Harcourt Brace had approached her about writing her memoirs. Her husband discouraged that project by asking, "Do you think people really care about your grandmother?" When asked about the validity of a rumor about her being approached to play the older Roberta in a Broadway revival of the musical, Irene admitted she had heard about the idea. "But why would I want to do that?" she asked. Irene professed to have liked sixteen of her forty-one films. She discussed her opinions of directors Gregory La Cava, Rouben Mamoulian, George Stevens, John Stahl, Richard Boleslawski, Victor Fleming, Tay Garnett, Michael Curtiz, and Leo McCarey, as well as her work in *The Awful Truth*, *Love Affair*, *My Favorite Wife*, *A Guy Named Joe*, *I Remember Mama*, *Back Street*, *The*

248   Irene Dunne

Mudlark, Joy of Living, and Show Boat. Irene judged Theodora Goes Wild very "unsophisticated" and could not understand its inital success or its respect from film students. She discussed her acting technique of becoming the character she played, a method which drove her family crazy. She said the only character she disliked was Vinnie in Life with Father, whom she described as "unbelievably rattlebrained." Irene claimed she never admired a comedienne or wanted to do comedy, perhaps because it came to her too easily. Fourteen stills from her films accompanied the article.

B-291   McDonough, John. "Irene Dunne: A Master with Staying Power." Kansas City Star [Missouri]. May 19, 1985.
Reprint of "Screening a Star: A Rare Interview with Irene Dunne (B-292).

B-292   _____. "Screening a Star: A Rare Interview with Irene Dunne." Chicago Tribune. May 12, 1985.
Irene Dunne reminisced about her career and technique. She discussed her preparation for film roles, writing character motivation between the lines in her script. Even when scenes called for her to ad lib, Irene planned her dialogue ahead of the shooting so she would be prepared. Irene compared directorial styles of Leo McCarey and George Stevens. Although Stevens worked at a much slower pace than McCarey, she praised Stevens's preparedness and called Penny Serenade one of her favorite films. Irene admitted that live television "scared the life out of [her]." Although she was quoted as saying she earned a doctor's degree from the Chicago Musical College, school records show that she earned an undergraduate degree in 1919 and was awarded an honorary doctorate in 1945. Article included a collage of photos from her films, as well as a picture of Irene receiving her honorary degree from Rudolph Ganz, and a 1979 photograph.

B-293   McGilligan, Pat. Backstory: Interviews with Screenwriters of Hollywood's Golden Age. University of California Press, Ltd. London. 1986. pp. 122-23, 222, 314, 320, 324-25, 343.
Screenwriters James M. Cain, Norman Krasna, Allan Scott, and Donald Ogden Stewart discussed their work on films in the 1930s and '40s. Cain claimed that When Tomorrow Comes bore little resemblance to the story on which it was based. He said, "...the girl was Irene Dunne, who had it in her contract that she had to sing at least one number. When Tomorrow Comes had a waitress who sings as good as Irene Dunne sings, and they made him [the character who was originally a Harvard man] a French pianist....That's how they mangle things up." Krasna recalled that it was a breakthrough in censorship when Irene and Cary Grant's characters in The Awful Truth got a divorce, indicating they had slept together. Scott remembered that Irene was the easiest of the major RKO actresses to please. He said,

"Being from the theatre, she always came to the set thoroughly prepared. If she had any problems with a scene, she would always select out the author, sit down with him, and talk it out - never making any suggestions but just saying she was having a bit of trouble and asking what she was doing wrong." Stewart recalled that the Hays office, Hollywood's censorship bureau, insisted that a sin must be followed by punishment on the screen. Therefore before Irene and Charles Boyer's characters could find happiness in <u>Love Affair</u>, she had to be injured to pay for a previous affair. He said, "You dissolved to her in a hospital with her realizing that God hadn't wanted her to meet Boyer until she was sorry for what she had done before."

B-294   McManus, John T.   "Magnolia of the Movies."   <u>New York Times</u>.   May 17, 1936.

Interview with Irene Dunne, who was in New York for the premiere of the film <u>Show Boat</u>. Irene was quite perplexed by erroneous information supplied by studio press agents about her background. When asked about her childhood entertaining on showboats, Irene explained that while she remembered watching the boats on the Ohio River as a girl, she was not allowed to attend the productions. Press reports said that her lawyer father wanted her to follow him into the legal profession and disapproved of her stage career. Irene corrected them, explaining that her father was not a lawyer and that her parents encouraged her to be an opera singer. Irene discussed her dislike of radio work, ironic since she later performed extensively in that medium. Although she had not performed on stage for six years, she believed in a few superstitions that were akin to theatre folk: never fix up too nicely or some other actress may take your part, never put a hat on the bed, never whistle backstage, never store shoes in overhead shelves, and be wary of passing a cemetary while on tour, a certain sign that the show will close early. Irene and Allan Jones were pictured in a scene from <u>Show Boat</u>.

B-295   Medini, Douglas A.   "Irene Dunne: The Most Versatile Leading Lady."   <u>Movie Collector's World</u>.   February 16, 1990.   pp. 62-63.

Medini complained that Irene Dunne was seldom remembered for anything but her ladylike roles, despite her versatility. He praised Irene's vocal and comedic talents, while giving an overview of her life and career. Medini's chronology was a bit confused, implying Mary Frances was adopted before Irene made <u>Roberta</u> and making no mention of her long distance marriage to Frank (mistakenly called Dennis) Griffin. Article included stills from <u>The Silver Cord</u>, <u>Love Affair</u>, and <u>This Man Is Mine</u>.

B-296   "Memos for the Boss."   <u>Lion's Roar</u>.   July, 1944.
Irene Dunne was mentioned in this in-house journal of MGM.

B-297   Milberg, Doris.   "Irene Dunne: Actress, Singer, Lady."   <u>Movie Collector's World</u>.   October 26, 1990.

250   Irene Dunne

p. 57.
As the second installment in a series entitled "Forgotten Stars of the '30s & '40s," the article was written before Irene Dunne's death, but ran as a tribute. Milberg said Irene was synonymous with the words "lady" and "versatility." The article presented a brief overview of Irene's life and career, touching on each of her films. Milberg concluded, "She was an original - her likes will not be seen again." Irene and Charles Boyer were pictured in a still from Love Affair.

B-298   Mitchell, Lt. Col. Curtis. "The Radio Front: Washington." Movie-Radio Guide. September 12, 1942. p. 8.
Among the stars mentioned as appearing on an upcoming special Command Performance broadcast from Washington, were Irene Dunne, Greer Garson, James Cagney, and Bing Crosby. Although Crosby was the only star who appeared on the broadcast, the other celebrities traveled to Washington to open a billion-dollar war bond drive the day after the broadcast.

B-299   _____. "The Radio Front: Washington." Movie-Radio Guide. September 19, 1942. p. 8.
A group of film stars, including Irene Dunne, Bing Crosby, Greer Garson, James Cagney, Ralph Bellamy, and Dinah Shore, traveled to Washington to launch a billion-dollar war bond drive on the steps of the Treasury. The crowd bought over a million dollars' worth of bonds from the stars.

B-300   Moak, B. "Happiness Guaranteed." Silver Screen. April, 1932.

B-301   Mordden, Ethan. Movie Star: A Look at the Women Who Made Hollywood. St. Martin's Press. New York. 1983. pp. 93, 100-101, 150-51, 216, 256.
Irene Dunne's versatility was discussed in a chapter entitled "Women's Women: the Ladies." Mordden observed, "...she seems a little put out by the hokum, high jinks, production numbers, and other commotions of the [musical] form." He continued, "In Roberta she has to play the love plot with Randolph Scott and make room for Fred Astaire and Ginger Rogers and Astaire's jazz band, and every so often she gives a look that says, 'Who are these people?' Surely that's why Dunne is arresting in screwball comedy. She's so lady that when she becomes antic it's like a Quaker going to war; take it very seriously." He described her role in Joy of Living as "American prim running wild." Mordden compared Irene's work in The Awful Truth to Katharine Hepburn's in Bringing Up Baby. While both films were screwball comedies with Cary Grant as the leading man, Mordden concluded that Irene's approach was more elegant. Adela Rogers St. Johns was quoted as saying, "Irene Dunne makes being good more fun." Despite Mordden's astute comments, he mistakenly said Roberta was filmed in 1953, rather than 1935.

B-302 Morehouse, Ward. "Theatre." *Theatre Arts*. Fall, 1948. pp. 34-42.
Chronicle of the 1923 Broadway season, including a photo of Peggy Wood and Irene Dunne in *The Clinging Vine*.

B-303 Morris, Bernadine. "A Lasting Hollywood Alliance." *New York Times*. October 17, 1967.
Irene Dunne discussed her admiration of the designs of Jean Louis, both on and off screen. Although Irene claimed he designed her costumes for *The Awful Truth* and *Theodora Goes Wild*, Kalloch and Bernard Newman were given the credit.

B-304 Moseley, Leonard. *Zanuck: The Rise and Fall of Hollywood's Last Tycoon*. Little, Brown and Company. Boston. 1984. pp. 269-70.
One of the reasons Darryl F. Zanuck chose to make *The Mudlark* was because it gave him the opportunity to cast Irene Dunne in a long-desired role. She had once confided in him that she wanted to play Queen Victoria. Zanuck saw the film as the perfect opportunity. Despite Zanuck's enthusiasm, the British press was outraged at the thought of an American actress essaying a British monarch. At the height of the controversey, Zanuck arranged for a private screening at Windsor Castle for King George and Queen Elizabeth (now the Queen Mother). The royals approved of Irene's performance. The King was quoted as saying, "It's a pity Great-Grandmamma wasn't really as pretty as the actress who played her. Much smaller and tubbier she was, and quite pasty."

B-305 Moseley, Roy with Masheter, Philip and Masheter, Martin. *Rex Harrison*. St. Martin's Press. New York. 1987. pp. 82, 87.
Biography of the actor, in which his work on *Anna and the King of Siam* was discussed. Rex Harrison and director John Cromwell disagreed on the speech pattern that the king should employ. Although Irene Dunne got along with Cromwell, Moseley noted that she went her own way during the production. He wrote, "She was a longtime Hollywood film actress, happily married for over twenty years and known for her professionalism and aloof cordiality. Rex did not find her an over-sympathetic leading lady, despite the fact that she was profoundly pro-British."

B-306 "Movie Dressographs." *St. Louis Post-Dispatch*. November 5, 1933.
Paperdoll of Irene Dunne with three costumes from *Ann Vickers*, *The Silver Cord*, and *The Secret of Madame Blanche*.

B-307 "The Movie Front." *Movie-Radio Guide*. August 29, 1942. p. 8.
Irene Dunne and her husband were pictured at the Stork Club during a recent trip to New York.

252   Irene Dunne

B-308   "The Movie Front." <u>Movie-Radio Guide</u>.
        September 19, 1942. p. 7.
Irene Dunne, Greer Garson, Ronald Colman, and Hedy Lamarr were pictured en route to Washington to sell war bonds.

B-309   <u>Movie Mirror</u>. May, 1939. p. 43.
Regal portrait of Irene Dunne, the star of <u>Love Affair</u>. Caption asked if Irene ever tired of being dubbed "the perfect lady."

B-310   "Movie of the Week: <u>Anna and the King of Siam</u>."
        <u>Life</u>. June 24, 1946.
Photos of the real Anna and the Siamese king were included in this pictorial preview of the film. The article noted, "Only disappointment is that the producers did not film it in color."

B-311   "Movie of the Week: <u>A Guy Named Joe</u>." <u>Life</u>.
        January 17, 1944.
Stills from the film were utilized to tell the story of <u>A Guy Named Joe</u>. Review compared the theme to <u>Here Comes Mr. Jordan</u>, but praised one unique aspect: "Its hero (Spencer Tracy) and heroine (Irene Dunne), a kind of Mr. and Mrs. Thin Man without benefit of clergy, talk and act like two people who have actually been at controls of a plane."

B-312   "Movie of the Week: <u>I Remember Mama</u>." <u>Life</u>.
        April 12, 1948.
Pictorial spread devoted to the film. Article said, "While <u>I Remember Mama</u> misses being completely enjoyable because most big scenes are tiresomely drawn out, it avoids the pitfall of oversentimentality and adds up to a first-class movie." In addition to stills from the film, author Kathryn Forbes, who wrote the stories on which the film was based, was pictured.

B-313   "Movie of the Week: <u>Life with Father</u>." <u>Life</u>.
        August 18, 1947.
Irene Dunne was pictured in four of ten stills from the film.

B-314   "Movie of the Week: <u>Love Affair</u>." <u>Life</u>.
        March 20, 1939.
Although <u>Life</u> claimed the film had little action, it said <u>Love Affair</u> was "told with the deft and charming touch at which Hollywood excels the world."

B-315   "Movie of the Week: <u>My Favorite Wife</u>." <u>Life</u>.
        May 13, 1940.
The film was called a "first-rate comedy" in this pictorial review. Article included other variations of the Enoch Arden story, in which a shipwrecked sailor returned to find his wife remarried.

B-316   "Movie of the Week: <u>Unfinished Business</u>." <u>Life</u>.
        September 15, 1941.

Director Gregory La Cava was profiled in this salute to his latest film. A former cartoonist, La Cava sketched plans for upcoming scenes in the margin of his script. La Cava's sketches were pictured, along with stills showing how the scene came out on screen.

B-317 "Movie Star in the U.N." New York Sunday News. December 15, 1957.

A color photograph of Irene Dunne and Dag Hammarskjold graced the cover of the Sunday magazine. Inside, Irene discussed her work with the United Nations. She confessed that she had stagefright throughout her film career, but found it easy to speak at the U.N. She theorized, "Maybe that's because, as an actress, I am impersonating someone else, while here I'm saying the things I myself feel." Irene claimed that life as a delegate was often more glamorous than life as an actress. Rather than going home at 6:00 after a day of filming, she was required to attend receptions and parties as a matter of diplomacy. Irene sometimes found it difficult to forget she was an actress. After finishing a speech at the U.N., pledging $21 million for aid to refugees, a man asked for her autograph. She thought it was an odd place for a fan to make the request, but took the paper he offered. She was surprised to see that it was the official agreement binding the U.S. to the $21 million aid. Irene was quoted as saying, "And I felt that, for at least one time, a star's autograph was really going to do some good."

B-318 "Movie-Radio Guide Recommends: Unfinished Business." Movie-Radio Guide. August 16, 1941. p. 5.

Pictorial review of the film starring Irene Dunne and Robert Montgomery. Critic pointed out the truth in the theme "Marry in haste and repent at leisure" by chronicling quick Hollywood courtships which ended in divorce. However, the critic concluded, "...director [Gregory] La Cava makes [Robert] Montgomery and [Irene] Dunne fall in love successfully after marriage. In Hollywood real life, it doesn't work out that way."

B-319 "Movie-Radio Guide Reports on: The Ten Richest Women in Movies." Movie-Radio Guide. September 20, 1941. p. 2.

Irene Dunne was named one of the highest paid actresses in Hollywood, with her earnings estimated at $405,000. Others included Bette Davis, Ginger Rogers, Loretta Young, Joan Crawford, and Greta Garbo. Only Claudette Colbert, whose earnings were estimated at $427,000, was richer than Irene. Although actresses earned substantial salaries, the article pointed out that income taxes were also high, with the government collecting close to 50% of a salary of $100,000.

B-320 "Movie-Radio Guide Reveals: Exclusive Stories Behind Stars' Great Love-scenes." Movie-Radio Guide. July 5, 1941.

254   Irene Dunne

Irene Dunne and John Boles were shown in a still from <u>Back Street</u>, representing one of the ten most famous love scenes of the past. Others included Robert Taylor and Greta Garbo in <u>Camille</u> and Janet Gaynor and Charles Farrell in <u>Seventh Heaven</u>.

B-321   "The Movies of 1948." <u>Life</u>. March 14, 1949.
Recap of films opening in 1948. <u>I Remember Mama</u> was heralded as the best of the "folksy pictures," which celebrated the virtues of home and family.

B-322   Mueller, John. <u>Astaire Dancing</u>. Alfred A. Knopf. New York. 1985. pp. 8, 65, 89, 94, 97.
Irene Dunne was mentioned in conjunction with <u>Roberta</u> and <u>Follow the Fleet</u> in this book saluting Fred Astaire's musical films. Producer Pandro Berman bought the film rights to <u>Roberta</u> as a vehicle for Irene, as well as for Fred Astaire and Ginger Rogers. <u>Follow the Fleet</u> was shaped like <u>Roberta</u>, in that Astaire and Rogers did not take the central romantic roles. Mueller pointed out that Irene was the initial choice for the role eventually played by Harriet Hilliard in <u>Follow the Fleet</u>. In fact, the screenwriters assigned the song "Let's Face the Music and Dance" to her character. However, when Hilliard was cast instead, they found the song was too rich for her voice and gave it to Astaire. Mueller suggested that a lyric soprano like Irene might have been able to minimize the "calculated naivete" of the song "But Where Are You?" from <u>Follow the Fleet</u>. He said Hilliard's performance only emphasized the rhyming lyrics.

B-323   "My Favorite Dress." <u>Hollywood Pattern</u>. December, 1937/January, 1938. pp. 14-15.
Irene Dunne was among the stars modeling their favorite film costumes. She chose a gown from <u>The Awful Truth</u>.

B-324   "New Faces Characterize Prudential's Family." <u>Variety</u>. September 21, 1949.
None of the previous season's rotating cast would be on hand for the <u>Prudential Family Hour of Stars</u>. The 1949 lineup consisted of Irene Dunne, Ronald Colman, Dana Andrews, Loretta Young, Jane Wyman, and Kirk Douglas. Irene kicked off the new season with an adaptation of <u>Love Affair</u>, but disappeared from the radio show after one more broadcast.

B-325   <u>New Movie Magazine</u>. September, 1932. p. 34.
Freulich portrait of Irene Dunne, striking an aloof pose. The caption stressed that she was one of Hollywood's mysteries. "Untheatrical, socially unambitious, sane in her viewpoint, normal and everyday in her life, she has the film colony mystified, yet without trying to do so," the caption read.

B-326   <u>New York Times</u>. August 26, 1934.
Jerome Kern planned to write two new songs for the film version of <u>Sweet Adeline</u>. The musical was Irene Dunne's

first movie under her Warner Bros. contract. Kern added "We Were So Young" and "Lonely Feet."

B-327   "News of the Screen." <u>New York Times</u>. March 24, 1937.
It was announced that Irene Dunne and John Boles would be reunited in a film, possibly <u>Joy of Living</u>. Although the article claimed they had co-starred in the musical comedy <u>Rio Rita</u> in 1929, Irene and Boles actually appeared in the melodrama <u>Back Street</u>. Bebe Daniels was Boles's <u>Rio Rita</u> co-star; Douglas Fairbanks, Jr. ended up appearing in <u>Joy of Living</u>.

B-328   <u>Nostalgia Book Club Newsletter</u>. November, 1977.
Club member Edward Smith gave his account of Irene Dunne's appearance at the the American Film Institute's tenth anniversary celebration. Smith, a longtime Irene fan, attended the showing of <u>Love Affair</u> and the discussion following it. When he asked her to autograph his 78 album, Irene invited him backstage so not to cause an autograph riot during the program. Smith arrived backstage and found Irene had already gone upstairs to the private reception being given in her honor. However, Irene had left a message for Smith to join her. Smith wrote, "She was as gracious and charming as one could have wished - and still as lovely as ever. A bit older in the face, of course, but she wears the years elegantly and they have been very kind to her." When Irene autographed the album, a <u>Washington Post</u> reporter picked up on the story, giving Smith the additional surprise of having his fairytale evening recounted in the newspaper (B-349).

B-329   Oates, Marylouise. "Art Fund-Raiser Honors Irene Dunne." <u>Los Angeles Times</u>. May 18, 1985.
Irene Dunne was honored by the National Art Association at a dinner at the Beverly Wilshire Hotel's Grand Ballroom. The evening included cocktails, a lavish dinner, dancing, musical selections sung by John Raitt, and clips from Irene's movies. After the film tribute, James Stewart spoke about his friendship with Irene. Although they never made a film together, Irene said she had always imagined it would be a western, which would end with a sunset and "a long, lingering kiss." Others in attendance included Roddy McDowall, Loretta Young, Bill Frye, and Father Maurice Chase. Article included a photograph of Irene with James and Gloria Stewart.

B-330   _____. "Irene Dunne's Movie-Idol Image Keeps on Playing Soft and Clear." <u>Los Angeles Times</u>. February 14, 1983.
Interview with Irene Dunne contrasting her film image with her private life. She discussed her friendship with then-President Ronald Reagan, her involvement with Saint John's Hospital, and her relationship with her husband Frank Griffin. Irene said she was surprised to learn after his death that he had kept every letter she had ever written

256   Irene Dunne

to him. When asked if she would write her memoirs, Irene responded, "The Lord never wrote a book, not that I knew about. Not really. And I don't think Abraham Lincoln ever wrote a book. So I have put it off again." A back accident prevented her from attending daily Mass, a condition she considered an "extreme sacrifice." Although Irene resisted attempts to bring her back to the screen, she kept up with the film industry and continued to be a voting member of the Academy of Motion Picture Arts and Sciences.

B-331   "Obituaries." <u>Variety</u>. December 23, 1936.
Irene Dunne's mother died in Beverly Hills on December 17, 1936. She had been Irene's companion throughout her career. A son Charles also survived.

B-332   "Obituaries." <u>Variety</u>. October 20, 1965.
Dr. Francis Griffin, Irene Dunne's husband, died on October 15, 1965, of a heart ailment. He was seventy-nine. Dr. Griffin began practicing dentistry in 1927. After his retirement in 1936, he became active in real estate in California and Nevada. In addition to being a director of the Beverly Wilshire Hotel, he was a founding member of the Los Angeles Music Center. Their daughter Mary Frances Shinnick survived.

B-333   O'Brien, Jack. "Voice of Broadway." <u>New Jersey Star-Ledger</u>. December 18, 1984.
When movie star lothario George Raft was asked which woman he ranked highest, he chose a woman he had never dated. He was quoted as saying, "No contest - Irene Dunne." Irene was pictured, with the caption, "A classic beauty."

B-334   O'Brien, Pat. <u>The Wind at My Back</u>. Doubleday and Company, Inc. Garden City, NY. 1964. pp. 163-64.
O'Brien discussed <u>Consolation Marriage</u>, which he called one of his favorite films. He recalled that he and Irene Dunne were sent to San Francisco to shoot a scene at the aquarium, despite the time and cost involved in transporting them. He also reminisced about the film's Hollywood premiere, which took place at the Carthay Circle Theatre. Irene and Spencer Tracy were pictured at the christening of their godson, Terry O'Brien, in 1941.

B-335   "On Rally Program." <u>Hartford Citizen</u> [Connecticut]. July 25, 1942.
Irene Dunne and Ed Wynn were among the celebrities scheduled to appear at a war bond rally at the Yale Bowl on Friday. The rally closed the Treasury Department's nation-wide, month-long campaign to sell a billion dollars' worth of bonds through retail trade outlets.

B-336   "One Man, Two Wives." <u>Movie-Radio Guide</u>. May 4, 1940. pp. 4-5.
<u>My Favorite Wife</u> received a two-page pictorial review as it was named "Picture of the Week."

Irene Dunne and her mother Adelaide Henry Dunn in the mid-1930s. Adelaide lived with her daughter until her death in 1936. (Wisconsin Center for Film and Theater Research)

B-337 "Opera and Comedy Win Favor." *Billboard*.
September 15, 1928.
Report from Atlantic City on the try-outs of *The Dagger and the Rose* and *Luckee Girl*. Irene Dunne was one of the actors mentioned in the "exceptional cast" of *Luckee Girl*. The musical was favorably received during its run at the Garden Pier. While *Billboard* also predicted that *The Dagger and the Rose* was "destined to be a hit," the show closed in Atlantic City before its scheduled Broadway opening. Ironically, one of its stars, Leota Lane, was in the Chicago company of *Luckee Girl* in 1929.

B-338 Ormiston, R. "To Make You Happier." *Photoplay*. April, 1944.

B-339 Osborne, Kay. "Portfolio of Fashion and Beauty; Ginger Rogers." *Motion Picture*. May, 1935. pp. 43-45, 62.
Bernard Newman, designer of *Roberta*, discussed his costumes and hats for the film. Irene Dunne modeled four outfits and talked about Newman's efforts.

B-340 Packard, Ruth Mary. "Seven Summer Favorites." *Ladies' Home Journal*. May, 1941. pp. 30-31.
Irene Dunne modeled a large red Milan hat.

B-341 Palmer, Gretta. "If I Were 21." *Ladies' Home Journal*. January, 1947. pp. 36-37, 155.
Celebrities in many fields discussed what they would do with their lives if they could begin again. Irene Dunne said she wasted much of her youth hesitating between a career in opera or musical theatre. She recalled, "I needed an immediate triumph to reassure me. And so, when I should have been singing scales, if I were to be a serious musician, I was headlong in the score of *Aida*." Irene wished she had married earlier and had several children, rather than adopting only one. She also regretted the years she and her husband were separated because of their careers. Admitting to a stubborn streak, Irene claimed she would not have taken advice at twenty-one. It was only later that she learned to listen to those who knew more than she. Irene concluded, "If I were 21, I'd aim high; mere security is too poor a bargain to strike with life." Photographs of Irene as an ingenue and as she was in 1947 accompanied the article.

B-342 "Pandemonium at the Palladium!" *Movie-Radio Guide*. May 9, 1942. p. 8.
Irene Dunne was pictured with Mrs. Sam Goldwyn at a military ball held at the Hollywood Palladium. The benefit raised money for the California State Guard to equip a hospital.

B-343 Parish, James Robert. *The RKO Gals*. Arlington House. New Rochelle. 1974. pp. 24, 27, 28, 29, 32, 127-92, 207, 214, 218, 279, 281, 283, 290, 291, 365, 399, 402, 470, 547, 648, 716, 761.

Detailed biographical essay on Irene Dunne's life and
career. The chapter on Irene, located on pages 127-92,
included a filmography and many photographs from her career
and private life. The book was a mini-history of RKO,
weaved into chapters on major studio contractees. Irene
also was mentioned in conjunction with her relationships
with other RKO leading ladies.

B-344   Parish, James Robert with Stanke, Don E. *The
        Swashbucklers*. Arlington House. New Rochelle, New
        York. 1976. p. 133.
Irene Dunne was one of fifty actresses who participated in a
1934 popularity contest. The actresses, who included
Loretta Young, Jeanette MacDonald, Norma Shearer, Bette
Davis, Barbara Stanwyck, and Ethel Merman, were asked to
pick their ten favorite actors. Ronald Colman topped the
list, followed by Fredric March, Clark Gable, Nils Asther,
Joel McCrea, Francis Lederer, James Cagney, Richard Arlen,
and Randolph Scott.

B-345   Parsons, Louella O. "*Cosmopolitan's* Movie
        Citations." *Cosmopolitan*. April, 1948.
        pp. 12-13, 164-66.
Parsons, the mother of *I Remember Mama's* producer Harriet
Parsons, praised her daughter's film and recalled how the
movie came about. Parsons claimed that she loved the film's
simple, human story, and that she would consider it one of
the finest movies ever made, even if she "never heard of
anyone connected with it." She gave *I Remember Mama
Cosmopolitan's* Citation for best picture of the month and
Irene Dunne the award for best feminine star, praising
"Mama's" compassion and imagination. Parsons said, "Irene
Dunne has never risen to the heights she reaches as 'Mama.'
You might expect a woman of [her] glamorous beauty to refuse
to hide these assets of loveliness. But no. She wears no
make-up [sic], and her clothes look as if 'Mama' had made
them, herself." Parsons continued, "She has thickened her
lovely voice with Norwegian gutterals - but her art shines
forth at its clearest."

B-346   Peak, Mayme Ober. "Study the Stars and Dress Your
        Line." *Ladies' Home Journal*. June, 1932.
        pp. 8-9, 105.
Costume designers discussed the stars' figure flaws, with
Max Ree, who designed the clothes for many RKO films,
commenting on Irene Dunne.

B-347   Peary, Danny. *Close-Ups*. Workman Publishing. New
        York. 1978. pp. 382-89.
Billed as "intimate profiles of movie stars by their
co-stars, directors, screenwriters and friends," *Close-Ups*
featured an essay about Irene Dunne by film
historian/screenwriter DeWitt Bodeen, and a profile of Cary
Grant written by Irene. In a chapter entitled "Irene Dunne:
Native Treasure," Bodeen, who wrote the screenplay for *I
Remember Mama*, recalled watching the actress bring his

script to life. In addition to wearing a wig and padded costumes, Irene hired a Norwegian woman to help perfect her accent. Bodeen recalled Irene's precision, making pauses and gestures at the exact same moment so that the film editor found it easy to put together her scenes. Irene claimed her best performance came on the third take. When the company filmed exterior shots on location in San Francisco, Bodeen said Irene was "in her element." She chatted with the public between takes and even had coffee in their homes. Bodeen also discussed Irene's popularity in France. <u>Back Street</u> was the best-loved of her films in Paris. Irene came to the conclusion that most French people knew of a woman like her character, who chose to live on a back street and spend whatever time she could with her married lover. Bodeen briefly touched on the highlights of Irene's career. The article included six stills. Irene described her frequent leading man in a profile entitled "Cary Grant: Working with a Man of Quality." She said, "I think we were a successful team because we enjoyed working together tremendously, and that pleasure must have shown through onto the screen." Irene called <u>The Awful Truth</u> her favorite of Grant's comedy performances. She recalled director Leo McCarey's improvisational techniques, of which she and Grant were both dubious at first. She compared Grant's comedy work with his dramatic performance in <u>Penny Serenade</u>, remarking that his concentration and preparedness could serve as an object lesson in professionalism for many an actor. In addition to stills of the team in <u>The Awful Truth</u>, <u>My Favorite Wife</u>, and <u>Penny Serenade</u>, Grant was pictured in three shots from his solo films.

B-348   Pendleton, Ed.   "Film Star Retains 'Title.'"   <u>Denver Post</u>.   June 19, 1968.
In Denver to present awards to the 1967 Colorado Women of Achievement winners, Irene Dunne discussed her career and image. She said, "I try to ignore the label of 'great lady' but it's something I just can't shake off." She recalled her first trip to Denver at age twelve when her mother bought her a postcard of Pikes Peak. "I've always wanted to see that mountain," Irene was quoted as saying, "But at the time I didn't get the chance." Her favorite film was <u>A Guy Named Joe</u>; her favorite leading men were Cary Grant and Charles Boyer. Pendleton concluded, "...the day-to-day activities of Miss Dunne still demands her most important role - that of carrying the grandeur of all that's good in the movie world."

B-349   "Personalities."   <u>Washington Post</u>.   November 8, 1977.   p. B-2.
As part of a twelve-day program celebrating the American Film Institute's tenth anniversary, Irene Dunne went to Washington for a screening of <u>Love Affair</u>. During a question-and-answer session following the film, longtime fan Edward Smith asked Irene to autograph her 78 album. When Irene saw that the album was empty, she asked what happened to the records. Smith said they were "too precious" to

tote from Baltimore. "What a diplomat," Irene told the crowd. Irene dispensed advice to aspiring actresses and explained why she retired. She compared herself to Mickey Mantle. "He had a good batting average and he quit while he was ahead," Irene explained.

B-350 "Photoplay." <u>Photoplay</u>. September, 1932. pp. 61-64.
Two sketches of Irene Dunne's costumes from <u>Thirteen Women</u> were shown.

B-351 Pickard, Roy. <u>The Hollywood Story</u>. Chartwell Books, Inc. Seacaucus, New Jersey. 1986. pp. 21, 34, 35.
Universal Studios was praised for its 1930s melodramas, including <u>Back Street</u> and <u>Magnificent Obsession</u>, starring Irene Dunne. She also was mentioned in a chapter on RKO's 1930s output: the epic western <u>Cimarron</u> and a series of profitable soap operas.

B-352 Plummer, Evans. "The Movie Front: Hollywood." <u>Movie-Radio Guide</u>. January 31, 1942. p. 8.
Irene Dunne joined Patric Knowles, Bob Hope, George Brent, and other stars at a Red Cross fund drive on January 19, 1942. Plummer reported that the day before the event, a rival columnist noticed that Irene had never been photographed with her legs crossed. Plummer observed, "Next morning there she was, big as peas, on the front page with her gams crossed as neatly, yet modestly, as we've ever gleaned a pair."

B-353 Plunkett, Walter. "Dressing Up the Movies." <u>California Monthly</u>. December, 1934. pp. 13-15, 43-44.
Irene Dunne's color preferences were mentioned in this article by costume designer Plunkett. He also discussed designing for Irene in <u>Cimarron</u> (credited to Max Ree) and <u>Stingaree</u> (uncredited).

B-354 Porter, Reed. "Plots and Pans." <u>Los Angeles Mirror</u>. September 19, 1949.
Father James Keller announced the Christophers's plans to make thirty non-profit shorts, which would help "throw out evil from American life." Irene Dunne was one of the stars mentioned who volunteered to donate her talent.

B-355 Prichard, Susan Perez. <u>Film Costume</u>. Scarecrow Press, Inc. Metuchen, NJ. 1981.
Extensive annotated bibliography of fashion pictorials and articles about costume designers, many from the pages of vintage movie magazines.

B-356 "Private Funeral for Dunne on Saturday." <u>Hollywood Reporter</u>. September 6, 1990.
Irene Dunne's funeral was scheduled for September 8, 1990. The Mass was held at Calvary Cemetery's Mausoleum Chapel.

Irene was entombed in a crypt beside her husband Francis Griffin, who died in 1965.

B-357 "Private Services for 5-Time Oscar Nominee Irene Dunne." *Daily Variety*. September 6, 1990. pp. 3, 18.

Obituary for Irene Dunne, who died of heart failure on September 4, 1990 in her Holmby Hills home. Irene's career was recounted. Several errors were present, including her age (eighty-eight instead of ninety-one), the labeling of the *Show Boat* tour as the "Chicago company," and identifying *Leathernecking* and *Present Arms* as two different features. The article pointed out that Irene was one of the first stars to negotiate a nonexclusive contract, which allowed her to free-lance between the studios. Former President Ronald Reagan praised Irene's acting talents. He was quoted as saying, "Irene Dunne was also a dedicated patriot who served our country with great distinction at the United Nations. By doing so, she set a wonderful example for so many of us in the motion picture business." In lieu of flowers, Irene requested that memorial donations be sent to Saint John's Hospital.

B-358 Proctor, Kay. "Play Truth and Consequences with Irene Dunne." *Photoplay*. July, 1942.

The actress discussed her reluctance to talk about her private life. Although she denied being overly discreet on purpose, she said, "It must be because I consider it so simple I don't see how it can interest anyone."

B-359 Pryor, Thomas M. "Hollywood Digest." *New York Times*. September 2, 1951.

Producers Jerry Wald and Norman Krasna asked RKO Radio Pictures to do a survey in eleven European countries, to see if European audiences had the same screen interests as Americans. Although Europeans were opposed to films with murder, war, poverty, recism, politics, and religion, their favorite performers were similar to those ranking high in American polls. Irene Dunne was one of the top fifteen actresses, along with Greta Garbo, Jane Wyman, Barbara Stanwyck, and Bette Davis. With the results, Wald and Krasna hoped to pick up pointers on how to make their films appeal to the widest range of tastes.

B-360 _____. "More or Less According to Hoyle." *New York Times*. July 14, 1940.

WGEO, a General Electric shortwave radio station in Schenectady, conducted a favorite film star poll among men living in the South Pole. Irene Dunne was the unanimous choice of the fifty-nine explorers, with Bette Davis and Olivia de Havilland following.

B-361 "Questions and Answers." *Photoplay*. April, 1931. p. 94.

Irene Dunne and Richard Dix were pictured in a still from *Cimarron*, a film which generated several questions for

Photoplay's forum. Allegedly, mail poured in, praising Irene's performance and asking where RKO had found such a perfect actress for the part. Article claimed RKO "gave her the part in Cimarron because she looked eighteen and could talk in the quavery voice of a woman of seventy." Article said Irene had grey eyes and copper-colored hair, stood at 5' 4 1/2", and weighed 120 pounds.

B-362 Quirk, Lawrence J. The Complete Films of William Powell. Citadel Press. Secaucus, New Jersey. 1986. pp. 235-38.
Credits and synopsis of Life with Father were given. Irene Dunne was seen in six of seven photos from the film.

B-363 _____. The Films of Myrna Loy. Citadel Press. Secaucus, New Jersey. 1980. pp. 139-41, 124-26.
Irene Dunne was pictured in two of four photos from Thirteen Women. Of her performance in Consolation Marriage, Quirk wrote, "Dunne is charming and low keyed in her histrionics."

B-364 _____. Margaret Sullavan: Child of Fate. St. Martin's Press. New York. 1986. pp. 26, 114, 115, 138.
After criticizing the 1932 version of Back Street, starring Irene Dunne and John Boles, Margaret Sullavan was asked if she could do a better job in a remake. Sullavan accepted the challenge and starred in the 1941 version of the film. Quirk said, "Irene Dunne reportedly took more than a little offense when it was reported to her that Sullavan considered her 'insipid' and Boles 'doltish' and 'wooden' in the film." Director King Vidor was quoted about Columbia mogul Harry Cohn's attitude toward women. "When it came to women, they were in his eyes either madonnas or whores, mostly whores," Vidor said. "He could be courtly and behave himself well enough with someone he sensed was a true lady, like Irene Dunne..."

B-365 Rankin, R. "Found, One Happy Actress." Screen Book. January, 1938.

B-366 Rankin, Ruth. "There's Gold in Those Frills." Photoplay. April, 1935. pp. 56, 62-63, 105.
Bernard Newman spared no expense in designing costumes for Roberta. Some of the fabrics he designed for Irene Dunne and Ginger Rogers's costumes cost twenty-five dollars per yard. Additionally, he made special stockings for each outfit and used a nineteen thousand dollar fur coat. The final costume budget was $250,000.

B-367 "Real Estate." Los Angeles Times. October 14, 1990. p. K-17.
After Irene Dunne's death, her French-colonial estate in Holmby Hills was put on the market for $6.9 million. The house, designed by Paul Williams, boasted four bedroom suites and three servants' rooms. Ironically, one of the

Irene Dunne's home at 461 North Faring Drive. (Author's collection)

realtors was William Bakewell, who co-starred with Irene in
<u>Back Street</u> in 1932.

B-368   <u>Real Screen Fun</u>. March, 1937. pp. 14, 28.
Melvyn Douglas kissed Irene Dunne in a posed still from
<u>Theodora Goes Wild</u>. In another shot, a maribou-clad Irene
tugged at Douglas's coattail to keep him from fleeing.

B-369   Reid, James. "No Sooner Said Than Dunne!"
        <u>Hollywood</u>. July, 1938.
Irene Dunne shared anecdotes about her impulsiveness. When
her husband Frank Griffin took her car one morning, Irene
was furious. She recalled chasing a man in a car, whom she
thought was Frank. When she realized she had stopped the
wrong car, her anger disappeared. She was quoted as saying,
"It's like that, with me. I can get <u>so</u> mad about things,
so burned up - and then I start laughing at myself, and it's
all over."

B-370   _____. "What Not to Discuss with Your Husband."
        <u>Motion Picture</u>. July, 1939. pp. 29, 78, 81.
Irene Dunne dispensed advice on what spouses should talk
about, using examples from her own marriage. She said her
long-distance marriage allowed her not to take her husband
for granted. The Griffins spent quality time, rather than
quantity time. Although she did not recommend separation,
Irene said it was important to use discretion in choosing
topics for discussion. Among those she said should not be
discussed were "the way the other drives a car," diets,
sports, clothes, and discipline. Irene concluded, "It
usually isn't fatal to discuss anything or everything with
your husband. But a little discretion can make what you do
discuss important and amusing and interesting to both of
you." Reid mentioned her upcoming film <u>A Modern
Cinderella</u>, which became <u>When Tomorrow Comes</u>.

B-371   "RKO's Pic-Tour of the Week." <u>Life</u>. June 16,
        1947. p. 4.
Irene Dunne discussed her wardrobe for <u>I Remember Mama</u>
with designer Edward Stevenson in this still promoting the
film.

B-372   "RKO's Pic-Tour of the Week." <u>Life</u>. August 11,
        1947. p. 2.
A glamour shot of Irene Dunne advertised <u>I Remember Mama</u>,
which <u>Life</u> called "the most unique vehicle of her career."

B-373   "RKO's Pic-Tour of the Week." <u>Life</u>. October 20,
        1947. p. 2.
<u>I Remember Mama</u> stars Irene Dunne, Barbara Bel Geddes,
Oscar Homolka, and Philip Dorn were pictured in a posed
still to promote the film. Caption proclaimed them the
"most lovable family you've ever met."

B-374   "RKO's Pic-Tour of the Week." <u>Life</u>. November 17,
        1947. p. 128.

266   Irene Dunne

Irene Dunne was seen in close-up in her I Remember Mama costume.

B-375 "RKO's Pic-Tour of the Week." Life. December 1, 1947. p. 6.
I Remember Mama stars Irene Dunne and Barbara Bel Geddes were pictured discussing script changes with producer Harriet Parsons.

B-376 Rodgers, Richard. Musical Stages. Random House. New York. 1975. p. 110.
The composer of She's My Baby recalled that the unsuccessful musical had an interesting cast. He wrote, "The ingenue was played by Irene Dunne, whose voice and beauty were then just beginning to be appreciated."

B-377 Rosen, George. "NBC Sets Velvet-Carpeted Spread for Fibber, Molly; 'Ghosts' Stand Out." Variety. September 21, 1949.
Review of the fifteenth anniversary broadcast of Fibber McGee and Molly. Although Rosen praised the show, he pointed out that the choice of guests reminded listeners how many NBC stars had defected to CBS.

B-378 Rothe, Anna, editor. "Irene Dunne." Current Biography 1945. The H.W. Wilson Company. New York. 1945. pp. 160-63.
Overview of Irene Dunne's life and career, encompassing her childhood, her stage roles, her films, and her marriage to Dr. Francis Griffin. Among the errors in the article were: Irene's year of birth was given as 1904 instead of 1898; her year of graduation from the Chicago Musical College was given as 1926 instead of 1916; and Leathernecking and Present Arms were implied to be two different films when, in fact, they were the same film. Irene was quoted as saying she preferred comedy roles to tragic ones. She said, "[Comedy] demands more timing, pace, shading, and subtlety of emphasis. It is difficult to learn, but once it is acquired it can be easily slowed down and becomes an excellent foundation for dramatic acting." Her hobbies were listed as golf, writing music, gardening, and cooking. Although Irene was quoted as saying, "I guess I'll go on acting until I'm old and feeble and nobody wants to look at me any more," she retired from the screen six years later.

B-379 Ruehl, Franklin R. "Hooray for Hollywood! Many Stars Have Adopted Children." National Enquirer. August 20, 1985.
Irene Dunne was among the list of celebrities who adopted children. Top adopters were Mia Farrow with five children, and Bob Hope and Fred MacMurray, who each adopted four.

B-380 Russell, Rosalind and Chase, Chris. Life Is a Banquet. Random House. New York. 1977. pp. 87, 109, 121.
Russell recalled that Irene Dunne, Jean Arthur, and Ginger

Rogers turned down the lead in <u>His Girl Friday</u> before
Russell was cast. She discussed her work with the Hollywood
Victory Committee during World War II. Russell said the
U.S.O. did not know what to do with dramatic stars like
Irene, Claudette Colbert, Loretta Young, and herself. With
Irene's musical background, it seems odd that the U.S.O. and
Russell would group her with the others.

B-381 Ryall, William J. "Irene Dunne Through the Years."
<u>Los Angeles Herald Examiner</u>. March 30, 1975.
Two samples of Irene Dunne's handwriting, taken some forty
years apart, were analyzed. Ryall revealed, "While at first
glance the signatures look quite different a study of the
two samples reveals that the circumstances of Miss Dunne's
life have changed very little over the span of many years."
He continued, "Irene Dunne, we remember was a woman of
classic beauty and feminine charm. We are happy she hasn't
changed." Photographs from 1941 and 1975 were included.

B-382 Saltzman, Barbara. "A Warm Reception for Irene
Dunne." <u>Los Angeles Times</u>. August 28, 1979.
Report on the American Film Institute's tribute to Irene
Dunne, the third in a series entitled "Best Remaining
Seats." The series honored people and movie palaces from
the golden age of films. Irene's tribute was held on August
25 at the San Gabirel Civic Auditorium. It included a
screening of <u>Love Affair</u> and film clips from <u>The Awful
Truth</u>. A question-and-answer session provided some
interesting insights to her career. Irene confessed that
her favorite role was in <u>I Remember Mama</u>. She said, "I
thought that she was a wonderful woman. It was probably the
only time I played a real character part."

B-383 Sarris, Andrew. "Rediscovering RKO." <u>Village
Voice</u>. January 8, 1979.
Article on RKO in conjunction with the Museum of Modern
Art's (MOMA) five-month retrospective of films by the
studio. The series was scheduled to fill in gaps for film
historians by focusing on seldom-seen movies. Sarris
claimed that even the studio's bad films were interesting.
He championed Irene Dunne, whom he said he would gladly see
in anything, "including the Terre Haute telephone book."
Irene was represented by <u>Cimarron</u>, <u>Symphony of Six
Million</u>, <u>Ann Vickers</u>, and <u>The Silver Cord</u> in the MOMA
retrospective. She was pictured in a scene from <u>The Silver
Cord</u>.

B-384 Saunders, A.W. "Irene Remembers Mama." <u>Life with
Music</u>. November, 1949.

B-385 Schickel, Richard. "Irene Dunne." <u>Architectural
Digest</u>. April, 1990. p. 169.
Irene Dunne's career was chronicled in an issue devoted to
movie stars' homes of the 1920s and 1930s. Schickel praised
Irene's multi-faceted roles, but said she would be best
remembered for her comic parts. He wrote, "When [film

268   Irene Dunne

historian] James Harvey visited with Irene Dunne in 1978, he still observed some secretiveness alight in her eyes, some bemusement - possibly with herself and her legend - that she did not choose to share. It remains quite the most attractive of all the movies' many mysteries." Inside and outside shots of Irene's Holmby Hills home were shown.

B-386   Schultz, Margie. "Hollywood's Great Ladies: Irene
        Dunne." *Hollywood Studio Magazine*. January, 1988.
        pp. 14-17, 40.
Overview of Irene Dunne's career, concentrating on her film roles. It pointed out the many remakes of her movies, illustrating that she chose roles with lasting substance. Seven photographs accompanied the article, including two candids taken after her retirement.

B-387   Schuster, Mel. *Motion Picture Performers: A
        Bibliography of Magazine and Periodical Articles
        1900-1969*. Scarecrow Press, Inc. Metuchen, NJ.
        1971. pp. 218-19.
List of periodicals with articles on film actors. Although the bibliography featured twenty-two pieces about Irene Dunne, from a variety of sources, *Photoplay* was the only vintage movie magazine cited.

B-388   _____. *Motion Picture Performers: A
        Bibliography of Magazine and Periodical Articles
        Supplement No. 1, 1970-1974*. Scarecrow Press, Inc.
        Metuchen, NJ. 1976. p. 230.
Second volume of Schuster's series, listing thirty-three additional articles by and about Irene Dunne from more obscure sources, including MGM's in-house magazine, *Lion's Roar*, and *Life with Music*.

B-389   Scott, Walter. "Walter Scott's Personality Parade."
        Parade Magazine. October 28, 1990.
Scott answered questions about celebrities in this national Sunday newspaper supplement. A Massachusetts woman asked why none of Irene Dunne's Hollywood colleagues attended her funeral. Scott explained that Irene requested no "showbusiness ballyhoo" at the service. Longtime friend Loretta Young was the only celebrity in attendance.

B-390   "Screen Notes." *New York Times*. August 20, 1934.
Announcement that Irene Dunne had signed a contract with Warner Bros. Her first film for the studio would be *Sweet Adeline*.

B-391   Sennett, Ted. *Lunatics and Lovers*. Arlington
        House. New Rochelle. 1973. pp. 17, 52, 54-56, 58,
        66-68, 197, 206-9, 217, 219, 221.
Book on screwball comedy featured synopses, quotes, and descriptions of the antics from *The Awful Truth*, *My Favorite Wife*, *Theodora Goes Wild*, and *Together Again*. Sennett praised Irene Dunne's merging of a "satirical air" and "touches of tenderness" in her role in *My Favorite*

Wife. He said, "The charm and urbanity that [Cary] Grant projects as Jerry combined with [Irene] Dunne's womanly grace and slightly tongue-in-cheek attitude, make The Awful Truth a special delight." Stills from the films were included.

B-392   Service, F. "My Screen Selves and I." Silver Screen. August, 1944.

B-393   "Set for Two." Movie Humor. August, 1935. p. 58. Although Irene Dunne signed a two-picture deal with Universal so that studio chief Carl Laemmle, Jr. could cast her as Magnolia in Show Boat, she ended up filming her second picture first. Director John Stahl demanded her services in Magnificent Obsession, therefore holding up the shooting of Show Boat.

B-394   "Shackled." Picture Play. August, 1932. p. 54. Caption heralded, "Love that can neither be realized nor shaken off keeps Irene Dunne chained in happy misery in Back Street." Irene was seen in three stills from the film.

B-395   Shipman, David. The Great Movie Stars: The Golden Years. Crown Publishers, Inc. New York. 1970. pp. 173-75.
Biographical sketch of Irene Dunne, with stills from Back Street, Magnificent Obsession, and Penny Serenade. Shipman said, "Irene Dunne's forte was indestructible dignity. In the slushy melodramas she made at the start of her career she suffered with patience....When she turned to comedy she was invincibly ladylike..." After describing a scene from The Awful Truth, Shipman declared, "...her gurgling, smothered laugh is more eloquent than many another's close-ups. She was airy and rather super."

B-396   "Show Biz on Trial with Uncle Sam, But Billion in Sept. Looks No Cinch." Variety. August 26, 1942. As the motion picture industry prepared to launch its billion-dollar war bond drive, plans of attack were discussed. The War Department's Command Performance radio program planned to record in Washington on August 30. The all-star line-up included Bing Crosby, James Cagney, Hedy Lamarr, and Abbott and Costello. On August 31, Treasury Secretary Morgenthau would host a luncheon, which included the Command Performance stars, plus Irene Dunne, Greer Garson, and others. Following the luncheon, the stars planned to launch the bond selling rally on the steps of the Treasury Department. During the month of September, the stars scattered to sell bonds, covering three hundred cities in thirty days. September 15 was designated "Carole Lombard Day," as a tribute to the actress who was killed in an airplane crash while returning from a bond drive.

B-397   "'Show Boat' to Open Monday at the American." St. Louis Globe-Democrat. January 19, 1930.

Article heralding the touring company of Show Boat and introducing its stars. Irene Dunne, who was described as a "former prima donna of the [St. Louis] Municipal Opera" during the 1926 season, was pictured.

B-398   "Show Girl Revue." Film Fun. February, 1937.
        pp. 65-69.
In a five-page pictorial featuring scantily-clad chorines, Irene Dunne appeared in a demure dress and hat, looking meek in a still from Theodora Goes Wild.

B-399   Shuler, M. "Working and Waiting." Christian
        Science Monitor Magazine. February 12, 1936.
        p. 3.

B-400   Sills, Claire. "Stars of 'The Late Show.'" TV
        Radio Mirror. November, 1972.
Irene Dunne, Noah Beery, Jr., and Norma Shearer were profiled in this where-are-they-now series. Sills recalled Irene's accomplishments, including the highlights of her film career, her honorary degrees, and her work with the United Nations. Although Sills reported that Irene was still beautiful and slim, she said the actress would not return to the screen. Instead, Irene busied herself with corporate responsibilites, working out of an office in her home, and spending time with her daughter and grandchildren.

B-401   Simonet, Thomas and editors of the Associated Press.
        Oscar: A Pictorial History of the Academy Awards.
        Contemporary Books, Inc. Chicago. 1983. pp. 29,
        92, 93, 239.
Photographs of actors who won Oscars. Irene Dunne was pictured in a still from Cimarron, which won the "Best Picture" Academy Award in 1931. Irene was also listed among the nominees and mentioned in a chaper on Oscar losers.

B-402   "A Sinclair Lewis Heroine - Irene Dunne." Vanity
        Fair. September, 1933. p. 31.
Irene Dunne was pictured, reclining on a zebra-striped pillow. She was heralded as the star of Ann Vickers, "the most important [role] hitherto attempted by Miss Dunne." Upcoming films included the musical Frivolous Sal and a movie with Francis Lederer. Neither project materialized.

B-403   "Singers and Dancers." New York Times.
        January 22, 1928.
Broadway performers Dorothy Dilley, Robinson Newbold, and Irene Dunne were profiled. Irene's life story was recounted, though she was mistakenly identified as a former law student. Allegedly, her father and mother insisted she finish her schooling before embarking on a show business career; in reality, her father died when she was eleven years old. The article concluded, "...but none of her musical comedy appearances mean as much to her as the final 'e' in her name, over the omission of which she is reliably reported to become annoyed."

B-404 "Sir Cedric Hardwicke Chides Fellow Britons for Barbs over American in Queen's Role." *New York Times*. March 15, 1950.
Sir Cedric Hardwicke, Irene's Dunne's co-star in *The Mudlark*, spoke out against criticism over the casting of an American as Queen Victoria. During a luncheon of the British-American Club of New York, Hardwicke explained that the disagreement had nothing to do with Irene's talent, but the fact that she was American. He said, "You might as well argue that a man has to be a murderer to play a murderer. It strikes at the very root of my craft."

B-405 Smith, Liz. "Playing Around." *New York Daily News*. August 31, 1977. p. 6.
Columnist Smith reported that Irene Dunne sang "Wishing," "Getting to Know You," and "I Only Have Eyes for You" at a party at Le Restaurant in Los Angeles.

B-406 "Speechmaker Listens." *New York Times*. October 11, 1952. p. 8.
General Dwight D. Eisenhower was flanked by Rosalind Russell and Irene Dunne on a train to Los Angeles in a photograph taken during the 1952 Presidential campaign.

B-407 Springer, John. *Forgotten Films to Remember*. Citadel Press. Secaucus, New Jersey. 1980. pp. 41, 44, 97, 104.
Chronicle of seldom-seen films that were considered worth viewing by film historian Springer. Irene Dunne was represented in stills from *The Silver Cord*, *Love Affair*, and *My Favorite Wife*.

B-408 Springer, John and Hamilton, Jack. *They Had Faces Then*. Citadel Press. Secaucus, NJ. 1978. pp. 94-96, 290.
Paean to 1930s screen actresses, including Irene Dunne. Her film roles were discussed, with Springer observing, "Miss Dunne's cool authority gave even worst [movies] some measure of distinction." Hamilton provided a brief biographical sketch, which claimed she was born in 1901, rather than 1898. The book included stills from *Back Street*, *High, Wide and Handsome*, *Love Affair*, and *Penny Serenade*, as well as a portrait of Irene.

B-409 Squire, Marian. "It's Fashionable to Be Feminine." *Modern Screen*. August, 1938. pp. 48-49, 79.
Irene Dunne modeled two costumes from *Joy of Living*.

B-410 St. Johns, Adela Rogers. "How Irene Dunne Succeeded without Glamour." *Photoplay*. May, 1939.

B-411 _____. "Thank You Irene Dunne." *Photoplay*. September, 1944.

B-412 *Stage*. December, 1935. p. 82.
Irene Dunne modeled a sable coat and a diamond and ruby

ring. The forty-carat star-ruby was set in diamonds with platinum.

B-413   "Stage or Screen Star - All Enjoy Their Motor Car." *Theatre Magazine*. July, 1926. pp. 46-47.
Ramon Novarro and Ernest Truex were among the celebrities posed beside their cars. Irene Dunne, the star of *Sweetheart Time*, was pictured with a Pontiac coach. She said, "It makes starring more brilliant when one has such a submissive escort take one to the theatre every day."

B-414   Stanley, Fred. "Hollywood Bulletins." *New York Times*. November 18, 1945.
Greer Garson and Bing Crosby were named America's favorite film stars in a poll conducted by *Boxoffice*. The trade journal quizzed independent theatre owners, as well as newspaper and radio critics, and members of educational and civic organizations. Irene Dunne was tenth runner-up in the poll, trailing Ingrid Bergman, Van Johnson, Bette Davis, Judy Garland, and others.

B-415   _____. "Hollywood 'Politics.'" *New York Times*. March 3, 1946.
The current standardized salary for free-lance stars was $150,000 per film. Among those receiving the salary were Irene Dunne, Barbara Stanwyck, Myrna Loy, Fred MacMurray, Charles Boyer, and Joseph Cotten. Stanley explained, "The deals generally specify fourteen weeks as a maximum engagement." Stars often obtained a share of the film's profits, in addition to their established salaries.

B-416   _____. "Hollywood Round-up." *New York Times*. August 20, 1944.
Irene Dunne and Charles Boyer were teamed for the third time in *Together Again*, then titled *A Woman's Privilege*. It marked the first time Irene had shown her legs and undergarments on screen. Some of the background scenes were filmed on location in Connecticut, although the movie was shot in Hollywood.

B-417   Stanyan, Mary. "Mr. John Is Old Hat These Days." *San Francisco Sunday Examiner and Chronicle*. May 27, 1979.
Profile of John P. John, who designed under the name John Frederics. He still owned a few hats, including one worn by Irene Dunne in *The Awful Truth*, although other creations were in the Metropolitan Museum of Art.

B-418   "Stars Take Have-a-Heart Tour." *Movie-Radio Guide*. November 22, 1941. p. 11.
Irene Dunne, Lew Ayres, Louis B. Mayer, and Hedy Lamarr were pictured viewing "a pitiful case" at the Los Angeles Orthopedic Hospital. The studio-supported Community Chest drive raised $467,000 in 1940. The hospital was one of the recipients of the fund.

B-419 "Stars to Twinkle on Treasury's Bond Drive." *Variety*. May 11, 1949.
Among the stars appearing on the Treasury Department's Opportunity Bond drive on May 16 were Irene Dunne, Bob Hope, Jack Benny, Al Jolson, and Humphrey Bogart. The program, which was broadcast on all networks, also featured a message from President Harry Truman.

B-420 "Stars Win Novel Contest." *New York Times*. August 26, 1938.
The American Society for the Hard of Hearing named Irene Dunne and Don Ameche as the most accomplished speakers in films. They were chosen in a survey conducted among the fifteen to twenty million hard-of-hearing citizens in the United States.

B-421 Stevenson, Edward. "The 'New Look' Is Not." *Silver Screen*. April, 1948. pp. 46-47, 75-76.
Irene Dunne modeled a costume from *I Remember Mama*, which designer Stevenson copied from his own family album. Stevenson discussed how the clothes from the film, which took place around 1910, were similar to current 1940s fashion trends. He included a sketch, adapting Irene's costume for modern wear.

B-422 "Stop-Press Bulletin." *Movie-Radio Guide*. November, 1941. p. 11.
Irene Dunne was announced as godmother of Pat O'Brien's newly adopted baby.

B-423 Strauss, Theodore. "A Rolling Milestone." *New York Times*. December 8, 1940.
Director Lewis Milestone discussed Group Productions' arrangement with 20th Century-Fox. Milestone and his colleagues, Ronald Colman, Irene Dunne, Charles Boyer, and Anatole Litvak, planned to produce films without supervision from Fox, but using the company's studio and assets. Strauss explained that the group would "pool their efforts on a minimal salary plus percentage basis." Colman was credited with the original idea, giving the creative forces more control of their films.

B-424 "Studio Makes 207 Corsets for '*Father*' Cinema." *Los Angeles Times*. September 9, 1947.
Irene Dunne and her *Life with Father* co-stars wore only 18 of the 207 corsets made by the Warner Bros. costume department for the film. The others were used in department store displays.

B-425 "Studios Picketed in Movie Walkout." *New York Times*. May 2, 1937.
Irene Dunne, then making *High, Wide and Handsome*, and other stars filming at Paramount Studios, were unaffected by a strike involving the scenic artists, hairdressers, painters, and draftsmen. Pickets let the stars pass and work went on as usual. The Screen Actors Guild planned a

meeting to decide whether or not to sympathize with the striking unions.

B-426 "Styles." <u>Movie-Radio Guide</u>. August 16, 1941. p. 10.
Irene Dunne was one of the stars sporting a new hairdo around Hollywood. Irene was pictured at Ciro's, with her hair high on her head and her ears exposed.

B-427 "Styles for That 'Siren' Mood." <u>Movie Mirror</u>. February, 1933. pp. 38-39.
Irene Dunne modeled three costumes for <u>No Other Woman</u>.

B-428 Swarthout, Gordon. "Clips from the Cutting Room Floor." <u>Film Fun</u>. March, 1940. pp. 24, 47.
After Irene Dunne spent almost an entire day filming a shower scene in <u>My Favorite Wife</u>, the crew realized that the glass stall was too transparent and too much of the actress could be seen. The problem was corrected and the scene was shot again. Irene was pictured, fully-clothed. Ironically, one of the highlights of the uncompleted remake, <u>Something's Got to Give</u>, was a nude swimming scene by Marilyn Monroe, who was reprising Irene's role.

B-429 "Sweet Adeline and Prize Pup." <u>New York Post</u>. April 15, 1935.
Photograph of Irene Dunne and a champion schnauzer, which was the first prize in a bridge tournament scheduled to raise money for Bryn Mawr College.

B-430 Swindell, Larry. <u>Charles Boyer - The Reluctant Lover</u>. Doubleday and Company, Inc. Garden City, New Jersey. 1983. pp. 115, 138-48, 194-95, 258-59.
In a discussion of star presence and acting ability, Swindell deemed Irene Dunne "underrated on every count." She was Charles Boyer's favorite leading lady, although they only made three films together. Boyer was quoted as saying that <u>Love Affair</u> was his favorite "because, for what it was, it was almost perfectly executed...it came closer than any of my other pictures to being exactly what it had hoped to be." Although <u>When Tomorrow Comes</u> garnered positive reviews and became Universal's most successful 1939 release, it was apparent that the film was trying to cash in on <u>Love Affair's</u> popularity by casting Boyer and Irene in similar roles. Because both actors appealed to the same audience, female moviegoers, they were teamed in a third film, <u>Together Again</u>. Swindell commented on the chemistry Irene and Boyer shared on and off screen, with the actors and their respective spouses often dining together. Swindell noted Irene's versatility, despite her never having played an unsympathetic role. She was among a small group of mourners at Boyer's funeral.

B-431 _____. <u>Screwball - The Life of Carole Lombard</u>. William Morrow & Company, Inc. New York. 1975. pp. 141, 188, 216, 217, 234, 242, 258, 259, 303.

Irene Dunne's screwball comedy roles were mentioned in this biography of Carole Lombard. Irene christened the U.S.S. Carole Lombard, a Liberty ship named for the late actress who lost her life in a plane crash returning from a war bond tour. Although Swindell claimed the launching took place in June, 1942, the ship was christened in January, 1944, marking the second anniversary of Lombard's death.

B-432 "Talkie Tips." <u>Film Fun</u>. March, 1935. p. 60.
Irene Dunne and Louis Calhern were pictured giving a toast in a still from <u>Sweet Adeline</u>.

B-433 Taviner, Reginald. "The Girl Nobody Knows." <u>The New Movie Magazine</u>. October, 1932.
Hollywood was trying to figure out Irene Dunne, who had been making movies for almost three years. Irene's background in Louisville and on the New York stage was recounted, but one of the things that puzzled the Hollywood community was her long-distance marriage. Irene explained that with three thousand miles between them, both she and her husband were able to pursue their careers without interference. Between films, she lived with Dr. Francis ("Frank") Griffin in their honeymoon apartment in New York. The remainder of the time, Irene lived with her mother in a house in Beverly Hills while Frank stayed with Irene's brother Charles at his club. Irene admitted that she had a terrible temper, which she tried to control by reading a book whenever she was angry. Although she was a member of the "Hole-in-One Club," Irene claimed that she often had to replace the golf clubs she broke after a particularly poor round. Irene said she preferred screen work to the stage and planned to stay in movies until she retired. She explained, "Here I play to a vastly greater audience....each role is different, and constant repetition of even a role like <u>Show Boat</u> becomes monotonous to me." Despite her love of the medium, Irene said she preferred to relax in the east. Because she was afraid of airplanes, she never traveled in them. Instead of sampling the Hollywood night life, Irene preferred to talk to her husband on the telephone. Perhaps her most unusual habit was singing over the radio incognito, to keep in practice.

B-434 Taylor, Robert. "Anything Can Happen in Hollywood." <u>Ladies' Home Journal</u>. September, 1936. pp. 8-9, 92-95.
After being named the favorite movie star of girls age sixteen to twenty in a national poll, Taylor discussed his rise to fame. Following success in <u>Broadway Melody of 1936</u>, MGM loaned Taylor to Universal for <u>Magnificent Obsession</u> with Irene Dunne. He said, "My reward for not doing a 'flop' with Miss Dunne was playing the boyfriend to Janet Gaynor in <u>Small Town Girl</u>." Taylor's leading ladies, including Irene, were pictured.

B-435 <u>Theatre Magazine</u>. March, 1931. p. 48.
Irene Dunne and Richard Dix were pictured in a still from

276   Irene Dunne

<u>Cimarron</u>, which critic called "[an] impressive screening of Miss Edna Ferber's novel of early Oklahoma days with the pioneers."

B-436   "They Never Forget." <u>New York Journal American</u>.
        April 18, 1941.
Although the script for <u>Unfinished Business</u> called for Irene Dunne to play a singer whose voice was so terrible that she could not get a job, the studio was afraid audiences would be too aware of Irene's real status as a singing star to believe the story. Instead, opera officials told her character that she was better suited for nightclub singing, and nightclub owners suggested opera. Article said that Irene never sang with the Metropolitan Opera, despite earlier reports to the contrary.

B-437   Thomas, Bob. "Film Queen Explains Her Clothes Cost."
        <u>Fort Wayne News-Sentinel</u> [Indiana]. April 3, 1952.
Irene Dunne offered hints for getting on the best dressed list. She said, "I don't buy many [clothes], but what I do buy are of the best....I make sure the clothes are well made and I generally pick things along the classic lines. It's not unusual for my things to last six or eight years." Irene claimed American designers had a better understanding of American women's clothing needs, but praised the enthusiasm the French had for fashion.

B-438   _____. <u>King Cohn: The Life and Times of Harry Cohn</u>. G.P. Putnam's Sons. New York. 1967.
        pp. 75, 126-29, 145-46, 176, 178, 217, 248.
Irene Dunne's Columbia films were mentioned in this biography of mogul Harry Cohn. Thomas said that Cohn alienated Irene, Cary Grant, and Jean Arthur, causing the three stars to refuse to finish out their commitments to the studio. Thomas also mentioned Irene's arguement with Cohn over <u>Theodora Goes Wild</u>. Thomas chronicled the filming of <u>The Awful Truth</u>, which was being rushed into production to fill a commitment with Irene. Cary Grant offered Cohn a commitment to another film if he would excuse the actor from <u>The Awful Truth</u>. Although Cohn was confused by Leo McCarey's unfinished script, he did not want to pay Irene her forty thousand dollar salary without having something on film, so he refused to release Grant. Despite the haphazard, improvisational shooting schedule, McCarey finished the film in only thirty-seven days, drastically under budget.

B-439   Thomas, Kevin. "The Best and Worst of '<u>Cimarron</u>.'"
        <u>Los Angeles Times</u>. August 25, 1984.
Comparison of the 1931 and 1960 screen versions of <u>Cimarron</u>, both of which were running on Los Angeles cable's Z Channel. Thomas preferred the first version, which starred Richard Dix and Irene Dunne, praising its "accurate reflection of attitudes and mores" of the frontier. Thomas also praised Irene's performance. He said, "Even this early Dunne,...is extraordinary, creating

a very proper, aristocratic Victorian woman who is warm, sympathetic and strong and who over the years outgrows the bigotry and puritanism of her class and generation."

B-440 _____. "Bing to Screen 'Best of Irene Dunne.'" *Los Angeles Times*. December 1, 1986.
The Los Angeles County Museum of Art presented a two-day tribute entitled "The Best of Irene Dunne." On December 5, 1986, *Back Street* and *Magnificent Obsession* were screened at the Bing Theatre. *Roberta* and *Sweet Adeline* were shown on December 6. Thomas said the title of the film tribute was inaccurate because, "It's unimaginable that Dunne ever gave anything less than her considerable best."

B-441 _____. "Permanent Exhibit of Movie Lore Opens." *Los Angeles Times*. December 9, 1970.
Irene Dunne and silent film star Betty Bronson were pictured at the opening of the Movie Hall of the County Museum of Natural History. The exhibit traced the development of motion pictures and displayed memorabilia from different eras of filmmaking. As she surveyed the displays, Irene said, "I always say I'm retired from acting but not from the industry. It's too fascinating for that."

B-442 Thomas, Tony and Solomon, Aubrey. *The Films of 20th Century-Fox*. Citadel Press. Secaucus, NJ. 1979. pp. 167, 169, 212, 216.
Studio history, featuring credits and a brief synopsis for films made between 1935 and 1979. Thomas and Solomon called Irene Dunne "elegant and thoroughly believable" in *Anna and the King of Siam* and said that her performance was "splendid" in *The Mudlark*. Irene was seen in stills from both films.

B-443 Thompson, Howard. *Fred Astaire: Hollywood's Magic People*. Falcon Enterprises Inc. New York. 1970. pp. 13, 16-17, 45-46, 155.
A photo of the *Roberta* poster and a two-page still of Fred Astaire, Ginger Rogers, and Irene Dunne were included in this pictorial history of Astaire's films.

B-444 "Three New Shows Take Top Position." *Variety*. December 10, 1920.
The touring company of *Irene* grossed twenty-four thousand dollars during its first six days in Chicago. *Variety* reported, "Not one newspaper critic failed to come through on this show, and it was an even split for honors between the piece and Helen Shipman. If there ever was a star made over night this little girl was, and deserves all that they gave her." Although many later sources claimed Irene Dunne played the title role in the Chicago company of *Irene*, she was in the chorus of this production.

B-445 Tobar, Hector. "Irene Dunne, Star of '30s and '40s." *Sacramento Bee*. September 5, 1990.
Irene Dunne died in her home around 6:20 PM on September 4,

1990. John Larkin, her business manager, said that she had been cared for at home by private nurses for the last year. She had been suffering from an irregular heartbeat. Her birthdate was incorrectly given as 1901. The article included a discussion of Irene's career, as well as her political and charitable efforts. Director Leo McCarey was quoted as saying, "There was nothing she couldn't play, nothing. I was always glad when she wanted me on a picture of hers. It meant I could relax - and still bring in a winner." Near the end of her life, Irene said she had only one regret: that she had so little time to enjoy her success. "My husband and I lived on opposite coasts, and saw each other only as often as our schedules would permit, which wasn't much." She continued, "We were together for a few years at the end. But it wasn't enough. Not enough at all."

B-446 "Topics for Gossip." Silver Screen. July, 1941. pp. 21, 69.
Irene Dunne and her husband loved unplanned trips. They often threw their golf clubs in the trunk in the morning, then took off for destinations unknown. The longest "surprise junket" happened when they headed for Santa Barbara for lunch one day. They returned seven weeks later, after an extended tour through the northwest and the Canadian Rockies. "They simply were having so much fun that they just kept on driving," item concluded. Irene Dunne was pictured with Robert Montgomery at a Screen Guild Theatre rehearsal (R-17).

B-447 "Topics for Gossip." Silver Screen. October, 1941. p. 82.
Irene Dunne planned to purchase "The Argosy," one of her father's favorite boats. She wanted to dock it in the Pacific and use it as a houseboat to get away from the pressures of Hollywood. Item implied that Captain Dunne owned many boats. While he was a steamship inspector, no other information confirms that he ever owned "The Argosy."

B-448 "Topics for Gossip." Silver Screen. November, 1941. p. 56.
Irene Dunne and Charles Boyer were pictured, riding in an open car during the Moon Festival. They were among the film stars who helped Los Angeles Chinese celebrate the festival by appearing in a parade through Chinatown.

B-449 "Topics for Gossip." Silver Screen. May, 1942. p. 19.
Irene Dunne, Bob Hope, Marlene Dietrich, and Deanna Durbin were pictured at a Red Cross benefit, which was broadcast on NBC. They were among many stars who appeared on the variety program (R-24).

B-450 Trent, Paul. Those Fabulous Movie Years: The 30s. Barre Publishing. Barre, Massachusetts. 1975. pp. 32, 130-31, 189, 191.

Credits, synopses, and stills from <u>Cimarron</u> and <u>The Awful Truth</u> were included in Trent's homage to 1930s films. Irene Dunne was given a one-page tribute, with four photographs from her films and an overview of her 1930s screen roles.

B-451 Twiggar, Beth. "Eighteen Inches from Camera, Well, Let Irene Dunne Tell of It." <u>New York Herald Tribune</u>. May 18, 1941.
Irene Dunne discussed <u>Penny Serenade</u> while visiting New York. She recalled filming a very long close-up. "In the final picture,...it is broken, but actually the shot was taken all at once, twenty-minutes' worth," she said. The usual close-up lasted only two minutes. Irene continued, "The camera was hardly eighteen inches away from me. I had to stand in a soundless room, recalling various parts of the story and letting my face reflect the memories. It required intense concentration." She praised the crew, who helped her shoot this difficult scene.

B-452 "2,850,000 to Fight Diseases of Heart." <u>New York Times</u>. June 5, 1949.
The American Heart Association presented its first annual gold awards for distinguished service and leadership in the 1949 national campaign. Among the recipients was Irene Dunne, chairman of the women's committee. The 1949 campaign raised almost $3 million.

B-453 "United Service." <u>New York Morning Telegraph</u>. June 29, 1941.
Photograph of Irene Dunne, who was scheduled to appear in a benefit for the United Service Organization (U.S.O.) at the Hollywood Bowl that evening.

B-454 <u>Universal Weekly</u>. June 29, 1935.
Irene Dunne was pictured in an announcement that she would star in Universal's screen production of <u>Show Boat</u>.

B-455 "Veteran Stars Rosalind Russell and Irene Dunne Shine at Premiere." <u>National Enquirer</u>. June 15, 1976.
Photograph of the two stars at the opening night of the 1976 Los Angeles International Film Exposition in Century City, where they attended the premiere of Alfred Hitchcock's <u>Family Plot</u>.

B-456 Vinson, James, editor. <u>The International Dictionary of Films and Filmmakers: Volume III Actors and Actresses</u>. St. James Press. Chicago. 1984. p. 205.
Brief career study of Irene Dunne, including a filmography and bibliography. Jeanine Basinger contributed an essay on Irene's talent for playing the modern lady on film. Basinger concluded, "In retrospect, Irene Dunne may be seen as an example of a type of actress that has almost disappeared from movies - a woman of intelligence and versatility who, no matter what the pressure, be it comic

280   Irene Dunne

or tragic, keeps going with humor, elegance, and dignity."

B-457   "Visits Madison before Leaving." <u>Louisville Courier</u>. May 6, 1940.
In Louisville for the world premiere of <u>My Favorite Wife</u>, Irene Dunne said, "It took me only three days to rediscover my Southern accent." While in her hometown, Irene attended the Kentucky Derby and journied to Madison, Indiana, where she spent her teenage years. Among the entourage in Louisville were Irene's husband Frank Griffin, director Leo McCarey, and RKO president George J. Schaefer.

B-458   <u>Vogue</u>. December 15, 1933. p. 55.
Irene Dunne modeled a black wool suit, which was trimmed in beaver.

B-459   Wald, Jerry and Macaulay, Richard. <u>The Best Motion Pictures of 1939-40</u>. Dodd, Mead and Company. New York. 1940. pp. 334, 352, 439-40, 489-90.
Credits, synopses, and comments about films released during the 1939-40 season were collected by screenwriters Wald and Macaulay. They concluded that <u>When Tomorrow Comes</u> did not meet its expected success, despite "two such sure-fire stars [Irene Dunne and Charles Boyer] in the leads." Wald and Macaulay trumpeted the popularity of <u>My Favorite Wife</u> with both press and public. They added, "The fact that Irene Dunne and Cary Grant, two of the most able farceurs in the business, played the leads didn't hurt the picture's success a bit."

B-460   Walker, Helen Louise. "Dress Up and Live." <u>Silver Screen</u>. May, 1938. pp. 18-19, 75.
Irene Dunne modeled a costume from <u>Joy of Living</u>, while designers Adrian and Edward Stevenson discussed current costume trends.

B-461   Wallen, Jim. "Life of Irene Dunne Is Related by Writer." <u>Madison Courier</u> [Indiana]. July 26, 1951.
Chronicle of Irene Dunne's early life, concentrating on her activities in Madison, Indiana. Wallen, editor of the Ashland Oil and Refining Company's <u>Ashland Oil Log</u>, wrote the article for the <u>Huntington Herald-Advertiser</u> [West Virginia]. He used records compiled by the late Harry Lemen, including financial records from the Madison Grammar School's production of <u>A Midsummer Night's Dream</u>.

B-462   Walters, Gwenn. "Photoplay." <u>Photoplay</u>. April, 1938. p. 76.
Irene Dunne modeled a hat she wore in <u>Joy of Living</u>.

B-463   _____. "Photoplay." <u>Photoplay</u>. October, 1939.
Irene Dunne modeled a costume from <u>When Tomorrow Comes</u>.

B-464   Wansell, Geoffrey. <u>Haunted Idol</u>. William Morrow and Company, Inc. New York. 1984. pp. 121-22, 125,

135-37, 141.
Irene Dunne's work in The Awful Truth, My Favorite Wife, and Penny Serenade was discussed in this biography of Cary Grant. Director Leo McCarey wrote The Awful Truth as he shot the film, often bringing bits of the script on brown wrapping paper to the set each morning. Grant was so distraught during the early days of filming, he asked studio head Harry Cohn if he could switch roles with Ralph Bellamy and even offered Cohn five thousand dollars to release him from the film. McCarey was furious with Grant, describing Grant as "nervous, uncertain, and insecure." Irene Dunne was quoted as saying, "Cary used to be very apprehensive about nearly everything in those days. So apprehensive in fact he would almost get physically sick." Despite Grant's apprehension, The Awful Truth was heralded by critics and public alike. Columbia tried to recapture its success by reuniting Irene and Grant with writer/director McCarey in My Favorite Wife. McCarey was replaced as director when he was injured in a car accident shortly before filming began. The studio could not afford to postpone the film because of the stars's salaries, which included $150,000 to Irene for ten weeks of shooting, so Garson Kanin was hired to replace McCarey. Irene was quoted as saying that Grant thought Penny Serenade was much too serious. He tried to convince Harry Cohn to release him again, but Cohn refused. Irene told the disgruntled Grant, "If you really stick with this and give it everything you have, I think you'll get an Academy Award nomination." Grant received his first Oscar nomination for Penny Serenade, but lost.

B-465   Warner, Alan. Alan Warner's Who Sang What on the Screen. Angus & Robertson Publishers. Australia. 1984. pp. 22, 23, 81, 106, 118, 128.
Although basically a list of songs and their performers, Warner included brief essays on a number of related topics, like TV songs, movie themes, and who sang what with big bands. Irene Dunne was mentioned as singing "I'll Get By" (A Guy Named Joe), "The Folks Who Live on the Hill" (High, Wide and Handsome), "Make Believe" (Show Boat), and "Smoke Gets in Your Eyes" (Roberta). Warner called Penny Serenade the best cinematic use of phonograph records, with its flashbacks segued by the playing of 78s. Before the film's release, RCA ran an ad, announcing which of the songs were available on Victor and Bluebird records. The uncredited vocalist in the film was Johnny Johnston, ironically, once the husband of Kathryn Grayson, who appeared in remakes of two of Irene's films. The book also reprinted ads for Penny Serenade.

B-466   Washburn, Dennis. "Six Will Be Honored on Friday." Birmingham News [Alabama]. December 22, 1985.
Preview of the telecast of the Kennedy Center Honors, which aired December 27, 1985. Honorees Beverly Sills, Irene Dunne, Bob Hope, Merce Cunningham, Alan Jay Lerner, and Frederick Loewe were profiled. Of her many post-film projects, Irene was quoted as saying, "Life goes on and

B-467 **Washington Post**. September 25, 1966.
Irene Dunne and her husband, accompanied by Mr. and Mrs. Spruille Braden and columnist Henry Taylor, stopped to watch the opera audience head into Lincoln Center after dinner at 21. Irene and Taylor were godparents for Mrs. Braden when she was converted to Catholicism in 1961. Taylor kidded that Mrs. Braden, the former Verbena Hebbard, spent a week at [famous milliner] Lilly Dache's "getting a hat with a hole in front, so she could be christened properly without getting her lid damp."

B-468 Watters, James. "Irene Dunne: No Oscar, Just Love."
       New York Times. September 23, 1990.
Paen to the actress following her death, written by the former entertainment editor of **Life**. Watters said, "She was a beloved public figure, not in the fantasy sense of Mary Pickford as America's Sweetheart..., but as the poised, intelligent and gracious vision of American womanhood." He continued, "Off-screen her ladylike personality was as real as Norma Shearer's was phony." Watters pointed out that Irene Dunne was one of the few actresses who excelled at both comedy and drama. He suggested readers imagine Claudette Colbert in **The Mudlark**, Joan Crawford in **I Remember Mama** or Jean Arthur in **Show Boat**. Watters recalled Irene's reaction to his wanting to include her in his book **Return Engagement**. The book consisted of "then and now" photos of veteran actresses. Irene finally turned him down, explaining that she wanted to be remembered as she was in the movies. She was quoted as saying, "I haven't held up as well as Loretta [Young], who is a marvel, hasn't changed or aged a day since I met her and that was 50 years ago." Watters pointed out that former First Lady Nancy Reagan and producer George Stevens, Jr. may have influenced Irene's being chosen as a Kennedy Center Honors recipient. (Stevens's father directed **Penny Serenade** and **I Remember Mama**.) Watters said another friend, who was a member of the Motion Picture Academy, wrote to Academy president Karl Malden, asking that Irene, Jean Arthur, Marlene Dietrich, and Myrna Loy be given honorary Oscars "before it was too late." In 1990, the honorary Oscar went to Akira Kurosawa, who already won several of the statues. Article included stills from **Show Boat** and **I Remember Mama**.

B-469 Watts, Stephen. "An American Plays Queen Victoria in
       London." **New York Times**. July 9, 1950.
While shooting **The Mudlark** on location in England, Irene Dunne discussed her portrayal of Queen Victoria and her first experience making a film outside Hollywood. Despite some early objections that a British actress was not cast as the queen, the hubbub had died down by the time **The Mudlark** began filming at Sir Alexander Korda's studio at Shepperton. Irene said she did not take the criticisms personally. She praised the way she was treated in England, with citizens going so far as to send her souvenirs of Queen

Victoria. Although the story occurred in a ten-day period
and was only a small portion of the queen's life, Irene did
a great deal of research so that her portrayal would be
authentic. Irene worried that her accent might cause some
controversy, as she spoke in a low English voice with a
slight German accent. However, the consensus of opinion
from the experts was that Queen Victoria spoke exactly that
way. Irene's only complaint was that the extensive makeup
and padded costume prevented her from being as free and
natural as she usually was on movie sets. In addition to
altering her laughing and eating habits, the makeup caused
cast and crew to give her added respect.

B-470 Weiler, A.H. "By Way of Report." New York Times.
       December 15, 1946.
Representatives for Irene Dunne and William Powell were
scheduled to toss a coin to decide whose name would be
top-billed at the New York premiere of Life with Father.
The loser's name would be top-billed at the Los Angeles
premiere. Half the prints shown around the country featured
Irene in the top spot, the other half had Powell, certifying
that the stars' billing was absolutely equal in the film.

B-471 _____. "By Way of Report." New York Times.
       November 16, 1947.
The eleventh annual "All-American Popularity" poll named
Ingrid Bergman and Bing Crosby as most popular stars.
Runners-up included Irene Dunne, Barbara Stanwyck, Claudette
Colbert, Bette Davis, and Betty Grable. The poll was
conducted by the weekly trade journal Boxoffice, which
canvassed the press, radio critics, independent theatre
exhibitors, and members of the National Screen Council.

B-472 Wells, Margery. "On Dress Parade." Modern Screen.
       June, 1934. pp. 77, 86, 88.
Costumes worn by Irene Dunne, Vivian Tobin, and Constance
Cummings in This Man Is Mine were among those discussed by
the film fashion writer.

B-473 _____. "You Can Have Clothes the Stars Wear..."
       Modern Screen. January, 1934. pp. 70-71, 87.
Cinema Shop sold costume copies, including an outfit worn by
Irene Dunne in Behold, We Live, released as If I Were
Free.

B-474 "What Happens to Your Fan Mail?" Screen Book.
       July, 1932. pp. 22-23, 64.
Irene Dunne was pictured holding a batch of letters in this
article on how stars handle their fan mail. Article noted,
"Since Cimarron, Irene Dunne has received hundreds of
letters from pioneer women who saw in her Sabra Cravat the
pioneer spirit of their youth."

B-475 White, Mary Linn. "Christmas Caravan Planners Gear
       Up." Cincinnati Post. September 21, 1990.
Dr. Joseph Link, a former professor at Cincinnati's Xavier

University and a longtime friend of Loretta Young, reminisced about his relationship with Irene Dunne. Link recalled attending several parties with Irene and visiting with her at Young's home. He said Irene often went on religious retreats with Young, Ann Blyth, Dolores Hope, Kathryn Crosby, and Ann Sothern. Link claimed Irene's husband was the brother of singer Dennis Day, however it was Ann Blyth's husband who was Day's brother.

B-476 "Who's Who at Who's Who." Los Angeles Herald Examiner. December 25, 1977.
Irene Dunne and Art Linkletter were guests of honor at the annual Christmas Who's Who International Ball. More than two hundred members of the Bel Air Country Club attended the black tie benefit for La Mission Orphanage in Mexico. Irene and Linkletter were pictured with Allen Chase, founder of the group.

B-477 "Who's Who on the Screen." New York Times. August 28, 1932.
Actresses Norma Shearer, Irene Dunne, Myrna Loy, and Mayo Methot were profiled. Irene, then on screen in Back Street, was mistakenly credited as having studied law.

B-478 "Why Irene Dunne Spent Her Last Yrs. Hiding from Old Friends." Globe. September 25, 1990.
An unidentified "friend" of Irene Dunne told the tabloid that the actress had spent her last years as a recluse because she wanted friends and fans to remember her as she was at the height of her career. "She didn't want people to see her so frail," the friend said. "She had too much pride and dignity for that." According to the article, Irene had refused to be photographed for a 1980 Life magazine spread on stars of the 1930s and '40s because she did not want people to see how she had aged. The friend claimed Irene's absence from the 1985 Kennedy Center Honors tribute was also due to her vanity. The friend said Irene had dreamed of being honored by her peers, but told the friend, "It breaks my heart, but I'd rather miss it than be wheeled in looking like a sick old lady on her last legs." Photographs of Irene in the 1930s and 1980s were included.

B-479 Wiley, Mason and Bona, Damien. Inside Oscar. Ballantine Books. New York. 1986. pp. 30, 31, 70, 77, 78, 79, 80, 96, 98, 174, 185, 240, 241, 299, 301, 397.
Irene Dunne's unsuccessful bids for the Academy Award were listed in this behind-the-scenes look at the Oscars. Cimarron director Wesley Ruggles was quoted as saying, "She can sing, play comedy or drama. She's bound to have one of the most enviable careers in Hollywood - if she gets a good agent."

B-480 Wilson, Craig and Williams, Jeannie. "Kennedy Honors: A Magical Night." USA Today. December 9, 1985. p. 2D.

Account of the two-day festivities surrounding the Kennedy Center Honors. Because of a back ailment, Irene Dunne accepted her medal at the Saturday evening dinner at the State Department, but could not attend the Sunday evening tribute, which was televised on December 27, 1985.

B-481 Wilson, Earl. "Just Like a Lady." <u>New York Post</u>. December 10, 1950.
Bedside interview with Irene Dunne, who was nursing a cold while in New York. Among the topics were her views on dieting. Irene said, "Personally, I'm not inclined to be the least bit heavy. But I know I could never be happy overweight." She also discussed the Queen of England, whom she met while filming <u>The Mudlark</u> and appearing at a Command Performance, and the difference between the English and American press. She said, "[The English press] just ask you right out how old you are. I just never tell them!"

B-482 Wilson, Elizabeth. "Dunne's Advice to Wives-to-be." <u>Silver Screen</u>. May, 1940.

B-483 _____. "Men She'll Remember." <u>Silver Screen</u>. April, 1941.

B-484 _____. "Playground of the Stars." <u>Screenland</u>. February, 1941. pp. 56-57, 92-95.
Honolulu was pictured as a getaway for the stars, although, Wilson reported, the Hawaiians often resented their presence. Wilson surveyed islanders from all walks of life and found the only actor whom they could agree on was Bette Davis. During Irene Dunne's visit, the crowds were pleased by her manners and cooperation, posing for pictures, chatting with the civilians, and allowing them to drape her with leis. However, they were not pleased when Irene pulled a "disappearing act." Having come to Hawaii for rest, she spent most of her time sunbathing, golfing, and sightseeing. Irene ran into some excitement while she was in Honolulu, witnessing her first wartime blackout from the roof of the Royal Hawaiian Hotel. Although some of the islanders thought Irene was the personification of good taste and breeding, others labeled her "snooty" and pronounced her "one of the most stand-offish stars ever to visit Honolulu." Irene was seen draped in leis.

B-485 _____. "Projections." <u>Silver Screen</u>. November, 1936.
Reporter Wilson claimed that she had described Irene Dunne as "Terrible copy - but awfully charming" in her diary. Wilson explained, "No matter how you look at it Irene just doesn't like to talk about herself (there are people like that, I'm told, but I never expected to meet one in Hollywood) and she can think up hundreds of cute little tricks to stall off an interview." Wilson described Irene's other idiosyncrasies: her tendency to daydream in the midst of telling a story, her lack of a sense of direction, and her vivid imagination. Irene recalled that she often told

people she had six brothers instead of one when she was a child. She explained, "I don't know why I was always pretending I had six brothers. Except that I liked to go to parties, and I was shy and wanted to assure myself of plenty of escorts." Irene also told how she met her husband at a party. Ironically, Irene did not want to attend the soiree at the Biltmore Hotel, but a group of friends insisted. When three succeeding dance partners asked where she was from, Irene told them each a different city, as she had grown up in Louisville, St. Louis, and Madison, Indiana. When the fourth gentleman asked her to dance, he told her that the other fellows thought she was crazy because she had given them different answers. Partner number four was her future husband, Dr. Francis Griffin. The article included several photographs of Irene, including a still from Magnificent Obsession with Robert Taylor, and a candid shot with her husband.

B-486 _____. "The First True Story of Irene Dunne's Baby!" Silver Screen. June, 1937.
The actress reminisced about her own childhood as she talked about her plans for her daughter Mary Frances Griffin. Although Irene complained about the constant music lessons she endured as a child, one of the first things she bought Mary Frances was a piano.

B-487 Wilson, Ivy Crane. Hollywood in the 1940s: The Stars' Own Stories. 1980.
Reprints of 1940s fan magazine articles.

B-488 "Women Near End of Busy Campaign." New York Times. November 4, 1956. p. 69.
Discussion of women in politics. Among the notable women involved in the arts who were active Republicans were Irene Dunne, Ilka Chase, Katharine Cornell, Helen Hayes, and Jinx Falkenburg.

B-489 Wyman, Jane. "The Lady's Not for Spurning Character Roles." New York Times. November 29, 1953.
The actress discussed her role in the remake of Magnificent Obsession. Irene Dunne had played the same part in the 1935 version of the film. Wyman called Irene a "superb actress" and said, "Whether or not my portrayal evolves as true and moving, it must certainly be my own."

B-490 Young, Loretta. "I Remember Irene Dunne." Photoplay. August, 1948.
The actress reminisced about her friend Irene Dunne in conjunction with the release of I Remember Mama.

B-491 "Your September TV Highlights." TV Star Parade. October, 1956. pp. 6-7.
Calendar of upcoming programs. Irene Dunne and Elinor Donahue were pictured as the stars of "Sheila," an episode of Festival of Stars, airing September 8, 1956. This was a rerun of the Ford Television Theatre episode, which

aired on May 24, 1956 (T-16).

B-492 "Ziegfeld to Present His '*Show Boat*' at Shubert."
Newark Evening News. September 21, 1929.
Newark audiences looked forward to seeing the touring production of *Show Boat*, which was scheduled to open the following week. Despite the reporter's enthusiasm for the musical, which starred Charles Winninger, Edna May Oliver, and Irene Dunne, he mangled the titles of several Jerome Kern/Oscar Hammerstein II songs. "Can't Help Lovin' Dat Man" became "I Can't Help Loving That Man" and "You Are Love" was listed as "You Are in Love."

Appendix: Magazine Covers

The following is a selected list of magazine covers which feature Irene Dunne.

<u>Modern Screen</u>   5.32
<u>Photoplay</u>   10.32
<u>Photoplay</u>   10.33
<u>Movie Mirror</u>   5.34
<u>Vanity Fair</u>   7.34
<u>Photoplay</u>   10.34
<u>Film Weekly</u>   10.12.34
<u>Photoplay</u>   6.35
<u>Hollywood</u>   7.36
<u>Movie Mirror</u>   7.36
<u>Screen Guide</u>   7.36
<u>Photoplay</u>   11.36
<u>Movie Story</u>   6.39   with Fred MacMurray
<u>Silver Screen</u>   9.39   with Charles Boyer
<u>Photoplay</u>   10.41
<u>Movie-Radio Guide</u>   4.25.42
<u>Movie Story</u>   9.47   with others
<u>Cine Revue</u>   2.2.51

Index

Entries are indexed as follows: page numbers refer to the Biography; coded enumerations refer to individual chapters: "P" for Plays and Personal Appearances; "F" and "FS" for Filmography; "R" for Radio; "T" for Television; "D" for Discography; "A" for Awards and Honors; "S" for Song Sheets; and "B" for Bibliography. The prefix "SP" refers to episodes of <u>Schlitz Playhouse of Stars</u>, which can be found in the Television chapter under T-1.

Abbott, Bud, P-18, R-58, B-54, B-396
Abel, Walter, P-18
<u>Academy Award</u>, F-34, R-41
<u>Academy Award Nominations Special</u>, T-9
Academy Awards, 7, 11, 13, 14, 18, 21, 24, F-2, F-21, F-23, F-25, F-38, F-40, T-5, T-9, T-19, T-28, A-6, A-11, A-12, A-15, A-32, B-75, B-192, B-255, B-266, B-401, B-468, B-479
Academy of Motion Picture Arts and Sciences, B-330, B-468
Ace, Goodman, T-17, T-21
Adair, Gilbert, F-3
Adrian, F-10, B-460
<u>Affair to Remember</u>, <u>An</u>, 25, F-25
<u>Age of Innocence</u>, <u>The</u>, 9, F-16, B-238
<u>Aida</u>, B-341
Albert, Eddie, SP-23
Alioto, Joseph, B-14
<u>All Quiet on the Western Front</u>, 8
<u>All This and Heaven Too</u>, 14

Allen, Fred, T-29
Allen, Gracie, P-14
Allyson, June, F-27, T-20
<u>Always</u>, 25, F-33
Ameche, Don, F-29, R-21, R-46, T-30, B-109, B-420
American Cancer Society, 18, A-24, A-26, A-37, B-222
American Film Institute, 25, P-26, P-27, A-65, B-12, B-328, B-349, B-382
American Heart Association, 18, A-30, A-33, B-170, B-452
<u>American Magazine</u>, F-33
American Movie Classics, B-31
American Red Cross, 18, P-16, FS-3, R-24, A-36, A-39, A-51, B-352, B-449
American Society for the Hard of Hearing, A-13, B-420
<u>America's Town Meeting of the Air</u>, R-37, R-39
Ames, Leon, F-39
Anderson, Doris, F-41

292   Irene Dunne

Anderson, Eddie "Rochester,"
  19, F-20, FS-4, R-65,
  T-29
Andrews, Dana, 20, R-45,
  B-204, B-324
Andrews Sisters, The, F-35
Angel Street, 17
Ann Vickers, 9, F-12,
  B-238, B-261, B-306,
  B-383, B-402
Anna and the King, F-38
Anna and the King of Siam,
  18, 25, F-38, R-44, R-66,
  D-11, B-164, B-175, B-263,
  B-266, B-277, B-305,
  B-310, B-442
Arlen, Harold, F-25
Arlen, Richard, B-344
Armstrong, Louis, FS-2
Arnold, Eddy, R-82
Arnold, Edward, P-18, F-29
Arthur, Jean, 11, 14, F-23,
  F-28, B-166, B-380, B-438,
  B-468
Ashland Oil Log, B-461
Astaire, Fred, 9, 10, 11,
  F-18, R-1, R-85, D-17,
  D-22, S-1, B-2, B-61,
  B-76, B-149, B-301, B-322,
  B-443
Asther, Nils, F-13, B-344
Astonished Heart, The,
  B-102
Ates, Rosco, F-2, F-4
Atwill, Lionel, F-16
Autry, Gene, P-14
Awful Truth, The, 13,
  25, P-27, F-23, F-28,
  F-30, R-9, R-32, R-83,
  A-12, A-65, B-24, B-31,
  B-35, B-43, B-84, B-114,
  B-120, B-140, B-145,
  B-151, B-160, B-165,
  B-166, B-175, B-177,
  B-215, B-235, B-245,
  B-258, B-261, B-266,
  B-277, B-290, B-293,
  B-301, B-303, B-323,
  B-347, B-382, B-391,
  B-395, B-417, B-438,
  B-450, B-464
Ayres, Agnes, F-23
Ayres, Lew, B-418

Babes in Toyland, 7, P-8,
  B-188

Bachelor Apartment, 7,
  F-3, B-238
Bachrach, Ernest, B-250
Back Street, 8, 25, 26,
  27, F-7, F-8, F-10, F-16,
  A-69, B-7, B-116, B-151,
  B-166, B-175, B-179,
  B-235, B-249, B-290,
  B-320, B-327, B-347,
  B-351, B-364, B-367,
  B-394, B-395, B-408,
  B-440, B-477
Bacon, Lloyd, B-185
Baer, Parley, R-69
Bagg, Elizabeth C., R-60
Bagnall, George, 24, T-28
Bailey, Pearl, T-21
Bainter, Fay, 7, F-2
Baker, Graham, F-24, B-59
Bakewell, William, 27, F-7,
  B-235, B-367
Ball, Lucille, F-18, F-24,
  T-23, B-18, B-176
Barnes, Binnie, B-102
Barnes, Margaret Ayer, F-16
Barrett, Elizabeth, R-72
Barry, Gene, T-8
Barrymore, Ethel, FS-2,
  R-46, R-64
Barrymore, John, P-14, F-29
Barrymore, Lionel, P-14,
  F-29, F-33, R-58, R-65
Barthelmess, Richard, FS-1
Baruch, Bernard M., B-10
Baryshnikov, Mikhail, T-30
Basinger, Jeanine, B-456
Baxter, Warner, F-29, FS-1,
  R-27
Beal, John, SP-12
Beckett, Scotty, F-25, F-28
Beery, Jr., Noah, F-35,
  B-400
Beery, Wallace, P-18, F-29,
  FS-1
Behold, We Live, F-13
  B-473
Bel Geddes, Barbara, F-40,
  R-54, B-373, B-375
Bellamy, Ralph, 9, 27, P-18,
  F-14, F-23, F-32, B-113,
  B-299
Bellarmine College, 24, A-57
Bells of St. Mary's,
  The, 18, B-250
Benaderet, Bea, R-69
Bendel, Henri, B-209

Bendix, William, R-68
Benefit Show for Retarded Children, T-13
Bennett, Constance, 6, 10, B-102, B-282
Bennett, Joan, P-18, F-35, T-1
Benny, Jack, 19, P-21, FS-2, FS-4, R-65, T-4, T-13, T-23, T-29, B-33, B-50, B-106, B-110, B-161, B-242, B-419
Bergen, Edgar, F-40, R-28, R-43
Bergman, Ingrid, 17, 18, B-32, B-250, B-414, B-471
Berman, Pandro S., F-6, F-11, F-12, F-14, F-15, F-16, F-18, B-322
Beverly Hillbillies, The, B-152
Beverly Wilshire Hotel, 23, 25, A-67, B-41, B-47, B-329, B-332
Bickford, Charles, F-9, F-22
Big Party, The, T-21
Bill and Coo, P-23
Billboard, 9, D-2, A-8
Bing, Herman, R-11
Bishop, William, SP-22
Blake, Amanda, SP-12
Blondell, Joan, SP-26
Blue, Ben, F-22
Blyth, Ann, 19, FS-4, B-475
Bob and Carol and Ted and Alice, B-177
Bodeen, DeWitt, F-19, F-40, B-347
Boe, Finn, B-218
Bogart, Humphrey, T-9, T-29, B-419
Boland, Mary, F-15
Boles, John, 11, 13, F-7, F-16, F-24, B-3, B-320, B-327, B-364
Boleslawski, Richard, F-21, B-88, B-205, B-290
Bond, Ward, F-33
Bondi, Beulah, F-30, B-18
Boswell, Connie, P-14
Boxoffice poll, A-10, A-22, A-25, B-62, B-414, B-471
Boyer, Charles, 13, 14, 15, 16, 17, P-14, F-7, F-25, F-27, F-36, R-14, R-25, R-42, R-46, R-67, R-76, S-5, B-30, B-32, B-54, B-60, B-128, B-161, B-293, B-297, B-348, B-415, B-416, B-423, B-430, B-448, B-459
Bracken, Ernest, 7, F-2
Braden, Spruille, B-467
Bradley, General Omar, T-23
Brady, Alice, F-24
Brando, Marlon, F-40
Brazzi, Rosano, F-27
Breen, Joseph, B-261
Brendel, El, FS-1
Brent, George, P-16, F-29, A-14, B-71, B-352
Breslow, Lou, F-41
Brice, Fannie, P-14
Bridges, Lloyd, SP-21
Bright Star, 20, R-78, B-269
Bringing Up Baby, B-301
Britton, Barbara, SP-4
Broadway Melody of 1936, B-434
Brodie, Steve, SP-5
Bronson, Betty, B-441
Brook, Clive, F-13
Brown, Joe E., FS-1
Browning, Robert, R-72
Bruce, Carol, P-17
Bryan, Jane, see Dart, Mrs. Justin
Brynner, Yul, F-38
Buchanan, Edgar, F-30, R-34
Burke, Johnny, FS-4, R-36
Burnett, Carol, T-30
Burns, Bob, P-14, F-7, F-29
Burns, George, P-14, P-21, T-23
Burrows, Abe, T-21
Bush, Anna Mary, see Griffin, Mary Frances
Bush, George, B-159
Butterworth, Charles, F-19, F-35, FS-1

Cabot, Bruce, F-12
Cagney, James, 16, P-18, B-254, B-298, B-299, B-344, B-396
Cain, James M., F-27, B-293
Cal York's, R-53
Calhern, Louis, F-17, B-432
California Arts Commission, 24, D-15, A-60, B-11,

B-13, B-14, B-77, B-156
Calkins, Johnny, F-39, D-14
Camden, Joan, SP-22
Camel Screen Guild
    Players, The, see
    Screen Guild Theater
Camille, B-320
Cantor, Eddie, R-37, B-38
Capra, Frank, A-58
Carlisle, Margaret, P-13
Carnegie, Hattie, B-27,
    B-250
Carrie, 11, B-57
Carrillo, Leo, P-14, P-18,
    R-58
Carroll, Anna Ella, 20
Carter, Jack, T-21
Cavalcade of America,
    The, 14, R-23, R-38,
    R-51, R-57, R-63, R-80
Cavanaugh, Rev. John J.,
    B-219
Cawthorn, Joseph, 7, F-17,
    D-21, D-26
CBS, P-14, F-39, F-40, R-26,
    B-125, B-136, B-377
Cerf, Bennett, T-2
Champion, Marge and Gower,
    T-13
Chaney, Jr., Lon, F-35,
    SP-18
Chang, Dr. T.K., B-103
Channing, Carol, T-23
Charlie McCarthy Show,
    The, R-28, R-43
Charlivels, Les, T-21
Charnin, Martin, F-40
Chase, Allen, B-476
Chase, Chevy, T-30
Chase, Father Maurice,
    B-329
Chase, Ilka, B-499
Chatterton, Ruth, F-10
Chevalier, Maurice, 9,
    FS-1, B-247
Chiang Kai-Shek, Madame,
    B-103
Chicago Musical College,
    3-4, 6, 19, A-2, A-3, A-4,
    A-5, A-21, B-45, B-90,
    B-239, B-265, B-292, B-378
Chicago Symphony, 3-4, 15,
    P-15
Chierichetti, David, 25,
    P-25, F-39, A-64, B-213,
    B-226

Chocolate Soldier, The,
    P-8
Christians, Mady, F-40
Christie, Audrey, R-52
Christine, Virginia, T-20
Christmas Stories from
    Guideposts, D-12
Christophers, The, 19, FS-4,
    FS-5, T-14, T-22, B-33,
    B-50, B-51, B-289, B-354
Christophers, The, 19,
    T-14, T-22
Chu Chin Chow, 3
Churchill, Marguerite, B-114
Churchman, The, B-134
Cimarron, 7, 9, 15, 25,
    F-2, F-5, F-15, F-26,
    F-29, R-23, R-55, A-6,
    B-25, B-29, B-84, B-167,
    B-175, B-213, B-238,
    B-277, B-279, B-351,
    B-353, B-361, B-383,
    B-401, B-435, B-439,
    B-450, B-474, B-479
City Chap, The, 5, P-6
Claire, Ina, F-23, B-16
Cleveland, Phyllis, P-6
Clinging Vine, The, 5,
    P-4, F-40, B-65, B-133,
    B-154, B-268, B-302
Cobb, Bob, B-185
Cobb, Lee J., F-38
Coburn, Charles, F-36, F-37
Cohn, Harry, 11, 13, F-21,
    B-364, B-438, B-464
Colbert, Claudette, 11, 14,
    20, P-18, F-23, F-29,
    R-47, T-4, B-80, B-161,
    B-286, B-319, B-380,
    B-468, B-471
Cole, Nat King, 21, T-18,
    T-23, T-29
Colgate Comedy Hour, 21,
    T-3, B-110
Collier, Sr., William, F-26
Colman, Ronald, 15, 19,
    P-18, R-31, T-29, A-7,
    B-60, B-161, B-204, B-308,
    B-324, B-344, B-423
Columbia Pictures, 10, 11,
    13, 14, 15, 17, F-21,
    F-23, B-80, B-177, B-258,
    B-364, B-438
Come Share My Love, F-41
Command Performance, R-36,
    B-298, B-396

Commonweal, The, B-134
Como, Perry, 27, R-68, T-17
Compton, Joyce, F-223, B-261
Conference on Family
  Security, P-22
Connolly, Walter, R-11
Consolation Marriage, 8,
  F-5, B-238, B-334, B-363
Conte, John, P-14
Conway, Tom, R-49
Cooper, Gary, 23, F-22,
  F-23, F-29, FS-1, T-29,
  B-161, B-173, B-248
Cooper, Gladys, F-34,
  B-102
Cooper, Jackie, P-14
Cooper, Jerry, R-8
Cooper, Merian, F-11, F-12,
  F-13
Corby, Ellen, F-40, T-24
Cornell, Katharine, F-16,
  B-488
Cortez, Ricardo, 8, F-6, F-8
Coryell, Bob, 23
Cosmopolitan's Citation,
  F-40, A-27, B-345
Costello, Lou, P-18, R-58,
  B-54, B-396
Cotten, Joseph, 27, R-34,
  B-32, B-415
Count of Luxembourg, P-8
Coward, Noel, R-4, R-49,
  B-71, B-102
Coy, Walter, SP-11
Crain, Jeanne, B-51
Crawford, Joan, 16, P-18,
  FS-1, D-32, B-71, B-319,
  B-468
Crenna, Richard, F-43
Crews, Laura Hope, F-11,
  F-13, F-16
Cromwell, John, F-11, F-12,
  F-14, F-38, B-164, B-261,
  B-305
Crosby, Bing, 18, P-18,
  FS-4, R-45, R-46, R-64,
  R-65, T-8, D-29, B-109,
  B-298, B-299, B-396,
  B-414, B-471
Crosby, Bob, T-13
Crosby, Kathryn, T-8, B-475
Crouse, Russel, F-39, B-92
Cukor, George, 13
Cummings, Constance, F-14,
  B-472
Cummings, Robert, P-20,
  T-10, B-122
Cunningham, Merce, T-30,
  A-68, B-136, B-159, B-466
Curie, Eve, 10
Curie, Marie, see Madame
  Curie
Curie, Pierre, 11
Curran, Homer, B-102
Curtiz, Michael, 18, F-39,
  B-290
Cut! Out Takes from
  Hollywood's Greatest
  Musicals, Volume 3,
  F-20, D-13

Dache, Lilly, B-467
Dagger and the Rose,
  The, B-337
Daily, Dan, R-64
Dale, Dr. Katherine, R-38
Daly, John, T-2
Dame in the Kimono, The,
  F-12
Daniels, Bebe, FS-1, B-327
D'Arcy, Alexander, F-23,
  B-140
Darnell, Linda, F-38, FS-2
Dart, Mrs. Justin (Jane
  Bryan), B-257
Dateline Disneyland, 21,
  T-10
Davis, Bette, 10, 14, 16,
  P-14, P-18, F-29, R-12,
  R-81, B-55, B-71, B-161,
  B-183, B-254, B-266,
  B-319, B-344, B-359,
  B-360, B-414, B-471,
  B-484
Davis, Rufe, P-14
Dawn, Gloria, 5, P-5
Day, Jr., Clarence, F-39
Day, Dennis, R-68, T-29,
  B-475
Day, Doris, F-28
Day, Laraine, P-18
de Cordoba, Pedro, F-28,
  R-64
Dee, Frances, F-11, B-18
Defense Advisory Committee,
  21, A-41, B-212
DeFore, Don, F-33, SP-16
de Havilland, Olivia, B-360
Dell, Claudia, FS-1
Demarest, William, F-41
DeMille, Cecil B., 15, F-29
Denning, Richard, T-15

296   Irene Dunne

Denny, George, R-37
Depinet, Ned E., 19
Derek, John, T-24
Descher, Sandy, F-43
Devine, Andy, P-18, F-15,
   F-35, F-41
Dewey, Thomas E., 21, P-14,
   R-58, B-194
<u>Dewey-Warren Bandwagon</u>,
   R-58, B-194
Dietrich, Marlene, F-35,
   FS-2, R-24, B-449, B-468
Dilley, Dorothy, B-403
"Dimension," 24, D-15, B-11,
   B-13, B-14, B-77
<u>Dinorah</u>, 4
Dinzel, Gloria and Rodolfo,
   T-30
Disney, Walt, F-24, T-10
Ditrichstein, Leo, F-4
Dix, Richard, 7, 9, F-2,
   F-5, F-15, F-19, FS-1,
   S-7, B-361, B-435, B-439
Dixon, Jean, F-24, B-18
<u>Don Giovanni</u>, F-4
Donahue, Elinor, SP-17,
   T-16, B-491
Donohue, Daniel, B-41
Dooley, Dr. Tom, T-23
Doran, Ann, F-30, F-41
Dorian, Bob, F-8
Dorn, Philip, F-40, B-373
D'Orsay, Fifi, FS-1
Dorsey Orchestra, Jimmy,
   R-19
<u>Double Indemnity</u>, B-139
Douglas, Kirk, 20, T-30,
   B-204, B-324
Douglas, Lloyd C., F-19
Douglas, Melvyn, F-21, R-5,
   R-10, R-30, B-88, B-168,
   B-368
Douglas, Paul, FS-4
Dreiser, Theodore, 11, B-57
Dressler, Marie, 7, F-2, A-6
Dreyfuss, Richard, F-33
Driscoll, Bobby, SP-8
Dunn, Adelaide Henry
   (mother), 1, 3, 4, 8,
   11-13, F-22, B-11, B-96,
   B-156, B-197, B-249,
   B-276, B-331, B-348
Dunn, Charles (brother), 1,
   8, B-11, B-331, B-433
Dunn, James, SP-17
Dunn, Joseph John (father),
   1, B-80, B-156, B-197
   B-294, B-403, B-447
Dunne, Irene (Irene Marie
   Dunn), acting technique,
   B-11, B-47, B-142, B-164
   B-292, B-347; age, 1,
   B-46, B-468, B-478;
   articles by, B-90, B-91,
   B-92, B-93, B-94, B-95,
   B-96, B-347; canceled
   films, 7, 9, 10, 11, 13,
   14, 15, 16, 17, 18, 20,
   21, B-3, B-16, B-32, B-55,
   B-57, B-75, B-80, B-266,
   B-329, B-402; censorship,
   F-12, F-24, F-25, B-138,
   B-261, B-293; charity
   work, 18, 23, 26, B-11,
   B-37, B-47, B-52, B-127,
   B-156, B-170, B-187,
   B-217, B-222, B-330,
   B-357, B-418, B-445;
   childhood, 1-3, B-294,
   B-348, B-378, B-433,
   B-486; death of, 26-27,
   B-5, B-6, B-46, B-82,
   B-117, B-120, B-123,
   B-126, B-165, B-187,
   B-215, B-225, B-231,
   B-232, B-233, B-237,
   B-356, B-357, B-367,
   B-389, B-445; home, 11,
   26-27, B-367, B-385; image
   as lady, B-90, B-140,
   B-160, B-262, B-301,
   B-309, B-395, B-484;
   marriage, 5-6, 8, 23-24,
   B-25, B-28, B-36, B-46,
   B-105, B-153, B-154,
   B-156, B-199, B-264,
   B-305, B-330, B-370,
   B-378, B-433, B-445; name
   change, 1, 3, 4, 5, P-13,
   B-81, B-403; politics,
   18-19, 21, B-19, B-20,
   B-173, B-194, B-208,
   B-406, B-445, B-488;
   religion, 19, 21-23, 24,
   26, F-8, B-5, B-10, B-23,
   B-28, B-96, B-109, B-166,
   B-217, B-219, B-222,
   B-223, B-228, B-230,
   B-256, B-330, B-352;
   World War II, 15-16, P-14,
   P-16, P-17, P-18, P-19,
   B-21, B-68, B-102, B-103,

B-124, B-125, B-161,
B-183, B-189, B-190,
B-254, B-298, B-299,
B-308, B-335, B-342,
B-396, B-449, B-453
Durante, Jimmy, R-64, T-23,
B-50, B-51
Durbin, Deanna, R-24, B-54,
B-449
Duryea, Dan, SP-2
Duse, Eleanora, B-99

Easter Parade of Stars, T-6
Eaton, Pearl, 7, P-6, P-11
Ebsen, Buddy, SP-26, T-10
Eddy, Nelson, 16, P-14, P-18, F-20, R-4, B-247
Egg and I, The, 20
Eggar, Samantha, F-38
Eileen, P-8, B-64
Eisenhower, Dwight, 21, T-18, B-203, B-406
Eleanor Roosevelt Cancer Foundation, T-23
Eleanor Roosevelt's Diamond Jubilee Plus One, 23, T-23
Elizabeth Blackwell Story, The, 13
Elza Schallert, R-6
"Enoch Arden," 14, F-28
Enter Madame, 10
Entwistle, Peg, F-8
Erickson, Leif, SP-4, SP-15
Erwin, Stuart, FS-1
Esmond, Jill, F-8, F-34
Etting, Ruth, D-29
Evans, Joan, F-43
Evans, Rex, T-4
Everything for the Boys, R-31

Faddiman, Clifton, R-33
Fairbanks, Jr., Douglas, 13, 16, F-24, FS-1, D-21, B-59, B-102, B-105, B-327
Falkenburg, Jinx, R-58, B-488
Family Plot, B-455
Family Rosary Crusade, B-5
Family Theatre, The, 14, R-45, R-48, R-56, B-5
Farrell, Charles, B-320
Farrow, Mia, B-379
Father of the Bride, B-289

Faust, F-15
Fay, Frank, FS-1
Faye, Alice, 16, P-18, R-68, D-32, B-254
Fein, Irving, T-29, B-110
Feldman, Charles, 11, 15, F-35, B-60
Ferber, Edna, 7, P-13, F-2, F-20, B-89, B-435
Ferris, Barbara, F-27
Festival of Stars, T-16, B-491
Fibber McGee and Molly (Jim and Marion Jordan), R-64, R-68, B-377
Field, Virginia, SP-13
Fields, Dorothy, F-18, F-24
Fields, Herbert, 7, F-1, F-24
Fields, W.C., F-23, F-35, F-39
Fifty Years of Film, D-14
Film Comment, B-166
Film Daily, F-40
Filmex, see Los Angeles International Film Exposition
Fio Rito Orchestra, Ted, R-1
Fisher, Eddie, T-18
Fleming, Rhonda, P-20
Fleming, Victor, F-33, B-153, B-290
Fletcher, Adele Whitely, B-119, B-264
Flynn, Errol, P-20, R-12
Focus on Film, B-250
Follow the Boys, F-35
Follow the Fleet, 10, B-322
Fonda, Henry, 16, 23, P-18, F-29
Fonda, Jane, B-153
Fontaine, Joan, P-20, R-81, B-122
Fontanne, Lynn, B-87
Footsteps in the Dark, B-63
Forbes, Kathryn, F-40, B-312
Ford, Glenn, F-2
Ford, Wallace, SP-19
Ford Television Theatre, 21, T-7, T-8, T-15, T-16, B-232, B-491
Foster, Preston, 15, F-31, B-240
Foy, Jr., Eddie, F-1

298 Irene Dunne

Fra Diavolo, P-8
France, Anatole, R-48
Francis, Arlene, T-2
Francis, Kay, FS-2
Franklin, Sidney, F-34, B-74
Frawley, William, P-11, F-22, D-26
Frederics, John (Mr. John), B-417
Frees, Paul, R-69
Friendship Bridge, R-18, B-124
Frivolous Sal, 9, B-402
From Here to Eternity, T-5
Front Line Theatre, R-30
Front Page, The, 14
Frontier Circus, 23, T-24
Frye, Bill, B-158, B-159, B-329
Furness, Betty, F-8, F-19

G.E. Theatre, 23, T-25, B-198
Gable, Clark, 23, B-62, B-161, B-344
Gabor, Eva, T-6
Gage, Mary Frances, see Griffin, Mary Frances
Gallagher, Richard "Skeet," P-6, FS-1
Ganz, Rudolph, B-292
Garbo, Greta, 11, 18, F-40, B-166, B-319, B-320, B-359
Gardiner, Reginald, B-102
Garfield, John, B-161
Garland, Judy, P-14, R-47, B-414
Garner, James, F-28
Garnett, Tay, 20, F-23, F-24, B-138, B-290
Garrett, Betty, R-65
Garson, Greer, 11, 16, 17, P-18, F-38, T-9, B-3, B-298, B-299, B-308, B-396
Gaslight, 17, B-32
Gavin, John, F-7
Gaynor, Janet, 16, P-18, B-320, B-434
Gehring, Les D., F-23
Gentleman's Agreement, F-40
George, Gladys, B-75
Gershwin, Ira, 14
Gibbons, Irene, see Irene

Gibson, Wynne, FS-1
Gigi, 21, B-16, B-249
Gilbert, Ruth, T-21
Gillmore, Margalo, F-11
Gilmore, Virginia, P-18
Girl from Utah, The, D-8, D-10, D-22
Gish, Lillian, F-39
Gleason, James, F-33
God and My Father, F-39
Goddard, Paulette, P-18
Goldwater, Barry, B-19, B-20
Goldwyn, Mrs. Sam, B-342
Gone with the Wind, 14, F-6, F-25, A-15
Good Earth, The, 13, F-23, A-12
Good Housekeeping, 6
Goodyear Program, The, R-32
Gordon, Ruth, F-37
Gorin, Igor, R-3
Goulet, Robert, T-30
Grable, Betty, 16, B-128, B-471
Grant, Cary, 13, 14, 15, 20, P-8, P-14, F-23, F-25, F-28, F-30, F-43, R-9, R-10, R-11, R-13, R-17, R-20, R-22, R-30, R-32, R-34, R-70, R-74, R-83, T-27, B-31, B-43, B-114, B-125, B-145, B-153, B-160, B-161, B-166, B-177, B-211, B-245, B-261, B-293, B-301, B-347, B-348, B-391, B-438, B-459, B-464
Grant, Kathryn, see Crosby, Kathryn
Gravet, Fernand, R-4
Grayson, Kathryn, F-18, F-20, F-30, T-18, B-165, B-465
Graziano, Rocky, T-3
Great Lover, The, 7-8, F-4, B-100
Great Ziegfeld, The, 11, F-21, A-11
Green, Mitzi, FS-1
Greer, Howard, F-25, F-27, F-28, B-150
Griffin, Dr. Francis (husband), 5-6, 8, 10, 11, 13, 14, 19, 23-24, 26, F-28, B-11, B-21, B-25,

Index   299

B-28, B-36, B-47, B-96,
  B-99, B-107, B-119, B-153,
  B-154, B-185, B-187,
  B-197, B-199, B-210,
  B-221, B-228, B-264,
  B-270, B-276, B-295,
  B-307, B-330, B-332,
  B-341, B-356, B-369,
  B-370, B-433, B-445,
  B-446, B-457, B-467,
  B-485
Griffin, Mary Frances (Anna
  Mary Bush, Mary Frances
  Gage, Mary Frances
  Shinnick, daughter), 11,
  13, 15, 19, 23, 26, F-7,
  B-6, B-15, B-109, B-119,
  B-144, B-156, B-187,
  B-210, B-228, B-234,
  B-276, B-281, B-295,
  B-332, B-341, B-400,
  B-486
Griffin, Stephanie, T-7,
  T-16
Grossman, John W., B-14
Group Productions, 15, B-60,
  B-423
Guide to "Dimension: An
  Exhibition of Sculpture
  for the Sighted and
  Blind", A, D-15, B-77
Guiness, Alec, F-42, R-77
Gulf Screen Guild Show,
  The, see Screen Guild
  Theater
Gulf Screen Guild Theater,
  The, see Screen Guild
  Theater
Guy Named Joe, A, 17,
  25, F-33, S-6, B-73, B-83,
  B-100, B-108, B-135,
  B-153, B-280, B-290,
  B-311, B-348, B-465
Gypsy, T-21

Hackett, Albert, F-10, B-289
Haden, Sara, F-19, R-3
Haines, Connie, R-36
Haines, William, FS-1
Hale, Alan, F-22
Hallmark Playhouse, R-55,
  R-71, R-73, R-75, R-79
Hamilton, Neil, 8, F-4
Hamilton, Vera, T-17
Hammarskjold, Dag, B-317
Hammerstein, II, Oscar, 5,
  13, 19, P-13, F-17, F-18,
  F-20, F-22, F-38, F-40,
  B-126, B-492
Harding, Ann, 6, 8, 9, 10,
  F-11, B-55, B-282
Hardwicke, Sir Cedric, F-40,
  SP-10, B-404
Hardy, Oliver, 7, F-23, FS-1
Harris, Marion, 5, P-10
Harris, Phil, R-68
Harrison, Rex, 18, F-38,
  R-44, R-66, T-30, D-11,
  B-164, B-305
Harrison, Ward, 1
Harrold, Patti, 4, P-3
Hart, Lorenz, 5, 7, P-11,
  F-1
Hart, Moss, 14, B-236
Harvey, James, F-33, B-166,
  B-290, B-385
Haver, June, P-20
Hawaii Calls, R-15
Hawks, Howard, B-166
Haydn, Richard, SP-1
Haydon, Julie, F-6, F-8,
  F-16
Hayes, George "Gabby," FS-1
Hayes, Helen, 21, F-10,
  F-22, T-18, B-488
Hayward, Susan, F-7
Hayworth, Rita, 16, FS-2,
  D-32, B-128
Head, Edith, F-26, B-73
Hearst, Jr., Mr. and Mrs.
  William Randolph, B-174
Heart Fund, R-82
Heart of the Rockies, 7,
  B-188
Hebbard, Verbena, B-267
Henreid, Paul, B-173
Henry, Charles
  (grandfather), 1
Hepburn, Katharine, 9, 10,
  13, 17, F-11, F-16, B-80,
  B-140, B-156, B-280, B-301
Herbert, Hugh, F-17, D-21,
  D-26
Herbert, Victor, 7, B-64
Here Come the Girls, D-16
Here Comes Mr. Jordan,
  B-311
Hersholt, Jean, 24, T-28
Hertz, Jr., John, 16, B-32
High, Wide and Handsome,
  11-13, F-17, F-22, R-8,
  D-21, D-26, S-3, B-4, B-9,

300   Irene Dunne

B-101, B-126, B-148,
B-172, B-178, B-248,
B-249, B-254, B-276,
B-408, B-425, B-465
Hill, Jack, FS-1
Hilliard, Harriet, 10,
B-322
Hilton, James, R-55, R-71,
R-73
Hirschhorn, Clive, 13,
B-177, B-178, B-179,
B-180
<u>His Girl Friday</u>, 14,
B-177, B-380
Hitchcock, Alfred, B-455
Hodges, Joy, R-1
Hodiak, John, F-33
Holden, William, 19, FS-4
<u>Holiday</u>, 13, B-177
Holloway, Jean, R-69
Hollywood Canteen, 16,
B-183, B-190
<u>Hollywood Fights Back</u>, 19,
R-47, B-173
<u>Hollywood Hotel</u>, R-1, R-3,
R-5, R-8, R-9
<u>Hollywood on the Air</u>,
R-85, D-17
<u>Hollywood on the Air
Presents "The Feminine
Touch"</u>, R-84, D-18
<u>Hollywood Sings</u>, D-19
<u>Hollywood Story</u>, D-20
<u>Hollywood without Makeup</u>,
P-23, T-27
Holmes, Phillips, F-10, T-7,
B-270
Holmes, Taylor, T-7
Holtz, Lou, R-26
Homolka, Oscar, F-40, R-54,
B-373
Hoosier Hot Shots, The, R-36
Hope, Bob, 19, 25, P-8,
P-16, P-21, FS-4, R-24,
R-65, R-68, T-19, T-23,
T-28, T-29, T-30, A-68,
B-33, B-41, B-106, B-136,
B-159, B-161, B-352,
B-379, B-419, B-449,
B-466
Hope, Dolores, B-41, B-475
Hopkins, Miriam, 10, P-18,
F-18, B-55
Hopper, Hedda, 20, FS-1,
B-193
Horne, Lena, D-32

House Un-American Activities
Committee (HUAC), 19,
R-47, B-173
<u>How the West Was Won</u>, 23,
B-187
Howard, John, SP-20
Howard, Leslie, R-13
Howard, Sidney, F-11, R-61
Howard, Trevor, R-49
Hoyt, Caroline, 1, B-197
Hudson, Rochelle, SP-20
Hudson, Rock, F-19
Hunter, Holly, F-33
Hunter, Ross, 24, B-147
<u>Huntington Herald-
Advertiser</u>, B-461
Hurst, Fannie, 8, F-6, F-7
Hussey, Ruth, R-46
Huston, John, R-47, B-173
Huston, Walter, F-12
Hutton, Robert, SP-25

<u>I Remember Mama</u>, 18, 19,
20, F-40, R-54, R-59,
R-65, A-27, A-31, A-32,
A-70, B-18, B-85, B-120,
B-166, B-187, B-202,
B-213, B-218, B-238,
B-278, B-290, B-312,
B-321, B-345, B-347,
B-371, B-372, B-373,
B-374, B-375, B-382,
B-421, B-468, B-490
<u>If I Were Free</u>, 9, F-13,
B-35, B-238, B-473
<u>Ike Day Surprise Birthday
Party</u>, T-18
<u>Il Trovatore</u>, P-8
<u>Indestructable Mrs.
Talbot, The</u>, 10, B-55
<u>Information Please</u>, R-33
<u>Inside Oscar</u>, 7
<u>Interlude</u>, 25, F-27
<u>Invitation to Happiness</u>,
14, F-26, F-41, B-58,
B-101, B-169
<u>Iolanthe</u>, P-8
Irene (Irene Gibbons), F-33,
F-34, B-207
<u>Irene</u>, 4, P-3, B-120,
B-146, B-154, B-197,
B-225, B-232, B-244,
B-247, B-444
<u>Irene Dunne American Red
Cross Fund Appeal</u>, 18,
FS-3

Index   301

Irene Dunne in Person with Love Affair, P-26
Irene Dunne in Songs by Jerome Kern, P-26, D-10, B-328, B-349
It Grows on Trees, 20, F-43, B-116, B-179, B-289

Jack Benny Show, The, 21, T-4, T-29, B-110, B-242
Jack Benny's Twentieth Anniversary Special, T-29
Jackson, Cornwell, R-65
Jackson, Mahalia, T-23
Jagger, Dean, F-43, T-14
Jamison, Anne, R-3, R-64
Jean Louis, F-36, B-250, B-303
Jeans, Isabel, B-16
Jerome Kern in Hollywood: 1934-1938, D-21
Jerome Kern in Hollywood, Volume 2, D-22
Johnny Belinda, 18, F-40, A-32
Johnson, Celia, R-49
Johnson, Edward, B-239
Johnson, Rita, R-64
Johnson, Van, 17, F-33, F-34, B-83, B-414
Johnston, Johnny, F-30, B-465
Jolson, Al, R-65, B-419
Jones, Allan, 10, F-20, R-16, D-13, D-24, D-25, S-2, B-131, B-294
Jones, Jennifer, 11, 16, B-57
Jordan, Jim and Marion, see Fibber McGee and Molly
Joslyn, Allyn, T-25
Jourdan, Louis, T-30
Joy of Living, 13, F-17, F-23, F-24, D-22, S-4, B-18, B-24, B-59, B-84, B-105, B-138, B-172, B-176, B-178, B-238, B-249, B-290, B-301, B-327, B-409, B-460, B-462
Joy of Loving, F-24, B-138, B-200
June Allyson Show, The, 21, T-20

Just a Woman, F-9

Kalloch, F-23, F-24, B-303
Kane, Eddie, FS-1
Kanin, Garson, 14, 15, F-28, B-245, B-464
Karloff, Boris, SP-6
Kass, Judith M., F-28
Keaton, Buster, FS-1
Keel, Howard, F-18, F-20, T-18
Keller, Father James, 19, FS-4, B-50, B-51, B-354
Kelly, Gene, R-65
Kelly, George, R-52
Kelso, Dan, B-194
Ken Murray's Hollywood, P-23
Kennedy, John F., T-23
Kennedy Center Honors, 25-26, T-30, A-68, B-47, B-48, B-53, B-132, B-136, B-137, B-158, B-159, B-466, B-468, B-478, B-480
Kern, Jerome, 5, 9, 10, 11, 13, 15, P-6, P-13, F-17, F-18, F-20, F-22, R-36, T-3, T-17, D-21, D-22, B-61, B-172, B-249, B-326, B-492
Kerr, Deborah, P-21, F-25, F-38
Kersten, Dr. Gina, T-20
Keyes, Evelyn, P-20
Kilgallen, Dorothy, T-2
King and I, The, 25, F-38
King George, B-227, B-304
Kirk, Phyllis, T-6, T-12
Knopf, Mildred, B-28
Knowles, Patric, 15, P-16, F-32, B-352
Knox, Alexander, F-37, R-40
Kobal, John, 24, F-20, B-29, B-248, B-249, B-250
Koehler, Ted, F-25
Korda, Sir Alexander, B-469
Krasna, Norman, B-293, B-359
Kreuger, Miles, F-20, B-252
Kruger, Otto, R-27
Kukla and Ollie, T-17
Kurosawa, Akira, B-468

La Cava, Gregory, 15, F-6, F-31, F-32, B-290, B-316,

302   Irene Dunne

B-318
Ladd, Alan, R-65
Lady, The, F-10, B-270, B-283
Lady Consents, The, 10, B-55
Lady Esther Screen Guild Theater, The, see Screen Guild Theater
Lady in a Jam, 15, F-32, B-94, B-116, B-179
Lady in the Dark, 14, B-236
Laemmle, Jr., Carl, F-7, F-20, B-393
Laetare Medal, 19, A-35, B-5, B-23, B-192, B-219, B-228
Lake, Arthur, R-58
Lamarr, Hedy, 17, P-18, F-35, FS-2, B-308, B-396, B-418
Lamour, Dorothy, 16, P-18, F-22, D-21, D-26, B-103, B-254
Land of Liberty, 15, F-29
Landi, Elissa, 10
Landon, Margaret, F-38
Lane, Artis, B-37, B-52, B-127
Lane, Leota, B-337
Langford, Frances, P-14, R-1, R-3, R-5, R-8, R-9
Langner, Lawrence, R-61
LaPlante, Laura, F-20
Larkin, John, B-6, B-82, B-117, B-445
Lateran Cross, 21, A-43, B-223
Laughton, Charles, P-18
Laurel, Stan, 7, F-23, FS-1
Lawford, Peter, F-33, F-34
Lawrence, Gertrude, 14, F-38, B-236
Leathernecking, 7, P-13, P-23, F-1, B-178, B-188, B-200, B-238, B-255, B-357, B-378
LeBaron, William, 7, F-2, F-3, F-5
Lederer, Francis, 9, B-344, B-402
Lee, Dorothy, 7, FS-1
Lee, Gypsy Rose, T-21
Lee, Michele, T-30
Leff, Leonard J, F-12

Leigh, Vivien, 14, F-25, A-15
Lemen, Harry, B-461
Leonard, Bill, R-60
Leonowens, Anna, F-38
Lerner, Alan Jay, 25, T-30, A-68, B-136, B-159, B-249, B-466
LeRoy, Mervyn, F-17, B-229
Leslie, Joan, 26, 27, P-18, F-25, SP-5, B-109
Let's Do It Again, 25, F-23
Letter of Introduction, B-176
Levant, Oscar, F-1, B-263
Lewis, Jerry, T-19
Lewis, Sinclair, F-12, B-402
Liberace, T-13
Liberty, F-18
Life, F-40, B-468, B-478
Life with Father, 18, F-39, D-14, B-18, B-38, B-92, B-129, B-134, B-180, B-278, B-290, B-313, B-362, B-424, B-470
Life with Mother, F-39
Life with Music, B-388
Lightner, Winnie, FS-1
Lillie, Beatrice, 5, P-11
Lincoln, Abraham, 20, FS-5, B-330
Linden, Eric, F-9, F-11
Lindsay, Howard, F-39, B-92
Link, Dr. Joseph, T-8, B-475
Linkletter, Art, P-21, T-10, T-13, B-476
Lion's Roar, B-388
Little Billy, FS-1
Litvak, Anatole, 15, B-60, B-423
Livingstone, Mary, T-29
Loewe, Frederick, 25, T-30, A-68, B-136, B-159, B-249, B-466
Lollipop, 5, P-5
Lombard, Carole, 11, 14, 15, F-31, B-140, B-161, B-286, B-396, B-431
London, Jack, SP-16, SP-25
Loretta Young Show, The, 21, T-11, T-12
Los Angeles County Museum of Art, 25, 26, P-24, A-62, A-69, B-440
Los Angeles International

Film Exposition (Filmex),
25, P-25, F-25, A-64,
B-49, B-80, B-81, B-213,
B-226, B-455
Los Angeles Times, B-257
Lost Weekend, The, B-139
Loudon, Dorothy, T-21
Louella Parsons Show,
The, R-50, R-59
Louisville Courier-
Journal, 3
Love Affair, 13-14, 19,
25, 27, P-25, P-26, P-27,
F-25, F-27, R-14, R-25,
R-69, A-15, A-64, A-65,
S-5, B-12, B-30, B-81,
B-87, B-104, B-150, B-151,
B-166, B-175, B-213,
B-226, B-233, B-238,
B-278, B-290, B-293,
B-295, B-297, B-309,
B-314, B-324, B-328,
B-349, B-382, B-407,
B-408, B-430
Love Among the Ruins,
B-80
Love Is the Sweetest
Thing - "Great Love
Songs of the 30s", D-29
Lovely to Look At, 25,
F-18
Lowe, Edmund, FS-1
Loy, Myrna, 8, 16, 17, F-5,
F-8, R-27, R-47, R-70,
B-32, B-161, B-177, B-243,
B-251, B-363, B-415,
B-468, B-477
Loyola University, A-49
Lubitsch, Ernst, 16, B-166
Lucas, Blake, F-25
Luckee Girl, 5, P-12,
B-337
Lux Radio Theatre, The,
14, 27, F-19, F-20, F-21,
F-23, F-25, F-31, F-38,
F-40, F-42, R-2, R-4, R-7,
R-10, R-12, R-14, R-16,
R-21, R-25, R-27, R-34,
R-42, R-44, R-54, R-66,
R-70, R-77, R-81, R-83,
D-11, D-25, B-206
Lynch, Christopher, R-64
Lyons, Ben, FS-1
Lytell, Bert, R-26

MacDonald, J. Farrell, FS-1

MacDonald, Jeanette, 9, P-3,
F-20, F-35, R-4, R-58,
B-247, B-344
MacLeish, Archibald, R-47
MacMurray, Fred, 14, 20,
P-20, F-26, F-41,
R-78, R-81, B-122, B-269,
B-379, B-415
Mad Miss Manton, The, 10
Madame Curie, 10, 11, 17,
F-21, B-3, B-22
Madame X, 9, F-10
Madison Courier, 1
Madison Herald, 4
Madison, Indiana, 1, 3, 4,
P-1, P-2, R-62, A-1,
B-169, B-220, B-244,
B-457, B-461
Magill's Survey of Cinema,
F-19, F-25, F-28
Magnificent Obsession, 10,
25, 26, F-19, R-3, R-7,
A-69, B-27, B-116, B-175,
B-179, B-201, B-278,
B-351, B-393, B-395,
B-434, B-440, B-485,
B-489
Mahoney, Francis X., P-13,
F-20
Makin' Whoopee - Favorites
of Stage and Screen,
D-30
Malden, Karl, B-468
Mama, F-40
Mama's Bank Account, F-40
Mamoulian, Rouben, 13, F-22,
B-248, B-290
Manning, Cardinal Timothy,
B-41
Mantle, Mickey, B-349
Marcellino, Muzzy, F-18, R-1
March, Fredric, F-29, R-72,
T-5, B-344
Margo, SP-23
Married in Haste, F-5
Marsh, Howard, P-13, F-20,
B-246
Marshall, Alan, F-34, B-100
Marshall, Herbert, P-18,
R-49
Martha, F-15, F-31
Martin, Dean, P-21, F-28
Martin, Mary, T-23, B-103
Martin, Tony, P-21, F-20
Marx Brothers, The, F-23
Mason, James, R-66

304   Irene Dunne

Maxwell, Elsa, A-18
Mayer, Louis B., 17, F-33,
   B-83, B-129, B-418
Mayner, Dorothy, R-64
<u>McCall's</u>, 11
McCarey, Leo, 13, 14, 19,
   20, F-23, F-25, F-28,
   FS-4, B-50, B-104, B-138,
   B-140, B-160, B-166,
   B-290, B-292, B-347,
   B-438, B-445, B-457,
   B-464
McCarthy, Charlie, R-28,
   R-43
McCrary, Tex, R-58
McCrea, Joel, F-11, F-29,
   B-250, B-272, B-344
McDaniel, Hattie, P-14,
   F-20, D-24
McDowall, Roddy, 25, 27,
   P-25, F-34, A-64, B-53,
   B-81, B-213, B-226,
   B-329
McHugh, Jimmy, R-36
McLaglen, Victor, FS-1,
   SP-14
<u>Melody of Life</u>, F-6
Melton, James, R-26, R-58
Menjou, Adolphe, 7, F-4
Merce Cunningham Dance Co.,
   T-30
Mercer, Johnny, R-36
Merkel, Una, 9, F-10
Merman, Ethel, P-8, B-344
<u>Merry Widow</u>, <u>The</u>, 9,
   B-247
Mesta, Perle, B-40
Methot, Mayo, B-477
Metropolitan Opera
   Association, 3, 4, 5,
   P-9, B-239, B-436
MGM, 7, 10, 11, 15, 17,
   21, F-2, F-4, F-18, F-19,
   F-20, F-29, F-33, F-39,
   B-3, B-32, B-83, B-100,
   B-129, B-135, B-161,
   B-188, B-270, B-296,
   B-388, B-434
Michael, Gertrude, F-12,
   SP-14
<u>Midsummer Night's Dream</u>,
   <u>A</u>, 3, P-1, B-461
Milestone, Lewis, 15, B-60,
   B-423
<u>Milk Maid</u>, <u>The</u>, D-1
Milland, Ray, F-23, R-27,
   R-58, B-194
Miller, Alice Duer, F-18,
   F-34, R-35
Milnes, Sherrill, T-30
<u>Min and Bill</u>, 7, F-2, A-6
Mineo, Sal, T-17
Miner, Mary, B-56
Mitchell, Thomas, 16, P-18,
   F-21, R-30, R-61, B-128
<u>Modern Cinderella</u>, <u>A</u>,
   F-27, B-370
<u>Modern Movies</u>, 6
<u>Modern Screen</u>, 1, 4, P-3,
   B-257, B-264
Mohr, Gerald, F-25, R-69
Monroe, Marilyn, F-28, T-29,
   B-428
Montgomery, Robert, 15, 21,
   F-29, F-31, R-17, R-21,
   R-58, R-81, T-4, B-240,
   B-318, B-446
Moore, Victor, R-58
Moran, Polly, FS-1
Moreno, Rita, SP-16
Morgan, Dennis, P-18, T-26
Morgan, Frank, P-14, F-34,
   R-58
Morgan, Helen, P-13, F-17,
   F-20, D-24, S-2, B-253
Mount Saint Mary's College,
   19, A-34, B-217, B-230
Mouseketeers, The, T-10
<u>Move Over, Darling</u>, 25,
   F-28
<u>Movie-Radio Guide</u>, R-12
<u>Mr. Deeds Goes to Town</u>,
   F-23
<u>Mudlark</u>, <u>The</u>, 20, F-42,
   R-77, P-8, B-29, B-34,
   B-227, B-276, B-289,
   B-290, B-304, B-404,
   B-442, B-468, B-469,
   B-481
Munshin, Jules, R-65
Murfin, Jane, F-1, F-11,
   F-12, F-14, F-18
Murphy, George, FS-2, R-18,
   R-46, R-58, T-10, B-124
Murray, Charlie, FS-1
Murray, Ken, P-23, F-1, R-9,
   T-27
Museum of Modern Art, 25,
   F-25, B-383
<u>Music in the Air</u>, D-3,
   D-10, D-22
<u>My Dear Lady</u>, 20

Index   305

My Fair Lady, 25
My Favorite Wife, 14, 25,
  P-26, F-28, F-30, R-17,
  R-65, R-74, A-70, B-12,
  B-18, B-31, B-43, B-72,
  B-140, B-145, B-160,
  B-165, B-185, B-211,
  B-214, B-215, B-238,
  B-245, B-277, B-290,
  B-315, B-336, B-347,
  B-391, B-407, B-428,
  B-457, B-459, B-464
My Man Godfrey, 15, F-31

Nagel, Conrad, F-12
Naish, J. Carroll, F-9,
  F-12, R-64
Nash, Mary, F-10
National Art Association,
  25, A-67, B-329
National Conference of
  Christians and Jews, 19,
  R-60, A-29, B-10, B-23,
  B-92, B-222
National Council of
  Catholic Youth, 23, A-46
NBC, 25, R-68, T-16, B-147,
  B-377, B-449
Neagle, Anna, F-29, R-4
Neal, Patricia, P-20, B-122
Negulesco, Jean, F-42
Nelson, Frank, R-74
Nesbit, John, R-48
Never a Dull Moment, 20,
  F-41, B-238
New Movie Magazine, The,
  14
New York City Opera, T-30
New York Foundling Home, 11,
  B-15, B-144, B-210
New York Herald Tribune,
  6, 19, 21
New York Times, 11, 14,
  16, R-47
New Yorker, F-12
Newbold, Robinson, B-403
Newley, Anthony, T-30
Newman, Bernard, F-18, F-21,
  F-32, B-143, B-162, B-303,
  B-339, B-365
Newman, Paul, T-23
Newsweek, F-42
Nicholas Brothers, The,
  P-14
Nightingale, Florence, R-73
Niven, David, R-12, T-19

Nixon, Marni, F-38
Nixon, Richard, T-23, B-19
No Other Woman, 8, F-9,
  B-238, B-427
Nothing Sacred, B-166
Novarro, Ramon, B-413
Now Voyager, 14, B-266

Oakie, Jack, FS-1, A-58
Ober, Philip, F-41, T-16
O'Brien, Margaret, R-49
O'Brien, Pat, F-5, R-46,
  SP-9, B-109, B-334, B-422
O'Brien, Virginia, P-14
O'Connell, Helen, R-19
O'Connor, Donald, F-35, T-5
Old Maid, The, 10, B-55,
  B-75
Oliver, Edna May, 7, P-13,
  F-2, F-12, B-492
Olivier, Laurence, 9, T-19,
  B-80
Once a Hero, B-56
O'Neil, Barbara, F-27, F-40,
  B-18
Oslo Aftenposten, B-218
Our Gang, F-23, FS-1
Ouspenskaya, Maria, F-25,
  B-104
Over 21, 17, F-37, R-40,
  B-139, B-177
Owen, Percival, 3
Owen, Reginald, F-15

Padula, Marguerite, 7
Paige, Raymond, R-3,
  R-5, R-8, R-9
Pallette, Eugene, F-31,
  F-32, FS-1
Paramount, 10, 11, 14, F-22,
  B-9, B-55, B-57, B-101,
  B-425
Parish, James Robert, 7, 8,
  F-32, T-9, B-343, B-344
Parker, Dorothy, F-31, F-37
Parker, Fess, T-10
Parker, Willard, SP-13
Parsons, Harriet, F-40,
  F-41, B-345, B-375
Parsons, Louella, 16, F-40,
  R-1, R-3, R-5, R-8, R-9,
  R-50, R-59, T-4, T-9,
  A-27, B-345
Patrick, Gail, F-28, R-65,
  B-18, B-185
Patterson, Elizabeth, F-22,

306 Irene Dunne

F-36, T-15
Peary, Harold, R-58, R-68
Peck, Gregory, 23
Pemberton, Mrs. Brock, B-282
Penny Serenade, 15, 27,
  F-30, F-40, R-22, R-34,
  B-18, B-31, B-43, B-63,
  B-140, B-145, B-160,
  B-175, B-177, B-245,
  B-258, B-266, B-278,
  B-292, B-347, B-395,
  B-408, B-451, B-464,
  B-465, B-468
Percy, Charles H., 21, T-18
Perlberg, William, 16
Perreau, Gigi, F-41
Perry Como Show, The,
  21, T-17
Peter Ibbetson, 10
Peyton, Father Patrick,
  R-45, R-64, B-5
Pfaff, Rosemary, 4
Philadelphia Symphony, 15,
  B-98
Photoplay, 8, B-151,
  B-167, B-387
Pickens Sisters, The, R-82
Pickford, Mary, 18, F-39,
  B-468
Pidgeon, Walter, 11, 16,
  P-18, R-32, R-42, R-67,
  B-3
Pink Lady, The, P-8
Pitts, ZaSu, F-7, F-21,
  F-39, R-58
Plummer, Evans, R-12, B-352
Plunkett, Walter, F-16,
  B-353
Pons, Lily, FS-2
Powell, Dick, P-14, R-1,
  R-3, R-5
Powell, William, 15, 16-17,
  18, F-39, R-14, D-14,
  B-32, B-129, B-177, B-251,
  B-362, B-470
Power, Tyrone, P-14, B-161
Present Arms, 7, F-1,
  B-188, B-255, B-357,
  B-378
Pretty Woman, B-237
Price, Vincent, T-4
Printemps, Yvonne, B-16
Prudential Family Hour of
  Stars, 19, R-69, R-72,
  B-204, B-324
Pryor, Roger, R-52

Puck, Eva, P-13, B-246
Puttin' on the Ritz, D-31

Queen Elizabeth, B-227,
  B-304, B-481
Queen Victoria, 20, F-42,
  B-8, B-34, B-227, B-276,
  B-289, B-304, B-404, B-469

Raft, George, P-6, F-29,
  F-35, B-333
Rainer, Luise, 11, 13, F-21,
  F-23, A-11, A-12
Raitt, John, 25, A-67, B-239
Randall, Tony, T-19
Rathbone, Basil, B-102
Ratoff, Gregory, F-6, T-4
Raye, Martha, T-3
Raymond, Gene, B-247
Reagan, Nancy, 26, B-13,
  B-14, B-468
Reagan, Ronald, 24, 26,
  P-21, T-10, B-14, B-82,
  B-132, B-156, B-330,
  B-357
Red Mill, The, P-8
Red Peppers, B-102
Ree, Max, F-1, F-2, F-3,
  F-5, B-346, B-353
Reed, Donna, T-9
Reed, Luther, 7
Regan, Phil, F-17, D-21,
  D-26
Return Engagement, B-468
Reynolds, Debbie, 23
Rigoletto, 3
Rio Rita, B-327
Ripley, Robert, R-58, B-194
Risdon, Elizabeth, F-21,
  F-39
Riskin, Everett, F-23, F-33
RKO, 6-10, 11, 13, 14, 18,
  19, 20, P-13, F-2, F-4,
  F-6, F-8, F-12, F-18,
  F-28, F-40, A-42, B-2,
  B-55, B-56, B-57, B-61,
  B-80, B-167, B-176, B-188,
  B-238, B-250, B-263,
  B-271, B-282, B-293,
  B-343, B-346, B-351,
  B-359, B-361, B-457
RKO Gals, The, 7, F-7,
  F-32
RKO Story, The, F-24,
  F-40
Roberta, 9, 15, 24, 25,

Index   307

26, 27, P-26, F-17, F-18,
   F-30, R-1, R-85, T-3,
   T-30, D-2, D-4, D-10,
   D-16, D-17, D-19, D-21,
   D-22, D-23, D-27, D-28,
   D-29, D-30, D-31, D-32,
   A-62, A-69, A-70, S-1,
   B-2, B-12, B-61, B-76,
   B-143, B-148, B-149,
   B-156, B-162, B-172,
   B-178, B-187, B-238,
   B-249, B-264, B-276,
   B-278, B-290, B-295,
   B-301, B-322, B-339,
   B-366, B-440, B-443,
   B-465
Roberts, Julia, B-237
Robertson, Liz, T-30
Robeson, Paul, F-20, D-24,
   S-2, B-253
Robinson, Edward G., P-14,
   FS-1, R-65, B-125
Rodgers, Richard, 5, 7, 19,
   P-11, F-1, F-38, F-40,
   B-376
Rogers, Buddy, FS-1
Rogers, Ginger, 9, 10, 11,
   14, F-18, FS-2, R-85,
   D-17, D-23, D-29, S-1,
   B-2, B-57, B-61, B-76,
   B-143, B-161, B-162,
   B-187, B-236, B-301,
   B-319, B-322, B-366,
   B-380, B-443
Rogers, Roy, R-65
<u>Romeo and Juliet</u>, 3, F-4,
   R-13
Romero, Cesar, SP-24, T-3,
   B-103
Roosevelt, Eleanor, 23,
   T-23, B-169, B-208
Rosenberg, George, 23
Ruben, J. Walter, F-3, F-6,
   F-9
Rubinstein, Arthur, F-35
Ruffner, Edmund "Tiny," R-19
Ruggles, Charlie, F-26
Ruggles, Wesley, 7, F-2,
   F-26, B-58, B-479
Ruick, Mel, R-12
Russell, Rosalind, 14, P-14,
   R-46, R-64, B-51, B-103,
   B-161, B-380, B-406, B-455
Rutherford, Ann, P-18, T-6
Rutherford, John, P-6
Ryan, Irene, B-152

Ryan, Robert, R-64

Sacerdote, Edouardo, B-90
Sahl, Mort, T-19
Saint John's Hospital and
   Health Center, 23, 26,
   A-40, A-52, A-55, A-66,
   B-11, B-37, B-47, B-52,
   B-127, B-156, B-187,
   B-330, B-357
<u>Saints and Sinners</u>, T-26
Savage, Ann, SP-24
Savage, Henry W., P-4, P-5,
   B-65
Scannell, Henry F., P-13
Scassi, Arnold, B-174
Schaefer, George J., B-457
Schallert, Elza, R-6
Schell, Maria, F-2
Schildkraut, Joseph, F-20
<u>Schlitz Playhouse of
   Stars</u>, 20-21, 27, T-1,
   B-110, B-198, B-232
Scott, Allan, F-18, B-293
Scott, Derek, F-39, D-14
Scott, Lizabeth, R-64
Scott, Martha, P-18, F-35,
   R-26
Scott, Randolph, 13, F-18,
   F-22, F-28, F-29, F-35,
   R-8, S-3, B-4, B-301,
   B-344
<u>Screen Directors'
   Playhouse, The</u>, F-28,
   R-62, R-74
<u>Screen Guild Players,
   The</u>, see <u>Screen Guild
   Theater</u>
<u>Screen Guild Theater</u>, 14,
   F-30, F-36, F-37, R-11,
   R-17, R-22, R-29, R-40,
   R-49, R-67, R-76, B-446
Sears, Zelda, 5, P-4, P-5,
   B-268
<u>Secret of Madame Blanche,
   The</u>, 9, F-10, T-7, A-70,
   B-35, B-39, B-100, B-270,
   B-283, B-289, B-306
Sedan, Rolfe, F-7, F-22,
   R-69
Seiter, William, F-18, B-2
Selznick, David O., 18, F-6,
   F-8, F-9, B-167, B-250
Selznick, Myron, F-31
<u>Separate Tables</u>, T-19
<u>Seventh Heaven</u>, B-320

308   Irene Dunne

Shakespeare, William, 3, P-1, R-13
Shaw, Winifred, F-17
Shearer, Norma, 17, P-14, P-18, FS-1, R-13, R-72, B-344, B-400, B-468, B-477
Shearing, George, B-13
Sherman, Lowell, 7, F-3, FS-1
She's My Baby, 5, P-11, B-376
Shinnick, Ann Marie (granddaughter), 23, 26, B-28, B-132, B-174, B-187, B-400
Shinnick, Mark (grandson), 23, 26, B-28, B-37, B-174, B-187, B-400
Shinnick, Mary Frances, see Griffin, Mary Frances
Shinnick, Richard Lee (son-in-law), 23
Shipman, Helen, 4, P-3, B-444
Shirley, Anne, FS-2
Shore, Dinah, P-18, F-35, R-68, T-29, B-299
Show Boat, 3, 6, 10, 25, P-13, F-17, F-20, F-22, F-23, F-30, R-16, T-17, T-30, D-13, D-24, D-25, S-2, B-18, B-21, B-26, B-44, B-45, B-84, B-87, B-89, B-116, B-123, B-126, B-131, B-148, B-165, B-172, B-178, B-179, B-188, B-193, B-232, B-246, B-248, B-249, B-252, B-253, B-276, B-277, B-290, B-294, B-357, B-393, B-397, B-433, B-454, B-465, B-468, B-492
Show Boat: The Story of a Classic American Musical, F-20
Show Business at War, 16, FS-2
Sidney, George, FS-1
Siepi, Cesare, T-21
Signoret, Simone, T-23
Sills, Beverly, 25, T-30, A-68, B-136, B-159, B-466
Silver Cord, The, 9, F-11, B-18, B-238, B-272, B-295, B-306, B-383, B-407
Silver Theatre, The, R-13
Simmons, Jerold L., F-12
Simms, Ginny, P-18
Sin of Madelon Claudet, The, F-10
Sinatra, Frank, P-21, FS-2, R-65, T-29
Sister Carrie, 11, B-57
Skelton, Red, R-65
Slippery Pearls, The, FS-1
Small Town Girl, B-434
Smith, Alexis, P-18
Smith, C. Aubrey, F-34, R-41
Smith, Edward, P-26, B-328, B-349
Smith, Glen, B-163
Society of Norwegian Playwrights, A-31, B-218
Something's Got to Give, F-28, B-428
Sondergaard, Gale, F-35, F-38
Song of Bernadette, The, 16
Song of the Islands, B-128
Sothern, Ann, 13, F-24, B-176, B-475
Sound of Music, The, T-23
Sparks, Ned, 7, F-1, F-17
Spellbound, B-139
Spellman, Cardinal, B-223
Spotlight Theatre, 20
Spring Maid, The, P-8
St. Cecelia, 3, P-2
St. Johns, Adela Rogers, B-301, B-410, B-411
St. Louis Globe-Democrat, P-8
St. Louis Municipal Opera, 5, P-8, B-64, B-397
Stafford, Hanley, P-14, R-30
Stafford, Jo, R-65
Stagedoor Canteen, R-26
Stahl, John, F-7, F-19, F-27, R-62, B-27, B-185, B-290, B-393
Stanwyck, Barbara, 10, P-14, FS-1, B-344, B-359, B-415, B-471

Stapleton, Maureen, T-30
Stars Over America, 16,
   P-18, B-254, B-298, B-299,
   B-308, B-396
Steiner, Max, F-5, F-6, F-8,
   F-9, F-11, F-12, F-13,
   F-14, F-15, F-16, F-18,
   F-39
Stephenson, Henry, F-13,
   F-15
Stevens, George, F-30, F-40,
   B-166, B-202, B-290,
   B-292, B-468
Stevens, Jr., George, T-30,
   B-268
Stevenson, Edward, F-24,
   F-25, F-40, B-371, B-421,
   B-460
Stevenson, Margot, R-13
Stewart, Donald Ogden, F-25,
   F-39, B-293
Stewart, Gloria, B-329
Stewart, James, 21, 23, 26,
   27-28, F-29, T-18, T-30,
   B-53, B-136, B-329
Stickney, Dorothy, F-39
Still Life, R-49
Stingaree, 9, F-15, S-7,
   B-84, B-238, B-271, B-353
Stockwell, Dean, R-64
Stolen Jools, The, FS-1
Stone, George E., F-2, FS-1
Stone, Lewis, F-29
Story of a House, 25,
   B-147
Story of Two Men, A, 19,
   FS-5
Sturges, Preston, B-166
Styne, Jule, T-21
Sullavan, Margaret, 14, 16,
   P-18, F-7, F-29, B-54,
   B-364
Swan, The, 21
Sweet Adeline, 9, 15, 26,
   F-17, R-84, D-6, D-10,
   D-18, D-20, D-21, D-22,
   D-26, A-69, A-70, B-172,
   B-178, B-180, B-229,
   B-326, B-390, B-432,
   B-440
Sweetheart Time, 5, P-7,
   B-141, B-413
Sweethearts, P-8
Swift, Kay, F-41
Swindell, Larry, F-31
Sydacker, H.M., 3, 4

Symphony of Six Million,
   8, 15, F-6, F-31, B-87,
   B-167, B-175, B-238,
   B-383

Tales of Manhattan, 16,
   B-128
Tamara, F-18
Tamiroff, Akim, F-22,
   SP-20
Taylor, Deems, R-33, R-47
Taylor, Elizabeth, F-34,
   F-39, B-38
Taylor, Henry, B-467
Taylor, Robert, 10, P-14,
   F-19, F-21, R-3, R-7,
   B-434, B-485
Technicolor, Inc., 24,
   A-56, B-208
Temple, Shirley, F-21
Tennyson, Alfred Lord, 14,
   F-28
Terris, Norma, 6, P-13,
   F-20, B-44
That Lady in Ermine, 16
Thayer, Tiffany, F-8
Theatre Guild on the Air,
   The, R-52, R-61
Theodora Goes Wild, 10-11,
   13, F-21, F-23, R-5, R-10,
   R-30, A-11, B-3, B-22,
   B-47, B-74, B-75, B-84,
   B-87, B-88, B-140, B-153,
   B-165, B-166, B-168,
   B-175, B-177, B-205,
   B-255, B-258, B-278,
   B-285, B-290, B-303,
   B-368, B-391, B-398,
   B-438
Thin Man, The, 16-17,
   18, B-32, B-243, B-251
Thin Man Goes Home, The,
   17
Thirteen Women, 8, F-8,
   B-35, B-238, B-251, B-350,
   B-363
This Man Is Mine, 9, F-14,
   B-1, B-35, B-113, B-186,
   B-238, B-295, B-472
Thomas, Danny, T-10
Thomas, John Charles, R-48
Those Legendary Ladies of
   Stage, Screen & Radio,
   D-27
Those Sensational Swinging
   Sirens of the Silver

310   Irene Dunne

Screen, D-32
Those Wonderful Girls of
    Stage, Screen & Radio,
    D-28
Three Minutes a Day, B-50
Tibbett, Lawrence, 9, B-247
Tierney, Gene, P-18
Till the Clouds Roll By,
    F-20
Tiller Sunshine Girls, The,
    7
Time, F-12, F-27, F-38
Titterman, Gayle, 20
TNT, A-70, B-233
Tobin, Genevieve, 5, P-7,
    B-141
Tobin, Vivian, F-13, F-14,
    B-141, B-472
Together Again, 17, F-36,
    R-42, R-67, R-76, R-74,
    B-97, B-112, B-177, B-250,
    B-258, B-391, B-416,
    B-430
Together Again!, 15
Tone, Franchot, P-18
Tonight at 8:30, B-102
Too Many Husbands, F-28
Top Hat, D-17
Torchia, Emily, B-153
Towne, Gene, F-24, B-59
Tracy, Spencer, 17, F-29,
    F-33, S-6, B-50, B-51,
    B-83, B-153, B-280, B-311,
    B-334,
Transient Love, F-14, B-1,
    B-186
Triumphant Hour, The,
    R-64
Truex, Ernest, B-413
Truman, Harry, R-65, B-419
Tucker, Sophie, F-35
Turner, Lana, FS-2
Turner Entertainment
    Company, F-28
Tuttle, Lurene, F-39
TV Radio Mirror, 24
20th Century-Fox, 15, 16,
    18, 20, F-25, F-28, F-38,
    FS-2, B-60, B-128, B-423,
    B-442
2001: A Space Odyssey,
    B-280

Ullman, Liv, F-40
Unfinished Business, 15,
    F-31, R-21, B-116, B-179,
    B-240, B-286, B-316,
    B-318, B-436
United Nations, 21, T-17,
    A-47, B-28, B-45, B-93,
    B-95, B-111, B-203,
    B-208, B-216, B-224,
    B-263, B-317, B-357,
    B-400
United Service Organization
    (U.S.O.), 16, P-14, F-35,
    R-20, A-17, B-125, B-189,
    B-380, B-453
United States Treasury
    Department, 16, P-17,
    P-18, P-19, R-65, A-19,
    B-85, B-419
Universal Studios, 8, 10,
    11, 14, 15, 16, 20, F-7,
    F-20, F-21, B-3, B-54,
    B-80, B-116, B-179, B-351,
    B-393, B-430, B-434,
    B-454
University of Notre Dame,
    19, 23, A-35, A-48, B-23,
    B-192, B-219, B-228
University of Southern
    California Cinema-
    Television Library, 4

Valiant Is the Name for
    Carrie, B-75
Valiant Is the Word for
    Carrie, B-75
Vallee, Rudy, F-40
Van Druten, John, F-13,
    F-40
Van Dyke, Dick, D-12
Van Heusen, Jimmy, FS-4,
    R-36
Variety, 4, P-3, P-18,
    D-2, A-9
Veeck, Bill, R-60
Very Good Eddie, D-7,
    D-10, D-22
Very Warm for May, D-5,
    D-9, D-10, D-22
Vidor, Charles, F-36, F-37,
    B-74
Vidor, King, B-364
Vinton, Doris, P-12
von Stade, Frederica, 26,
    T-30
Von Zell, Harry, R-78

Walburn, Raymond, F-22
Wald, Jerry, B-359, B-459

Index

Wallace, Jean, SP-11
Wanger, Walter, R-47
Waring, Fred, 21, R-58,
  R-65, T-18
Warner, Jack, 14, B-266
Warner Bros., 9, 10, 14, 18,
  F-23, F-39, D-14, B-55,
  B-129, B-180, B-229,
  B-266, B-326, B-390,
  B-424
Warren, Earl, R-58, A-28
Warren, Harry, F-25
Washington Post, B-132,
  B-328
Waterbury, Ruth, B-151
Wayne, John, 23, T-19,
  B-173
We the People, R-60
We Were Dancing, B-102
Webb, Jack, T-9
Weill, Kurt, 14
Welles, Orson, P-14, F-35,
  FS-2, R-26
Wellman, William, F-15
Werner, Oskar, F-27
West, Mae, F-23
Westley, Helen, F-16, F-18,
  F-20, B-18
Westman, Nydia, F-17, F-27,
  D-21, D-26
Westmore, Ern, 7, F-2
Westmore, Perc, F-39
Whale, James, B-249, B-253
Wharton, Edith, F-16
What's My Line, 21, T-2,
  B-110
Wheaton, Glenn, R-36
Wheeler, Bert, 7, FS-1
When Tomorrow Comes, 14,
  25, F-27, B-18, B-116,
  B-179, B-293, B-370,
  B-430, B-459, B-463
White, Sammy, P-13, F-20,
  B-131, B-246
White Cliffs of Dover,
  The, 17, 27, F-33, F-34,
  R-35, R-41, A-70, B-32,
  B-74, B-100, B-207
Whiting, Jack, 5, P-11
Whitty, Dame May, F-34
Who Could Ask for Anything
  More, F-41
Williams, Esther, F-33, R-65
Williams, Jane, R-1
Williams, Paul, 11, B-367
Wills, Chill, T-24

Willson Orchestra, Meredith,
  P-14, R-46
Wilson, Don, T-13, T-29
Wilson, Earl, B-146
Winninger, Charles, P-13,
  F-20, R-16, D-25, S-2,
  B-246, B-492
Withers, Jane, P-14
Witherspoon, Cora, F-37
Woman Overboard, F-28
Woman's Privilege, A,
  F-36, B-416
Wong, Anna May, B-103
Wood, Natalie, F-41
Wood, Peggy, 5, P-4, F-40,
  B-133, B-302
Woodland, P-8
Woodward, Joanne, T-23
Woolsey, Robert, 7, FS-1
World's Greatest Mother,
  The, R-46
Wrather, Bonita Granville,
  B-132
Wray, Fay, FS-1
Wright, Teresa, SP-3
Wyatt, Jane, SP-7
Wyler, William, R-47, A-58
Wyman, Jane, 18, 19, 21,
  P-18, F-19, F-23, F-40,
  A-32, B-204, B-324, B-359,
  B-489
Wynn, Ed, P-17, B-335

You Can Change the World,
  19, FS-4, B-33, B-50,
  B-51, B-354
You Can't Take It with
  You, B-24
Young, Alan, T-10
Young, Loretta, 19, 21, 26,
  P-14, F-29, FS-1, FS-4,
  R-46, R-64, T-11, T-12,
  B-21, B-33, B-50, B-82,
  B-109, B-204, B-250,
  B-319, B-324, B-329,
  B-344, B-389, B-468,
  B-475, B-490
Young, Robert, P-18, R-68
Young, Roland, F-23
Your Happy Birthday, R-19
Yours Truly, 5, P-10

Zamboni, Virginia, B-187
Zanuck, Darryl F., FS-2,
  B-304
Ziegfeld, Dr. Florenz, 3, 6

Ziegfeld, Florenz, 3, 6,
   P-13, B-45, B-492
Zinnemann, Fred, T-5
Zorina, Vera, P-18, F-35

About the Author

MARGIE SCHULTZ, a writer specializing in the entertainment field, is the author of a previous volume in Greenwood's performing arts series, *Ann Sothern: A Bio-Bibliography* (1990). She is a contributing editor for *Hollywood: Then and Now* and has published articles in *Show Music, Classic Images, The TV Collector,* and *Art Beat.*

**Recent Titles in
Bio-Bibliographies in the Performing Arts**

Julie Andrews: A Bio-Bibliography
Les Spindle

Richard Widmark: A Bio-Bibliography
Kim Holston

Ann Sothern: A Bio-Bibliography
Margie Schultz

Alice Faye: A Bio-Bibliography
Barry Rivadue

Orson Welles: A Bio-Bibliography
Bret Wood

Jennifer Jones: A Bio-Bibliography
Jeffrey L. Carrier

Cary Grant: A Bio-Bibliography
Beverley Bare Buehrer

Maureen O'Sullivan: A Bio-Bibliography
Connie J. Billips

Ava Gardner: A Bio-Bibliography
Karin J. Fowler

Jean Arthur: A Bio-Bibliography
Arthur Pierce and Douglas Swarthout

Donna Reed: A Bio-Bibliography
Brenda Scott Royce

Gordon MacRae: A Bio-Bibliography
Bruce R. Leiby